A RADICAL JEW

Contraversions

Critical Studies in Jewish Literature, Culture, and Society

Daniel Boyarin and Chana Kronfeld, *General Editors*

A RADICAL JEW

PAUL AND THE POLITICS OF IDENTITY

Daniel Boyarin

UNIVERSITY OF CALIFORNIA PRESS

Berkeley · Los Angeles · London

University of California Press
Berkeley and Los Angeles, California

University of California Press, Ltd.
London, England

© 1994 by
The Regents of the University of California

Library of Congress Cataloging-in-Publication Data

Boyarin, Daniel.
    A radical Jew : Paul and the politics of identity / Daniel
Boyarin.
        p.   cm. — (Contraversions ; 1)
    Includes bibliographical references and index.
    ISBN 0-520-08592-2
    1. Paul, the Apostle, Saint—Jewish interpretations.   2. Bible.
N.T. Epistles of Paul—Criticism, interpretation, etc.   3. Judaism
(Christian theology)—History of doctrines—Early church, ca.
30–600.   I. Title.   II. Series
    BS2506.B68 1994   93-36269
    227'.06—dc20

Printed in the United States of America
1   2   3   4   5   6   7   8   9

For W. D. Davies

רוֹדֵף הַשָּׁלוֹם, בְּהַגִּיעוֹ לִגְבוּרוֹת

Contents

Acknowledgments

I would like to thank the following people who took part in the production of this text:

First and foremost, an anonymous reader of my previous book for the University of California Press, who by commenting that I am (I hope, *was*) singularly uninformed about Paul set me going on the wonderful adventure (for me) that resulted in this book. This reader commented then that I should either drop all references to Paul in my work or learn something about him. I hope that she or he does not now regret having given me the second alternative. To somewhat garble a famous statement of William Wrede: "It is harder for one who half understands him to interpret Paul's doctrine than for one who knows nothing about him."[1]

Second, the friends and colleagues (and especially the patient Pauline scholars among them) who read and listened to and critically but fairly commented on various chapters of the book or, in some cases, the whole thing. I list them alphabetically here: R. Howard Bloch, Elizabeth Castelli, Ruth Clements, David Cohen, Carolyn Dinshaw, Moshe Halbertal, James R. Hollingshead, Karen King, Steven Knapp, Menahem Lorberbaum, Adele Reinhartz, Jonathan Schorsch, Alan Segal, Antoinette Wire, and Noam Zion.

I would especially like to mention here Professor W. D. Davies, who not only graciously accepted the dedication as a tribute but also offered his usual sharp critique and pointed out some of the places where my argument needed buttressing (against ideas of his). I hope that my buttresses hold up in his eyes. Richard B. Hays, a new friend and colleague whom Paul has brought me, has been supererogatorily generous to a usurper from another discipline into one that he has cultivated so assiduously for twenty years. He consulted with me tens of times on the telephone, read several chapters more than once, and read the entire book in a near-final version. There remain significant areas of disagreement between us in our interpretations of Paul, as well as equally important sites in which we agree totally. I have tried to take account of his objections, strengthening and clarifying my argument where I could, but at some level we continue to read Paul differently. For his Paul, the Jesus Christ of history, the Rabbi of Nazareth, is much more significant than for mine, and much follows from this difference of perception. I pray that this difference will be the sort of difference of which the Rabbis spoke when they said "Controversy for the sake of Heaven, in the end will perdure," by which I understand that it will be revealed in the end that somehow, "These and these are the words of the living God."

A first version of the overall thesis about Paul was presented at Duke University on the eightieth birthday of W. D. Davies. The frank but friendly responses of an extraordinary collection of Pauline scholars—and not least, the celebrant—on that occasion showed me much of what I had to do to make the theory at all plausible. Versions of the thesis have also been presented at the SBL, Pauline Epistles Section, at the Hartman Institute, and at a conference on "Jews and their Others" at Lehigh University. Chapter 7 was first presented at a conference on asceticism at Union Theological Seminary, for the invitation to which I thank Vincent Wimbush. I thank him as well for his encouraging critique of a very early version of this book. Chapter 8 was first presented (and published) as a colloquium of the Center for Hermeneutical Studies of the University of California at Berkeley and the Graduate Theological Union. It was also presented at the "Cultural Reading of the Bible" Cassassa Conference at Loyola Marymount University in May 1992. The formal responses and wide-ranging discussion on both of those occasions were of enormous help in reworking the chapter, as were also the responses and critiques of the editorial board of *Representations*, where another version has been published.

I would like to thank the University of California, Berkeley, for research grants proffered in the process of producing this book and the University of California President's Research Fellowship, during the tenure of which I did final revisions on this book while pursuing the project for which I received the grant. I also thank The Shalom Hartman Institute for Advanced Jewish Studies, an island of pluralism in a sea of reaction, without whose material and intellectual environment my work would have been a lot less pleasant and a great deal slower. The last chapter has been considerably reworked in the wake of a highly useful discussion there. Since I imagine that most of the participants would continue to vigorously disagree with me, I especially treasure their willingness to engage me seriously and critically.

Jonathan Boyarin, brother to me both κατὰ σάρκα and κατὰ πνεῦμα, has been so crucial in my intellectual and ethical formation that I cannot imagine my work without him. Chapter 10 in particular reflects our interaction, and a substantially different version has been published under our joint authorship in *Critical Inquiry*.

The members of my fall 1991 graduate seminar at Berkeley, "Paul, Platonism, and Palestinian Judaism," deserve a special vote of thanks for their critical patience. To a great extent, the ideas promulgated in this book are a product of our joint discourse. I am especially indebted to Charlotte Fonrobert, who has read through most of the Pauline corpus with me. I have benefited greatly from her knowledge and insight into Pauline exegesis. None of these people—especially not the graduate students—are in any way responsible for the defects of the discussion.

Finally, I thank Chana Kronfeld, perfect colleague and coeditor of our series in which this book is appearing, and Doris Kretschmer, an empowering and enabling editor.

Some of the chapters have appeared in earlier forms in the following publications: *Critical Inquiry, Paragraph, Representations, The Ascetic Dimension in Religious Life and Culture* (ed. Vincent Wimbush), *diacritics, Union Seminary Quarterly Review*. I thank the editors of all of these publications for permission to reprint material.

Introduction

Wrestling with Paul

You will surely not find it strange that this subject, so profound
and difficult, should bear various interpretations, for it will not
impair the face of the argument with which we are here concerned. Either explanation may be adopted.

Moses Maimonides

This book is the record of an encounter with some of the most remarkable
texts in the canon of western literature, the letters of Paul. If one measure
of the greatness of a work of literature is its ability to support many interpretations, then certainly these texts must rank among the very greatest
of literature, for they have spawned and continue to spawn—anew every
morning—not only new interpretations of particular passages but entirely
new constructions of their complete thought-world. Here, then, you have
a talmudist and postmodern Jewish cultural critic reading Paul. I think
that my particular perspective as a practicing Jewish, non-Christian, critical but sympathetic reader of Paul conduces me to ways of understanding
his work that are necessarily different from the ways of readers of other
cultural stances. This text fits into the tradition, then, of what has come
to be called cultural readings of the Bible, readings that are openly informed by the cultural knowledge and subject-positions of their producers.

I am going to begin this introduction by asking a question that I fan-
tasize will be asked by many of my readers: What motivated a scholar of
Talmud, virtually untrained in New Testament scholarship, to produce
an essay about Paul? What is my purpose in writing this book? What,
indeed, beyond the sensual pleasure of learning, impelled me to learn
Greek (of which I had only one year before this project) in order to read
Paul and write about him? There are several answers to these closely related questions.

First of all, I would like to reclaim Pauline studies as an important,
even an integral part of the study of Judaism in the Roman period and late

antiquity. Paul has left us an extremely precious document for Jewish studies, the spiritual autobiography of a first-century Jew. There is hardly another document, save parts of Josephus and Philo, which even comes close to fitting such a description. Moreover, if we take Paul at his word—and I see no a priori reason not to—he was a member of the Pharisaic wing of first-century Judaism, with which Josephus may have also been connected but with which Philo certainly was not.[1] In addition, Paul's activity and its consequences have had an enormous effect on the history of the Jews and Judaism in late antiquity (not to mention afterward). Much of that distinctive religious formation that we call rabbinic Judaism, which is the ancestor of virtually all Judaisms since late antiquity, was formed in the environment of a Pauline Christianity growing steadily in influence through the crucial formative centuries of this Judaism and culminating in the triumph of Christianity in the fourth century. I would like to make this absolutely clear. It is proper to speak of "rabbinic" Judaism only with regard to the second century and onward, because we have no direct evidence for such a movement prior to the Mishna formed in the late second century. The Rabbis see the first-century Pharisees as their spiritual ancestors, and there is no reason to doubt that sensibility, but, on the other hand, neither is there reason to assume that the later rabbinic reports about those Pharisees have not been substantially re-formed in the light of rabbinic Judaism itself. Accordingly, when we speak of rabbinic Judaism, we are speaking of a *post-Pauline* religious development. This means that Judaism formed itself for good and for ill in the context of Pauline (and other Christian) thought, sometimes undoubtedly reacting simply for the purpose of self-definition but also, more positively, answering in its own distinctive fashion theological and other challenges placed before it by Pauline Christianity.[2]

Second, I would like to reclaim Paul as an important Jewish thinker. On my reading of the Pauline corpus, Paul lived and died convinced that he was a Jew living out Judaism. He represents, then, one option which Judaism could take in the first century. Paul represents a challenge to Jews in the first century, and I will argue that he presents a challenge to Jews now as well. Assuming, as I do, that Paul was motivated not by an abnormal psychological state but by a set of problems and ideas generated by his cultural, religious situation, I read him as a Jewish cultural critic, and I ask what it was in Jewish culture that led him to produce a discourse of radical reform of that culture. I ask also in what ways his critique is important and valid for Jews today, and indeed in what ways the questions that Paul raises about culture are important and valid for everyone today. Further, I want to inquire into the limitations, inadequacies, contradictions, and disastrous effects of some of the Pauline solutions to those problems. Finally, I wish to interrogate our situation and ask whether we have better solutions to the cultural, social problems raised by the Pauline corpus.

In his very extremity and marginality, Paul is in a sense paradigmatic of "the Jew." He represents the interface between *Jew* as a self-identical essence and *Jew* as a construction constantly being remade. The very tension in his discourse, indeed in his life, between powerful self-identification as a Jew—in Romans 9, he expresses willingness to sacrifice his own salvation for that of "his brothers according to the flesh"—and an equally powerful, or even more powerful, identification of self as everyman is emblematic of Jewish selfhood. Paul represents in his person and thematizes in his discourse, paradoxes not only of Jewish identity, but, as we have come to learn, of all identity as such. When the Galatians wish to take on Jewish cultural practice, Paul cries out to them with real pathos: Remain as I am, for I have become as you are. The paradoxes and oxymorons of that sentence are, I submit, those of identity itself, and exploring the Pauline corpus with this kind of quest in mind will lead us to a deeper and richer appreciation of our own cultural quandaries as male or female, Jew or Greek, and human.

I am indeed wrestling here with Paul—a metaphor that I think he would have appreciated—in two senses: I am wrestling alongside of him with the cultural issues with which he was wrestling, and I am also wrestling against him in protest against some of the answers he came up with. Paul's discourse is supremely pertinent even today, and not only because there are millions for whom his word is Scripture. When Paul says, There is no Jew or Greek, no male and female in Christ, he is raising an issue with which we still struggle. Are the specificities of human identity, the differences, of value, or are they only an obstacle in the striving for justice and liberation? What I want to know is what Paul is saying to me, a male Jew, and how I must respond to it. How must I accept what he says as an ethical challenge and in what ways do I wish to reject that challenge and its implications? Finally, how might Paul's challenge and my response be of interest and importance to other people of difference?

Rather than seeing Paul as a text and my task that of a philologist, I see us engaged across the centuries in a common enterprise of cultural criticism. When, for instance, I deal with the question of the signification/ significance of circumcision in Paul and in the rabbinic response to him, I speak about it in terms drawn from post-structuralist inquiries into the significance of the "phallus," a seemingly appropriate line of inquiry which to my knowledge has yet to be pursued, although Derrida has, I think, been thinking along these lines for years.[3] When I inquire into Paul's pronouncements on the relations between the sexes, I do so with the full agenda of feminist cultural criticism in my personal reading agenda. And I am concerned as well to register the response of an actively practicing (post)modern rabbinic Jew to both Paul and Pauline interpretation, particularly insofar as these (especially the latter) have often been inimical to my religious/ethnic group and practice. My inquiry and response involve, as well, the ways that the Pauline discourse of the Jew as "figure" has heirs today in both marxian and other theoretical discourses.

This book is intended to be a cultural study of particular texts and issues within the Pauline corpus, especially those of gender and ethnicity. My underlying assumption is that in some fundamental ways Paul has set the agenda on these issues *for both Jews and Christians* until this day. The Pauline text that I most focus on is his Letter to the Galatians. This letter is in some respects the "sport" among the Pauline texts. One of the most obvious ways in which it is different from other documents in the corpus is that it does not speak, not even once, of the Parousia. Eschatology in Galatians—and there is much eschatology indeed—is realized eschatology, the ways in which the world is already changed by the coming and crucifixion and rising of the Christ from the dead. As J. Louis Martyn has expressed it, "Through the whole of Galatians the focus of Paul's apocalyptic lies not on Christ's parousia, but rather on his death" (Martyn 1985, 420). Second, in Galatians of all Paul's letters the theme of the new humanity—or rather, the new Israel—which includes both Jews and Gentiles is most powerfully expressed. Third, Galatians includes the stirring— for us particularly—declaration that there is "no male or female in Christ" (3:28), a gospel unknown from the rest of the corpus. Many Pauline commentators have reveled in the "difference" of Galatians—it was Luther's favorite—while others have virtually ignored it in their construction of Pauline thought. Martyn has even invented a charming technical term for this phenomenon: "Galatian embarrassment" (Martyn 1985, 411). This book, then, is conceived as a "reading" of Galatians, a reading in the contemporary sense of a particular putting together of a text and a reader, such that a particular construal of the text is undertaken.

Benjamin Harshav compares criticism to a kaleidoscope: neither mirror nor window. Each turn of the glass produces a new view and constructs the object; the view is never true and undistorted, but it does construct an object and not merely reproduce the eye of the beholder. Viewing Paul through the lens of Galatians, and especially through Galatians 3:28–29, the baptismal declaration of the new humanity of no difference, constructs a particular Pauline object, a different Paul from the one constructed by reading Paul through 1 Corinthians, Romans, or 1 Thessalonians. Choice of a hermeneutic and moral center from which to read the text is not a defect in but a starting point for the reading. This element of choice is inescapable, though less often acknowledged (even to the interpreter herself) than tacit.[4] Let me take a simple and dramatic example. Traditionally, Philemon has been read as a support for the institution of slavery, as a return of Onesimus to his former slave status, taking the moment in 1 Corinthians 7 where Paul tells slaves that they need not be free in order to be saved as determinative. If, however, we read Galatians 3:29 as our constant, with its declaration that there is no slave and free in Christ, then Philemon reads entirely differently, not as a commitment of Onesimus back into slavery but as a deft effort to pressure Philemon to free Onesimus. Though texts are not infinitely indeterminate, neither do they dictate ineluctably only one possible interpretation, and the interpreter must take, therefore, moral responsibility for her readings.

This point has been very well made by John Gager. He recognizes clearly that the choice of starting point will to a large extent determine one's reading of Paul. Thus, in producing his argument that for Paul Christ had not changed the status of the Jews at all but only of the gentiles, Gager cites such verses as, "Do we then overthrow the Law by this faith? By no means," as a starting point for his reading, arguing that such texts have always been an embarrassment to the traditional readings of Paul. He then argues:

> But to be embarrassed is not to be defeated. For those who do not
> simply ignore such texts, the solution lies in choosing not to begin
> with them, but to begin with passages that can be read as speaking
> of the demise of Israel and the abrogation of the Torah, for example
> Rom. 10:4, "For Christ is the end of the Law, that everyone who
> has faith may be justified," and treating other passages as anomalous

items which must be accounted for within this framework. It is apparent here that the beginning point has determined the final result.
The truth is a simple one and does not require elaborate exposition:
the end depends on the beginning. What does require explanation
is why particular beginning points are consistently preferred over
others.   (Gager 1983, 204–05)

This strikes me as one of the sharpest and clearest expositions of a simple
hermeneutical principle I have ever seen. Unless we simply abandon the
attempt to render the Pauline corpus more or less coherent, we will always
be choosing some starting point or other and trying to find how other texts
fit in with it. (Of course, this does not mean necessarily simply harmoniz-
ing texts but attempting to account for their sameness and difference.)[5]
And to put even a sharper point on it than Gager has, although the implication is clear in his works as well: The choice of starting point is primarily a theological, ethical, political decision, not a "scientific" one. I
have found that taking Galatians—particularly its stirring call for human
one-ness—as central to Paul treats us to a Paul who heightens our understanding of cultural dilemmas of both the first century and our own. Readings of Paul which either blunt the force of his critique of Judaism or
(much worse) render him a slanderer of Judaism seem to me much less
useful in appropriating the Pauline texts today.[6]

It is not, however, merely a question of starting point. While every
interpretation will require some effort to fit recalcitrant texts into its
scheme, for some the effort is greater than for others. In order, then, for a
reading of Paul centered on Galatians to carry any sense of conviction,
one of the factors has to be the entire context of the Pauline corpus. I will
have, therefore, many occasions to refer to others of Pauline letters, particularly the other *Hauptbriefe*, Roman and Corinthians, both of which
stand in very powerful and interesting interaction with Galatians. Indeed,
one of the tasks of some of the reading here undertaken is to relate the
ideas of Galatians to ideas expressed in the other letters, without, however, simply collapsing them. This reading of Galatians is pursued under
the sign of what I take to be the hermeneutical key to Paul, his allegorical
hermeneutic and a cultural politics which grow out of the hermeneutical/
intellectual and religious/moral world that he inhabits, the world of Hellenized Judaism of the first century. Let me hasten to add that I do *not* by
this intend a Hellenistic Judaism which is somehow less pure than a putative "Palestinian" Judaism. I hold, rather, that all of Palestinian Judaism

was also Hellenized to greater or lesser extent, although it is surely plausible that there were major cultural differences between Jews whose daily language was Semitic (Hebrew or Aramaic) and those whose daily language was Greek. Rabbinic Judaism, which I have interpreted in my previous book (*Carnal Israel: Reading Sex in Talmudic Culture*), is also Hellenistic. Its mode of Hellenization is, however, more often rejectionist than assimilationist, as I have argued in that book.

Paul was motivated by a Hellenistic desire for the One, which among other things produced an ideal of a universal human essence, beyond difference and hierarchy.[7] This universal humanity, however, was predicated (and still is) on the dualism of the flesh and the spirit, such that while the body is particular, marked through practice as Jew or Greek, and through anatomy as male or female, the spirit is universal. Paul did not, however, reject the body—as did, for instance, the gnostics—but rather promoted a system whereby the body had its place, albeit subordinated to the spirit. Paul's anthropological dualism was matched by a hermeneutical dualism as well. Just as the human being is divided into a fleshy and a spiritual component, so also is language itself. It is composed of outer, material signs and inner, spiritual significations. When this is applied to the religious system that Paul inherited, the physical, fleshy signs of the Torah, of historical Judaism, are re-interpreted as symbols of that which Paul takes to be universal requirements and possibilities for humanity. Thus, to take the most central of all Paul's examples, literal circumcision, which is for Jews alone, and for male Jews at that, is re-read as signifying baptism in the spirit, which is for all. Jewish history, the history of Israel according to the flesh, is taken as a sign for the meaning of Christ and the Church, Israel according to the spirit, in the world. I will argue throughout this book that many outstanding problems in Pauline interpretation can best be approached through this hermeneutical perspective. Just to take one example, E. P. Sanders's fine discussion of fulfilling the Law in Paul would be even stronger, I think, were he to adopt a hermeneutical understanding of Paul's antinomies between the Law under which Christians are not and the Law which they must fulfill and can fulfill by loving their neighbors as themselves (Sanders 1983, 93–105). The letter of the Law is abrogated; its spirit is fulfilled. This very old-fashioned (patristic!) interpretation of Paul must be integrated with newer understandings of the vital role that the integration of gentiles into the People of God played for Paul. It is this integration which my book attempts essentially by claiming that the two are one: The very impulse toward universalism, toward the One, is that which both enabled and motivated Paul's move toward a spiritualizing and allegorizing interpretation of Israel's Scripture and Law as well.

While Paul's impulse toward the founding of a non-differentiated, non-hierarchical humanity was laudable in my opinion, many of its effects in terms of actual lives were not. In terms of ethnicity, his system required that all human cultural specificities—first and foremost, that of the Jews—be eradicated, whether or not the people in question were willing. Moreover, since of course, there is no such thing as cultural unspecificity, merging of all people into one common culture means ultimately (as it has meant in the history of European cultural imperialism) merging all people into the dominant culture. In terms of gender, for Paul (as indeed, for nearly everyone until now), autonomy and something like true equality for women were bought at the expense of sexuality and maternity. Also, analogously to the culture question, the erasure of gender seems always to have ended up positing maleness as the norm to which women can "aspire."[8]

Rabbinic Judaism is in part a reaction formation against both of these Pauline moves—or, at the very least, a typological antithesis. Ethnic difference, cultural specificity, specific historical memory, and sexuality were highly valued in that cultural system, providing a partial, useful model for contemporary culture. If Paul's solutions were unsatisfactory from one point of view, however, those of rabbinic Judaism seem equally unsatisfactory from the opposite point of view. In terms of ethnicity, the Jewish system has created the danger (and in our times, the realization of that danger) of a racist social system, while rabbinic marriage, for all of its warmth and valorization of sexuality (including female sexuality) and childbirth, left precious little room for female autonomy, equality, and freedom. In my previous book, *Carnal Israel,* I have attempted a detailed description of the rabbinic side of this dialectical tension. In this work I hope to produce a more nuanced and rich account of the Pauline side of the dialectic. The mode of argumentation and thought in the book is thus one in which there is no winner or loser. My concern is not to promote or defend either the Pauline or the rabbinic discourse but to show how they participate together in the articulation of a set of cultural, social, and moral dilemmas which still plague us—"Gender Trouble" and the "Jewish Question."

The argument of the book is that this tension between the same and the different, in both gender and ethnicity, indicates the precise quandaries in which our sociocultural formation is trapped through the present; the dilemmas of multiculturalism and feminist theory seem to grow, then, out of cultural dilemmas that were first seriously encountered in the first century.[9] The Pauline corpus is, moreover, one of the main textual sources for Christianity, the most powerful of hegemonic cultural systems in the history of the world. Paul and the reactions to Paul are thus a major source for a historicization of our cultural predicament. In the reception history of Paul, his texts have generally served what might be broadly called conservative cultural-political interests; they have been used as props in the fight against liberation of slaves and women as well as major supports for theological anti-Judaism.[10] I am going to argue here that Paul need not be read this way, indeed, that his texts support, at least equally well, an alternative reading, one that makes him a passionate striver for human liberation and equality. I will further claim that this very passion for equality led Paul, for various cultural reasons, to equate equality with sameness, and that, despite what I take to be the goodness of his intentions, his social thought was therefore deeply flawed.

It is important that this claim not be misunderstood. I am not suggesting, of course, that Paul literally called for cultural uniformity in the sense that he demanded that people speak alike, dress alike, and eat alike. Indeed, one could argue—and it has been argued—that Paul's declarations that observances of the Law are adiaphora, matters of indifference, represent rather a cultural "tolerance." His argument is precisely *against* those who think that what one eats is of significance. It is, however, this very tolerance that deprives difference of the right to be different, dissolving all others into a single essence in which matters of cultural practice are irrelevant and only faith in Christ is significant. Thus for a Pharisee of Paul's day or a religious Jew of today, to be told that it is a matter of *indifference* whether Jews circumcise their sons or not, and therefore that there is no *difference* between Jews and gentiles hardly feels like regard for Jewish difference. Here differences persist, it seems, between many Jewish and Christian readers of Paul. A recent interpreter who argues strongly—and cogently—for the thesis that "Paul did *not* hold that Christians should lose their cultural identity as Jew or Gentile and become one new humanity which is neither"[11] shows this difference of perception in his very formulation, since the question for me is *not* the relative statuses of Jewish and gentile Christians but the statuses of those—Jews and others—who choose not to be Christians. Similarly, the claim of the same writer that "Paul believed that the Gospel gave him the freedom to be flexible in his keeping of Jewish food laws" (Campbell 1992, iii)—a claim with which I agree entirely—for me thoroughly undermines any argument that Paul intended Jews to remain Jewish, although Paul, were he here, would probably argue that he was redefining Jewishness in such a way that everyone could be Jewish. Those who would contend that the maintenance of Jewish practice is simply a life-style and that tolerance consists in insisting that it is a matter of indifference whether Jews follow that life-style or not are simply "buying into" Paul's ideology, not commenting upon it. Jewish difference does not mean only permitting Jews to keep kosher or circumcise within Christian communities; it means recognizing the centrality and value of such practices for Jews as well as their "right" to remain unconvinced by the gospel. This does not, however, constitute an accusation of intolerance on the part of Paul. Paul's gospel *was* one of tolerance. I claim rather that tolerance itself is flawed—in Paul, as it is today. Its opposite—by which I do not mean intolerance but insistence on the special value of particularity—is equally flawed. The theme of this book is that the claims of difference and the desire for universality are both—contradictorily—necessary; both are also equally problematic. The challenge of Paul's positive call to autonomy, equality, and species-wide solidarity cannot be ignored or dismissed because of flaws within it or because of the reactionary uses to which it has been put, but just as surely the insistence on the value of ethnic—even genealogical—identity that the Rabbis put forth cannot be ignored or dismissed because of the reactionary uses to which it can and has been put. The book will suggest in the end some dim glimmers of light to brighten this dark portrayal.

This reading of Paul will be supported, of course, by detailed analysis of his texts, a major part of the book. I have tried by my own efforts, and through seeking the help of experts, to keep my readings plausible both philologically and historically. One of the interesting issues that has come up in my interactions with professional Pauline scholars is a repeated response that I am reviving here in some ways currents in Pauline interpretation which were active in the nineteenth century and abandoned since. So be it. In the reading of texts, there may be progress in terms of our knowledge of the language or the historical and archaeological context; otherwise it may very well be that changed paradigms in reading owe as much to changes in our culture and politics as to real progress in knowledge. So, let the worm turn again. I suggest that this mode of reading Paul—which, once more, I have done my best to keep responsible in terms of scholarship—gives us a Paul who can live for us and work for us—not, of course (from my perspective) dictate to us—in our present wrestling with cultural and social dilemmas.

I would like to relate something of how this book was produced. It began with a careful but naive reading of Galatians virtually unaccompanied by any commentaries other than those designed primarily to aid in the construction of the Greek. This reading, having exposed to me what I took (and take) to be the central themes in the letter, led me to consider those themes within the context of Judaism. Having written that, I proceeded to "backfill" my text by undertaking an intensive reading of the voluminous literature on Paul published within the last twenty years or so. As I read, I discovered my predecessors and antagonists, *avant le lettre.* This is virtually nothing, it seems, that I have said which is not either asserted or denied at some point in the Pauline scholarship. The particular combination is, I hope, unique.

This book is thus related in different ways to different interpretative work currently being done on the Pauline corpus. I owe a profound debt to the rich re-reading of Paul undertaken in the wake of the treatises of Krister Stendahl, W. D. Davies, and his student E. P. Sanders. Richard Hays's *Echoes of Scripture in the Letters of Paul* has revealed Paul as a consummate reader of the Bible, answering my intuition that it is impossible to assume that Paul, any more than the Rabbis, would have been content to falsify or manipulate Scripture (in his own eyes) to win his arguments.[12] Perhaps not surprisingly, this book is part of the movement to thoroughly discredit the Reformation interpretation of Paul and particularly the description of Judaism on which it is based. I go further than some of the scholars in arguing that not only is this reading unsupportable in scholarly terms, but that it is an ethical scandal as well, and one that does Christianity no credit. On the other hand, I *do* (unlike Davies and Sanders) believe that Paul was motivated by a critique of Judaism, if not by the slanderous libel that Luther accused him of. In terms of specific understandings and interpretation, the reading of Paul which I undertake here seems to be closest in spirit (and often in detail) to the work of Ferdinand Christian Baur, produced over a century ago.[13] He also read Paul as primarily moved by a vision of universalism, although where I am generously critical, Baur waxed panegyrical. Moreover, where Baur, the consummate Hegelian, sees Paulinism as the triumph of a new and higher consciousness over Judaism which is a "lower state of religious consciousness," I can hardly accept such an evaluation. The great disappointments with universalism and human progress had not yet set in when he wrote, but his understanding of the essential issue at stake in Paul remains to my mind the most compelling. Two of the most effective contemporary representatives of a reading along these lines are James Dunn and Francis Watson (Dunn 1991, 125–46; Dunn 1990; Watson 1986). At many places in my text I will be engaging in dialogue (and not a little disagreement) with these two scholars. Finally, the book is most closely connected typologically (as far as I know) to a recent book, Elizabeth Castelli's *Imitating Paul: A Discourse of Power,* not so much for the conclusions (although many of hers *are* similar to mine) as for the explicit design to read Paul through the kaleidoscope of contemporary critical and cultural concerns.

By taking Paul seriously as an internal critic of Jewish culture, the value of his work for cultural criticism can be revealed. Marginalizing him as the founder of a new religion (a result which took place, I claim with many others, only after his death) deflects the force of his cultural challenge, which, even when its answers seem totally unsatisfactory, nevertheless calls us to provide answers of our own. I read Paul's discourse first and foremost as an inner-discourse of Jewish culture, one that was to repeat itself *mutatis mutandis* in the future development of Jewish culture as well. Both the passionate commitment to Jewish difference and the equally passionate commitment to universal humanity are dialectically structural possibilities of Jewish culture as it is (always) in contact with and context of the rest of the world.[14]

Sometimes this thesis and antithesis are present even in the same person, more often in contending political and social currents within any given Jewish chronotype. Paul's discourse, therefore, and its later analogues are a vitally important chapter in the cultural poetics of Judaism. I have several ambitions, or hopes, for this book. For scholars of Paul, at best it may prove some contribution to the interpretation of Paul's work; at worst it will be for them an object lesson in the dangers of going outside one's specialty. On the other hand, whether it achieves the first-mentioned aim or not, it still has a chance to participate in an activity even more important, to contribute in some small way to the improvement of human living together, that of Jews with Christians, Israelis with Palestinians, and all men with all women.

I

Circumcision, Allegory,
and Universal "Man"

THE LANGUAGE OF "MAN"

Behold Israel according to the flesh [1 Corinthians 10:18]. This we know
to be the carnal Israel; but the Jews do not grasp this meaning and as a
result they prove themselves indisputably carnal.

Augustine

When Augustine condemns the Jews to eternal carnality, he draws a direct
connection between anthropology and hermeneutics. Because the Jews
reject reading "in the spirit," therefore they are condemned to remain
"Israel in the flesh." Allegory is thus, in his theory, a mode of relating to
the body. In another part of the Christian world, Origen also attributed
the failure of the Jews to a literalist hermeneutic, one which is unwilling
to go beyond or behind the material language and discover its immaterial
spirit (Crouzel 1989, 107–12). This way of thinking about language had
been initially stimulated in the Fathers by Paul's usage of *in the flesh* and
in the spirit to mean, respectively, literal and figurative. Romans 7:5–6 is
a powerful example of this hermeneutic structure: "For when we were still
in the flesh, our sinful passions, stirred up by the law, were at work on our
members to bear fruit for death. But now we are fully freed from the law,
dead to that in which we lay captive. We can thus serve in the new being
of the Spirit and not the old one of the letter."[1] In fact, the same metaphor is used independently of Paul by Philo, who writes that his interest
is in "the hidden meaning which appeals to the few who study soul characteristics, rather than bodily forms" (*Abr.* 147).[2] For both Paul and
Philo, hermeneutics becomes anthropology.

Pauline religion should itself be understood as a religio-cultural formation contiguous with other Hellenistic Judaisms. Among the major supports for such a construction are the similarities between Paul and Philo—
similarities which cannot be accounted for by influence, since both were

active at the same time in widely separated places (Borgen 1980). The affinities between Philo and such texts as the fourth gospel or the Letter to the Hebrews are only slightly less compelling evidence, because of the possibility that these texts already know Philo (Borgen 1965; Williamson 1970). I take these affinities as prima facie evidence for a Hellenistic Jewish cultural koine, undoubtedly varied in many respects but having some common elements throughout the eastern Mediterranean.

Moreover, as Meeks and others have pointed out, in the first century it is, in fact, impossible to draw hard and fast lines between Hellenistic and rabbinic Jews (Meeks 1983, 33). On the one hand, the rabbinic movement per se does not yet exist, and on the other, Greek-speaking Jews such as Paul and Josephus refer to themselves as Pharisees. I am going to suggest, however, that there were tendencies which, while not sharply defined, already in the first century distinguished Greek-speakers, who were relatively more acculturated to Hellenism, and Hebrew- and Aramaic-speakers, who were less acculturated. These tendencies, on my hypothesis, became polarized as time went on, leading in the end to a sharp division between Hellenizers, who became absorbed into Christian groups, and anti-Hellenizers, who formed the nascent rabbinic movement. The adoption of Philo exclusively in the Church and the fact that he was ignored by the Rabbis is a sort of allegory of this relationship, by which the Christian movement became widely characterized by its connection with middle- and neo-platonism. In fact, this connection (between philonic Judaism and Christianity) was realized in antiquity as well, for popular Christian legend had Philo convert to Christianity, and even some fairly recent scholarship attributed some of his works to Christians (Bruns 1973; Williamson 1981, 313–14).

The congruence of Paul and Philo suggests a common background to their thought in the thought-world of the eclectic middle-platonism of Greek-speaking Judaism in the first century.[3] Their allegorical reading practice and that of their intellectual descendants is founded on a binary opposition in which the meaning as a disembodied substance exists prior to its incarnation in language—that is, in a dualistic system in which spirit precedes and is primary over body.[4] Midrash, as a hermeneutic system, seems precisely to refuse that dualism, eschewing the inner-outer, visible-invisible, body-soul dichotomies of allegorical reading (Boyarin 1990b). Midrash and platonic allegory are alternate techniques of the body.

In the hermeneutics of a culture which operates in the platonic mode of external and internal realities, language itself is understood as an outer, physical shell, and meaning is construed as the invisible, ideal, and spiritual reality that lies behind or is trapped within the body of the language. When this philosophy is combined with certain modes of interpretation current in the ancient East, such as dream-reading in which one thing is taken for another similar thing, then allegory is born—allegory in the most strict sense of the interpretation of the concrete elements of a narrative as signs of a changeless, wholly immaterial ontological being. Although there had been related techniques of Homeric interpretation, such as those of the Stoics who interpreted the gods as natural forces, it is really only with Philo's "allegory of the soul" that the specific western tradition of allegorical interpretation comes into being (Tobin 1983, 34–35). The drive toward allegoresis is the platonic valorization of unity and immovability over difference and change. In this tradition, language is a representation in two senses; in its "content" it represents the higher world, while in its form it represents the structure of world as outer form and inner actuality. As Sallust wrote, "The universe itself can be called a myth, revealing material things and keeping concealed souls and intellects," (Wedderburn 1987, 127). Origen expressed himself similarly, explicitly comparing the structure of the Bible as outer form and inner meaning to the ontological structure of the world (Boyarin 1990b). The human being is also a representation of world in exactly the same way; in her dual structure of outer body and inner spirit is reproduced the very dual structure of being.

My thesis in this book is that Paul also belongs, at least in part, to this tradition. It is for this reason that the "literal" can be referred to by Paul as the interpretation which is "according to the flesh" (κατὰ σάρκα), while the figurative is referred to by him as "according to the spirit" (κατὰ πνεῦμα). Literal interpretation and its consequences, observances in the flesh such as circumcision, commitment to the history of Israel, and insistence on procreation are all linked together in Paul's thinking, as are their corresponding binaries: allegorical interpretation, per se, and specifically of circumcision as baptism, of Israel as a signifier of the faithful Christians, and of procreation as spiritual propagation.

In order to keep a focus on Paul's dualism, *which does not radically devalue the body but nevertheless presupposes a hierarchy of spirit and body*, we do best by considering that the dual nature of Christ was so central in Paul's thought. Whether his christology is to be understood ontologically

or temporally, it involves in either case the positing of a Christ according
to the flesh and a Christ according to the spirit. It both inscribes a dualism
of spirit and body and valorizes the body, at least insofar as God became
flesh.[5] For Paul, certainly, just as the historical Jesus, while subordinate to
the risen Christ, is not thereby deprived of value, so also the individual
human body is not deprived of value vis-à-vis the soul, and as Romans 11
shows, neither is the historical Israel—Israel according to the flesh—vis-
à-vis "Israel according to the promise," the Christian believers.[6]

HERMENEUTICS AS POLITICS

Allegoresis finds its origin, on most current accounts, in the need to "up-
date" mythological texts no longer culturally applicable. The hypothesis
to be advanced in this chapter is that the attractions of allegory as a mode
of reading derive not from a need to apply ancient texts which are problematic but rather from a profound yearning for univocity, a univocity
which is only guaranteed by the positing of a spiritual meaning for language prior to its expression in embodied speech. In this sense, allegorical
interpretation is only a species of general European phallogocentric notions of meaning, including even Saussure's dualism of the signifier and
the signified; any notion of interpretation which depends on a prior and
privileged pairing of signifiers and signifieds is allegorical.[7] It follows from
this that the opposite of allegorical interpretation is not literal interpretation but rather midrashic reading as the very refusal of both univocity
and the very existence of a signified which subsists above, beyond, or
behind the signifier.[8]

Common to the phallos and the logos in the formation of phallogo-
centrism and thus of allegoresis is the desire for the One, for univocity in
interpretation as well as in ontology. A recent book by Arlene Saxonhouse has documented the origins and development of this cultural motif
in Greece (Saxonhouse 1992). Saxonhouse also documents the contestation of this "fear of diversity" within Greek culture, even, for instance,
within Plato himself.[9] In the Athenian tragedians, according to her, female characters are represented as a site of resistance to this drive for
unity, just as in the philosophers, the female is a disturbance in the One
(Saxonhouse 1992, 51). It seems nevertheless the case that in the early
centuries of our era it is the One rather than the many that attracts thinkers. In any case, Paul should be seen on my view as but one instance in
the working out of a cultural problematic set by the Greeks, not as the

representative of a positive Greek idea. Paul is, of course, a particularly interesting case both because of his synthesis of Greek and Hebrew cultures and because of his decisive influence on the later history of Europe.

The same cultural motives that produce allegoresis—logocentrism—as the primary mode of interpretation in Europe produce the Universal Subject as a Christian male. In both cases the passion for univocity seeks to suppress a difference, whether that difference be the signifier, women, or the Jews. Elizabeth Castelli has well formulated this cultural theme: "Sameness is valued above difference, and this valuing undergirds the entire mimetic relationship. . . . This treatment of difference has profound implications for processes of social formation, because it suggests that difference must be subversive of unity, harmony, and order" (Castelli 1991a, 86). As Jeremy Cohen has remarked of Origen, for that consummate allegorist, "Differentiation within the human species subverted primal perfection" (Cohen 1989, 236). The quintessentially "different" people for Paul were Jews and women. It is no accident, then, that the discourses of misogyny and anti-Judaism are profoundly implicated in projects of allegorical reading of the Bible.

The extraordinary alliance between hatred of Jews and hatred of women has been much remarked. Throughout the history of Christian Europe Jews and women have been vilified in many of the same terms. The (male) Jewish body has been feminized: male Jews menstruate in the folklore of much of Europe, and circumcision has been repeatedly blamed for the femaleness (weakness, passivity) of the Jew (Garber 1992, 224–31).[10] In this chapter I seek to explain the origins of western anti-Judaism and misogyny in the realm of a metalinguistic practice, the practice of allegorical interpretation, which I take to be not a local intervention in the meaning of texts but a global discourse on the meaning of language and the human body and especially on human difference. The desire for univocity manifested by allegoresis and frustrated by the material, embodied signifier is the same Hellenic search for univocity which the Universal Subject disembodies forth and which is frustrated by women and Jews as the embodied signifiers of difference.

WOMEN AS DIFFERENCE

The Greek desire for univocity motivates the canonical account of the origin of gender, the eighth-century B.C. poems of Hesiod. As Froma Zeitlin has stated:

The particularities too of Hesiod's extreme negativity towards woman, while open to compromise and mitigation in other texts and other spheres of interest, still remain the touchstone of an underlying attitude concerning this intrusive and ambivalent "other" who is brought into another man's household and forever remains under suspicion as introducing a dangerous mixture into the *desired purity and univocity of male identity,* whether in sexual relations or in the production of children.   (Zeitlin 1990)[11]

This desire for univocity of male identity which Zeitlin marks in the archaic Greek text becomes inscribed as a philosophical principle in Greek philosophy, and male becomes univocity as female becomes difference. As a long line of feminist thinkers beginning with Beauvoir has shown, western thought is dependent on the identification of the putative universal spirit with the male and the body of difference with the female (Lloyd 1984, 26). This dichotomy or opposition inscribes the opposition man ~ woman in a whole series of culturally charged binary oppositions, already in Pythagoras, although the actual list has changed (Lloyd 1984, 3). Thus man is to woman as

active:	passive
substance:	accident
form:	matter
soul:	body
univocity:	division and difference
meaning:	language
signified:	signifier[12]

These analogical sets of oppositions often seem to be so deeply grounded in western culture that they elude accounts of origins as well as attempts at transcendence. They seem to just be there. Even Jacques Derrida seems to imagine often enough that we can only "deconstruct" these oppositions from within them and never truly escape them (Derrida 1976, 24).

My hypothesis is that the discourse of gender in much of European culture has its sources in a particular metatextual combination of platonic philosophy and Hebrew myth, produced in the biblical hermeneutics of the first century, and that perhaps only this particular cultural combination could have produced the precise set of pernicious practices which mark western gender theory.[13] In other words, the same desire for univocity that Zeitlin has claimed for the Greek (Hesiodic) reign of the phallus is that which produces the reign of the logos as well. A series of very specific exegetical moves on the Genesis story proved to be the genesis as well of a certain type of allegory in western discourse, and that same allegory, in turn, thematized the supplementarity of woman in the culture.

PHILO, FEMALENESS, AND ALLEGORY

To establish the background for the interpretation of Paul, I would like first to briefly consider the writings of Philo (see also Boyarin 1993). I should make it clear that I am *not* claiming that Philo is the background for Paul, but only that he provides a background for my *reading* of Paul, that is, that certain themes which are explicit in Philo seem to me to be useful for understanding inexplicit moments in Paul's texts. The myth of a primal androgyny, a pre-lapsarian state before difference, was very widespread in late antiquity, particularly among platonists in the Jewish (and then Christian) traditions (Meeks 1973 and Crouzel 1989, 94).

As is well known now—largely through the efforts of feminist biblical critics—the Bible tells the story of the creation of humanity twice. In chapter 1 of Genesis, male and female are apparently created simultaneously, while in the second chapter, man comes first and woman is a secondary creation out of his body (Trible 1978; Bal 1987; Pardes 1989). In the interpretation of Philo, the first Adam is an entirely spiritual being, of whose non-corporeal existence it can be said that he is male and female, while the second chapter introduces a carnal Adam, who is male and from whom the female is then constructed.[14] Bodily gender—structurally dependent, of course, on there being two—is thus twice displaced from the origins of "Man":

> "It is not good that *any* man should be alone." For there are *two* races of men, the one made after the (Divine) Image, and the one molded out of the earth. . . . With the second man a helper is associated.
> To begin with, the helper is a created one, for it says "Let us make a helper for him": and in the next place, is subsequent to him who is to be helped, for He had formed the mind before and is about to form its helper.

Philo here regards the two stories as referring to two entirely different creative acts on the part of God and accordingly to the production of two different races of "Man."[15]

Philo here interprets Adam as the mind and Eve as the senses, the supplement, the "helper of the soul." The hermeneutic substance of the interpretation thematizes its own method, therefore, for the interpretation that distinguishes between primary substance and secondary form makes itself possible as an interpretation of the relation between Adam and Eve. Put perhaps in simpler language, the interpretation of Adam as spirit and Eve as sense-experience is what makes possible the interpretation of the *story*, the language of the Adam-and-Eve narrative, as matter to be interpreted by reference to the spirit of its true meaning. Or once more, to reverse the relation, the idea of meaning as pure unity and language as difference is what makes possible the interpretation of Adam as meaning and Eve as language. The nexus of allegoresis and contempt for the senses is tight. In both, a secondary carnal entity, respectively material signs, woman, the senses is contrasted to a primary, spiritual entity: allegorical meaning, man, mind. Significant in this context is the remark of Walter Burkert, that "In post-Platonic thought one can scarcely speak of imitation without assuming that it implies a gradation of kinds of Being, especially since Plato often characterizes the relation of sensible object and idea as *mimêsis*" (Burkert 1972, 45).

Philo explicitly marks the ontological implications of his interpretative practice: "Now these are no mythical fictions, such as poets and sophists delight in, but modes of making ideas visible, bidding us resort to allegorical interpretation" (Philo 1929b, 125).[16] The biblical story is not mimesis of the visible but representation of the invisible. Given this privileging of the invisible, it is not surprising that for Philo the story of Adam and Eve is one of the creation of sense-perception and its effects on Adam, who was formerly pure mind:

> For it was requisite that the creation of mind should be followed immediately by that of sense-perception, to be a helper and ally to it. Having then finished the creation of the mind He fashions the product of creative skill that comes next to it alike in order and in power, namely active sense-perception. . . . How is it, then produced? As the prophet himself again says, it is when the mind has fallen asleep. As a matter of fact it is when the mind has gone to sleep that perception begins, for conversely when the mind wakes up perception is quenched.   (Philo 1929b, 241)

The creation of sense-perception in the state of sleep, while recognized by Philo as a necessity, is profoundly and explicitly unwelcome to him: "But as it is, the change is actually repugnant to me, and many a time when wishing to entertain some fitting thought, I am drenched by a flood of unfitting matters pouring over me" (Philo 1929b, 245–46). And then:

> "He built it into a woman" [Gen. 2:22], proving by this that the most proper and exact name for sense-perception is "woman." For just as the man shows himself in activity and the woman in passivity, so the province of the mind is activity, and that of the perceptive sense passivity, as in woman.

And finally, the verse which in the Bible is one of the clearest statements of the non-supplementarity of gender becomes for Philo something else entirely:

> "For this cause shall a man leave his father and his mother, and shall cleave unto his wife, and the twain shall be one flesh" [Gen. 2:24]. For the sake of sense-perception the Mind, when it has become her slave, abandons both God the Father of the universe, and God's excellence and wisdom, the Mother of all things, and cleaves to and becomes one with sense-perception and is resolved into sense-perception so that the two become one flesh and one experience. Observe that it is not the woman that cleaves to the man, but conversely the man to the woman, Mind to Sense-perception. For when that which is superior, namely Mind, becomes one with that which is inferior, namely Sense-perception, it resolves itself into the order of flesh which is inferior, into sense-perception, the moving cause of the passions.   (Philo 1929b, 255–57)

It is easy to see here how for Philo the theory of the body and the theory of language coincide (Boyarin 1993, 37–42 and 57–60). His allegorical method, which privileges the spiritual sense ("the soul"), is exactly parallel to his anthropological doctrine, which privileges mind over the corporeal. The very necessity for humans to have senses is that which also generates the necessity "to make ideas visible" through the production of myth-like allegories. Both necessities are enacted in the story of the creation of woman, and together they resolve themselves into the "order of flesh." I am suggesting, therefore, that the western discourse of gender that finds its most specific point of origin in Philo owes its existence to the particular synergy of platonistic philosophy and the myths of Genesis. That is, on the one hand, the peculiar configuration of the biblical story which first describes a male-and-female creature, then gives it the name "man," and then reinscribes that very "man" as male, when combined with two peculiarly Greek cultural themes, the devaluation of the belated and the obsession with unity, produced the universal male.[17]

We thus see that the coordination of an allegorical perspective to language and a deep suspicion of human difference whether gendered or enculturated is not accidental at all. The two, in fact, seem on this analysis to be correlates of one another. The central thesis of this book is that the allegorization of the sign "Israel" in Paul is part and parcel of the very conception of difference within which Paul was to found his discourse on gender as well. As R. Howard Bloch has claimed, "We cannot separate the concept of woman as it was formed in the early centuries of Christianity from a metaphysics that abhorred embodiment; and that woman's supervenient nature is, according to such a mode of thought, indistinguishable from the acute suspicion of embodied signs—of representations" (Bloch 1991, 37). One such embodied sign was the sign "Israel," and its own most embodied sign, the seal of circumcision. Not so paradoxically then, Jewishness came to be a gender in much of the discourse of western Christianity, with all Jews (male and female) lumped together with women as the "same" Other. Paul, no less than Philo, sought to overcome that embodiment of the Jewish sign system.[18]

JEWS

The passage which begins with the last verses of Galatians 3 and continues through chapter 4 is the key text for reading this letter, and I read it as the hermeneutical key to Paul altogether. It is here that Paul makes most explicitly and passionately clear his stake in Christ, namely the erasure of human difference, primarily the difference between Jew and gentile but also that between man and woman, freeman and slave. In this section Paul also exposes the interpretative means by which erasure of difference is to be accomplished, in the famous allegory of Galatians 4:21–31. Making this the moral center of Paul's entire corpus is a hermeneutical choice, one which while not, of course, ineluctable generates a strong, (nearly) coherent, and important meaning for his work. Other choices can be made to center one's reading of Paul, and other results will obtain from them, including the moral monstrosity of reading all of Paul as generated by the vicious anti-Semitism of the possibly spurious 1 Thessalonians 2:14, engaged in by a recent writer (Hamerton-Kelly 1992).[19]

"There is neither Jew nor Greek"

For you are all children of God through faith in Christ Jesus. For as many of you as were baptized into Christ have put on Christ [saying]:

"There is neither Jew nor Greek; there is neither slave nor freeman; there is no male and female. For you are all one in Christ Jesus." If, however, you belong to Christ, then you are Abraham's offspring, heirs according to the promise.   (3:26–29)

In Deuteronomy 14:1 (and quite a few other places) we find the Jews referred to as the "children of God." Paul's theme in Galatians is his dissent from the notion that one particular people could ever be the children of God to the exclusion of other peoples, while other Christians sought to persuade his Galatian converts to become Jews as a condition of salvation. To disprove that claim and convince the Galatians of the rightness of his approach to Christianity, Paul cites the baptismal formula which the Galatians themselves had recited or heard recited at the time of their baptism. Paul's citation of a traditional baptismal liturgy here is thus very much to the point and cannot be adduced as evidence that this statement is not central and vitally important to him.[20] Moreover, he interprets the text. In the baptism there was a new birth (or a new creation), which is understood as substituting an allegorical genealogy for a literal one. In Christ, that is, in baptism, all the differences that mark off one body from another as Jew or Greek (circumcision considered a "natural" mark of the Jew!–Romans 2:27), male or female, slave or free, are effaced, for in the Spirit such marks do not exist. Thus, in this passage of Galatians that I have chosen as my key for unlocking Paul, Paul marks the analogous statuses of gender and ethnicity and the transcendence of both in the spirit: "For you are all children of God through faith in Christ Jesus."

Accordingly, if one belongs to Christ, then one participates in the allegorical meaning of the promise to the "seed," an allegorical meaning of genealogy already hinted at in the biblical text itself, when it said that in "Abraham all nations would be blessed," and even more when it interpreted his name as "Father to many nations." The individual body itself is replaced by its allegorical reference, the body of Christ of which all the baptized are part. This is what the "putting on" of Christ means, which is certainly a reference to the topos of the body as a garment, as in the Dominical saying Macdonald identifies plausibly as the source of (or if Macdonald is not accepted, certainly a reflex or analog of) the baptismal formula itself, to wit "when ye trample on the garment of shame, when the Two become One, and Male with Female neither male nor female." Alan Segal's comparisons with Second Enoch also seem apposite here, *if the text can be seen as pre-Pauline* (or if not, perhaps still significant as an early *reflex* or *interpretation* of the phenomenon):

[Enoch's] transformation is effected through a change of clothing. The clothing functions as or symbolizes Enoch's new, immortal flesh, as they are immortal clothes emanating from the throne room, not from the earth. This parallels Paul's future [?] glorification of the mortal body in 2 Cor. 5 : 1 – 10. Enoch has been put *in* the body of an angel, or he is *in* the manlike figure in 1 Enoch 71. This could explain Paul's use of the peculiar terminology in Christ.   (Segal 1990, 48–49, 62)

By entering into the body of Christ in the spirit, people become one with the seed to which the promise was made and thus themselves heirs of Abraham and children of God according to the promise. The garment of shame having been put off in the baptism and the spiritual body of Christ having been put on, the Galatians now propose by agreeing to circumcision, to return and put on again the garment of shame. They will thus show themselves precisely to be *outside of the covenantal promise and not within it as Paul's Jerusalem opponents would have it.* 4 : 19 should also be understood in this light. Christ taking shape "in you" means both within each individual in the ecstatic experience and through that their putting off of the body and entering into the spiritual body of Christ.[21] Scholars have recognized that Paul is citing here a traditional formula, one that refers back, moreover, to Genesis 1 : 27—"Male and female created he them"—as well as to the "myth of the primal androgyne" (Meeks 1973; Macdonald 1987). For Paul male-and-female means neither male nor female in the non-corporeal body of the risen Christ. The individual body itself is replaced by its allegorical referent, the body of Christ of which all the baptized are part. The parallel citation of the formula in 1 Corinthians 12 : 13 makes this even more explicit: "For in one spirit we were all baptized into one body."

Paul, however, adds to this traditional expression of the erasure of gender in the spirit the further erasure of ethnicity.[22] Both of these impulses are motivated, I argue, by the same desire for univocity—"when the two become one." In the process of baptism in the spirit the marks of ethnos, gender, and class are all erased in the ascension to a univocity and universality of human essence which is beyond and outside of the body.[23] Here allegoresis, the ultimate hermeneutical mode of logocentric discourse, unites both gender and ethnic identity as the secondary and devalued terms of the same binary opposition. This attitude toward ethnicity was, of course, not unique to Paul but once more part of a general Hellenistic longing for the univocal and the universal. Unique to Paul is the hermeneutic shift by which the allegorized particular Israel yields the universal "in Christ Jesus." The notion, however, that the body is the site of the particular and the spirit of the universal has deep roots in Greek culture.[24]

CIRCUMCISION, CASTRATION, CRUCIFIXION;
OR, THE BODY AND DIFFERENCE

As Jewish culture, both in Palestine and in the Diaspora, came into con-tact with other cultures in the Hellenistic and Roman periods, it was faced with the issue of how the biblical religion fit in a world in which Jews live among other peoples. The dualism of Hellenized Judaism provides one answer to this question by allegorizing such signifiers as "Israel," "history," and the practices of Judaism. Thus Philo interprets these signifiers as hav-ing meanings of universal applicability. The Bible, its prescriptions, and the history it relates are universal in that they teach everyone important truths. Philo was working within and from a cultural tradition which, as Gager has shown, was widely attested among *pagan* as well as Jewish writ-ers of the period "that regarded Judaism as a divinely revealed philosophy with Moses as its founder and spokesman" (Gager 1983, 69).

This "positive" and liberal perception of Judaism had negative conse-quences as well, however. As loyal a Jew as Philo was, he could not en-tirely escape the consequences of his allegorizing in a devaluing of the physical practices and genealogy of Israel. Where physical history and physical ritual exist only to point to spiritual meanings, the possibility of transcending both is always there. As Ronald Williamson has put it:

> It seems that for Philo, alongside traditional, orthodox Judaism, there
> was a philosophical outlook on life, involving the recognition of the
> purely spiritual nature of the Transcendent, in which one day, Philo
> believed, all mankind would share. In *that* Judaism the idealized Au-
> gustus, Julia Augusta and Petronius—among, no doubt, many others—
> had already participated.   (Williamson 1989, 13)

For Philo, such a spiritualized and philosophical Judaism, one in which a faith is substituted for works, remains only a theoretical possibility.[25] For Paul it becomes the actuality of a new religious formation which de-prives Jewish ethnicity and concrete historical memory of value by replac-ing these embodied signs with spiritual signifiers. These elements of em-bodiment are thus inextricable one from the other. If the body of language is its meaning and essence and the body of the person is his or her "self," then the history of Israel and the practices of that Israel are the physical history and practices of the body Israel.[26] Post-Pauline Christianity, with its spiritualizing allegorization of these signifiers, was universalizable but paid the enormous price of the suppression of cultural difference.

Philo indicates his disquietude with circumcision in his tract *On the Special Laws*, a tract whose name reveals what I take to be a common concern of such personalities as Philo himself, the author of *Wisdom of Solomon*, and Paul, that is, the specialness of Jewish rites and the ways that these mark off the Jews from others. Circumcision is in a sense the chiefest of these and, by Philo's own testimony, ridiculed in his environment (Philo 1937, 101; Hecht 1984). Philo offers four standard explanations and defenses of the practice, all of which promote rational and universal reasons for being circumcised. In fact, Philo emphasizes the fact that the Egyptians are also circumcised.[27] Finally, Philo offers in his own name two "symbolic" ($\sigma v \mu \beta o \lambda o v$) readings of circumcision. The more interesting of these is the second:

> The other reason is that a man should know himself and banish from the soul the grievous malady of conceit. For there are some who have prided themselves on their power of fashioning as with a sculptor's cunning the fairest of creatures, man, and in their braggart pride assumed godship, closing their eyes to the Cause of all that comes into being, though they might find in their familiars a corrective for their delusion. For in their midst are many men incapable of begetting and many women barren, whose matings are ineffective and who grow old childless. *The evil belief, therefore, needs to be excised from the mind with any others that are not loyal to God.*   (Philo 1937, 104)

The excision of the foreskin from the body is allegorically interpreted as the excision from the mind of an evil belief, indeed one that is intimately connected with the foreskin, as it has to do with generation. What we see, then, in Philo is a typical middle-platonist interpretation of the meaning of circumcision. Philo, however, typically berates those who, having a proper understanding of the meaning of circumcision, ignore the physical observance of the rite (Borgen 1980, 86; Collins 1985). The logic of his mode of interpretation is rather that others—not only Jews— should also be circumcised, a point which is supported by his aforementioned notice that the Egyptians follow the practice also.

In spite of his generally less extreme devaluation of the body, Paul goes further than Philo in a radical reinterpretation of circumcision. Where

Philo argues that circumcision both symbolizes and effects the excision of the passions, "symbolizes the reduction of all passion by effecting in the flesh of the penis a reduction of sexual passion," Paul "ties the removal of the fleshly desires exclusively to the believer's crucifixion with Christ" (Borgen 1980, 99). Baptism is also figured in Pauline language as putting off of the garment, namely the physical body, which is replaced by the corporate (resurrection) body of Christ. Baptism is a re-enactment for every Christian of the crucifixion of Christ, a putting off of the body of flesh and a recladding in the spiritual body of the risen Christ.[28]

"Circumcision" in its true meaning κατὰ πνεῦμα also means this. This is "the circumcision not made with hands." Since he allegorically interpreted circumcision as the outer sign performed in the flesh of an inner circumcision of the spirit, therefore, I would claim, circumcision was for Paul replaced by its allegorical signified and the embodied signifier "Jew" by its allegorical referent "believer in Christ." Paul returns over and over to this theme, most clearly in such passages as the following: Galatians 6:11–17; and Colossians 2:11, "In him also you were circumcised with a circumcision made without hands, by putting off the body of flesh in the circumcision of Christ." As Wedderburn has put it:

> Instead of the physical circumcision which was perhaps demanded of the Colossian Christians they are reminded of the circumcision that they have already received in their union with Christ, namely the far more drastic "putting away of the fleshly body" which comes from union with him in his death and burial; they have been raised with him in his resurrection.   (Wedderburn 1987, 84)

PAUL AND MIDDLE-PLATONISM

> Gentiles entering the new movement brought their culture with them, and Hellenism had already significantly affected Jewish culture both at home and abroad. Paul's Gospel . . . was at home in this milieu; and his universe, despite the foreshortened perspective he sees it in, is still very much the universe of late Hellenistic science.   (Fredriksen 1988, 63)

What was the substance of this late Hellenistic science to which Fredriksen alludes? While it had different varieties, one of its signal characteristics was a capacity to absorb and synthesize ideas from originally distinct philosophical traditions. Thus, for example among the philosophers known as the middle-platonists, both Aristotelian and Stoic logic were combined and considered platonist. It is not inconsistent, moreover, to find in one person elements of Cynic style combined with elements of platonistic thought.[29] The general outlines of the type of platonistic thinking which I ascribe to Paul have been delineated by John Dillon, one of the leading scholars of middle-platonism:

> We shall see throughout our period the philosophers of Middle Plato-
> nism oscillating between the two poles of attraction constituted by Peri-
> pateticism and Stoicism, but adding to the mixture of these influences
> *a strong commitment . . . to a transcendent supreme principle, and a non-*
> *material, intelligible world above and beyond this one, which stands as a*
> *paradigm for it.* The influence of Pythagoras and what was believed to
> be his doctrine was also dominant throughout our period. . . . Despite
> all the variations in doctrine that emerge, we can observe in this pe-
> riod the growth of a consistent body of thought, constituting a Pla-
> tonic heritage that could be handed on, first to Plotinus and his fol-
> lowers, and thence to later ages.   (Dillon 1977, 51 [emphasis added])

This philosophical tradition was widespread throughout the entire Mediterranean cultural area. There were prominent middle-platonists in Ascalon in Palestine, in Southern Anatolia, and in Syria. Thus, whether Paul got his education in Jerusalem, Tarsus, or even Damascus, the likelihood of his exposure to the central ideas of the platonistic philosophy current in his day is not at all implausible. Currently there is great resistance to the concept of a Paul nurtured by these philosophical traditions, resistance which Abraham Malherbe has described as belonging to an apologetic tradition (going back to Tertullian) for the absolute distinctiveness of Christianity. As Malherbe pithily remarks, "Why the New Testament, on *a priori* theological grounds, should have been kept safe from the taint of Hellenism requires a more cogent explanation than has been offered since early Christianity has become the object of modern historical research" (Malherbe 1989, 2). Indeed, the question is why should Hellenistic philosophy be considered a taint if it be found in Paul?[30] Malherbe himself documents the extent to which Paul was attuned to the style and methods of the popular philosophers of his day. The influence of this central platonistic notion of a higher world which stands as paradigm for this one and the importance of this conception for the reading of Paul will constitute a major claim of this book. The uniqueness of Paul—and I do think that he is unique—is not established by the lack of cultural input into his religious thought and experience but rather in the sui generis way that the different elements—Pharisaism, Hellenism, and belief in Christ—are combined to produce something absolutely new.[31]

JESUS ACCORDING TO THE FLESH:
THE CULTURAL POLITICS OF CHRISTOLOGY

According to my understanding, ontology, hermeneutics, anthropology, and christology are so intimately related in Pauline thought that they cannot be separated from one another.[32] The coming of Christ is, in fact, the perfect model for Paul's ontology, for just as Christ had a physical nature and a spiritual nature (Romans 9:5), and both are valuable, though the former is subordinate to the latter, so also the physical observances of the Torah and the people of Israel.[33] On the present reading, the fundamental insight of Paul's apocalypse was the realization that the dual nature of Jesus provided a hermeneutic key to the resolution of that enormous tension that he experienced between the universalism of the Torah's content and the particular ethnicity of its form. Paul understood both the dual nature of Christ's person as well as the crucifixion in the light of the familiar platonic dichotomy of the outer and the inner, the material and the spiritual, or in Paul's own terminology, the flesh and the spirit. Jesus was explicitly of a dual ontology, having an outer aspect of the flesh and an inner aspect of the spirit, or in more properly hermeneutic terms: There was a Christ according to the flesh (ὁ Χριστὸς τὸ κατὰ σάρκα [Romans 9:5])—which corresponds to the literal, historical Jesus—and a Christ according to the spirit—the allegorical, risen Christ:

> Concerning His son who was born of the seed of David according to the flesh, and declared to be the son of God in power, according to the spirit of Holiness, by the resurrection from the dead   (Romans 1:3–4).
>
> περὶ τοῦ υἱοῦ αὐτοῦ τοῦ γενομένου ἐκ σπέρματος Δαυὶδ κατὰ σάρκα, τοῦ ὁρισθέντος υἱοῦ θεοῦ ἐν δυνάμει κατὰ πνεῦμα ἁγιω- σύνης ἐξ ἀναστάσεως νεκρῶν

Jesus is the son of David according to the flesh but the son of God according to the spirit. This duality—if not dualism—is both ontological and hermeneutical or epistemological.

In the same category, it seems to me, is "So then, from now we know no man according to the flesh, and if we did know Christ according to the flesh, we will no longer [so] know him," Ὥστε ἡμεῖς ἀπὸ τοῦ νῦν οὐδένα οἴδαμεν κατὰ σάρκα εἰ καὶ ἐγνώκαμεν κατὰ σάρκα Χριστόν, ἀλλὰ νῦν οὐκέτι γινώσκομεν (2 Corinthians 5:16), in a context discussing the death and resurrection of Christ. There are two ways of construing this verse.[34] Most commentators nowadays understand that the κατὰ σάρκα here modifies the verb, ἐγνώκαμεν, and not the Χριστόν, while Bultmann held that it indeed referred to the Christ, who in his aspect of according to the flesh represented the historical Jesus, "Christ in his worldly accessibility, before his death and resurrection." Since we know for certain from Romans 9:5 that "Christ according to the Flesh" is a real entity in Pauline thought, I am inclined strongly to accept Bultmann's formulation.[35] It is not, however, crucial for my argument. If "according to the flesh" refers to the Christ, then it explicitly marks the site of Christ's dual ontology; however, the usage of κατὰ and not another preposition will, in any case, mark that ontological difference as an epistemological one as well, as a mode of knowing, experiencing, or interpreting Christ. On the other hand, if it is the knowing which is according to the flesh, the *hermeneutical* moment is explicit, even though the *ontological* point is muted. Once more, as Bultmann remarked, "A Christ known κατὰ σάρκα is precisely what a Christ κατὰ σάρκα is" (Bultmann 1951, 1, 231).

In 1 Corinthians 10:18, Paul interprets a verse having to do with the offering of sacrifices and remarks that the verse deals with Israel according to the flesh, which means both Israel in its corporeal aspect, the "historical Israel," as well as Israel interpreted literally.[36] Here, too, Paul contrasts two ways of knowing and interpreting Christ: The inferior (from his perspective) Christians focus on, know, Christ according to his human, outer, according-to-the-flesh aspect—which, while clearly lower, is *not* "without reference to God"—while Paul and his followers know the crucified and risen Christ, who is known according to the spirit. However, very significantly, Paul does not entirely deny, of course, the importance of "Christ according to the flesh" either.[37] The two Christs, or two ways of knowing Christ's dual nature, stand in the same axiological relationship one to the other as do the two Israels and, indeed, the two meanings (literal and spiritual) of the text as well.

Paul's entire thought and expression are generated by a very powerful set of analogical ratios. Among these sets of oppositions which can be gleaned from various places in his writings are

flesh	spirit
body	soul
humans	God
Jesus (before Easter)	risen Christ
literal	figurative
Israel	Church
works	faith
circumcision	baptism
traditional teaching	revelation
James	Paul
earthly Jerusalem	heavenly Jerusalem
(Jewish church)	(gentile church)
genealogy	"Promise"

Sets of binary relations like this are a prominent feature of Pythagorean thought and expression. We know that Paul thought in such terms, as at one point he even uses the Pythagorean terminology for it (Galatians 4:25), συστοιχεῖ. I suggest that in his thinking and writing, the analogies among the relations generated by these lists of related ratios provide much of the heuristic energy which makes possible Paul's religious critique and innovation.[38] Throughout this book I will be suggesting that the homologies of these ratios provide the force for Paul's thought and argumentation.[39]

Paul describes historical Israel's existence as carnal, physical, material, and literal, and therefore it follows that the hermeneutical practices by which that historical Israel constitutes itself are also carnal; the Jews read only according to the flesh. They do not see beyond the fleshly literal meaning to the spirit behind the language. This brings us to the question of supersession. Richard Hays denies that Pauline theology is supersessionist (Hays 1989, 98–102). For Paul the Christian community stands in continuity with and not against the historical Israel. There has been, moreover, no rejection of Israel owing to their faults or flaws, as in some other New Testament theologies, nor, finally are the Christian believers free of either ethical or moral requirements or unsusceptible to sin (as the Corinthians apparently thought). Hays's reading then defangs Paul of his "anti-Semitism" without, however, as in the case of some modern liberal apologists for Paul, removing the teeth of Paul's critique.[40] I would argue, however (and here, I think, the different hermeneutical perspectives of a self-identified Jew and a self-identified Christian show up): If there has been no rejection of Israel, there has indeed been a supersession of the historical Israel's hermeneutic of self-understanding as a community con-stituted by physical genealogy and observances and the covenantal exclu-siveness that such a self-understanding entails. This is a perfect example of cultural reading, the existence of at once irreconcilable readings gen-erated by different subject positions. What will appear from the Christian perspective as tolerance, namely Paul's willingness—indeed insistence— that within the Christian community all cultural practice is equally to be tolerated, from the rabbinic Jewish perspective is simply an eradication of the entire value system which insists that our cultural practice is our task and calling in the world and must not be abandoned or reduced to a matter of taste. The call to human Oneness, at the same time that it is a stirring call to equality, constitutes a threat as well to Jewish (or any other) differ-ence. While it is not anti-Semitic (or even anti-Judaic) in intent, it nev-ertheless has had the effect of depriving continued Jewish existence of any reality or significance in the Christian economies of history.

"NOW HAGAR IS MT. SINAI IN ARABIA": THE ALLEGORICAL KEY TO PAUL

It is in the famous allegory of the two wives of Abraham (Galatians 4:21– 31) that Paul explicitly develops the *theoretical* moment of his theological and political program, for it is here that he first (and solely) uses the actual term "allegory," which I am reading as the key to his discourse.[41] This is the climax of the entire argument and preaching of the letter, in which all of its themes are brought together and shown to cohere. Those inter-preters who regard this passage as out of place or an afterthought are, I think, quite mising the point of Paul's discourse.[42] Paul has just in the previous section railed once again against his Jewish Christian opponents for insisting that the Galatians must become Jews in order to be Chris-tians. He has used the language of inclusion and exclusion. There is no story more inherently exclusionary, and no text which more explicitly refers to both circumcision and conversion, than the text of Abraham, his wives Sarah and Hagar, and their respective children, the one included and the one excluded. For Paul's theology to work he must reverse the

terms of that constitutive biblical text and uproot the genealogical significance of the Promise. He must contrast, indeed, the Promise to the genealogy. Allegory is the perfect hermeneutic vehicle for this transformation, because it figures both the status of language and the status of the
body. Just as the language of the text is translated by an allegorical reading
into a spiritual meaning, so the body of the believer is translated out of
its ethnic status and into a spiritual body—again, the very notion that
verse 19 has insisted upon, for it is Paul who is going to give birth to the
Christians; he is pregnant and in travail with them until "Christ is formed
in them."

Paul here brilliantly sets up the terms of his onto-theology. Isaac's very
birth was not by natural means but through an angelic promise to his
mother.[43] This "promise" corresponds to the promise that was made to
Abraham that "his seed will inherit" and that through him all of the
peoples will be blessed, as well as to the promise to Sarah that she would
bear a son. On the other hand, Ishmael, the child born to Hagar, was
born by natural means. Isaac, accordingly, signifies "the spirit," and Ishmael, "the flesh." "The spirit" can thus be replaced here by "the promise,"
and "according to the promise" becomes a hermeneutical term, a way of
understanding Scripture.[44] In a recent paper, Barry Sang (1991) has elegantly described the exact methodology of Paul's allegory here: Paul gives
us a vital clue to his hermeneutic system, by using not only the term
ἀλλεγορέο (allegory) but also συστοιχέο (analogical ratios), a term related etymologically to the Aristotelian noun συστοιχεῖαι, which refers
to the Pythagorean practice. As Gaston had already shown, Paul's method
involves the use of the Pythagorean practice of establishing of parallel
columns of corresponding dichotomies (Gaston 1982).[45] We have already
seen such a Pauline list drawn from Galatians as a whole above. Sang
improves considerably on Gaston by demonstrating that it is precisely this
method of drawing up pairs of coordinate columns which enables Paul's
allegory. The two columns are set as opposites to each other, and accordingly each member of one column stands in an analogical (= equality of
ratios) relationship with any other member of the same column. Consequently, "according to the promise" is equivalent to "according to the
spirit." Since, as I have argued, "according to the spirit" is equivalent to
the allegorical meaning of the physical sign, it follows that being born
according to the spirit is the true meaning of descent from Abraham, of
which being born according to the flesh is only the signifier. This last fillip

brings Paul's hermeneutical method here even closer to Philo's, I think, than even Sang would have it.

As the commentators sense, this allegorical formation is also supported by the distinction between slave and free which Paul has developed at length in the previous chapter as marking the distinction between Christian freedom and Jewish and pagan slavery to the "elements of the world." It is the very concatenation of these several details that provides the extraordinary richness of the Pauline text here, which can be compared to an ornate tapestry for both its surface detail and depth:

> For it is written that Abraham had two sons, one from the slave
> woman and one from the free woman. The one from the slave woman
> was born "according to the flesh," however, while the one from the
> free woman "through the promise." These things have an allegorical
> meaning. For they are two covenants: one from Mt. Sinai, giving birth
> into slavery—this is Hagar. Now Hagar is Mt. Sinai in Arabia, but it
> also corresponds to the present Jerusalem, for she lives in slavery to-
> gether with her children. By contrast, the Jerusalem above is free—
> this is our mother. For it is written, "Rejoice, O barren one who does
> not bear: break forth and shout, you who are not in travail; for the
> children of the desolate one are more than the children of the one
> who has a husband." But you, my brothers, are children of promise,
> like Isaac. And just as in those days the one born "according to [the]
> flesh" persecuted the one "according to [the] spirit," so it is today.[46]

We thus see the political and theological themes of the entire Pauline enterprise in this letter coming together here in one brilliant stroke. All of the antitheses that he has set up until now work together to convince the Galatians that they have but one choice, to remain in the spirit and not recommit themselves to the flesh, to remain in the covenant that was made according to the promise to the one seed of Abraham, the (spiritual) body of the risen Christ, and not return to the slavery of the covenant with Sinai, which is the present Jerusalem—that is, both the symbolic present Jerusalem and the church in Jerusalem—by undertaking to fall back into the fleshly hermeneutic of literal interpretation of circumcision. Furthermore, at least in this passage we see how illusory is the contrast between allegory and typology.[47] Because the present Christian situation is to be interpreted spiritually, allegory is the appropriate mode for understanding it. To be sure, it is the historical event of the coming of the Christ, his crucifixion, and resurrection which has precipitated the reading, but that very historical event is itself not history but an event that signifies the end—*telos*, both the finish and the revelation of the mean-ing—of history.[48]

As a mode of reading events, apocalyptic is, accordingly, structurally homologous to allegory. Allegory, typology, and apocalyptic all equally figure an "end to history." The Christ event—Jesus' birth as a Jew and his transformation in the crucifixion—both signifies and effects the trans-formation/transition from the historical moment to the allegorical one, from the moment of ethnicity to the moment of the universal (spiritual) subject, from natural birth to spiritual rebirth in the Promise. That is, it signifies insofar as the allegorical meaning was always already there, and it effects insofar as only at the apocalypse is that meaning revealed in the world. This interpretation, i.e., that the true meaning always existed and only waited for the Christ event in order to be revealed, is strongly supported by Galatians 3:8: "And the scripture, foreseeing that God would justify the Gentiles by faith, preached the gospel beforehand [προε-υηγγελίσατο] to Abraham, saying, 'In you shall all nations be blessed.'" But "Now before faith came, we were confined under the law, kept under restraint until faith should be revealed" (3:23). The Christ event is thus precisely apocalyptic, in the strictest sense of that term—revelation; it has revealed the universally true meaning, faith, that always subsisted within and above history, works of the Law.

For Paul, allegory is indeed the speaking of the other; it reveals that the particular signifies the universal.[49] We must realize the depth of Paul's understanding of allegory not as a rhetorical device of language but as a revelation of the structure of reality (including historical reality) itself in order to have an appreciation for this passage and his thought in general. It is not that allegory and typology have been mixed here (*pace* Betz, 239), but history itself is transformed through this typology into allegory, and Paul's apocalypse is fully realized. Accordingly, interpretations of Paul which focus on his apocalypticism, understanding it as only a version of the general Palestinian Jewish apocalyptic, have also seriously mistaken the thrust of his gospel; it is not only that the fulfillment of time has come but more to the point that Paul understands it in a certain, specific way, as the revelation of the inner meaning of outward signs, an inner meaning which is always already there, whether the outward signs are the flesh, the Jews, the Law, or the historical Jesus. It seems to me to be a serious her-meneutic error to make one's interpretation of Paul depend on the apoca-lyptic expectation, which is after all not even mentioned once in Galatians, rather than the apocalyptic fulfillment which has already been realized in the vision of the crucified Christ according to the spirit, Christ's spirit, Paul's, and that of the Galatians.[50] Even J. Christiaan Beker, the most trenchant defender of Paul as apocalyptist, admits that "Galatians threatens to undo what I have posited as the coherent core of Pauline thought, the apocalyptic co-ordinates of the Christ-event that focus on the imminent, cosmic triumph of God" (Beker 1980, 100). This suggests that as central as expectation of the Parousia is for Paul, and Beker's reading is impressive indeed, it is not yet "the coherent core of Pauline thought" but a vitally important element of that thought whose core lies yet elsewhere. The "elsewhere" that I argue for is, of course, the unification of humanity, of which both the realized eschatology of the cross and the expected eschatology of the Parousia are equally vital parts.

WRITING ON THE PHALLUS: MIDRASH AND CIRCUMCISION

Paul, as is well known, was to win the field in Christianity, just as Christianity was to win the field in the western world. The true cultural issue dividing Christians from Jews by the second century was the significance of bodily filiation, membership in a kin-group, for religious life. As long as participation in the religious community is tied to those rites which are special, performed by and marked in the body, the religion remains an affair of a particular tribal group, "Israel in the flesh."[51] The fraughtness of circumcision (almost obsession with it) of all of these people is not to be found in the difficulty of the rite to perform but in the way that it is the most complete sign of the connection of the Torah to the concrete body of Israel. People of late antiquity were willing to do many extreme and painful things for religion. It is absurd to imagine that circumcision would have stood in the way of conversion for people who were willing to undergo fasts, the lives of anchorites, martyrdom, and even occasionally castration for the sake of God. The aversion to circumcision must have a different explanation, a cultural one.[52]

In early Christian writings from Paul on, there is a parallelism between the allegorical form and the content of hermeneutics. Thus, just as the materiality of the language is transcended in the spirituality of its interpretation, so also the materiality of physical, national, gendered human existence is transcended in the spirituality of "universal" faith. In midrashic interpretations of circumcision as well, there is a perfect homology between form and content of the interpretation. The midrashic interpretations of circumcision focused strongly, of course, on the physical rite itself and the inscription that it made on the body. In their writings, this mark of natural or naturalized membership in a particular people is made the center of salvation. These texts, in their almost crude physicality, register a strong protest, I suggest, against any flight from the body to the spirit with the attendant deracination of historicity, physicality, and carnal filiation which characterizes Christianity. The following text is exemplary. The role of the materiality of language and the significance of the physical body of σάρξ are both captured together in one image:

> All Israelites who are circumcised will come into Paradise, for the
> Holy Blessed One placed His name on Israel, in order that they might
> come into Paradise, and What is the name and the seal which He
> placed upon them? It is ShaDaY. The Shin [the first letter of the root],
> he placed in the nose, The Dalet, He placed in the hand, and the Yod
> in the circumcision.   (Tanhuma Tsav 14; Wolfson 1987a, 78)

In contrast to Paul and his followers, for whom the interpretation of circumcision was a rejection of the body, for the Rabbis of the midrash, it is a sign of the sanctification of that very physical body; the cut in the penis completes the inscription of God's name on the (male, Jewish) body. The midrash speaks of circumcision as a transformation of the body into a holy object. It constitutes, moreover, an insistence (typical of midrash) on the meaning of the actual material form, the shapes of letters and sounds of language. It is this insistence—and not "playfulness," as in some currently fashionable accounts—that leads to midrashic punning and seeking of significance in such very concrete, physical, material features of the Hebrew language. The penis—not phallus—in this text constructs precisely the refusal of logos. The insistence on the literal, the physical, is a stubborn resistance to the universal, a tenacious clinging to difference. At the same time, of course, the very claim that only the male, Jewish body has inscribed on it the full name of God reveals the real and present danger of both the gender and "racial" politics of commitment to difference, a theme to which I will return.

By substituting a spiritual interpretation for a physical ritual, Paul at one stroke was saying that the literal Israel, "according to the flesh," is not the ultimate Israel; there is an allegorical "Israel in the spirit." The practices of the particular Jewish People are not what the Bible speaks of, but faith, the allegorical meaning of those practices. It was Paul's genius to transcend "Israel in the flesh."

Thus, we see that the very same discursive moment, found in both Philo and Paul, which produced the devaluation of the ethnic body— Jewish—as the corporeal, produced also the devaluation of the gendered body—female—as the corporeal, and this is how the Universal Subject becomes male and Christian. For Paul, the "Jewish Question" and the "Woman Problem" were essentially the same, although the possibilities for "solving" them that he could imagine were substantially different.

2

What Was Wrong with Judaism?
The Cultural Politics of Pauline Scholarship

An enthusiastic first-century Greek-speaking Jew, one Saul of Tarsus, is walking down a road, with a very troubled mind.[1] The Torah, in which he so firmly believes, claims to be the text of the One True God of all the world, who created heaven and earth and all humanity, and yet its primary content is the history of one particular People—almost one family—and the practices that it prescribes are many of them practices which mark off the particularity of that tribe, his tribe. In his very commitment to the truth of the gospel of that Torah and its claim to universal validity lies the source of Saul's trouble. Not only he but many Jews of the first century shared this sense that something was not right. Philo in Alexandria and the anonymous author of the *Wisdom of Solomon* seem troubled by the same thoughts. Why would a universal God desire and command that one people should circumcise the male members of the tribe and command food taboos that make it impossible for one people to join in table fellowship with all the rest of his children? Now this Saul, as a loyal Jew, has in the past been among the most active persecutors of a strange messianic sect that has sprung up recently in Jerusalem. He knows something, therefore, of the claims and beliefs of the participants in that sect, little as they appeal to him. Walking, troubled and musing, all of a sudden Saul has a moment of blinding insight, so rich and revealing that he understands it to have been, in fact, an apocalypse: That very sect, far from being something worthy of persecution, provides the answer to the very dilemma that Saul is facing. The birth of Christ as a human being and a Jew, his death, and his resurrection as spiritual and universal was the model and the apocalypse of the transcendence of the physical and particular Torah for Jews alone by its spiritual and universal referent for all. At that moment Saul died, and Paul was born.

By telling the story of the conversion of Paul in this way, I am hardly making a claim to know things about "what really happened." Some

39

aspects of this story, such as the name change, seem highly unlikely to me. Still less am I claiming to know what was actually going on in the mind of Paul. Rather, I am using the narrative form to construct and communicate the "Paul" that I will present in this book. The Paul that I am constructing here is a highly politicized intervention in biblical interpretation and, I hope, more than that as well. This book is what has come to be known recently as a "cultural reading" of the Pauline corpus.[2] "Cultural reading" has two senses. On the one hand, it refers to the exegetical advances that "European" interpreters of the Bible gain by paying attention to the insights of Bible-readings from "other" cultures that may have practices and knowledges important for the understanding of biblical texts. It refers as well to the politicized readings of the Bible generated by people who have been the object of colonialist or racist practices carried out in the name of the Bible. In this book, I am contributing a cultural reading of my own, as a Jew, of certain key texts from the Pauline corpus, a cultural reading in both senses that I have mentioned. As a traditional Jew, steeped in the literature of rabbinic Judaism, I have intimate knowledge of a religious and hermeneutical tradition very close to that from which Paul presumably sprung. It is also, however, a cultural reading in the second sense, since Jews have certainly been the object of much violence brought about in the name of Paul's text. In this chapter I will present a brief account of developments in the study of Paul as I read them. This is not, however, intended as a history of research, a genre of writing belonging to dissertations, usually found in introductions to same, and ultimately dreary. Rather I intend here a highly political account of different interpretations of Paul from the perspective of a Jew committed to the significance and continuation of Jewish culture and particularity.

PAUL AND "THE JEWISH PROBLEM"

Since World War II, the study of Paul's letters has taken on a new sense of urgency and importance. Much of the horror inflicted on the Jews in this century can be traced at least partially to theologically informed attitudes of contempt for the Jews. These attitudes of contempt are partially produced in the context of a particular reading of Paul's texts, a reading which depicts him attacking Judaism as an inferior, mechanistic, commercialized religion, exactly paralleling portrayals of the Jewish People current in anti-Semitic Europe—witness even so relatively mild and nuanced a case as *The Merchant of Venice.* This reading of Paul's attitude toward Judaism usually goes along with two corollary propositions: that Paul converted to Christianity owing to his disgust with the ancestral religion, and that God had rejected the Jews because of their inferior religious stance. Following a spirited indictment of Paul by the important radical theologian, Rosemary Radford Ruether, various reinterpretations of his work have taken diverse directions (Ruether 1974).[3]

The "Old Paul"

Before World War II, and in certain circles until this day, Paul's oeuvre has been interpreted as a sustained attack on the Jewish religion. This is particularly the case in what has been (with some exaggeration) termed the "Lutheran" reading of Paul.[4] The best summary and critique of this view is found in E. P. Sanders's monumental *Paul and Palestinian Judaism* (Sanders 1977, and see Fredriksen 1988, 102–06). According to this interpretation, Paul became violently disillusioned with "Judaism" because of its commitment to "works-righteousness." These accounts of Paul (which also presented themselves as true statements about Judaism!), presented the Law as leading both to a sense of inadequacy, because of its alleged requirement that it be kept in its entirety for salvation, and also to self-righteousness and boasting before Man and God.[5] Furthermore, such a religion was arid and devoid of spiritual feeling. In its commitment to outer ritual (and ethical) action and not inner spiritual feeling, it produced a dry, spiritually deadly legalistic mentality. It was against this decadent and empty religion that Paul revolted. From the very beginning of any kind of scholarly dialogue, Jewish scholars had protested that this view of Judaism simply was not a fair representation of the religion. Jews had always had a notion and powerful sense of God's grace, חסד and רחמים, and of the necessity for grace in life and for salvation. Judaism, moreover, had always been inhabited by a profound spirituality experienced both through performance of the commandments and also in such experiences as prayer. The dramatic story of George Foote Moore's initially unsuccessful challenge to the reigning Christian accounts of Judaism, of the frustration of Jewish scholars like Samuel Sandmel who felt that nothing would ever change, and of the eventual triumph of a truer, fairer account of Judaism at the hands of Krister Stendahl, W. D. Davies, and especially Davies's student E. P. Sanders has been well told already (Watson 1986,

1–22). By now, in all but certain diehard Lutheran circles in Germany, it is well recognized that Luther's description of Judaism had more to do with his battles with Catholicism and his own personal spiritual conflicts than with either Paul or Palestinian Judaism. The question that remains, then, is: What about Paul? Did Paul simply misdescribe or misrepresent Judaism for one reason or another, or is it rather the Lutheran tradition which has misread Paul?

Five Current Views[6]

The Gaston-Gager Hypothesis   A very stimulating and moving attempt to totally revise our understanding of Paul was produced by Lloyd Gaston and developed further by John Gager.[7] The basic outlines of this view are that Paul never intended to replace "the Law" as the means of salvation and justification for Jews but only to add Christ as a means of salvation for ethnic gentiles. Paul's "attacks" on the Law are not directed at Jews at all but at Judaizers, that is, at missionaries who contend that gentiles must convert to Judaism and keep the Law, including circumcision, in order to be saved by Christ. Paul had no essential critique of Judaism at all but only a desire to produce "Moses for the masses." Gager has even written that "Jews of Paul's acquaintance resisted him *on the mistaken assumption* that he urged other Jews to abandon the Torah for allegiance to Christ" (1983, 200–201). This approach to Paul, termed by Gaston himself an experiment, is certainly a moving effort to rescue Paul from charges of anti-Semitism and thus save him for modern Christians.[8] Ultimately, however, it has proven exegetically unconvincing.[9] I need not rehearse here the objections to this view, since Thielman (and others) have already done the job (Thielman 1989, 123–33). It should be noted that while the thesis as a whole has been rejected, certain of its elements have stimulated valuable rethinking of Paul on various issues. Thus I would argue that there is something useful in the above-quoted proposition: Paul did not urge other Jews to abandon the Torah—except, of course, Peter. On the other hand, as I will suggest in Chapter 9 in my discussion of Romans 11, Jews who did not accept allegiance to Christ were considered by Paul to be lopped-off and abandoned branches of the People of God. Keeping the Law was for Paul adiaphora; faith in Jesus was most certainly not! Romans 14, especially if the "weak" and the "strong" are the law-abiding and the not-law-abiding, supports both halves of this proposition eloquently.[10]

E. P. Sanders: The Christological Interpretation of Paul   Recently, Frank
Thielman has presented the current state of Pauline scholarship in the
following fashion:

> Most interpreters, at least in the last decade, have concluded that
> Paul's view of the law can only be explained if we assume that he had
> abandoned Judaism and looked back on his "former way of life," in-
> cluding his devotion to the law, wholly from the standpoint of his ex-
> perience with Christ.   (Thielman 1989, 1–2)

The most prominent representative of this position is E. P. Sanders. Sanders argued that Judaism was not and had never been a religion of "works-
righteousness," by which is meant a religion in which meritorious works
automatically "earn" one's salvation (Sanders 1973, 1977). There had always been a recognition both of God's freedom and of God's mercy in
judgment. Judaism was rather a religion of Covenantal Nomism through
which salvation had been granted to Israel by a free act of grace, the
Covenant, to which the proper response was obedience to its terms. Jews
were saved through this grace unless their disobedience was such that it
marked them as having renounced the Covenant. This seems to me a
fairly accurate broad statement of "the Jewish pattern of religion." Note
its crucial point that in Judaism no one has ever completely fulfilled the
requirements of the Law, so God's justification will always have to be
informed by mercy or grace. Such a Judaism is clearly much less amenable
to treatment as a foil or background for a spiritual revolution by which
"legalism" was replaced by grace and spirituality in Paul. For Sanders, Paul
leveled no attack on Judaism at all, indeed hardly even a critique. One
way of summing up Sanders's position would be to say that the traditional
contents of a putative Pauline critique of Judaism cannot be accepted because they would make Paul a fool or a liar. Judaism was particularly
marked neither by self-righteousness nor by legalism, if by the latter we
understand a dry, nonspiritual or commercialistic religious attitude.

Therefore, claims Sanders, Paul's own soteriology can hardly be described as universalistic, since it was entirely dependent on faith in Christ,
a matter which is as particular as membership in (or conversion to) the
Jewish People (1983, 23). For Paul, argues Sanders in a famous formula,
the only thing wrong with Judaism was that it was not Christianity (1977,
552). On Galatians 3 (a text which will be discussed at length below)
Sanders writes:

In the midst of a sometimes bewildering series of arguments, quota-
tions, and appeals, there seem to be only two sentences in Galatians in
which Paul states unambiguously not only what his position is (which
is never in doubt) but *why* he holds it. These statements are [2:21 and
3:21]. Put in propositional terms, they say this: God sent Christ; he
did so in order to offer righteousness; this would have been pointless if
righteousness were already available by the law (2:21); the law was
not given to bring righteousness. That the positive statement about
righteousness through Christ grounds the negative one about the law
seems to me self-evident.   (1983, 27)[11]

Not quite self-evident, Sanders's interpretation depends (as all do) on
the choice of particular texts on which to hang the rest.[12] One could just
as easily suppose that in these verses Paul is arguing further for his view of
the Law, which is grounded, however, elsewhere. On my view, the elsewhere is, of course, the issue of salvation for all: Jews and gentiles alike.
Sanders's position in *Paul and Palestinian Judaism* requires that we assume
that there was nothing in Paul's position, thinking, or affect vis-à-vis his
prior Judaism that led to his experience on the Damascus Road.

Nor has Sanders substantially revised his position on this question. In
his *Paul, the Law, and the Jewish People,* he writes:

One of the most striking features of Paul's argument is that he puts
everyone, whether Jew or Gentile, in the same situation. This is best
explained by hypothesizing that he thought backwards, from solution
to plight, and that his thinking in this, as in many respects, was gov-
erned by the overriding conviction that salvation is through Christ.
Since Christ came to save all, all needed salvation. The fact that Paul
can equate the status of Jew and Gentile is explicable on this hypothesis and is simultaneously the best proof that Paul did not begin by analyzing the human condition.   (1983, 68)

This account, however, entirely begs the question of what brought Paul
to his recognition that salvation is through Christ. What happened to him
was either a psychological or a supernatural miracle.[13] If we, however,
reverse the logic, as I do, then he was prepared for his experience by a
deep sense of plight—not personal, but theological. We can account for
Paul's putting everyone in the same situation by assuming that this was
exactly what was bothering him about Judaism, namely that it *did not*
"equate the status of Jew and Gentile." Since, then, all need salvation,
Christ came to save all. The nature of the plight is derivable from his
letters and (as Sanders himself recognizes) it is consistent with what we

know of first-century Judaism in its several varieties. Accordingly, the view of Paul presented in this book accepts all of Sanders's claims above except the "solution-to-plight" direction and the argument that Paul's cannot be a universalist position because of its requirement of faith.[14]

Sanders has produced another powerful (but not irrefutable) argument for his position. He argues that there is a contradiction within Paul between repeated statements that the Law condemns and kills and also repeated statements that the Law (or the "old dispensation") was "glorious" (*both together* in 2 Corinthians 3). This apparent anomaly is explained by Sanders as a case in which the contrast is not between evil and good but between good and greater good:

> The simplest explanation of this dual form of contrast seems to be that
> [Paul] came to relegate the Mosaic dispensation to a less glorious place
> *because* he found something more glorious and that he *then,* thinking
> in black-and-white terms, developed the death/life contrast. I cannot
> see how the development could have run the other way, from an ini-
> tial conviction that the law only condemns and kills, to a search for
> something which gives life, to the conviction that life comes by faith
> in Christ, to the statement that the law lost its glory because a new
> dispensation surpasses it in glory.   (1983, 138)

As I have already said, this seems like an ineluctable claim. There is, however, another possible solution. Paul, while feeling that the Law was sweet and good (glorious) in his former life, was nevertheless deeply disturbed by its exclusive and ethnocentric implications.[15] Having discovered Christ as the solution to this plight, i.e., as the way to render Torah salvation for all, he now perceives that the former condition not only is less glorious than he thought and less glorious than the present condition but, in the absence of a turn toward the Lord, can only bring death and not life. When the Torah is read as a signifier for that which it truly signifies, its lesser glory is then apparent. When, however, it is read only for the letter, then that letter itself brings death and not life.

Thus even in the 1983 book, where he considerably clarifies his interpretation of Paul and definitively argues (to my mind) that the major thrust of Paul's thought on these topics was the salvation of *all* in Christ, Sanders still does not allow this to be the *motivating force* behind Paul's ministry.[16] Sanders's book contains the best single demonstration of the thesis that Paul's critique dealt not with individual self-righteousness on the part of Jews but with "their own righteousness," righteousness that is

reserved for Jews, namely, the Law (1983, 36–43).[17] But Sanders's ultimate understanding of Paul still wavers between two (partially incompatible) positions: According to one Paul was primarily motivated by christology, and according to another his primary motivation was the question
of inclusion of the gentiles. Thus Sanders writes:

> This gives us another way of defining Paul's attack on the law—more
> precisely, what he found inadequate in it. I said just above that it is
> the notion of Jewish privilege and the idea of election which he at-
> tacks, and I have elsewhere written that his real attack on Judaism is
> against the idea of the covenant and that what he finds wrong in Juda-
> ism is that it lacks Christ.   (1983, 47)

Which is it: the notion of privilege, or the lack of Christ? Here, I
think, Sanders tries to harmonize his previous claims that the only thing
wrong with Judaism was that it was not Christianity with his newer understanding that there *is* a genuine critique of Judaism in Paul's work,
although on an entirely different basis from the Lutheran slander. "The
argument is that one need not be Jewish to be 'righteous' and is thus
against the standard Jewish view that accepting and living by the law is a
sign and a condition of favored status. *This is both the position which, independently of Paul, we can know to have characterized Judaism and the position
which Paul attacks*" (1983, 46). This is just right, but despite mighty efforts
to harmonize—"What is wrong with the law, and thus with Judaism, is
that it does not provide for God's ultimate purpose, that of saving the
entire world through faith in Christ"—Sanders still leaves the christological and universalist aspects insufficiently integrated. Thus he can still
write, "Paul's view of the law depends more on the exclusivism of his
Christology than on anything else" (1983, 57, n. 64). Sanders still seems
to hold that Paul came to Christ, realized that faith in the cross was God's
plan for salvation, and then disqualified the Jewish Law for salvation; he
does not argue that Paul realized that the Jewish Law could not be the
means for salvation *because* it was only for Jews and came to Christ to *solve*
that problem.

Sanders has forever changed the way that Paul will be read by scholars
and interpreters of his work. In his masterwork, he finally achieved what
several Christian and Jewish scholars (including Davies) had tried for decades to achieve—to demonstrate that the slander of early Judaism promulgated by interpreters of Paul was simply and finally just that, a slander.

Pauline studies will never be the same, at least on English-speaking soil. New commentaries on the corpus advertise themselves as "the first full commentary on the Epistle" since the advent of the new paradigm (Dunn 1988; Barclay 1991). And indeed, Sanders has achieved a paradigm shift in the Kuhnian sense. Whatever criticisms have been leveled against Sanders's work, he has accomplished a gigantic breakthrough, which, I think, will never be reversed: He demonstrated that descriptions of the Judaism against which Paul is allegedly reacting *must be based first and foremost in realistic and accurate descriptions of actually known Judaism and cannot be simply "reconstructed" from the Pauline texts themselves.* Let me repeat this point: Whatever any interpreter ends up saying about Paul and Judaism from now on starts from actual Jewish texts and not from Paul.[18] Judaism must not be treated as an unknown to be reconstructed by Pauline scholarship.[19] Whether or not one agrees (and I often do and as often do not) with the details of Sanders's own interpretations of Paul, he has laid the foundations for a reading which neither slanders Judaism nor slanders Paul by making his account of Judaism a slander. As a professional and confessional student of rabbinic Judaism, I find Sanders's descriptions of my religious tradition unfailingly apposite to my own intuitions about this tradition. This is the gigantic advance which Sanders has wrought. The following brief quotation is exemplary of Sanders's clarity, accuracy, and intellectual integrity:

> The correct exegetical perception that Paul *opposed Judaism* and that he *argued christologically* becomes—without argument or exegetical demonstration, but on the ground of basic theological assumptions— an assertion that he opposed *the self-righteousness which is typical of Judaism.* This step has doubtless been facilitated by more than a century of reading Jewish literature as evidencing self-righteousness. *But the supposed objection to Jewish self-righteousness is as absent from Paul's letters as self-righteousness itself is from Jewish literature.* (1983, 156 [final emphasis added])

A Neo-Lutheran Reading Which Is Not Anti-Judaic: Stephen Westerholm   In his *Israel's Law and the Church's Faith,* Stephen Westerholm is a Pauline scholar who essentially maintains the view of Paul that Luther promulgated, without, however, allowing it to be or become a slander of rabbinic Judaism. He accepts Sanders's principle that we cannot describe Judaism on the basis of our reading of Paul, cannot assume that Judaism is in every way the antithesis of Pauline theology—e.g., cannot conclude that if Paul says that Christ excludes boasting, then Jews boast. Westerholm provides, however, an important counter-corollary, "The basis for Paul's rejection of the law must not be determined solely by asking what his foes were proposing any more than we may see Judaism's own perspective of the law in Paul's rejected version of it" (1988, 150). This is well put and means that the initial reasons for Paul's rejection of the Law and his later reflections and amplifications are both equally important. Westerholm argues that Luther understood Paul well but that Paul was representing not Judaism but Christian theology:

> There is more of Paul in Luther than many twentieth-century scholars are inclined to allow. But the insights of the "new perspective" must not be lost to view. Paul's convictions need to be identified; they must also be recognized as Christian theology. When Paul's conclusion that the path of the law is dependent on human works is used to posit a rabbinic doctrine of salvation by works, and when his claim that God's grace in Christ excludes human boasting is used to portray rabbinic Jews as self-righteous boasters, the results (in Johnsonian terms) are "pernicious as well as false." When, moreover, the doctrine of merit perceived by Luther in the Catholicism of his day is read into the Judaism of the first Christian centuries, the results are worthless for historical study. Students who want to know how a rabbinic Jew perceived humanity's place in God's world will read Paul with caution and Luther not at all.   (173)

Westerholm goes on to say, "On the other hand, students who want to understand Paul but feel they have nothing to learn from a Martin Luther should consider a career in metallurgy." The point is well taken, if exaggerated, and Westerholm has made a strong case for reading Paul as motivated by a sense of the universality of sin and a conviction that only grace can save. The important shift in his work from the neo-Lutheran interpretations of the Bultmann school is that for Westerholm it is not keeping of the Law which is sinful in Paul but failure to keep the Law. There is no doubt in my mind as well that Luther's emphasis on faith is a pivotal Pauline theme, once it is deprived of its anti-Judaic slander as Westerholm has done, but I am convinced that Luther (and Westerholm) have missed a major issue in Paul (perhaps *the* major issue). The issue of re-creation of Universal Israel was central for him, and justification by grace was a necessary condition for this; for Westerholm, the issue of universal sin and salvation by grace is the central point, and the salvation of the gentiles is almost epiphenomenal. While I am entirely in sympathy with Westerholm's sense that theological issues are central in the interpretation of Paul, I disagree strongly with his suggestion that the issue of unification of Jews and gentiles was a "sociological" and not a theological issue for Paul (122). This was no practical matter of "the promotion of the Gentile mission" but rather the very motivation *for* the gentile mission! It is this difference between us that ultimately determines, I think, the different emphases of our readings of Paul. Westerholm concludes his book by writing, "What influence Paul's discussions of the Gentile problem had in Galatia or Rome in the first century remains a mystery; their later effects in Hippo, Wittenberg, and Aldersgate are better known." Indeed, but I trust I will be forgiven the observation that this is a rather selective list of Christian "giants." Westerholm's interpretation is neither pernicious nor false but, I think, not sufficiently grounded in Paul's particular historical situation and that of first-century Judaism. What would have happened, on Westerholm's account, had the Jews been able to keep the Law? The question is, however, one of interpretative emphasis, not absolute disagreement.

The "Sociological" Interpretation of Francis Watson   Westerholm's Paul is quite different from that of Francis Watson in *Paul, Judaism and the Gentiles: A Sociological Approach* (1986).[20] Indeed, one might suggest that Watson would represent for Westerholm the classic candidate for a career in metallurgy. For him, the Jerusalem church was a reform movement, because it did not call for a radical change in Jewish self-understanding or practice, while Paul's was a sectarian and not reformist move. Watson not only dismisses the theological tradition and interpretation associated with Luther but seems to do away as well with the tradition of interpreting Paul as universalist that goes back to F. C. Baur, in spite of having very complimentary things to say about Baur at various points. He writes, "Thus, the origins of Paul's theology of the law are to be found in a specific social situation, and not in his conversion experience, his psychological problems or his insight into the existential plight of humanity" (28; see also 88–89). The possibility that Paul was a social and cultural critic (to use anachronistic terminology)—i.e., that the origins of his theology of the Law have to do with a critique of its social effects and meanings—seems not to have occurred to Watson as a real option at all.[21]

There is much in Watson's work that I find useful. For instance, his

reading seems entirely salutary in its clear recognition that Paul was breaking with the self-understandings of what constituted Jewish community on
the part of most Jews (63–69). There is much also that is quite similar to
the interpretation given here in the understanding that what was at issue
in "works of the Law" was membership in *historical Israel.* The fundamental difference between our interpretations lies in this: Where Watson over
and over sees Paul's objective as causing maximal separation of Christians
from Jews, I see his objective as creating maximal unity between Jews and
gentiles. For Watson the unity is epiphenomenal to the separation; for
me, the separation is an unfortunate consequence of the drive to one-ness
(130). According to Watson, the threat from the "men from James" was
mirabile dictu a threat "to break down the barrier he had built up between
his congregations and the Jewish community" (77)—not, that is, a threat
to rebuild the barriers that he had broken down between Jewish and gentile Christians in his congregations! On my view, the mission to the gentiles constituted the very essence of Paul's Christianity—just as Paul tells
it in Galatians 1; for Watson it is the product of disappointment at the
failure of the Jewish mission.[22]

Watson can write, "The Gentile Christian congregation does not observe the law, and to accept its legitimacy is to abandon the cardinal belief of the Jewish community, the absolute divine authority of the law of
Moses, even if one continues to observe it oneself. The antithesis between
faith and works is thus not a clash between two great opposing theological
principles. It must instead be interpreted sociologically; it expresses the
sectarian separation of Pauline congregations from the Jewish community"
(134). I find this statement quite astonishing. I agree entirely with Watson
that the antithesis between faith and works had nothing to do with
achievement versus grace and further that it had everything to do with
the question of Jews and gentiles in salvation. What I fail to understand,
however, is why this is not to be considered a theological issue par excellence in its own right and why it is not understood by him as the primary
motor of Paul's work. What, after all, could possibly be more theological
than abandoning a cardinal belief? I find that Watson's formalist sociological explanations of sectarian behavior beg precisely the question of
what motivates the break with the original community altogether. As
Watson himself remarks, "Once again, it is clear that Paul's use of antithesis *asserts* the separation of church from synagogue, but does not *explain*
theologically why such a separation is necessary" (69). This seems to me,

however, a singularly unsatisfying hermeneutical result. Watson's interpretative schema is also curiously non-historical in its apparent assumption
of a typology of sectarian behavior which always obtains in all historical,
cultural conditions. Thus, for example, his typology of reform movements
as distinguished from sects seems to me seriously inapt for the situation of
first-century Judaism, in which sects were the norm and there was no
formal hierarchical and hegemonic structure of either theory or practice
to reform.

James Dunn: Paul as Culture-Critic   James Dunn accepted that which I
have identified as Sanders's unimpeachable achievement, namely the insistence that any descriptions of the Judaism from which Paul came and
to which he reacted have to be based on Jewish texts and not on Paul
himself and that they may not distort Judaism in order to provide Paul
with an effective backdrop. He awarded Sanders, moreover, an extraordinary tribute, writing that while there had been much interesting Pauline
scholarship in the last years, "None have succeeded in 'breaking the
mould' of Pauline studies, the mould into which descriptions of Paul's
work and thought have regularly been poured for many decades now.
There is, in my judgement, only one work written during the past decade
or two which deserves that accolade. I refer to the volume entitled *Paul
and Palestinian Judaism* by E. P. Sanders" (Dunn 1990, 184). In spite of
this extraordinary and well-merited praise, Dunn was unhappy, however,
with one of the apparent consequences of Sanders's interpretation,
namely, that it left Paul appearing weak and self-contradictory: "But this
presentation of Paul is only a little better than the one rejected. There
remains something very odd in Paul's attitude to his ancestral faith. The
Lutheran Paul has been replaced by an idiosyncratic Paul who in arbitrary
and irrational manner turns his face against the glory and greatness of
Judaism's covenant theology and abandons Judaism simply because it is
not Christianity" (1990, 187).

Dunn's own understanding represents a tremendous advance over the
previous "Lutheran" reading of Paul, but it also corrects, in my opinion,
excesses of Sanders's (earlier) approach as well, for now we have a rational
basis for Paul's distress with Judaism, one that would lead him precisely to
the point where he would have a "conversion" experience but one that
does not slander Judaism, for there is no doubt that one of the major
problems with Jewish theology is to account for the gentiles in God's

plan. This is not to say that there were not Jewish thinkers before, con-temporaneous with, and after Paul who also confronted this problem. In-deed, the opposite is the case; I would claim that many Jews of late an-tiquity dealt with this issue, from Philo or the author of the *Wisdom of Solomon,* on the one hand, to the Rabbis, on the other—the Rabbis, especially, with their notion of the righteous of the nations.[23] This view takes Paul as a critic of Judaism and a reformer but not as an anti-Judaic thinker. Nor does the fact that this problem of Jewish theology implicitly raises a critique of Judaism itself render its author anti-Judaic. Judaism, like any culture, is obviously not above or beyond criticism from within or without.

Paul as a Jewish Cultural Critic

I read Paul as a Jewish cultural critic, and I ask what it was in Jewish culture that led him to produce a discourse of radical reform of that cul-ture. This question, moreover, raises two closely related but different points: What was *wrong* with Jewish culture in Paul's eyes that necessi-tated a radical reform? And what in the culture provided the grounds for making that critique? The culture itself was in tension with itself, char-acterized both by narrow ethnocentrism and universalist monotheism. I thus contend that Paul's motivation and theory were genuinely theologi-cal, but that his practice and preaching were directed toward radical change in Jewish society.

My fundamental idea, similar to Dunn's—and, as I have said, ulti-mately going back to Baur—is that what motivated Paul ultimately was a profound concern for the one-ness of humanity. This concern was moti-vated both by certain universalistic tendencies within biblical Israelite religion and even more by the reinterpretation of these tendencies in the light of Hellenistic notions of universalism (Hengel 1974). Paul was, therefore, troubled by, critical of, the "ethnocentrism" of biblical and post-biblical religion, and particularly the way it implicitly and explicitly created hierarchies between nations, genders, social classes. Despite this powerful, nearly irresistible concern for universal "Man" and critique of "Judaism," Paul nevertheless remained convinced that the Hebrew Scrip-tures contained God's revelation and that the Jews had been at least the vehicle for the communication of that revelation. In addition, moreover, to his plight having been motivated by a Hellenistic notion—one, I would emphasize, common to him and many other Jews—of the One or the universal, the solution for him was also generated by this idea. That is, Paul came to see, literally—via his vision on the road to Damascus—that the dual structure of outer, physical reality, that which he refers to as κατὰ σάρκα, which corresponded to and signified an inner, higher, spiritual reality, that which is κατὰ πνεῦμα, provided the answer to his socio-cultural problems. He could preserve both the significance of Israel and the Book, as well as include everyone in the People of God. This corre-spondence and signification holds on many levels at once: It explains the relation of the Jewish People to the Israel of God; it explains the relation of outer works to inner faith; it explains the dual nature of Christ; and it empowers the two-tiered theology of sexuality and the body which is characteristic of Paul as well. Following the view of Angus Fletcher that allegory and allegorical reading systems are not just literary but rep-resent profound ontological or metaphysical commitments, I call this dualist ontology, anthropology, hermeneutic, and christology, "allegory" (Fletcher 1970).

How does my view, then, relate to Dunn's, and how does it answer objections to his interpretation? The crux of the matter is the interpreta-tion of the much contested "works of the Law," ἔργα νόμου. In my opin-ion, the entire context of Pauline thought strongly supports Dunn's un-derstanding that this phrase refers precisely to those observances of the Torah which were thought by Jew and gentile alike to mark off the special status of the Jews: circumcision, kashruth, and the observances of Sabbath and the holidays. These are the three items which are mentioned by satir-ists *ad nauseam* as emblematic of Jewish cultural practice, of Jewish differ-ence (Gager 1983, 56–57). As Dunn so elegantly puts it, "If an unbap-tized Christian is for most of us a contradiction in terms, even more so was a Jew who did not practise the works of the law, circumcision, table regulations and sabbath" (1990, 194). Moreover, it seems likely that for many Jews of the first century, not only did these practices mark off the covenant community exclusively, but justification or salvation was depen-dent on being a member of that very community. At any rate, Paul seems to have thought so and expected Peter to assent to the proposition as well that gentiles are ipso facto sinners, as we learn in Galatians 2:15. The road to salvation for gentiles, according to such first-century Jews, lay in conversion and acceptance of the covenantal practices. Recent scholar-ship has made abundantly clear that conversion was a real political and cultural option for many gentiles in the Roman empire (Gager 1983, 77).[24] Nevertheless these practices remained essentially the rituals of a particular ethnic group. The doors were open, not closed, but one was saved by becoming *Jewish*. This is not, then, exclusiveness in the sense that it excludes, in principle, anyone, but neither does it conform to any Greek sense of the universal, of the One. It remains, after all, a valorization of difference. Now, on my hypothesis, this is precisely the motivating force behind Paul's entire conversion experience and mission, to transcend that very covenantal difference. As Dunn puts it: "The decisive corollary which Paul saw, and which he did not hesitate to draw, was that the covenant is no longer to be identified or characterized by such distinctively Jewish observances as circumcision, food laws and sabbath. *Covenant* works had become too closely identified as *Jewish* observances, *covenant* righteousness as *national* righteousness. . . . God's purposes and God's people have now expanded beyond Israel according to the flesh, and so God's righteousness can no longer be restricted in terms of works of the law which emphasize kinship at the level of the flesh" (1990, 197, 200).

Dunn's analysis has recently been challenged by Thomas Schreiner (1991), but I think that the particular turn that I have been giving to the thesis goes a long way toward answering Schreiner's arguments. Schreiner has rightly pointed out that there is in Paul a theoretical and theological attack on the doing of works of the Law, and not merely a critique of specific works of the Law as identity markers. On the other hand, Paul repeatedly makes distinctions between circumcision and "keeping the commandments." 1 Corinthians 7:19 is an excellent example of this: "For neither circumcision counts for anything nor uncircumcision, but keeping the commandments of God." There is, accordingly, no doubt but that Dunn is also correct in assuming that Paul singles out circumcision (and to a somewhat lesser extent the other "identity markers") and *opposes* them to the commandments of God, or even to the Law, which should be kept.[25] How then can these two seemingly contradictory moments of a general, theoretical attack on "works of the Law" and a specific set of oppositions between certain works and "the commandments of God" or "the precepts of the Law" be reconciled—at least if we do not intend to adopt Räisänen's notions of an incoherent Paul? I suggest that the two can be read as two sides of the same coin, because it is in the *doing* of the Law, that is, in the focus on the corporeal, that the identity of the ethnic group is marked and established.[26] On the other hand, in the spiritual Law, the Law of faith (Romans 3:27 and see below), there are no ethnic distinctions. Accordingly, when works of the Law are what is emphasized by the theology, then the focus is on the doing, on the external practices and especially on those which mark off the Jews from other peoples. In both Romans and Galatians Paul emphasizes circumcision and kashruth as the two most blatant examples of this. When, however, the theological emphasis is on "faith working through love," there will still remain room for that faith to be expressed in works—and indeed it must—, but only such works which are indeed an expression of such faith and love (cf. Romans 2:6).[27] Accordingly, Schreiner is right that "works of the Law" refers to the whole Law and not just the particular ethnic markers, and the question is indeed not one of a mistaken attitude toward the Law (229–30). Nevertheless, Dunn is also right. Emphasis on the doing, on the corporeal and literal doing of the Law, leads inevitably to the exclusion of those who have not shared that Law and the history which produced it, while emphasis on faith (as the allegorical interpretation of the Law) allegedly creates a universal People of God.

Dunn has got this just right in my opinion: "It is two ways of looking at the law as a whole which [Paul in Romans 3:27] sets in opposition: when the law is understood in terms of works it is seen as distinctively Jewish and particular features come into prominence (particularly circumcision); but when the law is understood in terms of faith its distinctive Jewish character ceases to hold center stage, and the distinctively Jewish works become subsidiary and secondary matters which cannot be required of all and which can be disregarded by Gentiles in particular without damaging (indeed thereby enhancing—v 31) its faith character" (Dunn 1988, 186–87). Watson has also emphasized this point: "'Works' refers to the way of life confined to the Jewish community, and 'faith' refers to a response to God which is open to Gentiles" (Watson 1986, 165). Watson and Dunn fail to ask how *Paul* would have justified his position hermeneutically—how he would have explained his "kind of understanding of the law," a point which is crucial considering that he and his interlocutors held the Torah to be revealed by God. To my mind, the thesis being put forward in this book, namely that Paul understood "works" as the material signifier of "faith," that is, his essentially allegorical appropriation of Scripture, solves this problem. This, then, leads once more to a reading of Paul which is in line with the traditional understanding of 2 Corinthians 3:6, namely, that the letter which kills is the literal meaning, while the spirit which gives life is the spiritual meaning of the text.

This connection between the keeping of the Law and ethnic particularity as Paul's main concern has been especially well made by Richard Hays, who summarizes Paul's concern (in Romans 3) as, "Is God the God of the Jews only (as he would be if justification were contingent upon keeping the Law)? Is he not the God of the Gentiles also?" (Hays 1985, 84). Since the emphasis is on the universal, many (if not most) works remain valid, insofar as they are universal. Although physical circumcision is excluded entirely, alms giving, for example, is not. The contrast is then not between the legalistic and the moral but between the particular and the universal, which corresponds to the flesh and the spirit.[28] This is particularly poignant in that the alms that were meant to be given were from gentile Christians to Jewish Christians, thus once more emphasizing both in form and in content the unity of all in the community of the new Israel.

The obsession with Jewish difference, so characteristic of western discourse until the present, finds one of its fountainheads in Galatians and Paul's oppositional emplacement of works and faith. Paul's expression of this opposition, particularly the famous passages in Galatians 3 that seem to refer to the Law as a curse, has been the foundation stone of anti-Judaic discourse and practice in the Church, as well as of accusations that Paul was an "anti-Semite." In this book, I am reading Paul otherwise.

3

The Spirit and the Flesh
Paul's Political Anthropology

GRECO-ROMAN JUDAISM AND
THE PROBLEM OF UNIVERSALISM

Paul was not the first or alone in the problem which I imagine concerned him, the relation of all of the other people of the world to the God of Israel. Judaism had been in increasing interaction with Greco-Roman—Hellenistic—culture for several centuries by the time Paul was born, and this interaction had led to several striking cultural developments. The most important of these developments for my present purpose was the transformation in the significance of universalism. Some notion of universal humanity had already existed in ancient Israel, particularly in certain of the prophetic texts, but this notion had—it seems almost imperceptibly—shifted in the centuries of Jewish contact with Hellenistic culture and Greek philosophy. To understand Paul, some appreciation of this development is necessary.

As Martin Hengel has shown, in antiquity there was great appreciation for Judaism on the part of Greek philosophy. The alleged abstractness of the Godhead and, of course, the pure monotheism greatly appealed to philosophically minded Greeks and Romans who commonly identified the Jews (and the Hindus) as philosophers (Hengel 1974, 255–61).[1] On the other hand, there were aspects of Jewish religiosity which were repellent to these same philosophers:

> The universal religious attitude of learned men which developed in the
> Hellenistic period through "*theocrasy*" regarded *the different religions as
> in the end only manifestations of the one deity*. Thoughtful Greeks like
> Hecataeus, and later Posidonius, may have acknowledged Jewish belief
> in its unfalsified form to be a high stage of spirituality, and Greek
> philosophy with an interest in religion had long been on the way to
> monotheism, but they found the claim of Jewish religion that it em-
> bodied the one revelation of the one God, to the exclusion of all else,

to be inacceptable. In their view the—relative—truth of even the
Jewish faith could be expressed only in a *universal* way without national and historically conditioned limitations.   (Hengel 1974, 261)

As Hengel shows, the notion that the different gods are manifestations
of the one deity has deep roots in Hellenistic culture. Thus, while biblical universalism was founded on a notion of the mission of Israel to save
all of humanity and bring them to the true worship of the only God,
Hellenistic notions of universalism involved the assumption that all the
gods were really different names for one God. It is not surprising, given
this double atmosphere of enormous respect for Jewish ideas about God
coupled with disdain for the particular, national, embodied, and practiced aspects of the religion, that thoughtful Hellenized Jews more and
more emphasized the former at the expense of the latter and that one of
the strategies employed in this shift of emphasis was the—again very Hellenistic—demonstration through allegoresis that the latter signified the
former. Moreover, once this type of exegesis was available, the very particularity of Judaism to the Jews could be called into question as well, for
there were others in their world who had similarly "philosophical" ideas
about God. Thus, the "'monotheizing' tendency and the strict way of
life practiced by Orphic conventicles with their esoteric, didactic house-
worship devoid of sacrifice early aroused the interest of Jewish circles in
Egypt who, as Aristobulus and Artapanus show, made Orpheus a witness
to the truth of the Mosaic law" (Hengel 1974, 262–63)—Mosaic law,
hardly, but better to the truth of the Torah. Importantly, this development was by no means confined to the Diaspora. Indeed, as Hengel has
argued, Palestinian Judaism was no less Hellenized than its Diaspora version. Alan Segal has aptly remarked, "Hellenistic Judaism, deeply influenced by classical thought, was the majority Jewish culture of the day"
(Segal 1990, 84).[2] On the other hand, in Palestine there had been and
was to be again a strong reaction movement against Hellenization. Within
this Hellenistic Judaism, Greek, universalist notions of God had taken
firm root:

> Since, as I have been at pains to discover, the God who gave them
> their law is the God who maintains your kingdom. They worship the
> same God—the Lord and Creator of the Universe, as all other men, as
> we ourselves, O king, though we call him by different names, such as
> Zeus or Dis.   (Ps. Aristeas 15/16)

Although in the text, this remarkable speech is placed in the mouth of a gentile, the text itself was written by a Jew, and as Hengel emphasizes, a Jew from circles not suspected of any sort of "assimilation or syncretism" (Hengel 1974, 264). This passage and the text in which it was embedded were quoted approvingly in their entirety by Paul's contemporary Josephus (Hengel 1974, 266). It was in this atmosphere that Paul grew up, whether his childhood home and education were in Tarsus, Damascus, or Jerusalem. By virtue of his training, he was a Hebrew of the Hebrews, while clearly, by virtue of his linguistic culture at least, he was also a Hellene. He could very well have been formed and informed by two nearly contradictory cultural tendencies, one toward a universalism which emphasized the capacity for all human beings to be saved and the other a reaction against this universalism which re-emphasized the particular privileges of the Jewish People in the eyes of the sole God. That powerful and tense combination, whereby Paul becomes a synecdoche of the Jewish cultural situation, gave rise to Paul's religious passion. One could say with only some extravagance that if Judaism is the mother of "Universal Man," then Hellenism is the father, and Paul the *shadkhen* who made the match.[3]

THIS DUALISM WHICH IS NOT ONE

My key claim is that Paul is mobilized by as thoroughgoing a dualism as that of Philo. I am quite aware of how heterodox such a claim will appear to the present community of Pauline scholarship, at least on English-speaking soil, so in this chapter I wish to establish the grounds and terms upon which I make it. Moreover, the morphology of Paul's dualism has to be carefully delineated, *because it does not imply a rejection of the body.*[4] Various branches of Judaism (along with most of the surrounding culture) became increasingly platonized in late antiquity. By platonization I mean here the adoption of a dualist philosophy in which the phenomenal world was understood to be the representation in matter of a spiritual or ideal entity which corresponded to it. This has the further consequence that a hierarchical opposition is set up in which the invisible, inner reality is taken as more valuable or higher than the visible outer form of reality. In the anthropology of such a culture, the human person is constituted by an outer physical shell which is non-essential and by an inner spiritual soul, which represents his [sic][5] true and higher essence. "In this life itself, what constitutes our self in each of us is nothing other than the soul" (*Laws* 12.959a7–8). For Philo, "The soul may be seen as entombed in the body" (Winston 1988, 212). This conception was commonly held through much of the Hellenistic cultural world.

Paul also uses similar platonizing dualist imagery, although significantly enough, without negative imagery of the body.[6] The clearest example of this in his writing is in 2 Corinthians 5:1–4:

> For we know that if the earthly tent we live in is destroyed, we have a building from God, a house not made with hands, eternal in the heavens. Here indeed we groan, and long to put on our heavenly dwelling, so that by putting it on we may not be found naked. For while we are still in this tent, we sigh with anxiety; not that we would be unclothed, but that we would be further clothed, so that what is mortal may be swallowed up by life.

Paul's whole point here is to insist on resurrection in the body; however, the body that is resurrected is not the same kind of body as the one "that we dwell in" now. He considers some kind of a body necessary in order that the human being not be naked and polemicizes here against those who deny physical resurrection.[7] He is not, then, to be understood as holding a radical flesh/spirit dualism that sees the goal of human perfection as liberation from the body. Nevertheless, the image of the human being which Paul maintains is of a soul dwelling in or clothed by a body, and, however valuable the garment, it is less essential than that which it clothes. (See also Käsemann [1933, 103] and especially Brandenburger 1968.) It is "the earthly tent that we live in"; it is not *we*.[8] The body, while necessary and positively valued by Paul, is, as in Philo, not the human being but only his or her house or garment.[9] The verse just preceding this passage establishes its platonistic context beautifully: "While we look not at the things which are seen [τὰ βλεπόμενα], but at the things which are not seen: for the things which are seen are temporal [πρόσκαιρα]; but the things which are not seen are eternal [αἰώνια]" (2 Corinthians 4:18). What could possibly be more platonic in spirit than this double hierarchy: on the one hand, the privileging of the invisible over the visible, and on the other hand, the privileging of the eternal over the temporal?[10] The continuation of the passage dramatizes this point even more: "We know that while we are at home in the body we are away from the Lord . . . and we would rather be away from the body and at home with the Lord." Bultmann recognized that these verses "are very close to Hellenistic-Gnostic dualism, but not identical because of the 'indirect polemic against a Gnosticism which teaches that the naked self soars aloft free of any body'" (1951, 102).[11] Bultmann further points out that Paul's famous report of his mystical experiences "either in or out of the body, I do not know" also supports an understanding within which self is in body (2 Corinthians 12:2–4). I could not agree more.[12]

That Paul holds an essentially dualist anthropology is also shown by such expressions in 2 Corinthians 7:1 as "let us cleanse ourselves of every defilement of flesh and spirit." Flesh can be cleansed of defilement in Paul, but it is a separate, distinct element of which human beings are composed and not, I suggest, the essential one. Indeed, Paul can recommend that a sinner be "delivered unto Satan for the destruction of the flesh, that the spirit might be saved on the day of the Lord" (1 Corinthians 5:5). Whatever the delivery unto Satan means and however the flesh is to be destroyed, it is clear that Paul holds that it is the spirit which will be saved at the end. This is in direct contrast to rabbinic eschatology within which, famously, the soul and the body will be rejoined for salvation or destruction at the end.

Paul is, however, not quite a platonist. As we have seen in the 2 Corinthians passage quoted, immaterial existence of souls without any bodies seems to arouse in him a sense of horror. There is, therefore, a body, but one entirely different from the body of "flesh and blood" in which we dwell today. Paul's very special dualism is also manifest in another text of his, 1 Corinthians 15:42–50:

> So it is with the resurrection of the dead. What is sown is perishable, what is raised is imperishable. It is sown in dishonor, it is raised in glory. It is sown in weakness, it is raised in power. It is sown a physical body [σῶμα ψυχικόν], it is raised a spiritual body [σῶμα πνευματικόν]. If there is a physical body, there is also a spiritual body. Thus it is written: The first man Adam became a living soul [ψυχὴν ζῶσαν], the last Adam became a life-giving spirit [πνεῦμα ζῳοποιοῦν]. But it is not the spiritual which is first but the physical, and then the spiritual. . . . I tell you this, brothers: flesh and blood cannot inherit the kingdom of God, nor does the perishable inherit the imperishable.

We observe here the absolutely astonishing combination in Paul of a biblical "positive" sensibility toward the *body*, combined with a Hellenistic/platonistic devaluation of the *physical*.[13] Even though for Paul there is no question, as we have already seen, of a human being persisting as a disembodied soul, nevertheless body itself becomes for him a dualistic term. There is a physical body and a spiritual body, a body of σάρξ και αἷμα (flesh and blood) and a body of πνεῦμα (spirit)! Moreover, these dyadic conjunctures are so necessary or so obvious in Paul's thought that he can use them as a logical argument. He says: If there is a physical body, there must be a spiritual body as well. This argument can only be explained, I submit, if we assume that for him everything physical has a spiritual counterpart—i.e., some version of platonism.[14] A further argument for this kind of platonism in Paul is the famous distinction in Romans 7:22–23 between the members and the inner self: "For I delight in the law of God in my inmost self but I see in my members another law at war with the law of my mind."

A solution to some conundra of apparent discontinuities in early Christian discourse, which seems at one and the same time to affirm bodiliness and disavow sexuality, is to emphasize the distinction between "body" and "flesh." The first is a term that often has positive valence, while it is the latter that is usually of increasingly negative connotation. It is in this sense of a body without flesh—that is, a body without sexuality, among other matters—that various early Christian thinkers can assert the positive status of "the body."[15] Thus that the Cappadocian Fathers held that the creation of humanity was for the purpose of bringing God into the material world, thus uniting the world with God, but they, nevertheless, considered sexuality as temporary and a sign of "man's" fallenness (V. Harrison, personal communication). Caroline Walker Bynum raises sharply the question of whether the "platonic" ideology of the person as soul was every fully accepted in Christian culture (Bynum 1991). This seems then to produce a moment of unresolved tension, or even incoherence in Christian platonism, beginning, I think, with Paul. In a stunning paper, Patricia Cox Miller has provided what I take to be an enormous contribution toward resolving this tension. Basing herself on Jean-Pierre Vernant's essay, "Dim Body, Dazzling Body" (Vernant 1989), Cox Miller argues that this distinction—between the sub-bodies of human beings and the super-bodies of the gods—explains as well Christian imaginings of the transformed body of the perfected Christian. She remarks:

> However, this perception of the body as the sign of human misfortune
> does not conform to the Platonic, and later Cartesian, dichotomous

model of human composition that splits the person into a positive soul or mind housed in a negative body construed as a prison or a mechanistic object in space. As Vernant says, "the human misfortune is not that a divine and immortal soul finds itself imprisoned in the envelope of a material and perishable body, but that the body is not fully one"— that is, for the archaic Greeks, the problem is that the human body is not fully a body.   (Cox Miller forthcoming)

The remarkable thing about Cox Miller's analysis from my point of view is that she shows its compatibility with an avowed, explicit, and extreme platonism, that is to say, she shows how even radical platonists in the patristic tradition, including especially Origen and the Cappadocians, can—nay, must—entertain at one and the same time "a dichotomous view of the human person" and an affirmation of "the positive valuation of the created world in the biblical book of Genesis." As Cox Miller shows by analyzing the imagery of the dreams of Gregory of Nyssa and Gregory Nazianzen, two of the most important of the Cappadocian Fathers, in their anthropology, Adam's body, Christ's resurrected body, the body of the ascetic in this life, and the resurrection body of all the saved are dazzling bodies, while the bodies of the rest of us are dim. Now Gregory Nazianzen—for example—is one of the wildest of the wild platonists (the term is Peter Brown's) in the early Christian tradition. As Cox Miller notes he considered the body an obstacle to insight and referred to it in terms reminiscent of the disgust of a Plotinus: "Bitter serpents biting, jackals swarming and snarling, wild animals with tusks, the sepia fish with its poisonous black vomit, herds of swine, lions, bears, the entrails of Jonah's monster: all these describe what it is like to live in a body." In classic platonistic fashion Gregory regards the physical world and material language both as illusions and mere signs of that which is higher. This man, however, when he dreams of his dead brother, dreams of him as inhabiting a heavenly body, not as a disembodied soul. And as Cox Miller demonstrates, Nazianzen was explicitly aware that this dreamed, brilliant, transformed body was that of his own desire. Gregory, like the other Gregory, his compatriot, whom Cox Miller also treats, found a way to balance the seemingly incompatible denigration of body of platonism and the valorization of body drawn perhaps from Jewish roots of Christianity (Genesis).

Although she does not say so, it seems to me that this hypothesis provides a hermeneutic key to Paul as well and particularly to such a text as 1 Corinthians 15. Paul, too, on my reading, was balancing platonistic and

"Hebraic" world views and anthropologies. Indeed, I would go so far as to argue that it may very well have been Paul who introduced into Christian thought this particular combination of a platonic dualism and an anthropology that does not regard the body as "problematic because of its sheer materiality as part of the physical world"—indeed, that 1 Corinthians 15 may be its most important source. At any rate, Cox Miller's analysis demonstrates the *possibility* of such a combination and the necessity of assuming that it has existed at some stage of Christian thought, and whether or not Paul is, as I claim, in some sense the author of this combination, its very existence increases dramatically the plausibility of reading such an anthropology in Paul.

Robert Jewett has provided another very elegant *exemplum* of Paul's dualism and its special character. In Romans 15:27 Paul writes that the gentiles are pleased to send alms to the church in Jerusalem, "for if the gentiles have shared in their spiritual things, they are obligated to share with them in the fleshly things." Jewett glosses this verse:

> The distinction between the fleshly and the spiritual things is therefore unrelated to the concrete problems in Rome; rather than being polemically motivated, it is something of an incidental reflection of Paul's thinking about the offering which shows the extent to which the technical flesh-spirit antithesis has come to affect his daily usage. . . . The assumption upon which the *a majori ad minus* argument is based is the intrinsic superiority of the spiritual over the fleshly things. Such an assumption in itself would point to Hellenistic dualism as the source of the categories, but Paul's argument would be impossible for the Hellenist. For how could a spiritual obligation be paid off by fleshly means if the two are completely incommensurable? And how could fleshly things be of such importance to the spiritual man that he would devote his attention to them to the extent that Paul confesses in these verses? (Jewett 1971, 165–66)

Aside from a strangely reified notion of the "Hellenist," I find this a perfect account of Paul's dualism. There is flesh and spirit. The spirit is higher and more important, but the flesh is not to be disregarded either. While I do not claim that these Pauline texts cannot be interpreted otherwise, I invite the community of Pauline scholars to recast their sense of what Paul *could* mean and observe the effects on reading his texts of an assumption that Paul held a dualist anthropology that does not abhor the body.[16]

What Is "Flesh"?

Σάρξ, "the flesh" is the most important term in Paul's anthropology, where it contrasts with πνεῦμα, "the spirit." A recent "history of research" by Robert Jewett counts the following interpretations:

1. Many of the Fathers of the church interpreted σάρξ "as material sensuality which solicited or directly induced sin" (Jewett 1971, 50).[17]

2. The Augustinian tradition which the Reformation continued understood the flesh as "man in revolt from God."

3. The "father" of modern critical study of the New Testament, Ferdinand Christian Baur, understood σάρξ, once more, as the material body which is the source of sin, however, for him, as for his follower Carl Holsten the πνεῦμα, spirit, is not the human spirit, soul, or mind but the Holy Spirit.

4. Holsten's contemporary, Hermann Lüdemann proposed that there is "within man himself a dichotomy of πνεῦμα ἀνθρώπου [spirit of man] (ἔσω ἄνθρωπος [inner man] which consists of νοῦς [mind] and καρδία [heart]) and σῶμα σαρκός [body of flesh] (ἔξω ἄνθρωπος [outer man] consisting of σάρξ [flesh], ψυχή [psyche] and σῶμα [body])" (Jewett 1971, 52). In a rather brilliant theorization, Lüdemann argued that Paul's anthropology was a unique blend of Hebraic and Hellenistic notions, such that while Paul did distinguish an inner man from an outer man in Hellenistic fashion, the inner man could be either controlled by the flesh or not, a more biblical notion. In spite of certain excesses, aspects of Lüdemann's contribution remain central, particularly the insight that for Paul, spirit and flesh were both inner- and extra-personal forces. These views, that is, various combinations of Holsten's and Lüdemann's, formed a sort of scholarly paradigm and consensus for Pauline interpretation that was challenged in the late nineteenth century.

5. One of the dominant trends developing in the second half of that century was a view that understood σάρξ to be simply the "whole human being," something like the "flesh and blood" of Hebrew usage, which certainly means the whole human being and not merely an aspect thereof. And the closeness to Hebrew usage in this view is no accident, for this interpretation in general sought to bring Paul

closer to "Old Testament" categories and paint him as relatively un-Hellenized and certainly non-dualistic. This was the view of, among others, Albrecht Ritschl.

6. In the next stage of research, as Jewett narrates it, there were two prevailing views: an apocalyptic conception which saw the flesh and the spirit as cosmic forces locked in combat in the last days and a gnostic one within which the fleshy human being is taken possession of by a divine fluid in the experience of gnosis and transformed. Jewett himself characterizes the ensuing situation as "The Resultant Confusion" (Jewett 1971, 63).

7. Dominant in current interpretation and scholarship is the Bultmannian-inspired "existential interpretation," within which $\sigma\acute{\alpha}\rho\xi$ is "the earthly sphere which becomes the source of sin only when man places his trust in it" (Jewett 1971, 67): "Each person is determined by either spirit or flesh, has a tendency towards one or the other; if one lives by spirit, he lives in midst of the indicative and the imperative and is enabled thereby to overcome the fragmentation of life and to achieve existential unity; but if one lives by the flesh, he does his own will and seeks to secure his own future by works" (Jewett 1971, 68–69). Bultmann's student and disciple Ernst Käsemann, about whom I shall have much to say in another context, took his teacher's views further by emphasizing the cosmological and eschatological dimensions, essentially, I think, by taking seriously the clear implication of Romans 7:5 that $\grave{\epsilon}\nu$ $\tau\widehat{\eta}$ $\sigma\alpha\rho\kappa\acute{\iota}$ (in the flesh) represents an eon. He remained, however, with the essentially existential definition of that eon as one determined by living according to the flesh defined as worldliness.

8. Egon Brandenburger has in some ways come closest to the view that I am espousing in the present work. In his *Fleisch und Geist*, Brandenburger proposed that Paul's $\sigma\acute{\alpha}\rho\xi$ ~ $\pi\nu\epsilon\widehat{\upsilon}\mu\alpha$ opposition bore significant parallels to Philo's dualism, a conclusion which I find compelling. This does not mean, however, that Paul has to be taken as a representative of the philosophical school of which Philo was a part or that Paul has been "influenced" (whatever that might mean) by Hellenistic Judaism, but it might very well reflect the existence of this dualism in the Jewish and wider cultural koine of the first century. On the other hand, there is no doubt that Paul manifests themes which

are quite unknown in Philo. Philo's platonism is such that cosmic history nearly drops out of the picture, whereas for Paul the apocalyptic sense of changing eons is powerful, as well as the cosmic drama between realms. Jewett has, I think, judiciously summed up the situation: "One would have to say that Brandenburger has succeeded in tracing a flesh-spirit antithesis in Hellenistic Judaism which offers some precedent for Pauline usage. But his attempt to document the cosmic dimensions of this antithesis is less than convincing because it does not properly relate to Philo's actual philosophical stance" (Jewett 1971, 92).

Jewett himself proposes an interpretation of Paul's σάρξ language which in one respect is close to the one that I am theorizing here. He argues that the origins of the term are in the controversy over circumcision, which is referred to as being "in the flesh." In Paul's conflict with the Judaizers in Galatia he came to portray his opponents as those who have confidence in the flesh in two senses: (1) they believe that circumcision as the entry marker into the Jewish People is the requirement for salvation, and (2) they wish to be saved themselves from zealot vengeance on the Judean church (Jewett 1971, 96; Jewett 1970). Then, "the fact that σάρξ had a negative connotation in the Hellenistic world made its polemic possibilities particularly attractive." Jewett's proposal, while in the right direction, is much too narrow in my view. First of all, it comprehends only one of the metaphorical senses of "flesh" allowed by the Bible and Jewish usage, namely, the penis which is circumcised. It thus ignores a second, equally powerful usage: kinship. When Jewett discusses the allegory of Galatians 4, therefore, he does not realize that there the child according to the flesh has to do not with nomism but with physical descent. Second, Jewett, in his zeal typical of moderns to deny any platonistic idealism in Paul, denies that which Paul himself asserts, namely, that his interpretation of the Hagar story is an allegory, because "it neither begins nor ends with abstract principles. It is a typological application of a past event onto a concrete present situation. The connection between past and present is apocalyptic rather than idealistic" (1971, 100). The move, however, from fleshy kinship to kinship according to promise and faith commitment, from earthly Jerusalem to heavenly Jerusalem, is certainly a move from the material to the spiritual. Since it is from the ma-

terial expressed in material language to a set of ideas more abstract than
the ones expressed *by* the material language, this is certainly allegorical,
just as Paul would have it, and eloquent evidence for a dualist sensibility.
What is so striking in Paul is precisely the way in which the apocalyptic
or typological is allegorical, that the world and history move from the
realm of the literal to the realm of the allegorical in time. Apocalyptic is
thus precisely, for him, a revelation, as its etymology implies. Third, Jewett falls back ultimately on the Bultmannian categories to explain what
Paul finds wrong with the flesh, namely, "It is religious man who rests on
his own virtuous obedience and thus enters into conflict with the spirit"
(1971, 101). Jewett thus nearly cancels out the virtues of his insight.
Fourth, Jewett locates the origins of the flesh ~ spirit opposition *in* the
Galatian controversy rather than seeing that it is this opposition which
occasions the controversy.[18] Fifth, I see very little evidence for Jewett's
understanding that σάρξ in Paul is demonic.[19] Finally, I disagree entirely
with the claim that "it was the concrete situation of conflict with the
Judaizers which led him to connect σάρξ with the old aeon" (1971, 101).
Σάρξ belongs to the old eon, because that was the eon in which the Torah
and physical Israel had a role, and it was always preparatory to the present
eon in which the Spirit has been revealed and the flesh of the Torah and
of Israel are superseded. Once more, this *explains* Paul's opposition to the
Judaizers and does not arise from it.

The upshot of my dispute with Jewett and the premise of this book is
that for Paul the term *flesh* enters into a rich metaphorical and meto-
nymic semantic field bounded on the one hand by the metaphorical usages
already current in biblical parlance and on the other hand by the dualism
of spirit and flesh current in the milieu of Hellenistic—that is, first-
century—Judaism. It was the working out and through of these multiple
semantic possibilities that generated Paul's major semantic innovations.
Flesh is the penis and physical kinship; it is the site of sexuality, wherein
lies the origin of sin; it is also the site of genealogy, wherein lies the
ethnocentricism of Judaism as Paul encountered it.[20] All of these could be
opposed, Paul came to see, by a spiritual or ideal set of counterparts which
would enable the escape from the two elements of human life that Paul
felt most disturbing: desire and ethnicity. The circumcision controversy is
not the fountainhead of Paul's theory of σάρξ, but the theory of σάρξ is
that which occasioned and fueled the controversy. Paul came to oppose

the Law because of the way that it literally—that is, carnally—insisted on the priority and importance of the flesh, of procreation and kinship, symbolized by the mark in the flesh, par excellence, the penis. This set of notions, then, expanded and complicated will be the foundation for my understanding of Paul.

"According to the Flesh" as the Literal: 1 Corinthians 10

The dyadic opposition between "flesh" $\sigma \acute{\alpha} \rho \xi$ and "spirit" $\pi \nu \epsilon \hat{\upsilon} \mu \alpha$ is central on all accounts to Pauline thinking and expression. Its interpretation, however, is as we have seen contested. Where once (i.e., since patristic times) they were understood as hermeneutical terms, referring to the "literal" and the allegorical respectively, it has become current in Pauline studies to understand the key terms $\kappa \alpha \tau \grave{\alpha} \; \sigma \acute{\alpha} \rho \kappa \alpha$ (according to the flesh) and $\kappa \alpha \tau \grave{\alpha} \; \pi \nu \epsilon \hat{\upsilon} \mu \alpha$ (according to the spirit) as axiological/sociological terms. In one typical formulation the former means, "human life organized without reference to God and his purposes," and the latter the opposite (Martin 1986, 151).[21] In other accounts, these terms are taken to refer only to types of people and/or the communities they form. Typical for recent sociological interpretation is the following remark of Alan Segal:

> All opponents boast of the flesh (Phil. 3:3; 2 Cor 11:18), since they hold their fleshly lives, their superior ritual status in Judaism over the gentile converts. *The language of flesh and spirit is not allegorical.* It is a reference to two kinds of Christian community—one priding itself in the flesh, circumcision; the other defining itself by means of a spiritual transformation, baptism, those who are converted in faith. (Segal 1990, 140)[22]

The hermeneutical aspect of this opposition has been marginalized (or even completely discredited) by these interpreters. I would like to revive it here, taking into consideration the difficulties raised by modern scholarship and attempting to include their valid insights as well. I suggest that seeing Paul's thought in terms of an opposition between the literal and the allegorical interpretations of the Law goes a long way toward answering the outstanding question of Pauline studies, the "contradictions" between

Paul's "negative" remarks about the Law and his "positive" ones. I place this interpretation, moreover, in context with recent advances in Pauline scholarship which demonstrate the social nature of much of his gospel.

"Having begun in the Spirit, are you now finishing up in the flesh," Paul rails at his Galatian converts (3:3). The ethical flaw in the Galatians' desire is not that they suddenly are becoming proud and self-righteous but that they are abandoning the higher condition of being "in the spirit" for a lower one of observance of circumcision *in the flesh, the penis* and all that this synecdochally signifies. "Perfected in the flesh" does indeed mean performance of the Law, but not reliance on the Law; nor is performance of the Law marked as human self-sufficiency as opposed to faith, but as outer, bodily activity, marked with the specificity of ethnic Jewishness, opposed to inner faith and spiritual experience. The observance of circumcision in the flesh becomes a veil that impedes attainment of the spiritual τέλος of the Law, as we will see in the discussion of 2 Corinthians 3 in the next chapter. Paul is arguing to his Galatian converts that they have already achieved a higher state, which is the purpose of the Law and should not wish now to regress to a lower state; he is not asserting here that there is something in itself morally or spiritually opprobrious in observance of Law. An important text for interpreting this passage is Colossians 2:16–23, whose author, Paul's disciple, argues similarly to Galatians that if the converts have achieved a higher state of having died with Christ, why do they now submit to regulations, "which are only a shadow of that which is to come" (17)! The Law is not opprobrious in itself, but it is surpassed in the Spirit.

Κατὰ σάρκα does, however, often enough have a pejorative sense. This is derived from its primary sense of the literal, concrete, flesh of the language. Those who remain enthralled by the literal in hermeneutics are necessarily enslaved as well by the flesh and the elements of this world. This explanation accounts for the slippage between κατὰ σάρκα understood as a hermeneutic term and its axiological or moral implications. Those who do not realize the true spiritual meanings of things are those who are trapped in their own flesh and cannot see beyond the flesh of the text as well.[23] This interpretation has the signal advantage of obviating the need to assume wide swings in Paul's usage of his technical terminology;[24] for example, many of the putative contradictions in Paul's usage which Robert Jewett alleges simply disappear (Jewett 1971, 2).[25] The pitfalls of the currently held interpretations of "according to the flesh" as an inherently pejorative term are perhaps most clearly exemplified in the tortuous interpretations of Romans 1:3–4:

> Concerning His son who was born of the seed of David according to the flesh, and declared to be the son of God in power, according to the spirit of Holiness, by the resurrection from the dead.   (Romans 1:3–4)
>
> περὶ τοῦ υἱοῦ αὐτοῦ τοῦ γενομένου ἐκ σπέρματος Δαυὶδ κατὰ σάρκα, τοῦ ὁρισθέντος υἱοῦ θεοῦ ἐν δυνάμει κατὰ πνεῦμα ἁγιωσύνης ἐξ ἀναστάσεως νεκρῶν

Paul is very likely citing a baptismal or otherwise confessional formula here (Schweizer 1957). The assumption that κατὰ σάρκα has, in itself, pejorative connotations leads one to the absurd conclusion that verses 3 and 4 contradict one another. As Jewett has put it:

> If the congregation were really Hellenistic as the opposition between κατὰ σάρκα and κατὰ πνεῦμα implies, it would scarcely be interested in claiming messianic honors for the fleshly Jesus; if the congregation were Jewish Christian as the messianic interest implies, it would scarcely contradict itself by the addition of the derogatory expression "in the realm of the flesh." Schweizer's article reveals first and foremost the impossibility of holding that this confession including the phrases "according to the flesh" and "according to the spirit of holiness" came from a single source.   (1971, 136)

Jewett seems unaware of the implications of this Schweizerian "revelation" for our apprehension of Paul. Wherever this formula "came from," Paul is now using it, and if the terms contradict themselves, how could he do so? It seems that an exegesis which leads to such conclusions ought to examine itself. If κατὰ σάρκα is a neutral hermeneutic term which takes on its value from its context, the problem simply disappears. Jesus is indeed the son of David, when interpreted according to the flesh, i.e., he is literally and physically a descendant of David, but he is the son of God when considered according to the spirit, that is, in the realm of the allegorical—which is, it must be emphasized, the revelation of a true ontological condition and not a mere metaphor. It is important to see that the gloss "according to the flesh" accomplishes the important hermeneutical task of resolving the apparent contradiction—as in Luke 1:34, for example—between Jesus as simultaneously son of David, which must mean "son of Joseph," and son of God (Fredriksen 1988, 28)!

The passage that proves this case is Romans 9:5: "The Christ which is according to the flesh [ὁ Χριστὸς τὸ κατὰ σάρκα]." I submit that it is impossible to gloss this expression as "The Christ who lives without reference to God"; or "The Christ who seeks justification by works." The passage must be understood as the Christ in his human aspect, Christ before Easter (without, of course, necessarily committing Paul to one or another later christology). We cannot, therefore, understand this as an essentially pejorative term, although, to be sure, this mode of Christ's existence is inferior to that of the risen Christ, κατὰ πνεῦμα, by implication. Other terms are simply neutral in their evaluative tone, such as "My brothers according to the flesh" (Romans 9:3), which surely means only my physical, Jewish kin, as opposed to the brethren in the spirit, the Christian believers.[26] In the context of that verse, understanding κατὰ σάρκα as a pejorative would be entirely inappropriate, as it would be in Romans 4:1, which refers to Abraham, our father "according to the flesh." In 1 Corinthians 1:26, σοφοὶ κατὰ σάρκα seems simply to mean those who are wise in worldly matters. Similarly, in 2 Corinthians 1:17, the phrase simply means in ordinary human fashion.

There are, accordingly, a significant number of passages in which κατὰ σάρκα is hardly to be understood in an axiological or evaluative sense as a term of opprobrium. I suggest that it is not necessary at all to regard these varied usages of κατὰ σάρκα as contradictory or inconsistent. The term κατὰ σάρκα itself is morally neutral, although always subordinated to κατὰ πνεῦμα. Its semantic value is one, with the variations in nuance directly contributed by the pragmatic context. In all of these passages, I think, it would be appropriate to say that Paul refers to an ordinary level of human existence that is, to be sure, lower than that of the spirit but not by any means stigmatized as being evil, venal, or without reference to God. Such an understanding of the term is particularly appropriate when the referent is either of two aspects of human existence: physical observances of Jewish ritual, especially circumcision in the flesh, and physical kinship—as opposed, in both cases, with their spiritual referents. This anthropological duality is thus matched by a homologous hermeneutical duality as well, which works perfectly, because that interpretation which is literal, "according to the flesh"—the outer meaning of the language—is precisely the mode of interpretation which on the plane of content privileges physical observances, physical kinship, and the paradosis (knowing) of the "historical Jesus," ὁ Χριστὸς τὸ κατὰ σάρκα, or "the physical knowing of Christ," which comes down to the same thing. Because the ways of both Jews and the Jerusalem Christians emphasize precisely these values (and not because they are self-righteous, without reference to God or against the will of God), they can be identified by Paul as "according to the flesh." Life and interpretation κατὰ σάρκα become pejoratively marked only when they have the negative social effects in Paul's eyes of interrupting the new creation of the universal Israel of God. The Law understood spiritually remains the ethical foundation of the new Israel, just as the Law understood carnally was the ethical foundation for the old.

In studying passages in Paul's writings in which "according to the flesh" is used as a hermeneutical term, we can see the intimate connection between hermeneutics and cultural critique in his thought. The crucial text for establishing such an interpretation is 1 Corinthians 10. I will begin by quoting the passage (with some ellipses):

> I want you to know, brethren, that our ancestors were all under the cloud, and all passed through the sea, and all were baptized into Moses in the cloud and in the sea, and all ate the spiritual food and all drank the same spiritual drink. For they drank from the spiritual Rock which followed them, and the Rock was Christ. Nevertheless with most of them God was not pleased; for they were overthrown in the wilderness. Now these things are warnings to us, not to desire evil as they did. . . . Consider Israel according to the flesh; are not those who eat the sacrifices partners in the altar?

The key to my understanding of this passage is the last verse. Almost precisely because it is so understated in its form, "Consider Israel according to the flesh" must be understood here as a hermeneutical term. In other words, while the phrase certainly includes all of the overtones that it does elsewhere, to wit, physical descent and over-literal understanding (and perhaps even "carnality" as a moral judgment), Paul is here appealing to the Corinthians to consider the verse/practice in its literal sense, not to concern themselves with axiological judgments of the Jews! RSV translates here simply, "Consider the practice of Israel," which is just what Paul means. I thus disagree with Richard Hays's implied interpretation that Paul refers here to "Israel according to the flesh" because he is discussing the golden calf episode (Hays 1989, 96). By verse 18, Paul is no longer referring to that story but rather to Israelite sacrifice in general. He wishes here to draw an analogy for his argument from that concrete, historical fact. Just as the literal Israel—according to the flesh—when they eat the sacrifices are partners in the altar, so also the figurative Israel—according to the spirit—are partners in the altar when they eat the Eucharist, and they should behave accordingly. If, at this point, the text is understood allegorically, the point of the analogy is lost.[27] Paul calls to his Corinthian readers to take a look for the moment at the literal, concrete, and historical meaning of a particular textual moment.[28] Accordingly, he insists on the literal meaning, κατὰ σάρκα of the verse, at least momentarily.

I think we learn much from this utterance. First of all, as earlier commentators have pointed out, the very positing of an "Israel according to the flesh" implies *necessarily* the existence of an "Israel according to the spirit" as well. Now, in light of the resonance created by the reference to "Israel in the flesh" in verse 18, I think we go back and interpret the references to spiritual food and drink in the previous verses and understand them as hermeneutical utterances as well. Thus, the food and drink may literally [!] have been spiritual in nature, but they are also to be *understood* spiritually (that is typologically/allegorically) as signifying the food and drink of the present Christian ritual. The Israel of that story signifies the present Israel which is the church—not, I emphasize, the institutional church of, e.g., Hebrews, but the present Christian congregations characterized and defined by the inclusion of ethnic gentiles into "the Israel of God" (Hays 1989, 86).[29]

This interpretation is further dramatically strengthened by Paul's explicitly hermeneutic statement that "the rock was Christ." Once again, there has been much discussion of the exact mode of figurative interpretation that Paul is here supposing, but in any case, it is very telling that he uses the past tense here: The rock was always Christ. Paul's "in-the-spirit" interpretation, whether typological or allegorical (or, as I claim, both at once), represents a dehistoricization of the text as well as an implicit claim that Christ is the always-existent Christ in heaven and not his temporary historical avatar on earth. Paul certainly held that the literal, historical meaning of the text was true—Consider Israel according to the flesh—but just as unquestionably he also located its significance not in its concrete historical moment but in that which it signified and which one way or another stops time and exits from history.[30]

The platonic preference for the immovable supersedes temporality, and this is the essence of allegory as I understand it. Having demonstrated that Paul interweaves his discourse here with a series of allusions to Deuteronomy 8 and 32, as well as Psalm 106, Hays reads the discourse as essentially midrash and even explicitly argues that "there is nothing distinctively Christian in the lessons that Paul draws from the Scripture that he cites here. Deuteronomy has already performed the imaginative act of turning the exodus into a paradigm for Israel's future experience; consequently, Paul's typological reading of the story is nothing other than a fresh performance within Israel's long-established poetic-theological tradition" (94). Yes—and no. On the one hand, Hays is undoubtedly correct; Paul draws here a lesson from the concrete historical events which is not entirely dissimilar from the lesson that Deuteronomy wishes Jews to learn from the same story, "And you shall remember. . . ." Paul, however, supplements that hermeneutic of memory of historical events with claims that the historical events *already* figured the current situation; the food and drink were spiritual and the rock was Christ. As in so much of my reading of Paul, I see here a brilliant conflation of hermeneutical cultural traditions, such that the "platonistic" moment of his spirituality is made wholly one with the biblical sensibility. Paul produces here an extraordinary synthesis between Palestinian and Hellenistic Judaisms.[31] On the one hand, Paul is not denying significance to the concrete, historical Israel, neither now nor a fortiori in the past, as can be clearly demonstrated by, among other places, Romans 11, which also entertains the idea that in the end historical Israel will repent and rejoin the New Israel. On the other hand, however, there is a strong implication that this Israel finds its true meaning and always did as a signifier of the community of faith which would include all humanity and not only the ethnic Israel. The story of Israel exists for two purposes: to prefigure and figure the Israel of God and to teach that Israel of God how it should behave. Both of these moments are uncovered together in 1 Corinthians 10. "Israel according to the flesh" is thus the *literal, concrete, historical Israel,* while Israel according to the spirit would be the allegorical, spiritual, ontological, and ideal Israel—ultimately the Church.

The dual person of Christ in the world is a perfect homology, then, to the dual nature of language and the necessity for allegorical interpretation to fulfill the spiritual meaning of concrete expression. Corporeal difference yields to spiritual universalism.[32] This structure is manifested beautifully in our passage from 1 Corinthians, where the manna and water given the Jews in the wilderness is called "spiritual" ($\pi\nu\epsilon\upsilon\mu\alpha\tau\iota\kappa\acute{o}\varsigma$), and the rock which followed the Jews in the Wilderness is interpreted as Christ (10: 3–4). Thus, "*our* ancestors were *all* under the cloud" (10:1), that is,

Paul's and the Corinthians' ancestors were all under the cloud, interpreted as baptism! Thus, the "all" of this verse is the same "all" as the "we all" of the passage from 2 Corinthians above. As Conzelmann remarks, "οἱ πατέρες ἡμῶν, 'our ancestors': Paul is speaking as a Jew, but includes also his Gentile-Christian readers. The church is the true Israel" (Conzelmann 1976, 165). The point has been made even more eloquently by Gordon Fee:

> By calling Israel "*our* Fathers," he emphasizes at the outset the Corinthians' continuity with what God had done in the past. Since this is being written to a Gentile congregation, this language is sure evidence of the church's familiarity with the OT as their book in a very special sense, and of Paul's understanding of their eschatological existence in Christ (cf. v. 11) as being in true continuity with the past. God's new people are the true Israel of God, who fulfill his promises made to the fathers. This identification is precisely what gives the warning that follows such potency.   (Fee 1987, 444; see Hays 1989, 96)

It does even more than that. Through its interpretative method it establishes the very hermeneutic by which the Corinthians can be considered members of the new Israel, indeed, by which the new Israel is constituted.

The crucifixion is what makes possible the fulfillment of Israel in the flesh by Israel in the spirit as well, and thus the erasure of the difference between "Jew and Greek" and their reconstitution as the new single People of God. Those who remain enthralled by the literal in hermeneutics are necessarily enslaved as well by the flesh and the elements of this world, and they, therefore, render Jesus's sacrifice in vain. This, to my mind, is the fundamental message of Galatians and ultimately of all of Paul, fully revealed already in that one moment in which the risen Christ—Christ according to the spirit—appeared to Saul the Pharisee, he who had never known Jesus according to the flesh and was about to transform that apparent disability in his apostleship into an advantage.[33] A platonic hermeneutic, similar to that of Philo, is what empowers and energizes Paul's gospel, however otherwise different are the moral and religious visions of these two first-century Jews.

Answering Davies's Objections   In his now-classic *Paul and Rabbinic Judaism*, W. D. Davies has argued against a hermeneutical reading of the flesh ~ spirit opposition in Paul. Davies has two major objections to the notion that in the usage of σάρξ Paul accepts "a typical Hellenistic dualism" (Davies 1965, 18). In the first place, he argues that "the ascription of Hellenistic dualism to Paul involves us in a psychological, ethical and spiritual impossibility. It would be to make Paul's faith in the real coming of Christ into the world an absurdity. To Paul Christ was of the seed of David, a figure in history, a man after the flesh. If the latter was intrinsically evil, as Hellenistic dualism maintained, then Paul's faith in the historic Christ was in vain" (18). The second argument that Davies mobilizes is a lexical one. He claims, correctly it seems, that σάρξ almost never (but not quite never) refers in Hellenistic Greek to the material as opposed to the ideal.

The first of Davies's arguments can be easily answered. Paul's "dualism" was precisely *not* a typical Hellenistic dualism, one that would maintain that the flesh is intrinsically evil. Davies is absolutely correct; such a value system would make very difficult the notion of a real human Christ, and indeed, "gnostics" who held such views have also held a docetic christology, that Jesus only appeared to be a man of flesh.[34] A dualism, however, of another sort, one that values the flesh, albeit considering the spirit to be the essence of the human and the essential meaning of things and of language as well, would explain precisely the coming of Christ, as a visible manifestation of God, into the world. Such a dualist mode of thinking will account for both the literal, physical Jesus who is the son of David according to the flesh and the pre-existent, spiritual Christ who is the son of God. On the other hand, a monistic ontology, such as that of much of rabbinic thinking, will not dematerialize Godhead to begin with, and will accordingly not require an Incarnation (or the Pauline equivalent thereof).

My explanation of Paul also accounts for the second objection as well. Σάρξ, בשר, flesh has two well attested metaphorical usages in Jewish parlance. It refers on the one hand to the penis and on the other hand to the physical connection of genealogy of filiation and of family relationship.[35] These are the primary senses in which Paul uses the term as well, thus referring to circumcision "in the flesh" and brothers "in the flesh" (Romans 9:3). And even "my flesh" as simply "my kin," e.g., Israel in Romans 11:14. However, Paul goes one step further in my view. Since for him, these physical entities and connections have been fulfilled/annulled by their spiritual referents, "according to the flesh" becomes a hermeneutical term referring to the literal, the flesh of language as well.[36] Let us see how this is achieved. In the wake of these familiar metaphors, Paul easily sets up a set of parallel ratios, a very common practice in Hellenistic argumentation. A quick look at Romans 2:28–29 will exemplify this procedure:

> Then those who are physically uncircumcised but keep the law will condemn you who have the written code and circumcision but break the law. For he is not a Jew who is one outwardly, nor is circumcision something external and physical. He is a Jew who is one inwardly, and circumcision is a matter of the heart, spiritual and not literal.
>
> οὐ γὰρ ὁ ἐν τῷ φανερῷ ᾽Ιουδαῖός ἐστιν οὐδὲ ἡ ἐν τῷ φανερῷ ἐν σαρκὶ περιτομή. ἀλλ᾽ ὁ ἐν τῷ κρυπτῷ ᾽Ιουδαῖος, καὶ περιτομὴ καρδίας ἐν πνεύματι οὐ γράμματι.

In this verse—which I discuss in much more detail in the next chapter—the relevant oppositions are:

outer	inner
in the flesh (penis)	in the heart
in the letter	in the spirit

We have here an absolutely marvelous syncretism of biblical and Hellenic notions, so organized that they become synonyms for each other. On the one hand, in the Bible itself, as is well known, the opposition between circumcision of the penis and circumcision of the heart is attested. In the second of these ratios, therefore, Paul is apparently just using the biblical formula. However, by combining them with the other two sets of oppositions new and additional meanings are generated as well. Thus, once "in the flesh" (meaning "penis") is on the same side of the ratio as "in the letter," and the latter is opposed to "in the spirit," then "in the flesh" can become opposed to "in the spirit" as well. The association of "letter" and "flesh" promotes an understanding of the flesh as the literal as well. Finally, the hermeneutical opposition of "outer" and "inner," which is purely Hellenistic, supports these transfers also, for the material language, the outer flesh of the language, is that which is opposed to its spirit, its true meaning, which is within it. It is further important to note that since "flesh" in Hebrew refers, as I have said, to physical kinship, exactly the same set of transfers will be possible for that term as well.[37] It is precisely this ability that Paul had—perhaps greater in him than in any other Hellenistic Jewish thinker—to discover and animate the ways in which Hellenistic and biblical ways of thinking could illuminate and enrich one another that constitutes his genius. And note that it is exactly this formal move that, on my account, makes his political, ideological, and theological passion. One could with justice say that in Paul, as in Christ, "There is no Jew or Greek." The ethical dualisms of the Bible are mapped onto hermeneutical, anthropological, and ontological dualisms of Plato in a way that often seems almost seamless. I think that Paul, unlike Philo, is not performing this mapping consciously but that it has become for him the very organic mode of his thinking. Jewgreek is Greekjew.

Furthermore, the usage of *body* and *soul*, respectively, for the literal and the allegorical is in fact known from Hellenistic language, namely from Philo, who writes that his interest is in "the hidden meaning which appeals to the few who study soul characteristics, rather than bodily forms" (*Abraham*, 147). Moreover, the radical allegorizers who deny the necessity of keeping the literal commandments are referred to by him as people who are "trying to live as souls without bodies" (ibid., 89). In Greek as well, σάρξ is more than occasionally used as a synonym or near-synonym for σῶμα, "body." [38] I hypothesize that two factors would have led Paul to choose the former over the latter for this meaning. The first is the powerful homology that is set up between the literal in language and those symbols of literality that are so central to his thinking, literal circumcision and literal connection with the family/tribe of Israel, by using the term *flesh*, which carries those metaphorical senses, and not *body*, which does not. Secondly, precisely because σῶμα had taken on particular significances for Paul (as we have seen in 1 Corinthians 15), including the notion of a spiritual body and often something like the whole person, it was not available to him for the sense of the outer, the merely physical. Accordingly, he could not use σῶμα for the physical, literal, outward sense, but only σάρξ. Finally, there are passages in which Paul himself indicates that σάρξ, flesh, is being used by him as a synonym for σῶμα, body: "So then, brothers, we are debtors, not to the flesh to live according to the flesh [οὐ τῇ σαρκὶ τοῦ κατὰ σάρκα ζῆν]. For if you live according to the flesh you will die, *but if by the Spirit you put to death the deeds of the body*[39] [εἰ δὲ πνεύματι τὰς πράξεις τοῦ σώματος] you will live" (Romans 8:12–13). Another such passage is Romans 6:12: "Let not sin reign in your mortal bodies, to make you obey their passions," where, as Bultmann has pointed out, "passions of the body" is equal to "passions of the flesh," as in Galatians 5:16 et al. Once more, as Bultmann has shown, "the body of sin [τὸ σῶμα τῆς ἁμαρτίας]" in Romans 6:6 is equivalent to "sinful flesh [σαρκὸς ἁμαρτίας]" of 8:3 (1951, 197). Furthermore, at several points in 1 and 2 Corinthians as well, the terms seem interchangeable (Jewett 1971, 58).[40] It is therefore not at all surprising to find that Paul uses "flesh" to mean the outer, literal sense of the language with all of its concomitant outer, physical referents, whereas Philo used "body" to mean these same things.

Circumcision in the spirit of the language, that is, the true allegorical meaning of circumcision, is also a spiritual experience, and it is this homology which makes Paul's expression so powerful. Paul's thought and mode of expression at this point are nearly identical to Philo's:

> It is true that receiving circumcision does indeed portray the excision of pleasure and all passions, and the putting away of the impious conceit, under which the mind supposed that it was capable of begetting by its own power: but let us not on this account repeal the law laid down for circumcising. Why, we shall be ignoring the sanctity of the Temple and a thousand other things, if we are going to pay heed to nothing except what is shewn us by the inner meaning of things. Nay, we should look on all these outward observances as resembling the body, and their inner meanings as resembling the soul. It follows that, exactly as we have to take thought for the body, because it is the abode of the soul, so we must pay heed to the letter of the laws. (Philo 1932, 185)

For Philo, as for Paul, the allegorical interpretation of circumcision, explicitly figured by Philo as "resembling the soul," refers to an event which takes place *in the soul,*[41] while the literal understanding, "resembling the body," refers to an event which takes place in the body.[42] It is this very homology between language theory and anthropological ontology that makes Paul's text so effective. Two very natural senses of "the flesh," namely, the observance in the flesh of circumcision and filial connection, are concatenated with embodiedness or fleshliness as an attribute of the literal meaning of language as well. Because the literal sense of the Hebrew Bible refers as well, par excellence, to these fleshy entities of genealogy and fleshly observance, such as circumcision and kashruth, the three senses of "flesh" all work together in Pauline rhetoric in synergistic fashion. The spiritual then refers to an observance such as baptism, which is not "in the flesh," made not with hands; to faith in general as opposed to physical observances; to the spiritual Israel, namely, the community of Christian believers; and to spiritual filiation according to the promise as opposed to the physical, genetic community of Israelites descended from

Abraham. All these denied senses are comprehended together in κατὰ σάρκα, which is not a term of opprobrium by itself but becomes so when the flesh is allowed to occlude the spirit.

"For we are the circumcision"

Philippians 3 gives an excellent illustration of the nexus linking circumcision, genealogy, and physical observance of the Law as coordinated terms in Pauline thought, indeed as "*the* flesh." It demonstrates as well that Paul's issue with the flesh was *not* self-righteousness and finally argues for my last point above, namely that the fleshy, literal interpretation of the Torah only becomes illegitimate when its true meaning is revealed through and in Christ Jesus. In words made particularly famous in modern scholarship for their role in making Stendahl's case for Paul's "robust conscience," Paul writes:

> Look out for the dogs, look out for the evil-workers, look out for those who mutilate the flesh. For we are the [true][43] circumcision, who worship God in spirit, and glory [καυχώμενοι] in Christ Jesus, and put not confidence in the flesh. Though I myself have reason for confidence in the flesh also. If any other man thinks he has reason for confidence in the flesh, I have more: circumcised on the eighth day, of the people of Israel, of the tribe of Benjamin, a Hebrew born of Hebrews; as to the law of Pharisee, as to zeal a persecutor of the church, as to righteousness under the law blameless. But whatever gain I had I counted as loss for the sake of Christ. (3:1–7)

This text renders highly problematic the regnant theological interpretations of several elements of Pauline language à la Bultmann. We see from here that καυχώμενοι—suddenly translated "glorying" and not "boasting" as elsewhere—is not a pejorative term in Paul's discourse or thought-world. One must "boast" in the right thing. Indeed, I would claim that the correct nuance for this verb is not *boast* in the modern English sense of *brag* but rather something more like "have confidence in," in accord with its parallel in the antithesis of verse 3.[44] We see that Paul's issue with the Law has nothing to do with an alleged self-righteousness to which it leads. Second, we have an exact and explicit definition of what Paul means by "the flesh" here, and it is not human striving for righteousness. He tells us just what he means: being circumcised, being genealogically Israelite, and being devoted to the literal, physical carrying out of the Law as opposed to the inner movements of its spiritual referent. "The flesh"—σάρξ—carries not the slightest shred of sinfulness, human arrogance, or any of the other burdens that translators lay upon it. These literal and physical marks of status—this commitment to the corporeal as locus of meaning and value—become mere dung (σκύβαλα) in Paul's eyes in the light of Christ's invitation to all people to join the spiritual circumcision.

Bultmann Against Bultmann   Paradoxically enough, the account I am giving here of the flesh ~ spirit opposition is similar in significant ways to that of Bultmann. However, as I will try to show, on this point Bultmann's exegesis and his theology are divided against themselves. I accept the exegesis and reject the theology (both as an account of Paul and in itself). As I have claimed above, Bultmann with his exegetical acumen correctly identifies the passages in which Paul clearly speaks of the body as a home for the spirit but immediately seeks to deny their theological import. Precisely the same thing happens when he speaks of another platonistic concept par excellence: the "inner self." Bultmann writes:

> What does Paul call man, and how does he regard him, when he is the *subject* of his own willing and doing, when he is his real self who can distinguish himself from his *soma*-self? In Rom. 7:22 and II Cor. 4:16 as a *formal designation* for that self he uses the term "the inner man" (ὁ ἔσω ἄνθρωπος), an expression *that appears to be derived from the anthropology of Hellenistic dualism*. But it has a *purely formal meaning* in Paul, as may be seen from the fact that it means two things of different content in the two passages cited. In Rom. 7:22, "the inner" is man's real self in contrast to the self that has come under the sway of sin: "the *soma* of death" (7:24) or "the *soma* of sin." In II Cor. 4:16 "the inner man" is still the real self, it is true, but in contrast to the physical body. Rom. 7:2 deals with the unredeemed man under the Law, II Cor. 4:16 with the Christian, in whom God's power is at work (4:7), and in whom the Spirit dwells (5:5). The "inner man" of Rom. 7:22 is identical in content with the *nous* ("mind"), which belongs to man's essence (note how "inner man" is picked up, v. 23, by the term "mind,") but the "inner man" of II Cor. 4:16 is the self transformed by the Spirit. Thus the term "inner man" as formal designation for the subject-self confirms our conception, derived from the interpretation of *soma*, of Paul's view of human existence as the having of a relationship to one's self.   (1951, 202 [emphases added])

This is an extraordinary combination, in my opinion, of brilliant exegesis and totally arbitrary theologizing. With unfailing accuracy, Bultmann has identified the Hellenistic, platonistic elements of Pauline expression and anthropology. In both the Romans and the 2 Corinthians passages (and for the Corinthians passage I have already argued its pervasive platonism above), Paul demonstrates the essentially dualistic nature of his understanding of human being. People have outer and inner selves, and while the outer is not rejected or despised, there is no question that it is lower on the scale of value than the inner. The association of the inner self with *nous* strengthens the platonistic connections of the thought sevenfold. But Bultmann's distinctions between the two passages make no difference whatsoever. Why one would want to assume that for Paul the *soma* of death is *not* the physical body and thus regard these usages as self-contradictory or inconsistent escapes me entirely. Indeed, the fact that in two different contexts Paul assumes the same dyad of inner and outer selves proves that this was for him the simple, natural way of thinking about human beings. Note that I am not claiming that Paul was in any way exceptional in this regard. I think virtually anyone in his Hellenistic-Jewish (and even gentile) world would have assumed the same things. That theologoumenon which Bultmann takes to be confirmed by the analysis of these texts is his alone and bears almost no relationship at all to the Pauline text.

These tensions within Bultmann are graphically manifest in the following quotation:

> To the category of conduct "according to the flesh" belongs above all
> zealous fulfillment of the Torah: it does so because a man supposes he
> can thereby achieve righteousness before God by his own strength.
> The Galatian Christians who want to adopt the Torah and be circum-
> cised are indignantly asked: "Having begun with the Spirit, are you
> now ending with the flesh?"—ending, that is, not in sensual passions
> but in observance of the Torah (Gal. 3:3). In fact, not only zeal
> for the Law but also pride in all the pious Israelite's merits and titles
> of honor belong to the attitude of the flesh—or, the Torah and the
> merits and dignities of Israel fall within the concept "flesh" as belong-
> ing to the sphere of the visibly occurring and the historically demon-
> strable.   (1951, 240)

What Bultmann seems not to have noticed is that the two interpretations he gives, of which the second one (marked by the dash and the
"or,") is an afterthought, are quite different from one another. The first
involves "according to the flesh" as a term of moral condemnation of the
Jews for pride and trust in their own powers to achieve righteousness. This

may be good Lutheran theology; I submit it is not Paul. Bultmann's second interpretation, which I think the exegete and scholar in him (as opposed to the Lutheran theologian) did not allow him to ignore, is that what "in the flesh" means is the outer, the visible, the historical, the ethnically specific, in short the literal interpretation of Torah, that which marks off Jews from gentiles.[45] I am convinced, of course, that only the second adequately characterizes Paul's expression.

This split between the exegete and the theologian is, I think, emblematic of Bultmann's interpretation of σάρξ in general. Thus in his *Theology of the New Testament* he correctly described the σάρξ as the natural, the physical, as referring to the activities performed in the flesh (circumcision) and filial descent and connection. He furthermore understood the hermeneutical aspect of the term as well:

> "Flesh" here means, first of all, simply the physiological flesh on which circumcision is performed, and flesh in this sense by the juxtaposition of "outward" is brought into the wider sphere of "the outward." But the antithesis, especially by using "spirit" as a contrasting term, makes it clear that the sphere of "the outward" is precisely the sphere of the "flesh." . . . This is also the sphere of "the letter" or "the literal."
> (1951, 234)

So far so good. In the very next section of the book, however, Bultmann leaves off the exegetical exactitude of his analysis of "flesh" as the literal, the concrete, the physical, and thus Jewish observance of literal, physical commandments such as circumcision in the flesh, kashruth, and Holy Days, and theologizes in ways slanderous of both Paul and the Jews. I will not rehearse this last point at length, since it has been much done already, and anyway my main point here is to argue that Bultmann's perception of Paul is correct and important, *until he begins his theologizing.* Let me just cite one example, however, to back up the claim:

> The sinful self-delusion that one lives out of the created world can manifest itself both in unthinking recklessness (this especially among the gentiles) and in considered busy-ness (this especially among Jews)— both in the ignoring or transgressing of ethical demands and in excessive zeal to fulfill them. For the sphere of "flesh" is by no means just the life of instinct or sensual passions, but is just as much that of the moral and religious efforts of man.   (1951, 239)

Paul, I am sure, would not recognize such sentiments as his own, not for one second. Yes, "flesh" does mean for him both giving in to the body

and observing the literal Jewish Torah, but not certainly because he ob-
jected to zeal in fulfilling ethical demands or was opposed to the moral
and religious efforts of "man," but rather because both the body and the
literal observance of Torah belonged to the sphere of the physical and outward. The physical Torah, moreover, in the way that it marked off Jewish
bodies from gentile ones frustrated God's plan for all humanity as "The
Israel of God." What concerned Paul, as I hope yet to make plausible, was
the literal observance of the Law insofar as it frustrated what Paul took to
be the moral and religious necessity of humankind, namely to erase all
distinction between ethnos and ethnos, sex and sex and become one in
Christ's spiritual body. The dualism of spirit and flesh was thus necessary
for his entire political and theological program to be carried forth. As we
have seen in the passage quoted above (from page 240), Bultmann understood this and could express it clearly, but he could not let it stand because
it was not consistent with his own theological positions.

PAUL'S "MAINLINE" PLATONISM

Once more, let me state the major thesis of this book. Paul's genius was
not as a philosopher, which he was not, but in his realization that the
common dualist ideology—ontology, anthropology, and hermeneutic—
which together for him formed a christology, provided the answer to the
theological problem that troubled him the most: How do the rest of the
people in God's world fit into the plan of salvation revealed to the Jews
through their Torah?[46] Let me be absolutely clear. I am not claiming for
Paul a radical dualism which denies value to the phenomenal world, but
rather a dualism of the sort which has characterized western thought practically since its inception, that is, the understanding of human beings, the
world, and language as all composed of a material and a spiritual component in correspondence with each other. In other words, what I am claiming is that Paul held to the kind of dualism, which N. T. Wright calls
"cosmological duality: the classic position of Plato," and identifies as "a
mainline belief of the Greco-Roman (and modern Western world)."[47]
There is, in this sense, nothing striking in claiming that Paul was such a
dualist; if anything the bold step that I am making is to claim that the
Rabbis (as opposed to both earlier Hellenistic Jews and later ones) *resisted*
this form of dualism.

4

Moses' Veil;
or, The Jewish Letter, the Christian Spirit

Throughout this book I claim that Paul's fundamental oppositions of the spirit and the flesh are hermeneutical in nature, that for Paul truth lies in the spiritual, allegorical interpretation of text, history, and world, while the physical is but a shadow of this truth. In contrast to regnant views claiming that Paul's hermeneutic is typological and not allegorical, I wish to unsettle this very opposition, claiming that typology is the revelation in time (apocalypse) of allegorical structures of signification that were always already in place. A key support for the hermeneutical nature—that is, its essential life as a response to the problem of language and interpretation—of Paul's binary opposition is the places where Paul draws a contrast between "spiritual" (ἐν πνεύμαρτι) and "literal" (ἐν γράμματι). These cases provide evidence that "spiritual" functions for Paul as a hermeneutic term, thus indicating that "according to the flesh"—the usual opposite of "according to the spirit"—does as well. There are three verses within the Pauline corpus in which the opposition is explicit: Romans 2:29, 2 Corinthians 3:6, and Romans 7:6. In this chapter, I will try to establish the necessity of a hermeneutical dimension of the first two of these texts, as well as its fundamentally allegorical nature, through detailed readings of them in their contexts. (Romans 7:6 will be interpreted in Chapter 7.) At the same time the participation of allegory as a mode of reading in an entire thought-world which structures it and which it in turn structures will be exposed through these readings.

READING THE BODY IN ROMANS 2

Romans 2:29: "He is a Jew who is one inwardly, and [real] circumcision is a matter of the heart, in the spirit and not in the letter [ἀλλ' ὁ ἐν τῷ κρυπτῷ Ἰουδαῖος, καὶ περιτομὴ καρδίας ἐν πνεύματι οὐ γράμματι]." The semantic opposition between "in the spirit" and "in the letter" in this verse suggests strongly that "in the spirit" is a hermeneutical term. "In the spirit" means, then, in the spirit of the language, as opposed to its letter. In order to understand the hermeneutical radicality of the end of Romans 2, a detailed reading of the entire chapter will be necessary.

This chapter, a stone ignored by the builders of Reformation Paulinism, has become the cornerstone of a new interpretation of Paul, one that is directly contradictory to that of the Reformation. The reason that the chapter has been a scandal for Lutheran theology is that it seems to assert strongly the value and necessity of works over mere "hearing" of the Law, which seems to contradict Paul's insistence in Galatians 3 on precisely the "hearing" of faith in opposition to the despised "doing of works." Since Lutheranism had understood that Paul's major message is that Judaism is inadequate—or even sinful—because of its valorization of good works, such verses as 13—"For it is not the hearers of the law who are righteous before God, but the doers of the law will be counted righteous"—seemed directly contradictory.

On the present reading, however, in Romans 2 Paul is not condemning Jews who *keep* the Law—as Reformation readers would have it—and certainly not attacking Judaism in general but rather criticizing Jews who believe that they are exempt from divine judgment, or even that they will be favored at the divine Assizes, simply by virtue of their being Jewish, without respect to their actual performance of the Law (Wilckens 1982; Dunn 1988; Watson 1986, 109–22).[1] In other words, he is attacking Jews who think that works are not necessary for salvation, since God saves Israel, and only Israel, by grace alone. Such chauvinist notions, by no means universal in first-century Judaism, did exist.[2] This interpretation can be supported from the very beginning of Romans 2 where in verses 1–3 Paul's diatribe is directed against one who condemns others for sins that he engages in himself. This condemnation is often taken to be an attack on simple hypocrisy, while I am suggesting that the person being attacked is not so much a hypocrite but rather a Jew who believes sincerely that mere possession, hearing, of the Law will save him.

Although at this stage, Paul addresses Everyman ($\tilde{\omega}$ $\check{\alpha}\nu\theta\rho\omega\pi\varepsilon$), this is, as Dunn perceptively suggests, to win rhetorical assent from his Jewish interlocutor, much as Nathan the prophet tells David a story about a man in general in order to win his assent before revealing that "You are that man" (Dunn 1988, 79).[3] Paul is cleverly employing here topoi of Jewish attacks on gentile lawlessness, but will turn them, in the end, against the very Jews who employ them. As Dunn has shown, verse 2 is almost a parodic citation of the *Psalms of Solomon:*

PSS. SOL.   And those who do lawlessness shall not escape the judg-
            ment of the Lord.
ROM   (Do you suppose you) who do the same things that you
            shall escape the judgment of God?
[PSS. SOL. καὶ οὐκ ἐκφεύξ ονται οἱ ἀνομίαν τὸ κρίμα κυρίου
ROM   καὶ ποιῶν αὐτα, ὅτι οὐ ἐκφεύξῃ τὸ κρίμα τοῦ θεοῦ].

(Dunn 1988, 81)

The passage in the *Psalms of Solomon* is typical in that it is a condem-nation of gentiles who do not have the Law, but Paul will turn it against the Jew who has the Law but does not keep it. His rhetorical strategy is, however, even more complex than that, for here he can be understood to be condemning simple hypocrisy, which his pious hearer will certainly condemn along with him: "The imaginary interlocutor is envisaged not as objecting to what Paul had said but as agreeing with it very strongly" (Dunn 1988, 81). This interlocutor will end up condemning himself through this very agreement when it is revealed later on in the chapter that Paul has a Jew specifically in mind and that it is not simply hypocrisy that Paul attacks here but the confidence of the Jew that his ethnic status will make the divine judgment lighter for him. That such confidence is not foreign to Pharisaic Judaism (or at any rate its successor) may certainly be established by such utterances as, "All Israel have a share in the Next World" without, of course, necessarily assuming that this rabbinic state-ment was already current at the time of Paul.[4] Paul is systematically un-dermining a series of Jewish theologoumena, all of which would have been strong underpinnings for Jewish confidence in God (καυχάομαι ἐν θεῷ), not, I think, to be understood as boasting in the sense of prideful speech so much as a false sense of soteriological status by virtue of being part of the chosen People itself.[5] I think that Dunn has put the matter with par-ticular exactitude and sensitivity:

> In all this it is very difficult to avoid the conclusion that Paul's aim is
> directed at what he sees to be the overconfidence in their election on
> the part of many of his fellow Jews. We of the twentieth century lis-
> tening to this can point to other statements from the Judaism of the
> same period . . . but we cannot assume that these writings are typical
> of the actual Judaism of Paul's time, any more than we can assume that
> Deuteronomy and Jeremiah are representative of the Israelite religion

of their time. The passages from Jewish writings already adduced, when set alongside the attitude Paul attacks, provide sufficient evidence that Paul's interlocutor was no straw man. The dominant or at least a prominent mood within Judaism prior to A.D. 70 may well have been more buoyant and self-confident than that which the sayings and writings actually preserved from the period represent.   (Dunn 1988, 91)

There certainly is one theological tendency within Judaism which ascribes a privilege with God to the chosenness itself.[6] It is this tendency—more or less typical of the Judaism of his time and place—which Paul attacks, not because of its association with complacency or self-righteousness but because of its implications for Jewish relations with Others.

This tendency is countered from within Judaism itself with another that regards chosenness not as privilege but as obligation. As Dunn has remarked, in verses 4–5 Paul is essentially appealing to biblical theology itself, as revealed in such Deuteronomistic sources as Deuteronomy 9–10 and Jeremiah:

Or do you think lightly of the wealth of his goodness and of his forbearance and patience, disregarding the fact that the kindness of God is to lead you to repentance? As a result of your hardness and impenitent heart you are storing up for yourself wrath in the day of wrath when will be revealed the righteous judgment of God.   (Romans 2:4–5)

In Deuteronomy 10 it is clear that the only privilege that Jews have owing to their ancestry is to have it demanded of them that they repent and "circumcise the foreskins of their hearts." Indeed, it is the very appeal to the ancestors and the choice of their descendants that issues in the charge, "So now you must circumcise the foreskin of your hearts," because God "is no respecter of persons" (verse 17). A persistent danger in the concept of chosenness is that it leads to a conviction that one is privileged with God, while the Deuteronomist (and Paul in his wake) argues that chosenness is rather a special burden, a demand for repentance. Since Paul's Jewish interlocutor is not repentant but rather relies on the privilege to save himself, he is storing up not merit but rather wrath for the day of judgment (verse 5), and because God is no respecter of persons, therefore the judgment will fall equally on Jew and gentile alike—the Jew first simply because she has been given the special commandment and the special opportunity to repent and circumcise the foreskin of her heart.[7] Now when Paul in verse 6 argues that God will render to each according to his works, he is *not* contradicting his doctrine of justification by faith but rather using a Jewish topos to convince (or trap) his Jewish hearer: Do not be confident in your Jewishness to save you, O Jew, for this serves only to increase the obligation upon you to repent and do good. God judges all according to their works and not according to their ancestry. Paul is engaging here not the contrast of works of the Torah, i.e., ritual acts, to faith but rather the contrast of privileged and static possession of the Law to doing that which God wants of us.[8] In verse 11, Paul clearly echoes Deuteronomy 10:17 by clinching his argument that Jew and gentile will be judged alike with the claim that "there is no respecting of persons with God" (οὐ γάρ ἐστιν προσωποληµψία παρὰ τῷ θεῷ—אין משוא פנים לפני ה'). Election will not avail on the day of judgment.

However, Paul is also setting another rhetorical trap for the Jew, because once more, the Jew will nod her head and indicate that she agrees that God will judge people by their works, but the Jew will have in mind both ethical behavior—faithfulness to the Covenant—and the performance of such rituals as circumcision, kashruth, and keeping of the Sabbaths. In the context of this reading of Romans 2, the next section is crystal clear in its meaning and no scandal for Pauline interpretation at all:

> For as many as have sinned without the law shall also perish without the law; and as many as have sinned within the law shall be condemned through the law. For it is not the hearers of the law who are righteous before God, but the doers of the law will be counted righteous. For when Gentiles who have not the law do by nature what the law requires, they not having the law are the law for themselves: they demonstrate the work of the law written on their hearts.   (2:12–15)

Dunn has already written on this passage, "The aim of this argument is clearly to puncture a Jewish assurance falsely based on the fact of having the law, of being the chosen people of God. His argument is that this assurance must be false simply because there are Gentiles who show more evidence in themselves of *what the law points to* than many Jews . . . who keep the law *at one level* (circumcision) but who are not properly to be described as real Jews, as 'doers of the law'" (Dunn 1988, 107 [emphasis added]). This talk of "what the law points to" and of levels of understanding certainly implies ascribing to Paul willy-nilly an allegoristic notion of hermeneutic. I will argue that this ascription is correct, and that even those Pauline scholars who most vigorously deny it are in fact assuming it unconsciously.

Let us look more closely at the text. Paul's argument here is actually twofold. He continues his critique of a Jewish theological notion—mightily contested by both the prophetic and Pharisaic traditions within Judaism—that mere possession of the Law counts for righteousness for all Jews. It is this which Paul refers to as "hearing of the law"—here to be understood as listening to it being read (Dunn 1988, 104–05). Paul, however, goes further than this, for he argues as well that gentiles who do not have the specific, the written Law can yet be a law unto themselves. It is possible to do what the Law requires without having the Law at all. How can this be so, since the Law requires such practices as circumcision about which without the Law one would not even know? Only because the true interpretation of circumcision is the allegorical one, the one available to all, men and women, Jews and Greeks, not an inscription of the flesh, σάρξ, בשר, penis, but an inscription in the spirit, figured as a writing on the heart, thus continuing the allusions to Deuteronomy 10 and Jeremiah 4! The connection between the allegorical interpretation of the Torah and its universal applicability is compelling. In a sense, what Paul says here is not unique, because certainly for many first-century Jews, the notion of a natural law (whether already figured as commandments to the children of Noah or not) which gentiles could keep, and indeed the concomitant possibility of gentiles being fully acceptable to God, would not have been foreign.[9] Once more, I think that what renders the Pauline move so special is the factor—not, to be sure, emphasized particularly here—that Jews and gentiles will be justified in the *same* way, by the same standard.[10] This point has been made by several commentators on this verse cited by Dunn, who insist that "the whole point of what Paul is saying here would be lost if νόμος was understood as other than as a reference to *the* law, the law given to Israel" (Dunn 1988, 99). Note the difference between "works of the law," ἔργα τοῦ νόμου, and here the singular ἔργον τοῦ νόμου. The first, the specific physical works of the Law, which represent difference, is a pejorative term in Paul's economy, while the second, the singular spiritual universal one *work* of the Law is positive.

In the next several verses, Paul addresses a "Jew":

> But if you are called a "Jew" and rely on the law and boast in God, and
> know his will and approve the things that matter, being instructed
> from the law. . . . You then who teach another, do you not teach your-

self? You who preach "Do not steal," do you steal? You who say, "Do
not commit adultery," do you commit adultery? You who abhor idols,
do you commit sacrilege? You who boast in the law—through transgression of the law you dishonor God. For "the name of God is blas-
phemed among the Gentiles through you," as it is written.   (17–24)

Once again, the simplest and most straightforward interpretation of
this passage is that of Dunn, who sees it as a continuation of Paul's diatribe
against the Jewish assumption that being a member of the covenanted
People will provide some kind of privilege at the last Assizes. Paul argues—and here his argument, particularly in verse 24, could be found in
many rabbinic texts—that Jews who profess the Law and do not perform
it are worse, indeed, than gentiles who do not have the Law at all. Such
Jews profane the name of the Lord. I think, moreover, that the "you" here
is a figure for the Jews as a collective and Paul's argument is not so much
against hypocrisy but against a self-righteous assumption that Jews are
privileged as a whole because of their possession of the Law, when, in fact,
there are many Jews who steal: "The argument is that the transgression of
any individual Jew is enough to call in question the Jewish assumption
that as a Jew he stands in a position of privilege and superiority before God
as compared with the Gentile. The point is that once the typical Jew's *a
priori* status as Jew before God by virtue of his people's election is seen to
be called in question, then the broader indictment of man in general
(1:18–32) can be seen to apply more clearly to Jew as well as Gentile
(2:9–11)" (Dunn 1988, 116). The diatribe is, on this reading, a continuation of Paul's critique of religious chauvinism and nothing else. Furthermore, this passage makes manifest the precise connection between the
Jewish ethnocentrism and the Law. It is having the Law and knowing
God's will that leads the Jews to their assumption of privilege vis-à-vis the
gentiles (Dunn 1988, 117).

As I have said, up to this point in Romans 2, Paul has essentially produced a sermon to which many if not most Pharisaic preachers as heirs of
the prophets could have and would have assented. Although there certainly was a doctrine that Jews have a privileged position in salvation
history, it is a perversion of that doctrine to imagine that it therefore did
not require them to be faithful servants of the Law (within human limitations and possibilities) in order to earn that privileged position. Indeed,
the privilege consists primarily in the guarantee that in the end of days
they will be able to repent, and then God will restore Israel to its glory as

he had promised to her ancestors, Abraham, Isaac, and Jacob. God's covenant with Israel is exactly as Paul represents it in Romans 11, a covenant of grace enabling Jews to repent and be saved. Generally, Jews would have held exactly what Paul argues for, namely that only repentance will guarantee the Jew justification. Jewish theology did not provide for justification on the basis of being Jewish alone, although there were some strains that came close to such a view.[11] The sense of Jewish privilege was rather that at the last all of the lost sheep would indeed repent and return to the fold—a position that even Paul did not abandon (see Romans 11:24). Dunn has gotten this just right in my view:

> Paul does not imply that the typical Jew is content simply to have the law; what the law supports is a whole way of life, as Paul knew well (Gal. 1:14; Phil. 3:6). But it was a way of life where distinctiveness of the Jew from the non-Jew was always to the fore (as the next clauses confirm). What Paul is attacking, therefore, is precisely the Jewish reliance on this distinctiveness.   (Dunn 1988, 111)

Insofar as Paul here is simply attacking hypocrisy, then, there is nothing in his preaching that is foreign to the prophets or indeed the Rabbis. Undoubtedly, certain Jews misunderstood the notion of Chosenness and indeed were led into the error of *sola gratia*.

At the end of the chapter, however, in verses 28 and 29, Paul draws a conclusion that would have shocked his Pharisaic teachers.[12] The rhetoric of the chapter as a whole would have led an imaginary Jewish listener to assent to it at every point, and then the ending would have the effect *mutatis mutandis* that "You are that man" has at the end of Nathan's speech to David.

> Then those who are physically uncircumcised but keep the law will condemn you who have the written code and circumcision but break the law. For he is not a Jew who is one outwardly, nor is circumcision something external and physical. He is a Jew who is one inwardly, and circumcision is a matter of the heart, spiritual and not literal.
>
> οὐ γὰρ ὁ ἐν τῷ φανερῷ Ἰουδαῖός ἐστιν οὐδὲ ἡ ἐν τῷ φανερῷ ἐν σαρκὶ περιτομή. ἀλλ' ὁ ἐν τῷ κρυπτῷ Ἰουδαῖος, καὶ περιτομὴ καρδίας ἐν πνεύματι οὐ γράμματι.

Paul argues that the "Jew" is characterized by inner, invisible dispositions and not outer, visible circumcision, by circumcision of the heart, the spiritual (allegorical) circumcision, and not by the literal circumcision of the flesh.[13] Note that here Paul goes beyond the claims he has been making in the chapter. This is not mere recapitulation but a fundamentally new idea, one that requires us to reinterpret the first part of the chapter in its wake. Up to this point, Paul has been arguing that mere possession or hearing of the Law will not justify any Jew, i.e., that being a member of the covenant people carries with it no grace; only works will do. A typical Jewish recipient of that message—particularly one "softened" up by Romans 1, with its fairly typical denunciation of gentile immorality—could easily assent to Paul's argument. After all, as I have claimed, the extreme notion that membership in the Jewish People was enough alone to guarantee salvation was hardly widespread.

But now we come to the climax and crux of the chapter, for here Paul thoroughly redefines precisely those theological terms to which we can expect that his Jewish interlocutor would have been assenting until now. The Jew has agreed that being Jewish is not sufficient for salvation, and one needs works as well. However, as Paul reveals now, when he speaks of good works, he does not mean what Jews intend by this—that is, he does not mean keeping (in theory and intent) all of the commandments, whether ritual or moral in nature, both those that divide the Jews from other peoples and those that bind them to others. The first category—synecdochized here by circumcision but certainly including food rules and Sabbaths—means nothing in the work of salvation. Such rules are only outer practices that signify the second category, that which Paul calls otherwise "the law of faith working through love." In other words, in this coda to the chapter which seems until now to be calling Jews to repent and keep the Law as *they* have understood it—a keeping that maintains ethnic identity and specificity—, Paul introduces his major concern throughout his ministry: producing a new, single human essence, one of "true Jews" whose "circumcision" does not mark off their bodies as ethnically distinct from any other human bodies. Paul has been hinting that this is his theme throughout the chapter. Twice he has told us that judgment and reward will come to "the Jew first and then to the Greek." He has, moreover, informed us that the gentiles, even though they do not have *the* Law, nevertheless have a law written on their hearts, to which the evidence of their ethical debates and attacks of conscience attest. Paul's universalist theme is thus clearly announced, and this ending merely confirms it powerfully. "True Jewishness" ends up having nothing to do with family connection (descent from Abraham according to the flesh), history (having the Law), or maintaining the cultural/religious practices of the historical Jewish community (circumcision), but paradoxically consists of participating in a universalism, an allegory that dissolves those essences and meanings entirely. As we shall see in the final chapters of this book, this dissolution of Jewish identity by spiritualizing and allegorizing it is a familiar move of European culture until today.

Hermeneutics or Ethics? Westerholm's Reading

Some modern interpreters contrast their interpretations of the end of Romans 2 with that current among earlier interpreters as ethical versus hermeneutical. Objections have been raised to the hermeneutical interpretation which I am espousing here. In a recent article, Stephen Westerholm has argued very cogently that the opposition of "spirit" and "letter" is an ethical one for Paul. His interpretation of Romans 2 runs as follows. Paul's target in Romans 2 is hypocrisy, and "in 2.17 he names his imaginary interlocutor a Jew, and notes the things of which the Jew boasts: he possesses the law of God, which embodies knowledge and truth; instructed in its precepts, he can play the role of leader for the blind, of light for those in darkness (vv. 17–20)" (Westerholm 1984, 233). At this point, according to Westerholm, Paul argues (similarly to the interpretation that I have proposed above) that Jews who do not keep the Law will be judged according to the Law. We now come to the crux of the interpretation, verses 27–29. Westerholm convincingly argues that διὰ γράμματος καὶ περιτομῆς in verse 27 does not indicate that the letter (written code) and circumcision are liabilities; they are not indices of a perverted understanding of the commands of God, but they are simply not sufficient in themselves.[14] I am in complete agreement with this interpretation thus far; however, at this point I part from Westerholm.

Westerholm himself remarks:

> When in v. 26, Paul writes that the "uncircumcision" of a Gentile who keeps the law will be counted as circumcision, his argument is admittedly one which most Jews of this time would have rejected, believing that literal circumcision was a prerequisite for a Gentile's admission to the people of God. Still, Paul evidently feels that he is simply pressing the logic of the situation to its conclusion: just as the (physical) circumcision of the Jew will be disregarded if he transgresses the law, so the (physical) uncircumcision of the Gentile will be disregarded if he keeps it.   (Westerholm 1984, 235)

Perhaps it takes a rabbinic Jew to sense the oddity—from our perspective—of this sentence, which simply repeats the oddity of Paul's formulation itself. Everything makes sense until the very last clause, *but keeping
the Law while being uncircumcised is simply an oxymoron from the perspective
of rabbinic Judaism, because being circumcised is part of the Law!* On the one
hand, rabbinic Judaism was to develop (and perhaps the Pharisees already
had) a doctrine whereby gentiles do not need to keep the Law at all in
order to be justified. There is a separate Law for them: the seven commandments given to Noah. On the other hand, "the" Law can only mean
one thing: the aggregate of all of the commandments both ritual—between humanity and God—and ethical—between humans and other humans. To be sure, there is a disagreement between Paul and "most Jews"
as to whether gentiles need to be circumcised in order to become part of
the People of God, but even more to the point, there is a fundamental
gap in the definition of the Law.[15] For prophet or Pharisee, it is possible
to preach: "What good is keeping this ceremonial part of the Law, if you
do not keep that ethical part of the Law?"[16] For Paul alone is it possible
to generalize the one part as the Law *tout court*. For Paul, Law has come
to mean something new, vis-à-vis Pharisaic Judaism; it has come to mean
"the law of faith working through love," in which "circumcision is nothing and uncircumcision is nothing" (1 Corinthians 7:19). Now whether
he has crossed the line or not into true allegory, and I believe he has, in
any case, once this new law of faith is defined as being that which is "in
the spirit; not in the written," ἐν πνεύματι οὐ γράμματι, we already
have a hermeneutical moment, a moment of interpretation. Furthermore,
the written is particular, the spiritual universal in Paul's scheme of things,
a point to be further supported below. One of the best examples of Paul's
allegorical readings of the commandments—in addition, of course, to his
reading of circumcision—is found in 1 Corinthians 5:6–8, where the
commandment to purge the house of leaven for Passover is reinterpreted
ecclesiologically to mean that one must purge the Christian communities
of the old leaven of the puffing up of pride (verse 2), as well as the leaven
of "vice and wickedness." Paul's reading here is very similar indeed to
that of Philo in the Special Laws, where leaven is also interpreted as pride
(Philo 1937, 193). The historical rite of a particular tribe has been transformed into an ahistorical, abstract, and universal human "truth," the very
essence of allegory.

Westerholm's own conclusions regarding the usage of "letter" and "spirit" in Romans 2 brings this point out clearly. Westerholm adheres to the view that "'Letter' in Rom. 2.27 does not refer to a particular interpretation of the Old Testament law, but to the possession of God's commands in written form." Paul is then preaching against a view that mere possession of the written text is sufficient for divine approval, whereas in truth only observance will win such approval. So far, so good—that is, the same as I wish to interpret. In the next paragraph of Westerholm's text, however, the enormous difference appears, for there he argues, "Similarly, circumcision which is (ἐν) γράμματι in v. 29 does not refer to a particular interpretation of circumcision, but simply to circumcision in a physical, external form. . . . Physical circumcision is contrasted with circumcision ἐν πνεύματι, which may or may not be meant to refer to the mark of the new age. In any case, it speaks of an inner reality which is not content with external forms, whatever limited legitimacy the latter may possess" (Westerholm 1984, 236). This very opposition, however, between a circumcision which is physical and one which is an inner reality is in its very essence a "particular interpretation of circumcision"! What else can it possibly be, especially if Paul argues that this inner reality is more important than and supersedes the physical observance? This does not preclude the ethical interpretation of "in the spirit" which Westerholm argues for; Paul is protesting an ethical defect in Romans 2— whether hypocrisy, as Westerholm would have it, or excessive reliance on ethnic privilege, as I interpret it. But there is no contradiction between an ethical reading of the opposition and a hermeneutical one. They go together and are homologous with each other.

HERMENEUTICS AS ETHICS: 2 CORINTHIANS 3

A similar relation obtains in 2 Corinthians 3, arguably the most important passage in all of Paul for reading his hermeneutic of the Torah and of "Old Israel." Richard Hays unsettles the opposition between two modes of interpreting the 2 Corinthians passage that have been considered mutually exclusive. In the tradition of the Church, 2 Cor. 3:6 has been understood from nearly the very beginning as denoting an opposition between literal and allegorical interpretation. This reading has in recent years been called into question by Pauline scholars, who argue that the opposition is rather between a written text of any kind and the fleshy [!] embodiment of Christian covenant in the actual community of the faithful. Hays refers to this embodiment as an Incarnation and remarks, "The traditional English translation of *gramma* as 'letter,' based in turn on the Vulgate's *littera*, is an unfortunate one . . . because it suggests that Paul is distinguishing between literal and spiritual modes of exegesis. This is the construal against which the advocates of a nonhermeneutical interpretation of 2 Corinthians 3 rightly object." Hays goes on strikingly to remark, "Thus, the Christian tradition's reading of the letter-spirit dichotomy as an antithesis between the outward and the inward, the manifest and the latent, the body and the soul, turns out to be a dramatic misreading, indeed a complete inversion. For Paul, the Spirit is—scandalously—identified precisely with the outward and palpable, the particular human community of the new covenant, putatively transformed by God's power so as to make Christ's message visible to all. The script, however, remains abstract and dead because it is not embodied" (Hays 1989, 130). This formulation, however, discounts one very important fact: The script had not remained abstract and dead, because it was already embodied in the living practice of Jewish communities. There must always be, then, a hermeneutical dimension to such a claim, almost by definition. And indeed, Hays himself argues very perceptively that whether or not the letter ~ spirit opposition is in itself the index of a dichotomy of hermeneutical practices, in any case Paul posits a hermeneutical shift from the reading of Moses to the experience of the Spirit.[17] There has, after all, been a change in the status of Scripture. The hermeneutical and ethical moments are indeed homologous with each other.

Of Veils and Fading Glory

I would further claim that the very notion of language as abstract and disembodied—that is, the very notion of the necessity for the word to become flesh, as it were—is already, in itself, an allegorical conception of language, paralleling the platonistic notions of non-corporeal Godhead which the Incarnation presupposes.[18] Analysis of the continuation of the Pauline text, 3:7–18, will bring out this point more clearly:

> Now if the ministry of death, chiseled in letter on stone, took place
> with such glory that the Israelites could not bear to gaze at Moses's
> face, even though it was fading,[19] will not the ministry of the Spirit be
> with greater glory? For if there is glory with the ministry of condemna-
> tion, how much more does the ministry of righteousness abound with

glory. Indeed, what has had glory has not had glory, in this case, because of the glory which so far surpasses it. For if what was fading [τὸ καταργούμενον] was with such glory, how much more the glory of that which endures!

Having, therefore, such a hope, we act with much boldness, and not like Moses when he used to put a veil over his face so the Israelites could not gaze at the end [= true meaning] of what was fading [καταργουμένου]. But their minds were hardened. Right up to the present day the same veil remains at the public reading of the old covenant—unlifted, because it is in Christ that it is fading [καταργεῖται]. Indeed, to the present, whenever Moses is read a veil lies over their hearts. Whenever anyone turns to the Lord the veil is removed. Now "the Lord" is the Spirit, and where the Spirit of the Lord is, is freedom. And we all, with unveiled face, beholding [as in a mirror] the glory of the Lord, are being transformed into the same image, from glory to glory, as from the Lord, the Spirit.

Hays reads the τέλος of verse 13, at which the Israelites could not gaze, not as the "end" but as the "goal" or "fulfillment"; note the parallel to the old hermeneutic problem of "Christ is the τέλος of the Law."[20] The veil, for Paul, as in the Torah itself, was to prevent those who were not capable of standing it from seeing the glory of Moses' transformation. Paul's allegorical reading of this is that until this day those Jews who deny Christ show themselves not capable of bearing the true meaning of the text in Christ and so still read it with a veil. Because their minds were hardened, they are prevented from perceiving the true meaning of the text, which is the glory, the spirit that transfigured Moses. That is, the reading of "Moses" prevents the Jews from seeing the glory of the Lord, and this is typologically/allegorically signified by the covering of Moses' face when he gave the Law. The word is meant to point to the Spirit which lies behind it (and always did), but the Jews remain at the level of the literal—literally, at the level of the letter, the concrete language which, of course, epitomizes midrash, and this is the *gramma* which kills.

Once more, in Hays's excellent formulation:

For those who are fixated on the text as an end in itself, however, the text remains veiled. But those who turn to the Lord are enabled to see through the text to its *telos,* its true aim. For them, the veil is removed, so that they, like Moses, are transfigured by the glory of God into the image of Jesus Christ, to whom Moses and the Law had always, in veiled fashion pointed. . . . The telos of Moses' transitory covenant (which remained hidden from Israel in the wilderness) was the same thing as the true significance of Moses/Torah (which remained hidden from Paul's contemporaries in the synagogue). . . . The veiled telos is, if we must express it in a discursive proposition, the glory of God in Jesus Christ that makes itself visible in fleshy communities conformed to God's image. . . . All the elements are necessary to express the hermeneutical and ethical significations that are packed into his metaphor.   (Hays 1989, 137, 146)[21]

This passage is thus typological and allegorical in its structure: That is, like the Spirit which must be incarnated in the Corinthian community and which Paul calls a writing, language always consists of a spiritual meaning which is embodied in the material. I think that Paul's argument is even more complex than this, for there are, in fact, four terms here, not two: Old Testament, its Jewish readers, Spirit, "we all." The lesser glory, the Old Testament, is both revealed and annulled by the greater glory of the Spirit. As the sun reveals the moon during the night and conceals it by day, so the Spirit was reflected indirectly in the Old Testament, which is now completely obscured by the greater light of the Spirit directly shining from the New. Even that lesser glory, Paul argues, lesser *because* it is transitory, was too much for the Jews to stand, and they had to be protected by a veil. Even more so is it the case that the glory which will not be annulled is too much for them to see, and they remain blinded to it by a veil. What even Hays does not make explicit, although it is implicit in his text, is that Paul is, in fact, playing with both senses of τέλος in this passage and doing so brilliantly. Those who do not see that there is a τέλος beyond the text reach a dead end in a veil, while those who *do* see that Christ is the τέλος of the Law see through the veil—that veil which is the letter itself—or better, the veil is removed, and they see the true glory of which the physical, material, literal glory of the text was only a shadow which passes away. Moses, then, provided the veil presumably because the time was not yet ripe for the τέλος, the true meaning, to be perceived, but this very veil has resulted in a hardening of the minds which prevents the turning toward Christ which alone removes the veil.

Paul, in fact, enacts the kind of reading that the Jews do *not* do at the same time that he talks about it. Whatever this passage is, it is not midrash, because it does not involve a close contact with the language of the verses of Exodus with which it deals, while midrash is precisely characterized by its attention to the physical, material details of the actual language (compare Hays 1989, 132; Davies 1965, 106–07). Paul's is typological/ allegorical reading, whereby the events of the "Old Testament" signify realities in the present life of the Christian community.[22] The metaphor of the veil is exact. Midrash, the way the Jews read Moses, is a hermeneutics of opacity, while Paul's allegorical/typological reading is a hermeneutics of transparency. Paul can boldly go where no Jew has gone before and reveal the true telos of the text because of the spiritual condition of his listeners who, protected by the Spirit, need not fear death. Paul thus asserts that the veil Moses put over his face symbolizes a veil the Jews had put over their hearts at the reading of the Law, because they do not expound it spiritually, which prevents them from perceiving the glory of the truth. Paul identifies the new readers of the Bible as "we all," thus asserting the universalism of the Christian dispensation over and against the particularities of the Jewish reading of Moses.

With this, we can answer another conundrum of this chapter, most fully explicated by Morna Hooker: "He has told us that Israel could not gaze on Moses' glory: how, then, does it come about that Christians can now gaze on the overwhelming glory which belongs to Christ?" (Hooker 1981, 298) Paul, however, has given us the answer to this question himself. "The letter kills but the Spirit gives life." And: "Now the Lord is the Spirit, and where the Spirit of the Lord is, there is freedom. And we all, with unveiled face, beholding the glory of the Lord, are being changed into his likeness from one degree of glory to another; for this comes from the Lord who is the Spirit." In other words, all Christians now have the experience of Moses himself! He, after all, beheld the face of the Lord, through an undarkened glass, and was not destroyed, but all of the other Jews had to perceive even the reflected glory that was in his face through a veil. When Moses turned to the Lord, he removed his veil. Now, all Christians who turn to the Lord are in the condition of Moses, and because the Spirit, which is the Lord (= Christ), gives life, therefore they can perceive the τέλος without fear of death.[23] The use of the verb κατοπτριζόμενοι, "looking as in a mirror," is fully explained by the traditional topos that Moses saw God through a glass which was not darkened, while all the other prophets only saw God through a glass darkly.[24] It thus strengthens the point that only the new Jews attain to the status of Moses himself.

This proposition is thus buttressed by the allusion to Exodus 34:34 in which we are told that Moses removed his veil when he went in before the Lord (Hooker 1981, 301). There is, however, a problem with this interpretation, a problem built into Exodus 34 itself: And the Children of

Israel saw the face of Moses, that the face of Moses was shining with light, and Moses replaced the mask (veil) on his face until he went to speak with Him. As Hooker acutely notes, in Exodus 34:34 it seems that Moses only replaces his veil *after* communicating the words of God to the people. This raises two questions: (1) if the people could not stand to see the face of Moses because of its glory, how come they were able to stand it later on, and every time he came out from the tent? and (2) What was the purpose of his placing the veil over his face after delivering the Divine discourse? One possible strategy for dealing with this (presumably the one that Hays would adopt) is to regard the clause "And the Children . . . with light" as a pluperfect, referring back to the first instance in which Moses came down and did not know that his face was shining and created the veil in order to protect the people. We would read verse 34 to mean that he put on the veil before speaking to the people.

Another line of interpretation, however, reads verse 34 as meaning indeed that Moses replaced the veil after speaking with the people, thus raising the questions above. Now, if we assume that *this* is how Paul interpreted the verse, then we can interpret Paul's midrash quite differently—and this is what Morna Hooker has done. If Moses replaced the veil only *after* delivering God's word, then the reason might very well have been that the glory was fading from his face, and he did not want the Jews to see this fading. Such a reading is known from Jewish texts of the early Middle Ages. The fourteenth-century Spanish commentator Abraham Ibn Ezra says:

> There are those who say that the light would be replenished when he went into the Tent of Meeting and spoke with God. And he would go out and the light would remain all of the time he was speaking the words of God with the Israelites. And when he would finish, he would put on the mask, for he knew that the light would disappear, and his face would return to its normal state, and it would be a stigma to Moses if the people would see his face without the light.

Paul's interpretation would be virtually identical to that of this anonymous ("those who say"; are they Jewish, or maybe Christian?) reader—whose view, I might add, was vigorously rejected by Ibn Ezra, citing a commentator from the tenth century. The reason for the energetic repudiation of this interpretation could quite plausibly be reconstructed as the fact that Christians were citing such a reading as typological evidence for the fading glory of Moses' text![25] There is no need, however, to go along with Hooker's assumption that Paul is inconsistent and simply changes horses in midstream from a story in which the glory was too much for the Jews to one in which the veil serves to hide precisely the fading of the glory, since any interpreter who takes 34:34 to mean what it seems to mean on the surface will have to confront the question of Moses' replacement of the veil only after speaking to the Jews.

As Hooker herself notes, Paul does not explicitly mention the veil in the first part. He only remarks that the Israelites could not bear to gaze at Moses' face. The text of the Torah does not make explicit—and verse 34 seems to contradict—the notion that the purpose of the veil was to prevent the Jews from seeing the glory which was too much for them! Indeed, they could not bear to gaze, but the reason for the veil was something else entirely, namely Moses' desire that they not perceive that his glory was transient. As we have seen, at least one apparently Jewish interpreter (cited by Ibn Ezra) reached the same conclusion. Paul, of course, made use of it by allegorizing it: The glory that faded from Moses' face signifies the glory that will fade from his literal, physical text, while the glory of the Lord, from which his reflected glory was replenished, is everlasting. Paul's own methods of interpretation here thus enact a reading of the Torah which enables the view beyond the letter into the glory of the Spirit, while the Jews who insist only on the historicality of Moses' veil and not its figurative, hermeneutical sense remain unable to perceive the true meaning of Moses. Another way of saying this is that the assertion of the concreteness of Moses' mask, its literality, renders it opaque and thus a veil which prevents seeing of the truth, while believing in its translucence renders it transparent and the true message lucid. Those people (Jews and gentiles) who manage to set aside the veil that prevents them from perceiving that the glory of the letter is transient and only a pointer to the glory of the Spirit, which is forever, perceive that greater glory indeed, while the Jews who persist in looking only at the letter and not through it remain trapped behind the veil which that letter is.

On this interpretation, as on Hays's, the issue is hermeneutics: "Once again, we see how Paul makes a statement about Judaism which certainly would not have been accepted by his Jewish contemporaries—namely, that the true meaning of the old covenant is hidden from them" (Hooker 1981, 300). When someone turns to the Lord, as Moses himself turned to the Lord, then the veil is removed and they can see the glory directly, just as Moses did.[26] The Lord is, however, the τέλος of the Law, that is, Christ:

> But just as it seems as if the veil is being lifted from our minds, too, and we think that we begin to grasp Paul's meaning, he confounds us all by declaring: "Now the Lord is the Spirit." Paul is not, of course, concerned here with the niceties of trinitarian theology. Rather, he is returning to the contrast with which he began—the contrast between letter and Spirit. The Lord is the Spirit who writes directly on men's hearts. In turning to the Lord, Israel not only experiences the removal of the veil, but moves from a relationship with God which is based on letter to one which is based on Spirit.   (Hooker 1981, 301)

The very ministry chiseled in stone signifies and is replaced in history by the ministry of the Spirit, which has been revealed in the New Covenant, which is not, of course, for Paul a text, a γράμμα, but it is an interpretation of a text (Hooker 1981, 299, 304). When Paul refers to the Old Covenant, he means both the historical covenant with the Jews and also their text. He thus implies *avant le lettre*, as it were, predicts or enacts the coming into being of the New Testament, and the relation of these two is figured as that of "letter which kills" to the "Spirit which gives life." Thus, the move of the modern readers of Paul, such as Hays, who deny the allegorical and supersessionist movement of Paul's text is ultimately not convincing. The supersessionism cannot be denied, because there already and still was an enfleshed community living out the "Old" Covenant. It certainly had not remained an affair of mere words on stone. "As the result of a gigantic take-over bid, we find all the functions of the Law attributed to Christ" (Hooker 1981, 303). Since the glory of the spirit hidden within the text is what Moses' veil conceals, and that hidden glory is the life of the Christian community, the Pauline structure is profoundly allegorical after all. He cannot mean, of course, that the text of the Torah has been abolished, so, therefore, he must mean that the literal meaning is what will be abolished. "It is clear that Paul—however inconsistent he may sometimes be—could hardly have referred to scripture itself as 'abolished,' when scripture provides him with his primary witness to Christ" (Hooker 1981, 303). The "letter" is not only the written word but certainly, as Paul says almost explicitly, the literal reading of "Moses" by the Jews. Augustine read Paul well: "In the Old Testament there is a concealment of the New, in the New Testament there is a revelation of the Old." A hermeneutic theory such as Paul's, by which the literal Israel, literal history, literal circumcision, and literal genealogy are superseded by their allegorical, spiritual signifieds is *not* necessarily anti-Semitic or even anti-Judaic. From the perspective of the first century, the contest between a Pauline allegorical Israel and a rabbinic hermeneutics of the concrete Israel is simply a legitimate cultural, hermeneutical, and political contestation. The denotation of "Israel" was to a certain extent up for grabs.[27]

To be sure, Paul does not mean by *spirit* the spiritual meaning in the sense of a detailed allegorical consultation of the written text (as perhaps an Origen would mean), but he does mean literal Israel as the signifier of the new Israel "according to the spirit," and literal circumcision as signifier of the inner disposition to which he referred in 2:29, and the letter of the Law as signifier of the Law of faith working through love, the Law of Christ, which is here called service in the new being of the spirit. The psychological and ethical dimensions are thus a consequence of the hermeneutic. In pursuing a fairly detailed reading of passages in Galatians, we will be able to trace these themes in their most concentrated form in Paul's writings.

5

Circumcision and Revelation; or, The Politics of the Spirit

UNIVERSAL MAN CONFRONTS DIFFERENCE: THE CRISIS IN GALATIA

The argument that I have begun to develop is that it is productive to read Paul as a Jewish cultural critic. My suggestion is that there is a great deal in his letters that suggests that the primary motivation, not only for his mission but indeed for his "conversion," was a passionate desire that humanity be One under the sign of the One God—a universalism, I have claimed, born of the union of Hebraic monotheism and Greek desire for unity and univocity. In this chapter I would like to continue making the case for this as a plausible reading of Paul (especially in Galatians) and also to begin to explore some of the cultural issues that the Pauline move was to raise. We see Paul here actually confronting and attempting to deal with real social issues to which his theory gave rise. As E. P. Sanders has pointed out, "When it came to cases, Paul's easy tolerance, which he effortlessly maintained in theory—it is a matter of individual conscience what one eats and whether one observes 'days'—could not work. It was not only a matter of individual conscience, it turned out, but of Christian unity, and he judged one form of behavior to be wrong. The wrong form was living according to the law" (1983, 178).

The major argument of this book, then, is that what drove Paul was a passionate desire for human unification, for the erasure of differences and hierarchies between human beings, and that he saw the Christian event, as he had experienced it, as the vehicle for this transformation of humanity. Paul operated with what I call an allegorical hermeneutic (of language, of the Jews, of history, of Christ) which was fully homologous with an allegorical anthropology and axiology. The text which establishes this understanding of Paul's gospel most clearly is his Letter to the Galatians, which is entirely devoted to the theme of the new creation of

God's one people, the new Israel through faith and through the crucifixion and resurrection of Christ. In my reading of selected passages from that letter in this and the next chapter, I wish to establish the plausibility of two claims: (1) that the social gospel was central to Paul's ministry, i.e., that the eradication of human difference and hierarchy was its central theme, and (2) that the dyad of flesh and spirit was the vehicle by which this transformation was to take place. In the opening paragraph of the letter, the prescript, the major themes of Paul's thought are introduced and particularly the nexus between Christology and the mission to the gentiles.

"An apostle not from men"

Paul, an apostle not from men nor through a man, but through Jesus
Christ and God the Father who raised him from the dead.   (1 : 1)

Dyadic opposition is introduced in this, the very first sentence of Galatians.[1] Paul is not a human apostle but an apostle of the risen Christ. As commentators have pointed out, the form of the expression is certainly strange and very pointed rhetorically. Accordingly some exegetes have argued that Paul must be directly addressing his opponents' charge here, that is, that they had indeed charged him with being an apostle from men, the Church in Jerusalem, and that, therefore, he should submit to the authority of his principals (Bruce 1990, 72–73; Longenecker 1990, 4). Betz has already dismissed this interpretation, as had Burton long before, as there is no evidence anywhere else that this was the nature of the charge, and to assume that every bit of pointed rhetoric found in Paul is in direct response to the opponents seems methodologically unnecessary and therefore unsupportable (Betz 1979, 39, 65). Further, this reading makes sense of only one of the two parallel phrases ("from men"), and not the other. This interpretation does, however, have the advantage of taking account of the energy of this expression, which the suggestions of Betz and Burton do not. In my reading, Paul here, in the prescript, in his very identification of himself, provides a proleptic summary of his entire theme and argument. Paul is not an apostle from men, that is, not from those who are authorities "in the flesh," as it were, those who have known or are related physically to Jesus, "a man," but he is the apostle through the resurrected Christ "in the spirit," and from God who raised him. This interpretation, which is plausible in itself, not least because it makes sense of both halves of the chiasm, does in fact provide an answer to the otherwise attested charge against Paul, to wit, that his apostleship was inferior because he had never had contact with the historical Jesus (Burton 1988, 5; Betz 1979, 39). Paul's argument is to be taken as a direct counter to such charges as the following from the *Pseudo-Clementine Homilies*:

> You see now how expressions of wrath have to be made through visions and dreams, but discourse with friends takes place from mouth to mouth, openly and not through riddles, visions, and dreams as with an enemy. And if our Jesus appeared to you also and became known in a vision and met you as angry with an enemy, yet he has spoken only through visions and dreams or through external revelations, but can any one be made competent to teach through a vision? And if your opinion is, "That is possible," why then did our teacher spend a whole year with us who were awake? How can we believe you even if he has appeared to you, and how can he have appeared to you if you desire the opposite of what you have learned? But if you were visited by him for the space of an hour and were instructed by him and thereby have become an apostle, then proclaim his words.   (Betz 1979, 333)[2]

Even if, as seems plausible, this text is a later Jewish Christian text written in response to Paul and not the occasion of *his* response, I think it still indicates well what the nature of the conflict between Paul and his Jerusalem opponents would have been like. There is, after all, other evidence, from within Paul, for such a view. The allegory of the lower and the upper Jerusalem (Galatians 4:21–31) points in this direction. Moreover, in 2 Corinthians 5:16 Paul insists that his community no longer knows (that is, recognizes!) Christ according to the flesh but only recognizes Christ according to the spirit. To my mind, that polemic is similar to what we have in Galatians against those who claim that their authority derives from closeness, even family ties, with Jesus, the Jew born of a woman. Finally, it has been suggested that Romans 1:3–4 ("Concerning His son who was born of the seed of David according to the flesh, and declared to be the son of God in power, according to the spirit of Holiness, by the resurrection from the dead") represents a Pauline gloss on a liturgical formula of the early Church for describing Jesus as the son of David and thus as ethnically Jewish.[3] Paul reverses the value of this formula by insisting that this refers only to Jesus' birth according to the flesh, while according to the Holy Spirit, Jesus is the son of God thus rendering his ethnic and family ties, if not worthless—Romans 9:5—, of decidedly less importance![4] Paul's genius is to be found in this: That which his Jewish Christian opponents cited as the defect in his authority becomes for him precisely its point of greatest strength. I am not imputing to Paul a mere rhetorical or political ploy but an argument which fits perfectly with the entire structure of his thought. Maintaining the structure of binary oppositions that I have cited above in Chapter 1, the apostleship of Peter and James is of an inferior nature, because it is only from Jesus in the flesh (a man); it is the human teaching of a human teacher, while Paul's revelatory vision is not of the human Jesus but of Christ according to the spirit.

"Or am I seeking to please men?"

> Or am I seeking to please men? If I were still pleasing men, I would
> not be Christ's slave. For I would have you know, brothers, that
> the gospel preached by me is not human in nature. For I did not re-
> ceive it from man, nor was I taught, but through a revelation of
> Jesus Christ.   (1:10b–12)

In direct counter to the charge of the Jewish Christians that I have just cited, Paul argues that while their gospel is only a human teaching, and therefore not truly a gospel but only a teaching like any other, his gospel came directly through a revelation of Jesus, that is, of course, Jesus in the spirit (Longenecker 1990, 5). The defect in his apostleship has been turned into its very source of strength.

"I did not confer with flesh and blood"

> For you have heard of my former way of life in Judaism . . . and that I
> advanced in Judaism beyond many among my people who were of the
> same age, since I was far more zealous for the traditions of my forefa-
> thers. But when it pleased him who had set me aside from my mother's
> womb and called me through his grace to reveal his son in me, in or-
> der that I might preach him among the gentiles, immediately I did not
> confer with flesh and blood, nor did I go up to Jerusalem, to those who
> were apostles before me.   (1:13–17)

Betz understands these claims of Paul's to be in a philosophical tradition whereby the autodidact and the pneumatic is superior to the one who has received teaching through sane and rational means. I would like to argue that the burden of Paul's argument is different. Once more, on my view, he is contrasting the source of knowledge of his Jerusalem opponents, Peter and James, with his own, and his opponents are found wanting. Why precisely does Paul mention here his zeal and his advancement in learning of the traditions of his forefathers? I think it is because the precise claim that Peter and James had made against him is, in effect, that they have a *paradosis* of Jesus which Paul does not. Paul then says: If it is paradosis that is required, then I have had a greater paradosis than yours. If all that the coming of Christ means is some correctives to the teaching of traditional Judaism, of the traditions of the Fathers, then what did it accomplish? If there has not been a fundamental change in the structure of salvation, then the sacrifice of Jesus on the cross would have been in vain, as Paul will say openly later on. The source of my knowledge, he says, is not of the same type as the source of knowledge that I had when I was advancing in the traditions of genealogical fathers, but rather the direct revelation in the spirit of Christ is *in me.*[5] Paul's next sentence—"immediately I did not confer with flesh and blood"—is now fully intelligible, whereas until now it has been held to be puzzling. As Betz puts the problem: "Strangely, he does it first of all negatively, saying what he did *not* do: 'immediately I did not confer . . .'. It is obvious that Paul wants to underscore his immediate reaction to the call. Why does he not simply state his obedience, as he does in Acts 26:19–20? The negative statement is indeed mysterious" (Betz 1979, 72). This is one of the points where I believe that my interpretation solves exegetical problems which previous theses have not: Paul's "negative" statement is exactly the essence of his argument. Paul is emphasizing the superiority of his gospel precisely because it has no human, no fleshly, origin but only the content of the revelation of Christ in him. Therefore, he did not go up to Jerusalem or consult with *flesh and blood* (a calque on the normal Hebrew expression בשׂר ודם for human beings, as opposed to God),[6] having been vouchsafed a source of knowledge so far superior to the knowledge that the flesh and blood possessed. Paul's usage of this precise term here is not fortuitous, since for him, as we have seen, "Jesus according to the flesh" and "Israel according to the flesh" are both technical terms. He is making the case for his dualist hierarchy, here at the level of epistemology. Paul's revelatory experience was, indeed, of supreme importance to him, as we shall also see below in discussing Galatians 3. To deny the supreme importance to him of this experience would be to call Paul a liar, something which is entirely against my intent. The issue is not whether Paul was a mystic but rather what function his mysticism played in the formation of his doctrine and practice.[7]

Paul sets up here the argument that will serve him well throughout the letter: If business is to continue as usual, with the traditions of the Fathers in place and observance of the commandments still required, and, more-over, with the Church claiming another sort of flesh-and-blood paradosis as well, then what possible purpose did the crucifixion serve? Notice that this obviates the old exegetical question of the relationship between Paul's vision of the risen Christ and the content of his gospel (cf. Betz 1979, 64–65).[8] The vision and gospel are one, because the vision of the risen Christ is what enabled Paul to understand the allegorical structure of the entire cosmos as the solution to the problem of the Other and thus to set out on the road to Arabia, "in order that I might preach him among the gentiles."

CONFERENCE IN JERUSALEM: CONFRONTATION IN ANTIOCH (2:1–2:14)

The famous and notoriously difficult reports of Paul's two face-to-face con-frontations with the leaders of "Jewish Christianity" must be understood in the light of an overall construction of Pauline thinking. The crux of the matter, to my mind, is the question of when (or indeed whether) Paul argued that circumcision and observance of such commandments as the laws of kashruth were abrogated not only for ethnic gentiles but for ethnic Jews as well. I suggest that for the logic of Paul's theology, which was complete in its entirety from the first moment of his revelation, there was not the slightest importance to the observance of such rites for Jews or gentiles.[9] This does not mean, however, that such observances and their historical meanings are coded by Paul as "bad." They are simply lower on the hierarchy of values and thus sacrificeable to a higher cause. My inter-pretation is somewhat different in nuance from that of Davies, who writes: "Nevertheless, although the universalism that we have noticed was im-plicit in the depth of Paul's experience of God in Christ from the first, its explicit formulation in thought was a slow process, and its strict logical expression in life was never achieved" (1965, 58). Davies further regards the "inconsistencies" of Paul as engendered by unresolved personal con-flicts: "In fact, both in life and thought, the Book of Acts and the Epistles of Paul reveal a conflict between the claims of the old Israel after the flesh

and the new Israel after the spirit, between his 'nationalism' and his Christianity. It is, indeed, from this tension that there arose most of the inconsistencies that have puzzled interpreters of Paul; and it is only in the light
of the Judaism of the first century A.D. that this is to be understood" (59).
I would argue that Paul's "universalism" was complete from the first moment, and that Galatians, one of the earliest of his letters, demonstrates
this. On the other hand, his dual valorization of both spirit and body did
not allow him to discount entirely the claims of the literal, physical Israel
according to the body. I will make a similar case in Chapter 8 vis-à-vis
gender also. In my view, the tension is not a residue of unresolved inner
conflict in Paul so much as a necessary tension of his ontology, hermeneutics, and anthropology—even his christology—which are, for me, all
strongly parallel.

Owing, therefore, to Paul's conviction that literal observance was
merely irrelevant, being only in the flesh (i.e., it was not sinful striving
for works-righteousness à la the Lutheran tradition), he was willing to
allow Jews to continue observing such commandments if they chose to,
*until such observance conflicted with the fundamental meaning and message
of the gospel as Paul understood it,* namely, the constitution of all of the
Peoples of the world as the new Israel (Segal 1990, 215–16; Sanders 1983,
178; compare Davies 1984, 139). Paul says as much when he writes in 1 Corinthians 7:19 that neither circumcision nor uncircumcision is anything.
The practices themselves are adiaphora; it is their interference with the
one-ness of the new Israel that disturbs the apostle.[10] The two most obvious such conflicts possible would be any attempt to suggest to the gentiles
that in order to be full members of the People of God they must observe
the commandments of the Law, such as circumcision and the rules of kashruth, or any observance on the part of Jewish Christians which would lead
to a social split and hierarchical structure for the relations between ethnic
Jews and gentiles within the Church, thus defeating Paul's whole purpose.[11] In the light of this consideration I think we can read the accounts
of Jerusalem and Antioch confrontations with Peter and his associates.

At stake at the Jerusalem conference was the first of the two possible
threats to the integrity of Paul's gospel, namely, the claim of the Jewish
Christians that gentiles must be circumcised (which alone counts as conversion to Judaism) in order to join the People of God. Yielding or losing
this point would, indeed, have resulted in his having run in vain, just as
losing the analogous point now with the Galatians would also result in his

and their having run in vain (cf. 3:4), because the whole content of Paul's gospel, as I have understood it, is that the physical observances *that constitute the physical Israel as the People of God* have been transmuted and fulfilled in the allegorical signification in the spirit, thereby constituting the faithful gentiles as Israel in the spirit. This is why it is absolutely vital for Paul that he prove that he has not given in on the question of circumcision as a conversion ritual and requirement, and the ocular proof of Titus's uncircumcision makes that point as no other could: "Yet not even Titus who was with me was compelled to be circumcised" (Galatians 2:3).

This also provides us with an explanation of the difficult expression at 2:6, that "what they were makes no difference to me, God does not show partiality." I emphatically endorse, with Betz,

> the position of a long line of scholars who believe that Paul means
> to refer to the life of the apostles before Pentecost: they may have
> had fellowship with the historical and, in particular, with the resur-
> rected Jesus-Messiah; they themselves or others may base their repu-
> tation upon that fellowship; or James may even be a relative of the
> ["Christ according to the flesh"] (cf. 2 Cor 5:16), [yet] God did
> not pay attention to these historical qualifications when he called
> Paul.   (Betz 1979, 93)

The operative word here is "historical," because history—to be sure, the concept is somewhat anachronistic—for Paul has the same valence as "according to the flesh." Israel according to the flesh appealed to history to validate its claim that it alone was the People of God, so once more, as above, were Paul to accept the claim of superiority on the part of Peter and James owing to knowledge of the historical Jesus, and even worse to genealogical connection with him, he would have completely undermined and destroyed the point of his whole mission and spiritual life. Again we see Paul's cultural/religious politics and his political struggles converging brilliantly at a single point, the point of distinction between that which is merely κατὰ σάρκα and that which is κατὰ πνεῦμα.

In the incident at Antioch we see the conflict over the other possible threat to Paul's gospel of inclusion of the gentiles qua gentiles in the People of God, that is, the disruptiveness of Jews and gentiles having different and inherently divisive food practices, when they are living together in the same community as they are at Antioch. According to the narrative that Paul presents, Peter himself had realized this originally, and he also had eaten together with the gentiles, which certainly means he had eaten the non-kosher food of the gentiles. Otherwise, there would have been no violation at all of Jewish Law.[12] As Betz puts it, "he [Peter] had the same theological convictions as Paul, but he did not dare to express them" (Betz 1979, 108).[13] This provides strong evidence in my view that Paul himself had not ever agreed (at least not in his heart) that there were really two gospels, one to the circumcision (and preaching circumcision) and one to the uncircumcision (and preaching uncircumcision). His statement about the Jerusalem conference to the effect that there were two gospels simply reflects the compromise agreement that he made and not his true theological understanding. Else, how could he possibly object to Peter, the apostle to the circumcision, continuing or returning to the performance of Jewish rites? Since Paul's concern was to include the gentiles and not to disabuse the Jews of their outmoded notions, he was able to conclude the agreement on those terms, as long as it did not threaten his mission (Engberg-Pedersen 1992, 688–89). Peter, by acceding to the demands of the "people from James" that he return to Jewish food practices, provided that threat (cf. the excellent formulation of Betz [1979, 112]), and Paul met it vigorously.

"It is not by works of the Law that all flesh will be justified"

We who are Jews by birth and not sinners from Gentiles know that a human being is not justified by works of the Law except through faith in Christ Jesus. So we have also come to believe in Christ Jesus [καὶ ἡμεῖς εἰς Χριστὸν Ἰησοῦν ἐπιστεύσαμεν], in order that we might be justified by faith in Christ [ἐκ πίστεως Χριστοῦ] and not by works of the Law, since it is not by works of the Law that all flesh will be justified. If, however, we who are seeking to be justified in Christ are also found to be sinners, is Christ then a servant of sin? This can never be. For if I establish again what I have dissolved, I set myself up as a transgressor.   (2:15–18)

This passage is only intelligible, in my view, if it is addressed to Peter.[14] It is irrelevant to me whether it was actually said to Peter at Antioch or whether it is a hypothetical speech reconstructed by Paul for the benefit of the Galatians, but its implied addressee is certainly Peter. He is using the language of Jewish Christians to argue against them, for Paul himself, of course, does not regard the gentiles as essentially sinners as opposed to Jews. He thus states: You and I were born Jews and under the Law. That is, according to Jewish theology as we have known it until now, we already possessed the means to salvation. We had no need of justification by faith, according to that very theology. But we, you *and* I, came to the realization that that theology was mistaken, and that by works of the Law, no one would be justified.[15] Therefore, we turned to faith in Christ Jesus (Hays 1985, 85).[16] Now, if you by your actions imply that we have been sinners in abandoning the Law, that very Law which you and I have confessed is inadequate to redeem, then is our faith in Christ the testimony of sin? Clearly not so! However, by reestablishing that which you have dissolved—namely, by returning to the observance of the Jewish food rituals and taboos—you have confessed yourself to be a transgressor, have "set yourself up" as a transgressor by doing so.[17] As for me, it is the very opposite.

It seems to me that a major interpretative issue has been often missed in the commentaries on Galatians, to wit, answering the question of *why* Paul is reciting here the entire narrative of the conference in Jerusalem and the confrontation at Antioch. To my mind, this lengthy narration is only intelligible if it is intended as a sort of parable or analogy of the situation in which the Galatians now find themselves.[18] The application of the present verse to the situation of the Galatians is crystal clear. If you now take on yourself the obligations of the Law, you are then declaring that until now you have been sinners, and thus undermining completely the doctrine of justification by faith, and it will have all been in vain. The crucial issue for Paul is not the theological question of what pleases God, but rather is the relations of the Jews and the Nations (Hays 1985, 84). Paul is convinced that the *Jewish-Christian* doctrine of justification by faith, which he assumes as a given both by him and his "opponents," provides the answer to this question, for in faith, all people are one, while in practices they are divided into different tribes. Accordingly Paul argues with Peter: Since you have come to the realization that these works are insufficient for justification and that what is necessary is faith, why, then, do you continue to insist (or allow yourself to be bullied into insisting) that works are necessary? You thus defeat the whole purpose of Christ's coming, which was to free us from the practices of Israel in the flesh by teaching us of their allegorical meaning for Israel in the spirit, through his crucifixion which revealed his own dual nature and thus figured our transformation.

It is really only at the very end of his letter that Paul reveals the application of the Antioch parable to the Galatians situation: "It is those people who wish to make a nice appearance in the flesh that compel you to be circumcised—only so that they may not be persecuted because of the cross of Christ. For not even the circumcisers[19] themselves keep the Law, but they want you to be circumcised, in order that they may boast in your flesh" (6:12–13).

This is absolutely the key passage to the understanding of Paul's opponents in Galatia. It has to be read in the context of Paul's narration of the events at Antioch, which as I emphasized above (not originally, of course) is recited by Paul as an analogy, almost a typology, of the events in Galatia. Paul's opponents are not actually Jewish Christians who insist on circumcision for salvation but essentially are in consonance with Paul's theology; they hold that circumcision is *not* necessary. When pressed, however, by the contemporary antitype of the "men from James," they have their gentile proselytes circumcised in order to escape persecution, that very persecution that Paul himself alludes to when he writes, "But if I, my brothers, still preach circumcision, why am I still persecuted?" (5:11) These men, themselves, do not keep the Law, nor do they intend that their converts will keep the Law—they are essentially in agreement with Paul—but they cave in to pressure from the conservative wing of the Jerusalem church.[20] The analogy with Peter's behavior in Antioch is perfect, as well as with Paul's charge against Peter: How can you ask these people to be circumcised when you do not yourself keep the Law? The charge is not of hypocrisy, but of not standing firm in that which is absolutely essential to the Christian message in Paul's view (Cosgrove 1988, 132–39). As I have already observed, the term "boast" in Paul is often better translated "have confidence in" or "rely on" than "boast about." Paul is adamant in his integrity. If the Galatians accept circumcision, the whole purpose of the Christ event is destroyed. It will all have been in vain. When Paul tells them, "Look, I, Paul, tell you that if you become circumcised, Christ will be of no benefit to you. I testify again to every man who has become circumcised, that he is obliged to do the whole law" (5:2–3), his point is that by becoming circumcised they reject the message of the Law of Faith or the Law of Christ, which he goes on to detail in the next and final chapter. Willy-nilly, they will be acceding to the Jewish Christian doctrine of James and his followers that only through entrance into the Law (that is, conversion to Judaism) can anyone be saved.[21] By showing their lack of faith in the power of the cross to save, they give up their right to salvation by the cross, as opposed to Paul him-self who writes, "But far be it from me to boast [again, to have confidence in] anything but the cross of our Lord Jesus Christ, through which [the cross] the world has been crucified to me and I to the world" (6:14). Paul ends his letter on a note of absolute insistence: "For neither circumcision nor uncircumcision is anything, but a new creation" (6:15). Only by en-tering into the new creation of Christ's spiritual body, that is, into the New Israel that came into existence with the crucifixion of his fleshly body, is anyone saved. When that fleshly, Jewish body (born of a Jew, under the Law) was crucified, then the new spiritual universal body was created, thus erasing the difference between the circumcised and the uncircumcised.

THE MEANING OF JUSTIFICATION

The term *justification* itself must be explicated. I have suggested that Paul shares this terminology and even the specific term *justification by faith* with his Jewish-Christian opponents, here personified by Peter. It is important to realize, moreover, that the term *justification* itself is not a novum of Christianity but simply a basic Jewish notion. It refers to the situation of the believer at her last judgment (whether eschatological or merely after death is irrelevant here), when the question is: Will I be acquitted by the divine court? Justification means acquittal. The Greek is a calque (loan translation) on the Hebrew צד״ק, which means both to be just or righteous and to be *declared* or *recognized* as just or righteous.[22] In addition, there is already biblical speculation on *how* one becomes justified, whether through God's justice or through his mercy. The novelty of Christianity is that faith in Christ is what counts (either alone or in combination with works) at the divine Assizes. Paul's thought is therefore primarily soteriological, and his determination is that all shall be saved by the same means. Such ethnic practices as circumcision and refraining from eating shrimp could not possibly be the mechanism by which Scythians and Celts (in Galatia) would be acquitted at the Last Judgment, because these practices are spe-cifically Jewish, whereas, as Sanders precisely formulates it, "Christ is the end of the law, so that there might be righteousness for *all* who have faith." And therefore, according to Paul:

> God's righteousness is, through Christ, available on the basis of faith
> to all on equal footing. If God's righteousness is the righteousness

which is by faith in Christ and which is available to Gentile as well as Jew, then the Jewish righteousness which was zealously sought is the righteousness available to the Jew *alone* on the basis of observing the law. *"Their own righteousness," in other words, means "that righteousness which the Jews alone are privileged to obtain" rather than "self-righteousness which consists in individuals presenting their merits as a claim on God."* [23]

It is because it is God's righteousness that it could not possibly be for Jews alone, as Paul explicitly says in Romans 3:29: "Is God the God of the Jews alone?" To support this construction of the theology, detailed exegesis of Paul's hermeneutic is necessary. [24]

PAUL'S MIDRASH

Now, although I am claiming in this book that in one major way Paul's hermeneutic stands in opposition to midrash, in another way he is very much within a midrashic tradition. The fundamental hermeneutical stance which he takes to the text is allegorical; that is, the language and even its apparent referents are understood as pointing to a reality beyond themselves. This is then an entirely different orientation to language from midrash in which the concrete reality both of the language and the history which it encodes is absolutely primary. Paul, however, seems very able indeed to make use of midrashic *techniques* of manipulation of biblical language. In a sense, this is exactly what we would expect of Paul if we take his descriptions of himself seriously. A Hellenistic Jew, thoroughly imbued with the ideology of middle-platonism but just as thoroughly trained in contemporary Palestinian biblical hermeneutics, would perhaps predictably produce biblical interpretation that is Hellenistic in ethos but often Pharisaic in method. [25] The following section of Galatians provides some excellent examples of Paul's use of midrashic method.

The first example of how important this observation is for understanding Paul is Galatians 2:16. It has already been recognized that the argument of this verse is dependent on Psalms 143:2, but I think that the full measure of the midrash has not yet been appreciated (Betz 1979, 118). Even James Dunn, who has made this verse the cornerstone of his argument, and with whose approach I largely agree, has not fully plumbed the depths of this verse (Dunn 1990, 183–214). [26] Paul assumes as a *given* of his argument that works do not justify. This is not, then, what he is trying to prove here. What the commentators seem to have missed is that Paul is not reading Psalms 143:2 alone but together with its preceding verse. The two verses are:

> Lord, hear my prayer, listen to my supplication in your faith. Answer me in your justice.
> Do not reproach your servant with statute, for no living being will be justified [declared just] before you.

I think that Paul's only extravagant exegetical move here is to read "your faith" as "faith in You."[27] All the rest of his doctrine then follows. No living being will be justified (= acquitted) before you by "statute"; therefore, we are dependent on our supplication in faith in order for us to be answered by Your justice (= justification, acquittal).[28]

This interpretation accomplishes several purposes. First of all, I think that it definitively establishes Dunn's point that justification here is simply the *Jewish* doctrine of vindication by God and not transfer terminology.[29] Second, it strongly argues for Dunn's other main point, that what is bothering Paul is the ethnic exclusivity of Torah-righteousness. The word מִשְׁפָּט, which I have translated "statute," in other contexts in Psalms itself, refers precisely to the Jewish Law of the Torah which explicitly marks off the Jews from others. "He has spoken his words to Jacob, his laws and *statutes* to Israel. He has not done so for any other nation, and *statutes*, they do not know" (Psalms 147:16–17). Accordingly Paul's interpretation of these verses is just perfect for his argument. David is asking for God to acquit him on the basis of his supplication in faith, because if no human being can be righteous, then failure to keep the statutes (which are specifically and explicitly special to Israel) cannot be the determining factor of salvation.[30] All this becomes a powerful argument in favor of the replacement of "works of the Torah," Jewish ritual observances by faith, and Paul's argument against Peter is complete.[31] Note that David's supplication to God to "answer me in Your justice" is paradoxically that he come to judge not on the basis of "statute" but on the basis of faith!

While with regard to the specifics of the midrash, I have departed from Dunn's reading, it should be emphasized that in respect to the content, I am in full agreement with him, and I believe that this reading only strengthens his point that "works of the law, epitomized in this letter by circumcision, are precisely acts of the flesh. To insist on circumcision is to give a primacy to the physical level of relationship which Paul can no longer accept" (Dunn 1990, 199). The only thing that puzzles me is why

Dunn, having come this far, writes "by that course, Paul will not intend a dualism between spirit and matter, however dualistic his antithesis between spirit and flesh may seem later on in Galatians 5. . . . *But* the word 'flesh' also embraces the thought of a merely human relationship, of a heritage determined by physical descent, as in the allegory of Galatians 4" (199 [emphasis added]).[32] On the contrary, it is precisely the dualism between flesh and spirit which makes possible this very allegory, so this is exactly what Paul intends. This "physical descent" is an affair of matter, just as spiritual kinship is an affair, tautologically, of the spirit, so there is no "but" here. And this is just what makes Paul's gospel new vis-à-vis traditional Jewish ideologies of sin and redemption (including this very Psalm), which, as has been often shown, *also presuppose the need for God's mercy, since no one can be completely righteous.*[33] What is new in Paul is not the notion that one cannot be justified by acquiring merits but the notion that faith is the spiritual signified of which convenantal nomism is the material signifier, and that in Christ the signified has completely replaced the signifier. As Dunn has put it, "The new age calls for a practice of the law *(including circumcision) that need not include the outward rite*" (Dunn 1988, 121). Physical relationship = physical practices (circumcision the very symbol of genealogy) = literal meaning, but spiritual relationship (Israel in the spirit) = faith = allegory. It is in this sense that Paul can appear to be abrogating the Law at the same time he claims to be fulfilling it; he fulfills the alleged allegorical sense, while abrogating the literal (doing). The allegorical is universal while the letter is particular. The allegorical gives life, but the letter kills.

CIRCUMCISION AND THE SPIRIT:
THE MEANING OF PAULINE CONVERSION

A very important line of modern Pauline scholarship regards Paul's conversion experience as primary and derives all of Paul's reflections from that fundamental moment. In its religious form, this view is simply that Christ appeared to Paul, and Paul drew the consequences of this revelation. In its secular form, this way of thinking about Paul has been considered most elaborately by Alan Segal in his *Paul the Convert* (1990). Segal applies insights from the social psychology of conversion and argues by analogy to modern conversion experiences that only after conversion to the new religion does the convert identify what "was wrong" with her previous

religion. It seems to me, however, that whether or not converts can account for why they converted or whether or not it is possible to predict
who will convert to another religion, it is nevertheless the case that some
social or psychological factors must have prepared the potential conversion or mystical experience. In Paul's case, when it is possible to identify
a theme of critique of the previous religious system which is plausible in
itself—in other words, which corresponds to what we know of that system
and corresponds, moreover, to other contemporaneous critiques—it seems
to me a violation of Occam's razor to assume that this critique had not
motivated the conversion, and not vice versa. While the experience of
being in the Spirit as a mystical event is certainly essential in Pauline
religion, as my discussion of Galatians 3 below will show, I do not think
that Paul's own mystical experience was unprepared for by his past.

The principal area of difference is that I place much less weight on
Paul's mysticism than Segal does. Although I am impressed by Segal's
argument that Paul provides precious evidence for mysticism in first-
century Judaism, I am not persuaded that this is the primary explanatory
category for Paul's texts and activities (1990, 34–72). This is not to say
that I deny either the reality of Paul's mystical experience or its significance within his religious life; all I would deny is its primacy. For Segal
the experience of ecstasy was cardinal, and the christological interpretation a later phenomenon of Paul's experience in a Christian community.
This leaves somewhat unexplained Paul's turn to that very Christian
community, which Segal argues can be explained through the psycho-
sociological study of modern conversion experience: "A convert is usually
someone who identifies, at least retrospectively, a lack in the world, finding a remedy in the new reality promulgated by the new group" (1990,
75). My problem is, of course, with "at least retrospectively." If there were
no perception of lack in the world, then why would the convert be a
"religious quester" to start with? I think we *must* begin, then, with the
lack, that which I have called the critique. Since I do not imagine that
Paul was "psychologically abnormal," I ask what were the cultural and
social conditions that led Paul to have such an experience? None of this,
however, denies the reality or the central importance of the mystical experience as providing precisely the solution to the plight.

In an article otherwise quite compatible with the view of Paul adopted
here, Segal writes, "Paul himself essentially is converted by his vision of
Christ from the perspective of a Pharisee, a right-wing one at that, to a

perspective that is more characteristic of left-wing Pharisees and more 'Hellenistic' Jews" (Segal 1992). I find this an improbable formulation and strongly prefer a view which would perceive in Paul a conflict to begin with, one which his evident Greek linguistic culture would have prepared, which was resolved by his conversion. In Paul, I argue, the agony preceded the ecstasy. Nevertheless, no rich and responsible reading of Paul can ignore the vital role that pneumaticism does play in his thought, the Spirit not only as a hermeneutic principle but also as a vital force and experience in Christian life. Here, I wish to show that these two aspects of the meaning of "spirit" in Paul are homologous and contribute together to the production of the same system of meanings. N. T. Wright has suggested just the right balance in my view, in defining "Pauline theology":

> If we were to specify the content of this set of beliefs, it would be natural to begin with definitely Jewish categories, since Paul by his own admission continued to understand his work from the standpoint of one who had been a zealous Pharisaic Jew; and that would mean grouping them under the twin heads of Jewish theology, viz. monotheism and election, God and Israel. Indeed, my underlying argument throughout my discussion of Paul, here and elsewhere, is that his theology consists precisely in the redefinition, by means of christology and pneumatology, of those two key Jewish doctrines. (1992a, 1, 7)

Galatians 3 is the chapter in which Paul's pneumaticism, summed up by the phrase "baptism in the Spirit," is most richly shown, although, interestingly enough, the *term* does not occur in this letter. The relevant context begins, however, in chapter 2 of that epistle.

"For through the Law I died to the Law"

> For through the Law I died to the Law, in order that I might live for
> God. I have been crucified with Christ; and it is no longer I who
> live, but Christ lives in me; and what I now live in the flesh I
> live in faith in the Son of God who loved me and gave himself
> up for me. (2:19–20)

Paul's paradoxical formulation here is a crux. What does it mean to say that through the Torah he died to the Torah? My suggestion is that this must be understood in the light of Paul's paradoxical opposition of the true Torah to that which is understood as Torah by other Jews, as we have seen in our reading of Romans 2 above.[34] Paul's whole argument there is that there is a true Law (the Law of faith; 3:27), and that this Law is different from the false Law of the observances of physical rites and the trust in physical genealogical connection. The true Law is the spiritual, allegorical, inward interpretation of the external, which is only its sign. In our verse in Galatians, Paul is arguing exactly the same proposition and giving it its christological foundation as well. Through the true meaning of the Law, which was revealed in the crucifixion and resurrection of Christ *as a hermeneutic key* and as a mysterious transformation, I have died to the old (mis)understanding of the Law as the outward observance which makes one (so I thought) a real Jew. Paul is referring here to the christological apocalypse he experienced and which, I will argue, the Galatians experienced as well. This interpretation is certified by the phraseological identity of the ἐν ἐμοί both places (Betz 1979, 124). This is *gnostic* in the etymological sense of a knowledge which transforms the person of the knower entirely.[35] Bultmann's descriptions of the Hellenistic mystic fit Paul perfectly at this moment:

> Man is related to the other world by participation in it. Something in him has come from that other world, that world of light. Depending on which mythical or cultic tradition determines the thought patterns, it is there from the very beginning as a primeval portion of light that has descended into matter, or it is the result of some change or influx due to a sacrament or an ecstatic experience. This something in man is regarded as the essential element in the one born again. And yet it has no necessary connection with the empirical man, with his acts and his fate.   (1967, 19–20)

This is very close indeed to the Pauline discourse on the meaning of dying with Christ as an ecstatic experience and baptism as a sacrament in Galatians.[36]

Paul follows this with a remarkable and necessary corollary to his argument. His Jerusalem opponents could certainly have argued something to the effect that while it is true that Christ's coming has redeemed the spirit, we who still dwell in flesh must observe the Torah in order to control the flesh and make it as well obedient to God's will. Paul counters this by saying that the very dwelling in the flesh is only apparent. In reality, he is no longer living in the flesh but in a hidden spiritual existence called Christ living in me. A passage from the *Corpus hermeticum, Chapter xiii,* cited by Bultmann, provides an extraordinary parallel (however Bultmann himself quite puzzlingly fails to note this parallel):

Seeing in myself an immaterial vision, produced by the mercy of God,
I have left myself in order to enter into an immortal body, and I am
now no longer what I was, but I have been begotten in the intellect.
This cannot be taught, and it cannot be seen by means of the material
elements through which we see below. This is why I am no longer concerned with this initial created form which was my own. I have no
more color, cannot be touched, and do not extend in space; all that is
foreign to me. Now, my child, you see me with your eyes, but what I
am you cannot understand when you look at me with your body's eyes
and with the physical sight. It is not with those eyes that anyone can
see me now, my child.   (Bultmann 1967, 18–19)

Note the extraordinarily clear platonistic influence on this passage as
well. Although Paul has not physically died, it is Christ who lives in him.
He was crucified with Christ, and he has been transformed into the sort
of being that Christ was, only apparently fleshly but through faith entirely
spiritual.[37] Observances in the flesh would seem, then, totally irrelevant.
"The practical consequence of this can be either libertinism or asceticism"
(Bultmann 1967, 21). It is easy to see how the Corinthians "misunderstood" such preaching.[38]

"Having begun in the spirit,
are you now finishing up in the flesh?"

You foolish Galatians! Who has bewitched you, before whose eyes
Jesus Christ crucified was so vividly portrayed. This only do I want to
learn from you: did you receive the Spirit by works of the Law or by
the hearing of faith? Are you so foolish? Having begun in the spirit,
are you now finishing up in the flesh? Have you experienced such
things in vain? If so, it really was in vain. Does he, therefore, who
supplies the Spirit to you and who works miracles in you [do so] by
works of the Law or by the hearing of faith?   (3:1–5)

Paul is arguing here that the Galatians have partaken of exactly the
same sort of transformative experience that Paul himself underwent, and
now, in contrast to him, they wish to nullify it. He "does not deny the
grace of God. For if justification came through Law Christ has died in
vain" (2:21), but they, by their desire to accept the Law, do deny the
grace of God and show that Christ has died in vain.[39]

I suggest that this "before your eyes" suggests a platonic "eyes of the
mind," in which visions are seen.[40] Paul's depiction here is the implemen-

tation of *enargeia.*[41] In any case, the analogy between Paul's own vision of the crucified Christ and that of the Galatians is enhanced by the use of ἐν ὑμῖν, "in you," which echoes the ἐν ἐμοί by which Paul describes his own experience.[42] The "hearing of faith" has been much discussed (Hays 1983, 143–45). Does this refer to God's act of proclamation (which the Greek allows) or the human act of hearing? I think that it is both, understood as a single act. Paul exploits the very ambiguity of the Greek in order to make an extraordinarily rich and multivalent claim. This "hearing," because it is "of faith," I would suggest is a hearing with the ears of the soul—like the seeing with the eyes of the mind. God declares, and the humans hear, in one soteriological (and mystical) moment of Paul's preaching and the Galatians' baptismal response. This double motion of God's faith and human faith will connect the rest of the chapter as well. In Abraham we find both the promise, which will be fulfilled through the coming of Christ into the world, and the faith in the promise, which is fulfilled by people entering into Christ faithfully.[43] The beginning and the end of Galatians 3 hold together perfectly, as Hays has already argued, albeit on somewhat different grounds (1983, 193–214). Because the spirit is given through faith and not by works of the Law, therefore, "There is no Jew or Greek in Christ," ἐν Χριστῷ, which I take to be virtually equal in force to "in the spirit," ἐν πνεύματι.

The ratio, spirit is to flesh as faith is to law, is here made absolutely explicit, thus establishing the dualist movement of Paul's thought. "Spirit" here is functioning in two very closely related senses, which contribute enormously to the effectiveness of the argument. On the one hand, obviously, Paul is referring to the Holy Spirit which manifests itself as a gift in the life of the Galatian community, but, on the other hand, he coordinates with it spirit as one of the poles of the dyad: flesh ∼ spirit. We then get another one of the analogical equations that Paul, following common Hellenistic usage, finds so useful—and so obvious that they often do not need to be explicitly drawn. Cosgrove remarks that "The Spirit/flesh antithesis is put to a wide variety of uses by the apostle; it is not simply another way of expressing the polarity between faith and works of the law" (1988, 46).[44] True enough, but at the same time, I would argue that whenever Paul uses a dichotomy of this sort—and spirit/flesh is one of the most powerful for him—all of its associated, analogical dichotomies are being called into play at the same time. Since "flesh" means literal observance (works) and especially circumcision in the flesh, "spirit" *means* faith, so it is absurd in Paul's view, almost a contradiction in terms, to expect manifestations of the Spirit to be the product of works.[45] They belong on opposite sides of the dualist hermeneutical structure. I think we do better to listen closely to the rich overtones of Pauline language, the way its polysemy increases its power, rather than trying to resolve the ambiguities at every moment.[46]

The final two sentences, which have been the occasion of much exegesis, make perfect sense on my reading, for as I have argued, Paul's concern is that any notion of the obligatory nature of physical observances makes nonsense of the completion of the meaning of such observances in the spiritual signifieds. So if the Galatians now accede to the notion that they must be perfected "in the flesh," they would render the gifts of the spirit "in vain." "If so" then means, "If you do this thing and have yourselves circumcised." Since the Galatians have not yet done so, it is simply a conditional.[47] If they do not make this grave error, then it will not have been in vain. I would tentatively suggest that Paul's opponents here had been promoting a doctrine that vision in the Holy Spirit is only available to the circumcised.

"FROM MY *FLESH* I WILL SEE GOD"

From rabbinic texts—albeit quite a bit later than Paul—we actually learn of the view hypothesized as a genuine Jewish theologoumenon.[48] Some of the Rabbis read circumcision as a necessary preparation for seeing God, the *summum bonum* of late-antique religious life (Boyarin 1990a). This is, of course, an entirely different hermeneutic structure from platonic allegorizing, because although a spiritual meaning is assigned to the corporeal act, the corporeal act is not the signifier of that meaning but its very constitution. That is, circumcision here is not the sign of something happening in the spirit of the Jew, but it is the very event itself—and it is, of course, in his body.[49] Moreover, as I have argued elsewhere, for the rabbinic formation, this seeing of God was not understood as the spiritual vision of a platonic eye of the mind, but as the physical seeing of fleshly eyes at a real moment in history (1990a).[50] Thus, even when it spiritualizes, the rabbinic tradition does so entirely through the body. Spirit here is an aspect of body, almost, I would say, the same spirit that experiences the pleasure of sex through the body, and not something apart from, beyond or above the body.

Elliot Wolfson has gathered the rabbinic (and later) material connecting circumcision with vision of God:[51]

> It is written, "This, after my skin will have been peeled off, but from my flesh, I will see God" [Job 19:26]. Abraham said, after I circumcised myself many converts came to cleave to this sign. "But from my flesh, I will see God," for had I not done this [circumcised myself], on what account would the Holy Blessed One, have appeared to me? "And the Lord appeared to him" [Genesis Rabbah 48:1, 479].

As Wolfson correctly observes there are two hermeneutic moves being made simultaneously in this midrash (1987b, 192–93). The first involves interpretation of the sequence in the Genesis text of Genesis 17:1–14, which is the description of Abraham's circumcision and Genesis 17:23 ff., which begins, "And The Lord appeared to Abraham in Elone Mamre." The midrash, following its usual canons of interpretation, attributes strong causal nexus to these events following on one another. Had Abraham not circumcised himself, then God would not have appeared to him. This interpretation is splendidly confirmed by the Job verse. The Rabbis considered the Book of Job, together with the other Holy Writings, to be an exegetical text that has the function of interpreting (or guiding interpretation of) the Torah. In this case, the verse of Job, which refers to the peeling off of skin, is taken by a brilliant appropriation to refer to the peeling off of skin of circumcision, and the continuation of the verse, which speaks of seeing God from one's flesh, is taken as a reference to the theophany at Elone Mamre. The reading of sequence of the Torah's text is confirmed by the explicit causality which the Job text inscribes.[52] Circumcision of the flesh—peeling of the skin—provides the vision of God. As Wolfson remarks, this midrash constitutes an interpretation of circumcision that directly counters the Pauline one: "The emphasis on Abraham's circumcision . . . can only be seen as a tacit rejection of the Christian position that circumcision of the flesh had been replaced by circumcision of the spirit (enacted in baptism)" (1987b, 194). The physical act of circumcision *in the flesh,* which prepares the (male) Jew for sexual intercourse, is also that which prepares him for Divine intercourse. It is hard, therefore, to escape the association of sexual and mystical experience in this text.

The strongly eroticized character of the experience of seeing God, established by the interpretation of circumcision, is made virtually explicit
in another (later) midrashic text, Numbers Rabbah 12:10, also cited by
Wolfson (1987b, 196–97):

> O, Daughters of Zion, go forth, and gaze upon King Solomon, wearing the
> crown that his mother made for him on his wedding day, on his day of bliss
> [Song of Songs 3:11]: It speaks about the time when the Presence
> rested in the Tabernacle. "Go forth and gaze," as it is said, "And all
> the people saw and shouted and fell on their faces" [Leviticus 9:24].
> "The daughters of Zion," those who were distinguished by circumci-
> sion, for if they were uncircumcised they would not have been able to
> look upon the Presence. . . . And thus it says, "Moses said: This is the
> thing which the Lord has commanded that you do, in order that the
> Glory of the Lord may appear to you" [Leviticus 9:6]. What was "this
> thing"? He told them about circumcision, for it says, "This is the thing
> which caused Joshua to perform circumcision" [Joshua 5:4]. . . .
>
> Therefore, Moses said to them, God commanded Abraham, your
> father, to perform circumcision when He wished to appear to him. So
> in your case, whoever is uncircumcised, let him go out and circumcise
> himself, "that the Glory of the Lord may appear to you" [Leviticus
> 9:6]. Thus Solomon said, "O Daughters of Zion, go forth and gaze
> upon King Solomon," the King who desires those who are perfect, as it
> is written, "Walk before Me and be blameless" [Genesis 17:1], for the
> foreskin is a blemish upon the body.

This is indeed a remarkable text, not least for the blurring of gender
which it encodes in its interpretative moves. Consistently with the entire
midrashic enterprise of interpreting the Song of Songs, the verse in question is historicized as well. It is taken to refer to the event described in
Leviticus 9, in which the entire People of Israel had a marvelous vision of
God. This event is interpreted as a wedding between God and Israel, as
are other moments of revelatory vision of God, such as the hierophany at
Mount Sinai. The verse of Song of Songs that refers to King Solomon's
wedding is taken, then, as an interpretation of the wedding day between
God and Israel described in Leviticus. But complications begin. By a typi-
cal midrashic pun, King Solomon (*Schelomo*) is turned into God, the King
who requires perfection (*Schelemut*). If the male partner is God, then the
female partner must be Israel. Accordingly, the "Daughters of Zion" are
Israel. However, this also results in a gender paradox, for many of the
Israelites who participated in that Divine vision were men.[53] Those very
Daughters of Zion are accordingly understood as males. The word "Zion"

(Hebrew *Tsiyyon*) is taken as a noun derived from the root *ts/y/n,* to be marked, and accordingly the Daughters of Tsiyyon are read as the circum-cised men of Israel.

I would like to suggest that more than midrashic arbitrariness is at work here, for the mystical experience *au fond,* when experienced erotically, often involves (in the West?) gender paradox. The mystical experience is interpreted as a penetration by the Divine word or spirit into the body and soul of the adept. This is accordingly an image of sex in which the mystic is figured as the female partner. This paradoxical gender assignment (when the mystic is biologically male) is a problem for erotic mystic imagery (Eilberg-Schwartz 1991). Verna Harrison has described a similar issue in the work of Gregory of Nyssa:

> When the human receptacle is described allegorically in terms of sex-uality, it has to be represented as female. It is no accident that in his first work, *On Virginity,* and in one of his last, the great *Commentary on the Song of Songs,* Gregory chooses feminine language to speak of the human person, especially in describing our relations with God, which for him are the definitive aspect of human identity and exis-tence. . . . In the treatise *On Those Who Have Fallen Asleep,* he specu-lates that in the resurrection human reproductive faculties may be transformed into a capacity to become impregnated with life from God and bring forth various forms of goodness from within oneself. This suggests that although human persons can be either male or fe-male in this world and will be neither male nor female in the next (cf. Gal. 3.28), on a different level they all relate to God in a female way, as bride to Bridegroom.   (Harrison 1992, 118–19)

My perhaps too bold suggestion is that our midrashic text is related to the same paradox of mystical experience. Circumcision is understood by the midrash text as feminizing the male, thus making him open to receive the Divine speech and vision of God. My interpretation of this midrash is that of medieval mystics (E. Wolfson 1987b, 198 ff.): "R. Yose said, Why is it written, 'And the Lord will pass over the door [literally opening]' [Exodus 12:23]? . . . 'Over the opening,' read it literally as 'opening'! That is, the opening of the body. And what is the opening of the body? That is the circumcision" (Zohar 2, 36a, cited in E. Wolfson [1987b, 204]).[54] Although this text is a pseudepigraph of the thirteenth century, I am sug-gesting that the idea is already embryonic in the midrashic text, in which circumcised men are "daughters." The mystic pseudepigraph would then be making explicit that which is implicit in the earlier formation. Thus,

we have indeed evidence for the possibility of a Jewish (and Jewish Christian) view that regarded circumcision as necessary preparation for experiencing the Spirit. Note once more how that view is grounded precisely *in
the flesh*. "From my flesh [my circumcised penis] I will see God." Were
such a view current among Paul's opponents in Galatia we would easily
understand his charge, "Having begun in the spirit, are you now finishing
up in the flesh?"[55]

The reason that this suggestion must be very tentative is that, as far as
I know, the only evidence for such a doctrine is post-Pauline and therefore
could very well be interpreted as a *response* to Paul. Nevertheless it remains very attractive to me to speculate that such a doctrine already existed among the "Jews" and thus the Judaeo-Christians, for then Paul's
argument here has enormous force. "They are telling you that only the
circumcised can see God, but you yourselves have already experienced
visual experiences in the Holy Spirit, so their claim is shown to be a lie!
Moreover, since the spirit is higher than the flesh, and you have already
jumped (from the very beginning) to that level, will you now return to
the lower level of the flesh?"[56] Another possibility is that Paul is simply
contrasting two forms of initiation as such: the higher one, baptism, which
is in the spirit, and the lower one, circumcision, which is in the flesh. It
may even be that Paul's crucial flesh ~ spirit dyad is initially generated by
this very opposition.[57] In any case, it enters into a very rich texture of
associations and meanings in his thought that go far beyond the moment.
One way of saying this—and of seeing it—would be to understand this
fundamental opposition as reproduced entirely at every moment in his
discourse, as its foundational, structuring, generating "key" symbol.[58]

FREEDOM OR ANARCHY?

In order to understand Paul, surely one of the key texts is Galatians 5:14.
Paul's rhetoric in this passage is apparently confusing and has led interpreters to directly opposing conclusions. In verse 14—"For the whole law
is fulfilled in one word, 'You shall love your neighbor as yourself'"—he
seems to be upholding the Law. But just a few verses later, in verse 19 he
seems to speak of the Law as irrelevant: "But if you are led by the Spirit
you are not under the law." Some have seen here (in verse 14) an apparent
contradiction to his view that the Law is abrogated; after all, he cites the
Law here and ordains that it be kept in some sense or other, while others

with equal justice see this passage as the center of Paul's "attack" on the Law. Some of these interpreters have gone so far as to regard 5:14 as "ironic." A third view sees Paul as contradicting himself within the space of three verses. E. P. Sanders contributed a searching discussion of these passages in Paul. He has well demonstrated the inadequacy of all earlier interpretations (1983, 93–105; Thielman 1989, 50–54). He shows that Hans Hübner's distinction between "the whole law" (5:3) as the Jewish Law and "all the Law" (5:14) as a Law which has nothing to do with the Jewish Torah is impossible (Sanders 1983, 96). He moreover shows that the notion that Paul distinguishes between the Law perverted (by Jews) and the Law as it was intended does not hold because Paul never refers to Jewish practice of the Law as perverted. There is, moreover, as Sanders demonstrates, little in Paul to commend the view of Bultmann and his followers that Paul condemns the Law pursued for salvation, while he upholds the (same) Law pursued for the fulfilling of God's will, that it is the inner disposition of the person that counts (85–86). On the other hand, as in other cases, I find Sanders's objections to the current interpretations stronger than his own exegetical suggestions—his analysis of the plight is better than his solution. In this case, I think he starts off very well by observing that for Paul the observance of loving one's neighbor (Galatians 5:14) (and particularly in its concrete manifestation of bearing her burdens [6:2]) constitutes "the *real* way to fulfill the law" (97). Moreover, even though Pharisaic/rabbinic teachers also cite Leviticus 19:18 as a summary of the Law, none other than Paul (or such as Philo's extreme allegorizers) advocated that its observance *replaced* circumcision and the rest of the concrete Law. Sanders's summary of the problem is exemplary: "There is, then, appreciable tension between the view that Christians are not under the law at all—they have died to the law, not just to part of it and not just to the law as perverted by pride, but to the law as such—and the view that those in Christ fulfill the law—not just aspects of it, and not just the law when pursued in the right spirit" (99). Sanders, however, comes to the conclusion "that both positions cannot be maintained in detail." Obviously an interpretation which makes sense of both of Paul's statements would be superior to one that cannot. I think that Galatians 5:14 (and its associated texts) can be strongly read in the context of the general interpretation of Pauline thought that this book proposes.

To be sure, Paul does not propose a distinction between the Law pursued in the right spirit and the Law perverted. In this, as I have said,

Sanders completely convinces me. But Sanders's parallel denial that there is no distinction in Paul between the letter and the spirit of the Law does not convince. On the one hand, Sanders precisely distinguishes between two interpretations of the Pauline antinomy: (1) you are not under *the* Law, but nevertheless you are under *a* law, the Law of Christ, which commands love of the neighbor; and (2) you are not under the Law, but nevertheless you should fulfill it, not by being circumcised, but by loving your neighbor; that is real fulfillment.

He argues that the second is "by far the more likely meaning" (98). On the other hand, he is unable in my opinion to explain what it means to fulfill the Law without being circumcised. Sanders is effectively throwing up his exegetical hands when he writes with regard to 1 Corinthians 9:19–21, "Christians both stand in a right relationship to God and live in accordance with his will, but [this] is no more thought through in a systematic way than Gal. 5:14 and Rom. 8:4" (100). To bridge this gap, I submit that only a hermeneutic approach will do, one that understands that the Law is one—"But the readers would not understand that Paul intends by 'law' in 5:14 and 6:2 a law which is entirely distinct from the other one" (98)—but at the same time finds a way to relate systematically between that which is being affirmed and that which is being denied about the Law in Paul. My claim is that there is ample evidence throughout the corpus that what is being affirmed is the spiritual sense—the universal Law of Christ, of love, of faith—and what is being denied is the literal, carnal sense—the Jewish Law of circumcision, kashruth, and the Sabbath. This solution is explicitly denied by Sanders, who claims that Paul "does not define Christian behavior as keeping the 'spirit' of the law as distinct from observing it literally" (101). But Paul *does*—as Sanders himself admits—draw such a distinction at several prominent places. Why should Romans 2:29, which I have interpreted in detail in the previous chapter, not be understood as proposing precisely this distinction, whereby "true" circumcision is a matter of the heart and the spirit and not of the penis? The Jew who is one inwardly and not outwardly would be precisely the one who is characterized by loving his neighbor as himself and not by watching what he eats. Paul's references to "circumcision not made with hands" also strongly support precisely this interpretation, that Paul distinguishes between the physical and the spiritual interpretations of the Law and affirms the latter while denying the significance of the former. Once more, the physical observances correspond to difference, to the particular, while the spiritual interpretations are understood by Paul to correspond to sameness, to the universal.

Indeed, "The law, for Paul, is not only the will of God, it is the will of God as revealed in Jewish Scripture," but only, as Sanders notes by implication, after the veil has been removed. This veil is the carnal veil that occludes precisely the spiritual, inner meaning. In this way, we understand Paul's excision from the Law of precisely that which was particularly Jewish and thereby problematic for his project of the new universal Israel, without necessitating an assumption of either inconsistency or, worse, expediency, as Sanders is forced to by his insistence that "Paul himself offered no theoretical basis for the de facto reduction of the law" (102–03). The same point has been made in somewhat different terms by Westerholm. Sanders argues that Paul's point in Romans 10:5–8 is that "Moses was incorrect" (41). Westerholm is absolutely accurate in asserting, "But Moses could not be 'incorrect' for Paul" (1988, 145 n. 16). Therefore, there must be a rationally explicable theoretical basis for his approach to the Law. I hold that he did offer such a basis and did so, moreover, over and over again in his dyads of spirit/flesh, spirit/letter, inner/outer. Sanders agrees that 1 Corinthians 7:19—"Neither circumcision nor uncircumcision, but keeping the commandments of God"—is "one of the most amazing sentences that he ever wrote" (1983, 103). But he seems to think that it is possible to interpret Paul without accounting for that amazing sentence: "He seems to have 'held together' his native view that the law is one and given by God and his new conviction that Gentiles and Jews stand on equal footing, which requires the deletion of some of the law, by asserting them both without theoretical explanation" (103).[59] I will not propose that everything in Paul must hang together or that different circumstances may not ever have provoked somewhat different and partially contradictory responses, but I believe that here we can supply a theoretical explanation that precisely eliminates such a gross contradiction.

The point that Paul wishes to make here is that Christian freedom must *not* be interpreted as permission to do everything and anything. Paul already anticipates the sort of "misunderstanding" of his gospel with which he would have to deal in 1 Corinthians.[60] It would have been easy to misunderstand Paul's railing against the Law as a claim that there is no Law at all, but this is not what Paul ever meant. What he meant is that there is an outer aspect to the Law, the "doing" of the Law, which was special to the Jewish People alone and which has been abrogated in

Christ, and an inner, spiritual aspect of the Law which is for everyone and which has been fulfilled in Christ and is thus entirely appropriately styled as "the Law of Christ" (6:2). The "Law of Christ" is the allegorical, spiritual fulfillment of the letter of the Law of Moses, the Law according to the flesh (Hays 1987). "Flesh" has two seemingly opposite but paradoxically coordinated meanings for Paul; it is commitment to the literal, outward doing of the Law on the one hand, and it is sinning through the flesh on the other. These two are not, of course, identical, but they are related. Both of them are opposed in some sense to the spirit which alone provides assurance of fulfilling the Law (that is the spiritual referent of the Law, which is love). The apparent contradictions in Paul remarked by various commentators are, on this interpretation, entirely illusory (Barclay 1991, 140 and n. 113). Paul's expression here is thus no more contradictory of itself or of anything else in Paul than "For in Christ Jesus neither circumcision nor uncircumcision is of any avail, but faith working through love" (Galatians 5:6). Paul has in effect taken common sentiments of Judaism to the effect that the purpose of the whole Torah and its Laws can be summed up in one ethical/spiritual principle and drawn the logical conclusion suggested by his allegorical scheme, namely, that the spiritual signified can replace its literal signifier completely. This, then, counts for him as fulfilling the Law while the outward observances are the doing of the Law also referred to as being "under the Law."

Galatians 5:14 and 19 are thus in perfect consequence. The Christians are not $\check{\alpha}\nu o\mu o\varsigma$, without Law, nor $\acute{v}\pi o\ \nu \acute{o}\mu o\nu$, under the Law. Instead, they are $\check{\epsilon}\nu\nu o\mu o\varsigma\ X\rho\iota\sigma\tau o\hat{v}$, in the Law of Christ (1 Corinthians 9:20–21), which also proves that $\acute{v}\pi o\ \nu \acute{o}\mu o\nu$ is in opposition to $\check{\epsilon}\nu\nu o\mu o\varsigma\ X\rho\iota\sigma\tau o\hat{v}$) (Barclay 1991, 126–27). They are not lawless, nor under the Law (Galatians 5:19), but subject to the Law of Christ, which alone counts as *fulfilling* the Law (Galatians 5:14). This perspective helps us solve, as well, another outstanding problem in Pauline interpretation, the nature of the "Law of Christ." Is the Law of Christ a reference to Jesus' actual teachings or not (Barclay 1991, 126–35; Hays 1987)? Does $\nu \acute{o}\mu o\varsigma$ here mean "law" at all, or perhaps only "principle"? In my view, these questions are obviated, because the Law of Christ refers to the Law according to the spirit, the Law of faith working through love, which enjoins those practices of agape which Jesus has also in his person taught. The Law of Christ is thus the Law transformed by Christ's crucifixion and exemplified by his behavior.[61] Faith and love without "doing" are fulfillment, while doing without faith and love is nothing. Paul is thus completely consistent.[62] It is thus that Paul can say: "Neither circumcision counts for anything nor uncircumcision is anything but keeping the commandments of God" (1 Corinthians 7:19). Rabbinic Jews, understandably, reacted quite negatively to such sentiments. In the next chapter I will continue close reading of Galatians with a view to answering the question of whether Paul's discourse on the so-called "curse of the Law" is as anti-Judaic as it has often been claimed to be by both Jewish and Christian readers.

6

Was Paul an "Anti-Semite"?

> The supposed conflict between "doing" as such and "faith" as such
> is simply not present in Galatians. What was at stake was not a
> way of life summarized by the word "trust" versus a mode of life
> summarized by "requirements," but whether or not the require-
> ment for membership in to the Israel of God would result in there
> being "neither Jew nor Greek."
>
> E. P. Sanders

READING PAUL AS A JEW

One of the crucial passages in Paul for determining (or rather, constructing) his posture vis-à-vis the Jewish religion—the Law—is Galatians
3:10–4:7. Many interpreters, especially of the "Lutheran" school, have
read this passage as if the "curse of the Law" consists of the inability of
human beings to ever meet its demands fully and therefore the irreparable
curse that it places on all. The whole purpose of the Law, on this account,
is to *increase* sin in the world, so that the saving grace of the cross will be
even more abundant. As can be imagined, such an interpretation of Paul
leads easily to charges that he was rabidly anti-Jewish. Moreover, if such
views are asserted as a theologically correct view of Judaism and its historical role, then the theology is anti-Judaic (and later anti-Semitic).
While there are, of course, passages that *can* be read in support of such a
perverse notion of God—else it would not have achieved such widespread
acceptance—I would like to show (as have several other commentators by
now) that certainly in Galatians this is by no means a necessary construction of the text.[1] Much more plausible a priori, in my view, would be a
conception (closest to Dunn's) that the ultimate inadequacy of the Law
stems from its ethnic exclusiveness, from the fact that it represents the
practices of the Tribe of Israel and therefore is unsuitable as a way of life
and of salvation for the Universal Humanity which Paul seeks to institute.
E. P. Sanders's insight here is also very important, namely, that this sec-

tion consists not so much of Paul's critique of the Law but of his explanation of God's purpose in giving the Law, given its inefficacy for salvation
(1983, 65 ff.).

In the following section I will attempt to show that Paul produces a
sort of radical, "heretical" midrash—but midrash, nevertheless—in support of his new understandings of Judaism. The very fact, however, that
he supports his view with midrash indicates his conviction that he stands
in continuity with the Torah and not against it. To be sure, from a "Jewish" point of view, this "continuity" itself constitutes rejection of the Law.
The form of Paul's argument itself provides then an elegant analogue for
his character; in both we find an entity both inside and outside of Judaism
at the same time.

"Those who are men of works of Law are under a curse"

By contrast, those who are men of works of Law are under a curse. For
it is written, "Cursed is everyone who does not uphold everything that
is written in the book of the Law, by doing it" [Deuteronomy 27:26].
It is, then, obvious that nobody is justified before God by Law, because "The righteous shall live by faith" [Habbakuk 2:4]. The Law is
not by faith, but "He who does them shall live by them" [Leviticus
18:5].   (3:10–12)

A proper understanding of these verses of Paul is crucial for any evaluation of his ideology vis-à-vis the Jews, the Torah, and Judaism, as many
currently held readings end up claiming that Paul significantly distorts
Jewish doctrine here. Hans Joachim Schoeps largely based his claim that
Paul misunderstood/misrepresented Judaism on this very passage (Schoeps
1961, 175–83). A reinterpretation of the passage that will not lead to
such conclusions is therefore highly important for our general evaluation
of Paul on Judaism. In establishing the identity of Paul as a Jewish cultural
critic, it is important to demonstrate that he writes *as a Jew*.[2] Showing the
thoroughly midrashic character of the main arguments of the letter is then
directly relevant to the descriptive project as a whole. Paul's argument is
almost prototypical midrash.[3]

Most interpreters have quite missed the point here, in my view. Their
interpretations are dependent on theological presuppositions about Paul's
relation to the Law as generating sin, a proposition which seems a priori

implausible for Paul to have held. Dunn has produced the best arguments against this notion:

> Betz's own reconstruction of Paul's reasoning (the law was given in order to be broken and to generate sin) is hardly obvious from the text (even allowing for 3.19). It would hardly cut much ice with his readers, and on this point Paul could hardly simply assume that his readers shared his presuppositions. . . . Moreover, as Hübner points out, such a theology attributes a very perverse motive on the part of God in giving the law (*Gesetze* 27); it is hard to think that Paul would be unaware of such a corollary or would willingly embrace it.   (Dunn 1990, 234)[4]

Alternatively, interpretations are based on the notion that one who transgresses even one precept of the Torah is irredeemably cursed—a notion that has no support in Jewish texts of either the first or later centuries. As E. P. Sanders has written, "This sequence of views cannot be found in contemporary Jewish literature. The sequence of thought sounds plausible, but it does not appear to be Paul's, nor that of any form of contemporary Judaism" (1983, 27; 1977, 17–64). "All the rabbis whose views are known to us took the position that all the law must be accepted. . . . No rabbi took the position that obedience must be perfect. Pharisees and rabbis of all schools and all periods strongly believed in repentance and other means of atonement in the case of transgression" (Sanders 1983, 28). The only exception is *perhaps* 4 Ezra (Schoeps 1961, 19; Sanders 1983, 28). Krister Stendahl pointed out that this interpretation is implausible *on inner Pauline grounds*, because Paul himself in Philippians claims to have been "blameless as to the Law" (3:6). Sanders has further discredited on exegetical grounds the interpretation that Paul's claim is based on the word "everything" in the verse and means that one who does not keep *all* of the Law is accursed:

> These three considerations—the character of the terminological argument in favor of *Gentiles* being *righteoused* by *faith*, which is based on prooftexts; the fact that Paul states in his own words what he takes the prooftexts to mean; and the subordination of vv. 10–13 to v. 8— seem to me to be decisive against the view that the thrust and point of the argument are directed toward the conclusion that the law should not be accepted because no one can fulfill all of it. The argument seems to be clearly wrong that Paul, in Galatians 3, holds the view that *since* the law cannot be entirely fulfilled, *therefore* righteousness is by faith.   (Sanders 1983, 22–23)

Sanders's arguments against the standard reading seem impeccable to me. His own interpretation, however, leaves something to be desired in that it makes Paul depend on a purely associative connection between "the words *nomos* and cursed." Schlier, on the other hand, interprets that Paul's intention is that those who *do* the Torah are not *fulfilling* the Torah and are therefore accursed (Schlier 1965, 132).[5] However, since he misses the point of the midrashic form, his interpretation has not had the impact it ought to have had on the commentatorial tradition.[6] Dunn, also, I think correctly understands the import of the verse but does not even attempt to interpret the midrash. As Dunn understands:

> Most Jews of Paul's day would simply assume that to be ἐξ ἔργων νό-μου is to remain within all that the Torah lays down, *is* to do what the law requires. But Paul denies that equation. To be of the works of the law is *not* the same as fulfilling the law, is *less* than what the law requires, and so falls under the law's own curse. Why so? The answer is given by our previous exposition of "works of the law." Those who are ἐξ ἔργων νόμου are those who have understood the scope of God's covenant people as Israel *per se,* as that people who are defined by the law and marked out by its distinctive requirements. Such an understanding of the covenant and of the law inevitably puts too much weight on physical and national factors, on outward and visible enactments, and gives too little weight to the Spirit, to faith and love from the heart.   (Dunn 1990, 226–27)

So far, so good. But Dunn also does not answer the question of how this can be learned from Deuteronomy 27:26.

The answer is quite simple when looked at from a midrashic point of view. The verse reads, "Cursed is everyone who does not uphold everything that is written in the book of the Law, by doing it." The words "by doing it" at the end of the verse are syntactically and semantically superfluous—remove them, and the sense is not harmed. Paul, then, following a very standard midrashic move, rereads the verse (or indeed rewrites it syntactically), so that all of its elements will add to the meaning. He does so, in fact, by taking the "by doing it" as modifying the entire phrase "everyone who does not uphold everything that is written in the book of the Law." We could rewrite the verse, then, as: "Everyone, who [precisely] by *doing* it does not uphold all that is written in the book of the Law, is under a curse"; i.e., by *doing* it, by physical performance, works of the Law, one is *not* upholding all that which is written in the book of the Law, and *that* is the curse, because "all that is written" implies much more than mere doing! The hermeneutical move that Paul makes here is quite similar (although not identical) to that of the Rabbis in the Talmud on Exodus 23:2, who interpreted "After the majority you must not incline to do evil, and you shall not bear witness in a suit to incline after the majority" as meaning that one *must* follow the majority.[7]

As Stephen Westerholm has concluded in general, "What is crucial to note is that Paul consistently distinguishes between the 'doing' of the law's commands required of those subject to it and the 'fulfilling' of the law by Christians" (1988, 203; cf. Betz 1979, 275; Barclay 1991, 141).[8] Notice, however, the difference between my way of turning this interpretation and that of others who hold this view. Westerholm seems to regard this usage as a way of deflecting objections to Paul's position by exploiting the "ambiguity" of the term "fulfill." This is referred to explicitly as "looseness of speech" (Räisänen, supported by Barclay, 140, 142). Barclay also ends up with this sort of explanation: "Given the Galatians' attraction to the law, it would have been dangerous to dismiss the significance of the law altogether, but the positive statements Paul makes here about the law are hedged about with sufficient ambiguity to prevent the impression of reinstating the law" (141–42). I would phrase this entirely differently: Given the fact that Paul believes that the Torah was given by God, it would have been impossible for him to dismiss it altogether, and the positive statements that he makes are the essence of his hermeneutical theology by which Christianity fulfills and does not abrogate Judaism. Thielman, on the other hand, writes, "Paul, on this view, is not suddenly saying that the law has a place in Christian ethics (he has after all just forbidden the Galatians from practicing circumcision), but that Christian ethics overwhelm and, by overwhelming, supersede the Jewish law" (1989, 51). According to my interpretation, for Paul "Christian ethics" is simply the true interpretation of "Jewish Law" and always has been. As I have argued above in Chapter 4, this is supersessionist from the point of view of Jewish hermeneutics but not from Paul's point of view.

The end of Galatians provides an important parallel: "For the whole law is fulfilled in one word, 'You shall love your neighbor as yourself'" (5:14). In this verse, Paul speaks of "fulfilling" the Law, not of "doing" it. Barclay has made the very telling point that πληροῦν and its Hebrew equivalent מלא are never used in Jewish sources in either Hebrew or Greek with reference to the Law, and further that when Paul refers to Jewish observance of the Law he uses φυλάσσω (keep), ποιέω (do), and

πράσσω (practice) but not πληροῦν (fulfill) (Barclay 1991, 138–39).
Jews do the Law, but Christians fulfill the Law, and even more to the point
of this book, the very notion of fulfillment *is a Hellenistically inspired Pauline innovation in theology*, although obviously one for which the way was
prepared by the prophetic diatribes against the hypocrisy of bringing sacrifices while ignoring homeless people. It replaces the difference of the
doing of *many* material practices with the logos of one ideal fulfillment,
just as the difference of Jew and Greek or male and female is also to be
replaced by the Ideal One, spiritualized phallus which can be circumcised
not physically but only with a "circumcision not made with hands."[9]
Thus, precisely by dying to the Law according to the flesh, the Christian
believer can fulfill the Law of Christ. By crucifying the flesh, together with
its passions and desires *and its fleshly practices*, circumcision, the Christian
becomes able to walk in the spirit and fulfill the Law of faith working
through love. This is the true circumcision which defines the true Jew
(Romans 2:25–29).

This distinction is the clue to understanding the key verse, Galatians
3:10, where according to my interpretation Paul argues that those who
"do" the Law are not "fulfilling" the Law. I assume that the ἐμμενεῖ
(upholding) of the Deuteronomy quotation is semantically (or perhaps
theologically) roughly equivalent to πεπλήρωται (fulfilled) in Galatians
5:14.[10] The Hebrew מקיים of the verse certainly means "to fulfill the requirement of" as well as "to preserve." Men of works of the Law, those
who hold that works justify and practice accordingly, are accursed by the
Law itself, because of their misunderstanding of the true import of the
Law. It is these to whom Paul will later refer in Romans as "you who have
the written code and circumcision but break the law." This interpretation
is supported as well by Paul's own usage in other places, for instance,
Romans 3:27, where he explicitly contrasts "doing," which equals "the
Law of works," with "The Law of faith."

The next verse is also quite simply understood as a midrashic argument,
although from the rabbinic point of view surely a "midrash of lies."[11] Paul
wishes to prove that "nobody is justified before God by Law." He first cites
the verse of Habbakuk which reads that the "righteous live by faith."[12] It
follows from this that those who live by faith are the righteous, i.e., the
justified. He then argues that those who live by the Law do not live by
faith, since the verse in Leviticus explicitly reads "He who *does them* lives
by *them*," i.e., one who does the commandments lives by *them* and not by

faith. Since, then, we know from Habbakuk that the righteous live by faith, he who lives by *them* and not by faith (and, thereby, does not *fulfill* the Law) is not righteous—is not justified.[13] Paul has then a perfect proof that "nobody is justified before God by Law."[14] This interpretation obviates Sanders's claim that Paul is here denying the truth of a verse of the Torah (1978, 106, and 1983, 20 ff.). Paul is using methods of interpretation that would not surprise any Pharisee (I suspect) or Rabbi, although the results he arrives at would, of course, shock them to their depths.[15] The phrase "does them" in the Leviticus verse is precisely the same as "to do them" in the verse of Deuteronomy, so this argument is a direct sequel to the previous one.[16] Finally, it is highly significant that in the Leviticus context, the Law which one does is specifically marked as that which marks Jews off from gentiles:

> You shall not act according to the way of life of Egypt in which you lived. And you shall not act according to the way of life of Canaan, into which I will cause you to go, and you shall not live by their laws. You shall do my statutes [משפטים] and keep my laws and live by them. I am the Lord your God. And you shall keep all my laws and all my statutes and do them, which if a man does he will live by them.

Given the whole vector of Paul's argument in Galatians, it is hardly surprising that he would choose this set of verses as his negative example. As I have pointed out above, the word משפטים, "statutes," is a highly marked term for Jewish privilege in having been given the Law, because of its use in the Psalms verse: "He has spoken his words to Jacob, his laws and *statutes* to Israel. He has not done so for any other nation, and *statutes*, they do not know" (Psalms 147:16–17). Therefore, Paul argues, those who do them, and thereby mark themselves off from the Egyptians and the Canaanites, live by them and not by faith, but those who live by faith, which is for all, are righteous. Ergo, those who do them are not righteous.

It is not insignificant, moreover, that this verse of Leviticus that Paul has just treated so negatively appears in the context of justification of the laws against incest, which appear immediately following it, and it is precisely these sexual practices which are identified as the "way of life of Egypt and Canaan." If this was the nature and content of Paul's preaching on his first visit to Corinth as well, it is not entirely surprising that some of the Corinthian Christians "misunderstood" and concluded that Christian freedom consisted of abrogation of the laws against incest as well. This point will be very significant in the next chapters of this book.

"Christ has redeemed us from the curse of the Law"

Christ has redeemed us from the curse of the Law by becoming a curse for us, for it is written, "Cursed is everyone who hangs on a tree."   (3:13)

"In the context of the letter, he certainly assumes that the Law becomes a curse for those who seek justification before God 'by works of the Law,' because by doing so they deprive themselves of the blessing of Abraham given to 'men of faith'" (Betz 1979, 149).[17] The theological and christological notions are very clear here and well set out in the commentaries, for example, by Betz. Humanity has been enslaved by the "elements of this world," including, for Jews, the Law. (For the positive role of the Law as παιδαγωγός, see below on 3:24). Through the double sacrifice of being born a human, coming under the Law, and being crucified, Christ has freed Jews from the slavery of the Law and gentiles from the slavery of the elements of the world. All of this will be developed further in Chapter 4 of the letter and is prefigured in the verse here.

Once again, the crucial question is how to understand the prooftext that Paul cites. In fact, I think that the answer here is rather simple. The verse in Deuteronomy reads literally: A curse of God is hung, or, since there is no way to distinguish subject from nominal predicate in Hebrew other than context: The hung one is a curse of God. In Hebrew and Aramaic the verb "hang" is often used with the sense of "to crucify." One could very easily, then, interpret the verse to read that the crucified one is the curse of God, and from thence the substitutional christology that Paul here implies can be readily derived. It is a very interesting problem, however, that the verse as cited in Paul's Greek, presumably from a Septuagint form, actually supports the midrash less well than would the original Hebrew. I would suggest, therefore, with a certain degree of trepidation that we may have here, in fact, a fragment of Palestinian Christian midrash that Paul is reproducing. The "scapegoat" christology, generally held to be an earlier christology than Paul, would support this hypothesis as well.

"The promise of the Spirit through faith"

That the blessing of Abraham might come upon the Gentiles through Jesus Christ, and that we might receive the promise of the Spirit through faith.   (3:14)

Paul here, as elsewhere, spiritualizes and allegorizes the notion of kinship. If for rabbinic Jews the crucial signifier is actual, physical descent from Abraham, for Paul, it is descent from Abraham according to the spirit, which is constituted by entry into the faith community of Christ. He equates the promise made to Abraham that Sarah would bear Isaac to Abraham's spiritual paternity of Jesus, "the seed" to whom the promise was made, and through Jesus, the seed of all who believe. Thus the exegetical notion that the blessing is for the descendants of Abraham by the "promise" and not to those who are his descendants "by the flesh" is fulfilled in time by God through the sending of the Messianic seed through which the promise was made. The fulfillment of the promise is, however, through the participation of the people in the spirit which has been offered them by Christ's crucifixion. Entering into the spirit, by participating themselves in the experience and commitment of the crucifixion and resurrection, constitutes acceptance of the gift and thus entering into the descent by the promise, the type of which was the birth of Isaac through the promise and not by the natural carnal means.[18] Indeed, it is not so much Abraham who is the type of Christ but Isaac. God offers adoption as spiritual children through the sacrifice of his son, but people either accept it or reject it. They accept it by allowing the gifts of the spirit into their hearts. If they reject it by going back to the works of the Law, implying thereby that only physical descent or physical adoption into the Jewish family saves, then Christ died on the cross in vain. As Ferdinand Christian Baur put it so precisely at the end of the nineteenth century, "According to the [Jerusalem apostles], it is in vain to be a Christian without being a Jew also. According to [Paul], it is in vain to be a Christian if, as a Christian, one chooses to be a Jew as well" (Baur 1875, 57).

In Galatians Paul is supporting the connection between the allegorical theory of the Law and christology. The two midrashim together provide the argument. The Law itself has already informed us of its own dual nature by telling us that anyone who remains with the physical level of "doing the Law" has not fulfilled the Law. This is then followed by the midrashic argument that anyone who merely does the Law is not living by faith, which alone justifies, and finally that Christ through his crucifixion has revealed the true meaning of the Law, namely, that its material signifier is to be replaced by its spiritual signified. In the next section Paul will turn to the third aspect of the triad, the question of physical descent and genealogy, which he will also read in accord with the allegorical structure.

> *"Brothers, I draw an example*
> *from common human life"*

> Brothers, I draw an example from common human life: likewise, nobody annuls or adds a codicil to a covenant of a man, once it has been ratified. Now the promises were spoken to Abraham "and to his seed." It does not say "and to his seeds," as about many but about one: "and to your seed"—which is Christ. But this is what I mean: the Law which came 430 years later does not make void a covenant previously ratified by God, in order to nullify the promise. Hence, if the inheritance comes through Law, it no longer comes through the promise. However, by promise God has granted it to Abraham as a gift of grace.   (3:15–18)

In these verses, Paul sets up his opposition between physical descent and genealogy—which are equal to the literal, to Israel according to the flesh, which corresponds as well to the historical Jesus—and descent according to the promise, Israel according to the spirit, which corresponds to the risen Christ. N. T. Wright has recently contributed what I take to be a new and correct interpretation of this passage. "Seed" here does not mean Christ per se but rather "family," as its Hebrew original often does as well.[19] In order for the traditional Jewish theological conviction that in the end all will be saved through the covenant to be true, the promise must devolve on all in the end. Now it does not say "seeds," families, but "seed," family, so it follows that for the covenantal promise to come true, all of humanity must be constituted through Christ into a single seed (Wright 1992a, 162–68). The Law, which came later and serves a temporary function, could not be the means by which this will come about, since it divides humanity into families and does not join them into one seed. In any case, God's promise is a "gift of Grace," a term which certainly echoes the Hebrew מתנת חינם, where the Hebrew root for grace is used adverbially to mean a free, unconditional gift.

"Why then the law?"

Why then the law? It was added because of transgression, until the seed should come to whom the promise had been made; and it was ordained by angels through an intermediary. Now an intermediary is from more than one, but God is one.   (3:19–20)

Proper clarification of this and the following passage is crucial to any construal of Paul's theology of Judaism. There seems to me to be not the slightest reason in this text to understand the word χάριν as telic, namely that Paul wishes to say that the Law was given in order to produce transgression, as Betz, following many modern commentators, argues.[20] The simplest explanation of the verse is that the Law was given as a temporary and secondary measure, because of the existence of sin in the present age, in order to restrain people from transgressing until the coming of Jesus who is the seed (Lull 1986, 481–98).[21] Thielman has proposed another interpretation which seems to me also to be a distinct possibility. He reads τῶν παραβάσεων χάριν προσετέθη, "added because of transgression," as having causal force, not in the sense of preventing transgression but in the sense of providing an answer to transgression, namely, punishment. This also helps make good sense of the συνέγκλεισεν ἡ γραφή, "Scripture consigned or confined under sin," of verse 22 below (1989, 74).[22]

After hundreds of years and hundreds of interpretations, I believe that Wright has solved the problem of these verses (1992a, 168–72). The "seed" to whom the promise was made is the new one human family of Christ, and it was ordained by angels through an intermediary, Moses. Wright's reading decisively clarifies the next verse. The translation given above follows standard interpretations, none of them successful, which in one way or another find here a logical argument that the Law must have been given by angels and not by God. Wright translates rather, "Now he [the mediator] is not a mediator of one, but God is one." Having established above that "one" here means the new unified single family of humanity in Christ, we understand the verse to mean that Moses was the mediator not for this one family of humanity but for only a part of it, for a difference within the sameness, so this cannot be the fulfillment that God looks for, because God is one. The verse becomes on this reading an exact parallel to Paul's argument in Romans 3:20: "Is God the God of the Jews only? Is he not of gentiles also? Yes, of gentiles also." As Wright sums up his interpretation:

The problem of v. 20b can be solved quite easily once 20a is read
in this way. Moses is not the mediator of the "one family," *but God
is one,* and therefore desires one family, as he promised to Abraham.
The presupposition of Paul's argument is that, if there is one God—
the foundation of all Jewish belief—there must be one people of God.
Were there to be two or more "peoples," the whole theological scheme
would lapse back into some sort of paganism, with each tribe or race
possessing its own national deities.   (1992a, 170)

The Rabbis, however, did not see it that way, allowing that others
could worship God and be saved without joining into one People of God.
Once more, I think the passion for unity must be ascribed to Paul's Hellenistic Jewish *Weltanschauung.*

The Law is thus demoted in importance vis-à-vis the promise, but
whether it was given to prevent or to punish transgression, there is no
suggestion here that it has a demonic function or that these angels are to
be understood demonically. It is easy to see, however, how gnostics could
find such a meaning here. In any case, the important point is that there is
no warrant here to understand that the function of the Law was to produce
transgression in order to increase the scope of the working of God's
grace—rather like a doctor making the patient sicker in order to increase
the scope of her healing power. Nor do the next verses argue for such an
interpretation either.

"Is the law then against the promises of God?"

Is the law then against the promises of God? Certainly not. For if a law
had been given which could make alive, then justification would indeed be by the law. But the scripture consigned everything under sin,
in order that the promise, by faith in Jesus Christ might be given to
those who believe. Before the faith came, we were kept in custody
under the Law, confined until the coming faith was to be revealed.
Therefore, the Law has been our guardian until Christ, in order that
we might be justified by faith. But since the faith has come, we are no
longer under a guardian.   (3:21–25)

Paul begins this argument with another logical proof. If the Law, as he has
just said, is given for the purpose of preventing sin, does it not annul the
promise—in other words, does it not substitute itself for the promise and
obviate the promise?[23] This seems to me a strong argument against the
interpretation of the previous verses that the Law was given to increase

sin, in order that the grace of the promise would be necessary, for if that were the case then the question of the Law being against the promise would not arise! Only if the Law is accorded the positive role of confining sin would it be possible even to imagine that it somehow cancels the promise of a "free gift of grace." Verse 23, "But the scripture," seems difficult for my interpretation, however. It seems strongly to promote a reading that the Law itself produces, and thus confines everyone under, sin. However, this problem is illusory. Note that Paul switches here from "The Law" to "Scripture" as the subject of the sentence, and this shift must be significant.[24] He is not speaking here of "The Law" at all, but of the text. The action of the text is linguistic, so "consigns/confines everyone under sin" must be understood as "predicates of all humanity that they are sinful." To understand this point, the following linguistic parallel may be helpful. In his book on Paul, John Barclay has written the following sentence: "The peculiar pessimism about 'mankind' and 'flesh' in the Dead Sea Scrolls arises from an apocalyptic and sectarian perspective which consigns everyone to doom unless they experience the grace of God within the elect community" (1991, 205). Just as Barclay does not mean to say here that the sectarian perspective *caused* (performative) everyone to be doomed but only that it *declared* (constative) everyone doomed, so also could we understand Paul's Scripture as "confining" everyone under sin, in other words, declaring that all are sinful. This interpretation also obviates the difficult conclusion that Paul is equating "under sin" in this verse with "under the Law" in the next; therefore, the Law = sin (Longenecker 1990, 181–82). For ὑπὸ ἁμαρτίαν in the sense of "sinful," see Romans 3:9. It may be that Paul holds, as indeed he seems to, that the Law cannot redeem from sin (Romans 6:14), but this still does not mean that he holds that the Law produces, increases, or causes sin. Thielman offers an attractive alternative interpretation, that Scripture (which he takes as equal to the Law here) confines everyone who is sinful and does not allow them to escape the consequences of their sin.

In either case, however, the function of the Law is not to give life. The answer to the question about the Law being against the promises, then, is No, of course it is not. Now comes Paul's proof: If there were a law which could make alive (= justify), then indeed justification would come from the Law and the promise would be nullified. The function of the Law, however, is not to give life. All it does is confine all under sin, or by reason of sin, so that they may continue until the promise is given to those who believe. Therefore, the original premise is proven wrong: The Law does not annul the promise. Paul then explains the positive function of the Law as a pedagogue who makes it possible for people to be justified by faith, and now that this function has been fulfilled is no longer required.[25]

Accordingly, we need not see the παιδαγωγός in a negative light, as Betz implies (177), in order to follow Paul's argument. If the pedagogue is a guide and baby-sitter appropriate for the small child, then we understand Paul's *mashal* perfectly. In the infancy of humanity the pedagogue was necessary because of sin (not to produce sin, a bizarre and near Marcionite notion, which Lutheran theologians refer to as "God's strange work"![26]), but now with the maturity of the coming of Christ the pedagogue is no longer necessary. If we do not accept the essentially Lutheranizing interpretation of Paul's Law doctrine to the effect that it has never been a way of achieving virtue, then we do not need to render Paul's notion of the Law as a pedagogue so discontinuous with the topos of Law as educator which as Betz remarks was common from Plato on. On the other hand, there may be no doubt that Betz is correct that it is wrong to see here an argument that the Law prepared for the coming of Christ by educating people in that direction (Betz 1979, 177–78). The *mashal* in the beginning of chapter 4 completely disables such an interpretation. The pedagogue is not a teacher in the sense of one who prepares the child for adulthood but a guardian in the sense of one who keeps him or her out of trouble while waiting for adulthood. This does not, however, translate into such terms as "ugly" or "demonic" that Betz uses, nor to a notion that the pedagogue was sent to increase transgression!

> *"And because you are sons, God has sent the Spirit*
> *of his Son into our hearts, crying, 'Abba! Father!'"*

I mean that the heir, as long as he is a child, is no better than a slave, though he is the owner of all the estate; but he is under guardians and trustees until the date set by the father. So with us; when we were children, we were slaves to the elemental spirits of the universe. But when the time had fully come, God sent forth his Son, born of woman, born under the law, to redeem those who were under the law, so that we might receive adoption as sons. And because you are sons, God has sent the Spirit of his Son into our hearts, crying, "Abba! Father!" So through God you are no longer a slave but a son, and if a son then an heir.   (4:1–7)

Paul develops and interweaves here two themes that he has set forth, the metaphor of the pedagogue and the Galatians' memory of their baptism. He conjoins them through the slave-freeman antinomy of the baptismal formula by insisting that the child is alike in status to the slave. Further, the childhood image, which has until now only been used to explain the status of the Law, given 430 years after the promise and only temporary, is now used analogously to explain the situation of the Galatians under paganism. We, all of us, I as a Jew and you as pagans, we were all under the elemental spirits of the universe: You under the pagan gods and I under the Law. I wonder if Paul is thinking here of the verse in Deuteronomy 4:19, which seemingly ordains the stars as the proper worship of "The Nations." Thielman has, once more, made an attractive and simple alternative suggestion. He argues philologically that $\tau\grave{\alpha}\ \sigma\tauo\iota\chi\varepsilon\hat{\iota}\alpha\ \tauo\hat{\upsilon}$ $\kappa\acuteo\sigma\mu o\upsilon$, "the elements of the world," simply means the world itself, and the reason that Paul uses this "roundabout" term is that $\sigma\tauo\iota\chi\varepsilon\hat{\iota}\alpha$ is also used metaphorically for the "elements" as that which a child learns first in school, thus effectively continuing Paul's figure of a child's education and maturity (1989, 82).[27] But when we had grown up, then God the Father sent forth his son to redeem us born under the Law, that we—and you as well—might receive adoption as sons. Because you are also sons, at the baptismal ceremony God sent his spirit into our hearts, and we all cried out "Abba! Father!"

The explicit citation of the Aramaic usage alludes, I think, to two things: Jesus' own crying out of "Abba" to God and the traditionary pre-Pauline liturgy of the baptism. Therefore, through God, you (and we) have been recognized as a son, by entering into the spiritual body of the Son, and therefore no longer a slave but an heir. (See also Schweizer, in the *TDNT* VIII 391–92 and 399.) Paul's figure for the condition of Israel under the Law demonstrates beyond doubt, I think, that he does not hold the Law to be demonic or evil, or the commitment to keeping the Law to be contemnable in the way that the variations of the "Lutheran" interpretation would have it. This "slavery" is the benevolent and beneficial slavery of the child. It is for his own good. Only a fool, however—You foolish Galatians—would prefer to remain in such a state and not grow up into the status of heir. In an unpublished paper, David Henkin has analyzed this text brilliantly:

> Significantly, the elevation of the Christian to the status of son is not
> an adoption in the ordinary sense of a superimposition of a natural title

on someone who has no natural claim to the title. As the metaphor of the custodian (the *paidagogós*) in the preceding verses implies, the apocalyptic moment is one in which sons (who were always by nature sons, though their contingent historical position obscured this fact) are recognized and redeemed by their rightful father. The reshuffling of the lines of genealogy is presented here as an act of restoration. The historical signifiers that Jewish law prescribed to represent a kind of paternal bond with God are peeled away and sons are recognized by their father by virtue of their faith, which is to say by virtue of the capacity to recognize him as their father.   (Henkin 1991)

This, I think, provides the perfect summation of Paul's theology of Judaism and the Jews. They and their Law had literal value at a certain point in human history, in the childhood of humanity. However, now that maturity has come in the guise of the coming of Christ, his crucifixion, and his rising from the dead, the value of the signifier has been superseded. There is no more role for Israel as such in its concrete sense— except always for the promise of Romans 9–11 that in the end it will not be abandoned but redeemed by coming to faith in Christ. At stake is not Paul's love for Jews. I take very seriously his anguish in the beginning of Romans 9 over his brothers in the flesh. This very anguish, however, is precisely what signifies that as Jews—that is, as the historically understood concrete community of the flesh—Israel has no more role to play in history. A true parable may help make the point clearer. A Jewish friend of my family's was in the business of importing equipment for chicken farmers. As such, among his major customers were Anabaptists in Pennsylvania, with whom he became very friendly over a number of years. At one point, at a meal, the wife of his customer became distraught and began to cry. When asked why she was crying, she answered: Because Sidney is such a lovely person, and he is going to go to hell. I have no doubt that her love for Sidney was real—and specific, not merely abstract love for all human beings—just as was Paul's for his Jewish relatives. Nevertheless, it would be hard to claim that this woman valued Sidney, *as a Jew,* and this is my point about Paul. If the only value and promise afforded the Jews, even in Romans 11, is that in the end they will see the error of their ways, one cannot claim that there is a role for Jewish existence in Paul. It has been transcended by that which was its spiritual, allegorical referent always and forever: faith in Jesus Christ and the community of the faithful in which there is no Jew or Greek.

On my reading, then, it is totally inappropriate to think of Paul's thought as anti-Semitic, or even as anti-Judaic (except for perhaps the occasional outbursts of temper and frustration in 1 Thessalonians 2:14 [if genuine] and Philippians 3). Paul loves his relatives according to the flesh, anguishes over them, and is convinced that in the end they will be saved. This salvation, however, is precisely for those Jews a bitter gospel not a sweet one, because it is conditional precisely on abandoning that to which we hold so dearly, our separate cultural, religious identity, our own fleshy and historical practice, our existence according to the flesh, our Law, our difference. Paul has simply allegorized our difference quite out of existence.

PAUL'S ALLEGORIZATION
OF THE TORAH

He who loves his neighbor has fulfilled the Law.
Romans 13:8

To the ears of a rabbinic Jew, this statement sounds totally familiar but also totally discordant. It is of a piece with Galatians 5:14 discussed above and with such other Pauline statements as "neither circumcision counts for anything nor uncircumcision is anything but keeping the commandments of God" (1 Corinthians 7:19) or, even closer to home, "For in Christ Jesus neither circumcision nor uncircumcision is of any avail, but faith working through love" (Galatians 5:6). Romans 8:4, with its talk of the "just requirement of the law," also fits into this category. This is not an accident or a sport in Pauline discourse, therefore, but a very central moment. The "just requirement of the Law" is defined as one thing and one thing only: faith working through love. Moreover, here as elsewhere, Paul refers to "fulfilling the Law" and not to "doing" it. I have already observed this crucial distinction more than once.

Frank Thielman has tried very hard to bring this complex of Pauline texts close to some form of Judaism contemporary with Paul. He considers these passages as evidence that Paul "says straightforwardly that believers should keep the law," which from my point of view is an astonishing remark and one that simply swallows whole Paul's revolutionary redefinition of "the Law" (1989, 90; and see Barclay 1991, 135–36, who certainly understands the revolutionary implications of Paul's talk here). Thielman, of course, attempts to support this point of view by claiming:

Paul has, of course, defined obedience to the law in a way different from his Judaizing opponents. They took a strict attitude toward ob-

serving such particularly Jewish commands as circumcision whereas
Paul took a more liberal attitude toward these requirements (1 Cor
7:19, Gal. 6:15). Nonetheless, as we have seen in chapter three, the
argument between Paul and his opponents is not between a renegade
Paul who has redefined the law at will and normative Judaism, but, to
a large measure, between two Jewish ways of looking at the law.   (90)

This is simply not adequate for several reasons. First of all, such modern
terms as "strict" and "liberal" are entirely anachronistic in this context. If
the Torah is the word of God, as all Jews, including Paul, held, something
more than attitudes of strictness or liberality will be required in order to
distinguish between parts of God's word which are or are not valid or
binding. Secondly, since Paul is a Jew and since we no longer use such
terminology as "normative Judaism" outside of theological discourse, the
statement that the argument between Paul and his opponents is one of
two Jewish ways of looking at the Law is tautological and therefore empty
of content. The question is rather whether Paul's Jewish way of looking at
the Law is or is not part of larger movements of Jews of his time and how
the different Judaisms relate to each other typologically and historically.[28]

Thielman claims to have presented evidence that Paul's position was
not substantially different from that of other Jewish groups of his time.
This evidence, when examined, however simply does not hold up. "Thus
it is difficult," Thielman writes, "to see any great difference between what
Paul says in 5:14 and what Philo describes as the principle theme of ser-
mons heard in the synagogues of 'every city'":

> But among the vast number of particular truths and principles there
> studied, there stand out practically high above the others two main
> heads: one of duty to God as shewn by piety and holiness, one of duty
> to men as shewn by humanity and justice. . . . (*Spec. Leg.* 2.62–63
> [282]).   (Thielman 1989, 52)

I submit that Paul's doctrine has very little to do with what Philo's text
describes. Where Philo's preachers argue that these principles are the most
important of the Torah, this does not in any sense constitute a claim that
one has fulfilled the Torah by observing these principles while not, for
instance, circumcising male infants or observing the food laws and Sabbaths. To be sure, there apparently were Jews in Philo's world who thought
so, but in the passage I have discussed in Chapter 1, Philo himself rails
against such views:

> It is true that receiving circumcision does indeed portray the excision
> of pleasure and all passions, and the putting away of the impious con-

ceit, under which the mind supposed that it was capable of begetting by its own power: but let us not on this account repeal the law laid down for circumcising. Why, we shall be ignoring the sanctity of the Temple and a thousand other things, if we are going to pay heed to nothing except what is shewn us by the inner meaning of things.

To be sure, the point of the Law is to teach these "two main heads" of piety toward God and justice toward man, but for Philo, as for virtually anyone else calling him or herself Jewish at that time, as far as we know, this did not abrogate "particularly Jewish commands," and there were not, except perhaps in very minute groups, "two Jewish attitudes toward the Law." [29]

Nor are any of the other texts that Thielman cites any more convincing. Eleazar's argument in the Letter of Aristeas that the purpose of the peculiarly Jewish commandments is to be "symbolic reminders of the virtues by which the people of God should seek to order their lives: justice, peace and the contemplation of God" certainly does not bespeak the abrogation of those commandments, and neither the apologetics of a Pseudo-Phocylides nor the lack of mention of "ceremonial" commandments in the Testaments of the Twelve Patriarchs demonstrates any such notions of Judaism. What all of these texts do demonstrate is something that I am claiming from the very opening sentences of this book. Paul was troubled by something that troubled many Jews, particularly Greek-speaking Jews of the first century: the "special laws" of Judaism, those that marked off Jews from the rest of humanity. Even stories about the "Pharisees" encode this issue. Perhaps the most famous is the one of the gentile who came to Hillel to be taught the Torah while standing on one foot. Hillel, in accordance with his fashion, answered gently: "Do not do unto others what you hate done to yourself." But then he added: "Now go learn the rest!" It is that addition which Hillel (according to the story) makes and Paul does not which marks the Pauline off from virtually any other Jewish discourse. The others wish gentiles to appreciate Judaism, perhaps to join it; Paul wishes all humanity to become one unit in love working through faith in Christ. The "plight" was a common one; his solution, I maintain, was an uncommon one—although perhaps not unprecedented. [30]

There is a further very elegant argument that allegorization and spiritualization represented Paul's hermeneutic approach to the Law. I refer to 1 Corinthians 9:8–11, where Paul uses precisely an *allegorical* interpretation of a law in the Torah which he explicitly applies to the Christian situation:

> Do I say this on human authority [κατὰ ἄνθρωπον]? Does not the law say the same? For it is written in the law of Moses, "You shall not muzzle an ox when it is treading out the grain." Is it for oxen that God is concerned? Does he not speak entirely for our sake? It was written for our sake, because the plowman should plow in hope and the thresher thresh in hope of a share in the crop. If we have sown spiritual good [τὰ πνευματικὰ ἐσπείραμεν] among you, is it too much if we reap your fleshly benefits [τὰ σαρκικὰ θερίσομεν]?

Paul engages in a double spiritualizing move in interpreting the verse of the law. In the first place he explicitly denies that its literal sense—Do not muzzle an ox—is relevant at all. Indeed, one might ask whether, according to Paul, it is *forbidden* to muzzle an ox while it treads.[31] To this point, however, Paul's interpretation is not entirely unlike a fairly rare but attested midrashic move that reads certain halakhic verses as metaphors for something else. Thus, for example, the verse of Leviticus which prohibits placing a stumbling block before the blind is understood by the Rabbis as a prohibition on aiding someone to sin. Paul's next move, however, seems to me to leave midrash behind and enter allegory, namely his re-reading of the grain which is trodden as "spiritual good," suggesting also the familiar hermeneutic antinomy of the spiritual and the physical as well. It follows that even though Paul refers to the Law as an authority here, this is the Law as understood κατὰ πνεῦμα, in accord with its spiritual sense and not its literal, physical sense.[32]

By understanding that the Law according to the flesh was the signifier of an allegorical Law of love according to the spirit, and that those, *including ethnic Jews,* who received the spirit were absolved of the requirements of the Law according to the flesh, Paul was not apologizing for Jewish Law and particularity, for Jewish difference, like the other Hellenistic Jewish writers cited, but *annulling* Jewish difference (Dunn 1988, 89). "Remain as I am, for I have become as you are" (Galatians 4:12). In the pathos of this verse is the center of Paul's ministry. He has given up his specific Jewish identity in order to merge his essence into the essence of the gentile Christians and create the new spiritual People of God. If they now turn away from this transumption into the allegorical and become Jewish Christians, they will have thereby lowered themselves and left Paul alone. The entire force of his apocalypse will have been annulled. It is difficult for me to understand how scholars can assume that Paul remained Law-observant given this verse. The entire continuation of this passage through verse 20 can easily be understood in the light of this interpretation. The theme of exclusion and inclusion that Paul develops in verse 17 is central and refers once more to inclusion in and exclusion from the Jewish People, and this leads with perfect naturalness into the allegory of Ishmael and Hagar, perhaps the biblical text that most explicitly thematized exclusion. For Paul, the only possibility for human equality involved human sameness. Difference was the threat. If Paul is not the origin of anti-Semitism (and I hold that he is not), it may certainly be fairly said that he is the origin of the "Jewish Question."

The upshot of the above discussion is that there is no evidence in Galatians, on my reading, that Paul's problem with the Law was connected with the impossibility of keeping the Law fully, or that the Law was given in order to increase sin so that grace might abound more fully. The Law was rather given to the Jews, as a temporary measure for specific historical reasons, meant to be superseded by its spiritual referent, faith, when the time would come, which, of course, it has. Paul's argument is not anti-Judaic, then, in the sense that certain interpretations of it would have it be. It is not a claim that God has rejected the Jews because they were inadequate in some sense or another, not an assertion that their keeping of the Law was a striving against God!, an attempt to force God to justify them, a form of boasting, self-righteousness, and pride, a religion of Sacred Violence, or any of the other variations of this essentially anti-Judaic topos. The Jews as concrete signifier of the fulfilled spiritual signified, the body of Christ, the Church, had simply outlived their usefulness. They stood in the world now only as the sign of something else. They had been allegorized out of real historical existence, and their concrete, separate existence and cultural difference were now vestigial, excepting only the faithful promise that in the end God would keep His promise to them, and they would be redeemed—as Christians. Paul's hermeneutic of the Jews as signifier of the faithful body of Christians, of the Jews as the literal—κατὰ σάρκα—of which Christians are the allegorical signified, κατὰ πνεῦμα, even if not the "origin of anti-Semitism," certainly has effects in the world until this day. In other words, I argue that while Galatians is not an anti-Judaic text, its theory of the Jews nevertheless is one that is inimical to Jewish difference, indeed to all difference as such.[33]

For the rest of this book, I am going to begin to explore how the "Jewish Question" and the "Woman Question" are related historically and typologically in Paul. I will be developing my suggestion that both of these "problems" for western culture are produced by the same metaphysical commitments to an ideal One—logos and phallus—and thus that allegory, the mode of reading which desires to transcend the material differences of language in search of its ideal logos, is essentially, paradigmatically, imbricated in these cultural politics.

7

Brides of Christ

*Jewishness and the Pauline Origins
of Christian Sexual Renunciation*

ROMANS 5–8
AND THE FAMILY OF GRACE

Romans 5–8 is often held to be a digression in the argument about the
status of Israel carried on in Romans 1–4 and 9–11. Another line of
interpretation and theology regards these chapters as the real center of
Romans and all the rest as ancillary material. Recently N. T. Wright has
argued that these chapters carry on in a direct way the argument of 1–4
and lead directly in turn into 9–11 (1992a, 193–230). "It is the continuation of the same argument, the necessary bridge between the discussion of
the family of Abraham defined by faith in Jesus Christ (3.21–4.25) and
the family of Abraham defined by grace not race (9–11)" (194). In general, I agree with both this point and some aspects of the particular interpretation that Wright gives as well. He writes:

> The position Paul is arguing, just as in Galatians 3, is that the Torah
> has not alleviated, but rather has exacerbated, the plight of Adamic
> humanity. This can only mean that the recipients of the Torah, i.e.
> Israel, have found themselves to be under its judgment because of their
> participation in Adamic humanity. Since therefore Christians have left
> the realm of the παλαιὸς ἄνθρωπος in baptism, they have also left
> the realm of Torah, coming out from the place where it could exert a
> hold over them. (195)

I absolutely concur in this interpretation, which accounts for much of
the language of these chapters. But I dissent from, or rather offer an alternative to, Wright's interpretation of what this means in terms of Paul's
religious world view.[1] Wright argues that the essential point of Romans 7
is that the Torah has had the function of concentrating sin in Israel, so
that the Christ, Redeemer of Israel, could redeem the whole world as

well.[2] What I will propose in this chapter is that the Torah has exacer-
bated the plight of Adamic humanity essentially because of one provision
it contains, and not because of its character as law as such. This Law,
which Paul refers to in verse 23 as "an Other Law" (ἕτερος νόμος), is the
command to procreate, and the desire that it produces in the members.[3]
Dealing with this command is the necessary bridge that Paul must build
between the family of Israel defined by race and that defined by grace,
since for old Israel procreation as the means of continuation of God's
People was *the* central and highest of goods and of religious values, but at
the same time, for Israel by the first century sexuality had become thoroughly anxiety-ridden and guilty as well (Biale 1992, 39–40). Many Jews
of the first century had a sense that they were commanded by God to do
that which God himself considered sinful.

Sexuality and Sin in First-Century Judaism

The Palestinian Judaism of Paul's time was strongly dualist in mood and
at best powerfully ambivalent about sexuality.[4] In *The Testament of the
Twelve Patriarchs*, a Hellenistic Jewish text from Palestine dated to some-
time approximately in the late second century B.C., each human being is
inhabited by a "good spirit" and an "evil spirit." The evil spirit is explicitly
defined as sexuality and opposed by a good spirit, which is anti-sexual:
"And the spirits of error have no power over him [the genuine man], *since
he does not include feminine beauty in the scope of his vision*" (Kee 1983, 803).
"For the person with a mind that is pure with love does not look on a
woman for the purpose of having sexual relations" (Kee 1983, 827).[5]
Other passages in this same text also indicate an extremely anxious affect
around sexuality. The text speaks of seven "good spirits" inhabiting human beings. Of these,

> the sixth is the spirit of taste for consuming food and drink; by it
> comes strength, because in food is the substance of strength. The sev-
> enth is the spirit of procreation and intercourse, with which come sins
> through fondness for pleasure. For this reason, it was the last in the
> creation and the first in youth, because it is filled with ignorance; it
> leads the young person like a blind man into a ditch and like an ani-
> mal over a cliff. With these are commingled the spirits of error. First
> the spirit of promiscuity resides in the nature and the senses. A second
> spirit of insatiability, in the stomach.   (782–85)

The distinction between the spirit of taste for food and the spirit of pro-creation is striking. Although both are listed among the good spirits, the former contributes strength to the body. We would expect, therefore, that the clause on "the spirit of procreation and intercourse" would similarly continue; "by it comes the continuation of the race, because in intercourse the race is maintained." But instead we read, "with which come sins through fondness for pleasure." While the spirit of taste is commingled with a spirit of insatiability, the spirit of intercourse induces to sin, even before being commingled with the spirit of promiscuity. Philo, famously, expresses himself similarly. There may be no question, then, that Helle-nistic Judaism, including in Palestine, had developed extremely pessimis-tic notions of sexuality. The clearest expression of this Palestinian Jewish negative affect around sexuality is, of course, the term יצר הרע itself, the evil inclination as a near synonym for sexual desire.[6]

In a thinking person, such judgments would inevitably have been in powerful conflict, indeed creating a sort of double bind, with the command-ment to procreate. The fact that sexuality, the יצר הרע, is the agent of the first positive commandment in the Torah is an irony that neither Paul nor the Rabbis could escape. The very efforts which the Rabbis were to make a century or two later to overcome the negative encoding of sexual-ity and desire as ipso facto evil provide eloquent testimony to the strength and problematicity of this ideology of sex for a community insisting on the unqualified goodness of procreation, owing to the doctrine of the holiness of its physical existence (Boyarin 1993, 61–64). The Rabbis for their part heavily ironized the notion of the Evil Instinct through paradoxical for-mulations, such as calling the Evil Instinct "very good" (Boyarin 1993, 167–96). Paul, I suggest, found a different way out. Through readings of three Pauline texts—Romans 5–8, 1 Corinthians 6, and Galatians 5–6—I hope to make a case that for Paul encratism was the ideal, procreation of no value whatsoever, and marriage indeed merely a defense against desire for the weak. The politics of this move, of course, are intimately bound up in the transcession of Israel according to the flesh by its spiritual signified.

THE LAW AS STIMULUS TO SIN

In Romans 5:12–14, Paul explicitly discusses Adam and draws a distinc-tion between his sin and the sin of all others from Adam to Moses:

Therefore as sin came into the world through one man and death through sin, and so death spread to all men because all men sinned— sin indeed was in the world before the law was given, but sin is not counted where there is no law. Yet death reigned from Adam to Moses, even over those whose sins were not like the transgression of Adam, who was a type of the one who was to come.

Although the wording is somewhat confusing, I think that very important points can nonetheless be derived from this passage. Paul is making a distinction between "sin" on the one hand and "transgression" on the other. Adam's transgression was correctly accounted to him, because he had been given a law: the law, of course, forbidding him to eat of the tree of knowledge.[7] Sin is separate from the Law. It is not caused by the Law; all men sin and the (natural?) consequence is death, even for those for whom sin cannot be accounted, because their "sins are not [accountable because they are not] like the transgression of Adam." Adam ends up here being prototypical of two human groups: those who have the Law and thereby are subject to have their transgressions accounted (Jews) and those who are affected by unaccountable sin but nevertheless die as a result of it (gentiles).[8] "Adam's sin was παράβασις obviously = 'sin accounted' since it was an act of disobedience to what he knew to be a command of God" (Dunn 1988, 276). Paul is at pains that we realize that even without accounting, sin itself nevertheless results in death, so that even those who have not sinned as Adam did—that is, even those who do not know the Law—are in exactly the same situation as those who know the Law. Paul's overall theme in Romans that Jews and non-Jews are *in exactly the same situation* is thus well supported by this argument. Paul is further counteracting, however, a Jewish argument or attitude which we have already seen him critiquing in Romans 2, namely, the attitude that having the Law provides some sort of immunity to sin or redemption from sin. This is the source of his assertion here and below that having the Law makes sin greater, not lesser. "God's purpose for the law was not to distinguish Jewish righteous from gentile sinners, but to make Israel more conscious of its solidarity in sin with the rest of Adam's offspring" (Dunn 1988, 286).

The only way to understand verse 20, "Law came in to increase the trespass," is in context, in reference to Adam—one man's trespass—so Adam is clearly here the type of the Jew, human being under the Law.[9] The content of this verse is interpretable in two ways, neither of them, at any rate, nearly so antithetical to rabbinic theologoumena as the Reformation tradition would have it. Either the knowledge of that which is forbidden increases culpability, or having the knowledge of that which is forbidden increases the desire to sin.[10] Either way, the point is that Jews cannot claim any privilege, because they have the Law. Having the Law makes their salvation more difficult, not easier. Paul is fighting against a Jewish theology—held by some, not all, first-century Jews—which argues that just having the Law provides a privileged place in salvation for the Jews.

THE "LAW OF SIN
IN OUR MEMBERS" IS SEX

Starting from the assumption that Romans 7 continues Romans 5, I want to propose that the entire discourse about Law and commandment in this section of Romans has to do with sexuality. Of all the myriad interpretations that have been offered for the soliloquy of chapter 7, the one that makes the most sense to me, for all its problems, is the interpretation that the speaker of these verses is Adam. Watson has recently presented a strong argument in support of this reading.[11] He presents a series of detailed comparisons between the speaker of Romans 7:7 ff. and Adam:

1. Only Adam was alive before any commandment was given (v. 9).
2. The commandment not to eat of the fruit of the tree of knowledge came and gave Sin (the Serpent) an opportunity to bring death to Adam (v. 9).
3. "Sin deceived me" (ἐξηπάτησεν) is the same term that Eve uses to describe what happened to her, namely, that the Serpent "deceived me" (ἠπάτησεν με) (v. 11; cf. Gen. 3:13).
4. The result of the transgression is death, so "the very commandment which promised life proved to be death to me." (Watson, 152)

Westerholm and other scholars had already rejected this interpretation, arguing that "You shall not covet" refers to the prohibition in the Decalogue and not to Adam (1988, 59).[12] Watson, however, completely finesses this objection by interpreting the negative command involved as *both* the commandment to Adam not to eat of the fruit of the tree of knowledge and the command against desire in the Decalogue. They are, as I shall suggest below, in a sort of type/anti-type situation. He is thus not constrained to ignore the obvious allusion to the Decalogue in the chapter in order to maintain his reading that the speaker is Adam, for

Adam's commandment is a type of the commandment to all—In Adam, all have sinned.[13] This argument that Paul could appropriately use the verse of the Ten Commandments as a sort of catchword referring to Adam's sin can be further strengthened. First of all, the commandment in the Decalogue refers precisely to sexual lust. In the version of Deuteronomy, this is the entire content of the verse: Thou shalt not desire thy neighbor's wife (οὐκ ἐπιθυμήσεις τὴν γυναῖκα τοῦ πλησίον σου). To be sure, the verse goes on, in a separate sentence, to list other objects of one's neighbor that one should not covet as well. Furthermore, in the version in Exodus 20:17, where the Hebrew reads: Thou shalt not desire thy neighbor's house or his wife, the Greek has οὐκ ἐπιθυμήσεις τὴν γυναῖκα τοῦ πλησίον σου as the first item and as a separate sentence, precisely as in the Deuteronomy version. It is thus entirely plausible that Paul has the sentence "Do not desire the woman—of your neighbor" in mind when he cites οὐκ ἐπιθυμήσεις. This verse of the Decalogue is the only negative commandment in the whole Torah that refers to desire and not to an action. It is thus the very anti-type, as it were, of the prohibition on Adam, if that prohibition is understood, as it most often was, as a prohibition against sexual desire (Wright 1992a, 197). Furthermore, as Watson argues:

> The serpent's use of the commandment to deceive leads to sin: "Sin . . .
> wrought in me every kind of desire" (Rom. 7:8). . . . "Desire" means
> primarily sexual desire, and this may be linked with Gen. 3:7: "Then
> the eyes of both were opened, and they knew that they were naked;
> and they sewed fig leaves together and made themselves aprons." This
> suggests that the "sin" of v. 6 was sexual in nature, and for this reason
> Paul can identify the commandment of Gen. 2:17 with the command-
> ment, "You shall not desire," just as he can identify the transgression
> of the commandment in Gen. 3:6 f with the awakening of "every kind
> of desire" (Rom. 7:7 f). (Watson, 152)

Watson's argument can be amplified. The story that Paul tells in verses 8 and 11—"But sin, seizing an opportunity in the commandment, produced in me all kinds of desire. Apart from the law sin lies dead. . . . For sin, seizing an opportunity in the commandment, deceived me and through it killed me"—seems most specifically intelligible as a gloss on the Genesis story. It was indeed the serpent (= sin) in that story who by subtly manipulating the terms of the prohibition caused Eve and Adam to eat the fruit and die. "Now the serpent was more subtle than any beast of the field which the Lord God had made. And he said unto the woman,

Yea, hath God said, Ye shall not eat of every tree of the garden? And the woman said unto the serpent, We may eat of the fruit of the trees of the garden: But of the fruit of the tree which is in the midst of the garden, God hath said, Ye shall not eat of it, neither shall ye touch it, lest ye die. And the serpent said unto the woman, Ye shall not surely die." Here we indeed see sin seizing an opportunity in the commandment! It thus seems to me that this reading makes the best specific and sharp sense of Paul's first-person narrative. Thus, although Westerholm's objection cannot be dismissed entirely, the other strong considerations in favor of Watson's interpretation should lead us to consider it very favorably. I believe that the speaker of Romans 7 is indeed Adam, the same Adam of whom Paul speaks in chapter 5.

If we take seriously the suggestion that the speaker here is Adam and that what he is speaking of is sexual desire, I think that we must also take into consideration the fact that Adam and Eve had been positively commanded to "Be fruitful and multiply." In my opinion, only the interpretation that Paul is speaking of sexual lust, inflamed by the positive commandment to procreate, which "Sin" does indeed know how to exploit, accounts for such expressions as the "Law of Sin in our members" and all the talk here of inflamed passions.[14] Sexual desire was referred to among Jews in the first century unambiguously as the יצר הרע, the Evil Inclination. As David Biale has written, "For other writers of the time, sexuality was dangerous because even if it began licitly, it could, once aroused, slide all too easily into sin" (1992, 40). This is how Sin has used the commandment to procreate in order to arouse sinful desire (Watson 1986, 152).

SIN AND THE LAW

It follows that Paul would be making a much stronger statement—but also a much more "localized" one—about the relation between sin and the Law. If the sin of Adam and Eve was sexual—either the discovery of sexuality itself or a change in the nature of sexuality—, a view that was held throughout much if not most of ancient interpretation—then it was the positive commandment to have children that led them into it, through the occasion of Sin's (the Serpent's) manipulations. They had been commanded to procreate but also to avoid sexual desire. No wonder that the Serpent (Sin) was able to exploit the commandment to cause them to sin! Within any interpretation that begins with the assumption that sexuality is sinful, as it certainly was for many Jews and Christians in late antiquity, the blessing of procreation is going to be a logical and hermeneutical conundrum, as witness the myriad difficulties of the Church Fathers in sorting out the sequence of events here (Anderson 1989).

Adam's double bind, commanded on the one hand to procreate and on the other to avoid eating of the fruit of the tree of (carnal) knowledge, is the type of Jewish humanity under the flesh, commanded to procreate but also to not have lustful desires, let alone act on them. The Christian, however, having been released from procreation and thus from sexuality, can conquer her desires and bear fruit for God. On this reading, Paul's references to "bearing fruit," καρποφορήσωμεν, whether for God, i.e., spiritual fruit in verse 4, or for death, i.e., children in verse 5, are precisely an allusion to the commandment: Be fruitful and multiply, of Genesis 1:28.[15]

CHILDREN AS FRUIT FOR DEATH

However we understand the soliloquy of Romans 7, I think a strong case can be made for the interpretation that Paul's theme in this chapter is sexuality and redemption from it, as from the flesh through Christ's crucifixion, which make possible the crucifixion of the flesh in everyman. Paul opens chapter 7 with the analogy of the married woman whose husband dies:

> Do you know brethren—for I am speaking to those who know the law—
> that the law is binding on a person only during his life. Thus a married
> woman is bound by law to her husband as long as he lives; but if her
> husband dies she is discharged from the law concerning her husband.
> Accordingly, she will be called an adulteress if she lives with another
> man while her husband is alive. But if her husband dies she is free
> from that law, and if she married another man she is not an adulteress.
> Likewise, my brethren, you have died to the law through the body of
> Christ, so that you may belong to another, to him who has been raised
> from the dead in order that we may bear fruit for God.   (7:1–4)

This parable or analogy has often been regarded as clumsy by even the most friendly of Pauline interpreters. Typical is Stephen Westerholm: "The analogy is not the most perspicuous in the literature" (1988, 206). The problem with the analogy is that Paul's parable is of a woman no longer subject to the law of adultery because her husband has died, but its application is about one who is no longer married because she herself has died. There seems to be a lack of fit. This slippage between parable and application is, however, rather typical of the parabolic structure. In the parable itself, which refers to actual human life, obviously it is the husband who must die, for otherwise his wife could not remarry. However, in the application of the parable, the Christian reality, within which, as Paul argues in chapter 6, the believer dies to one kind of life and is reborn to another, even within this world and this body, the wife through dying becomes released from her obligations to her former husband and is free to marry again. Christians, having died to their first husband, the Law, are brides of Christ, married to him, in order that they may bear fruit for God. It is indeed the Christian who dies *to* the Law—not the Law which dies—, but the result is equivalent to the Law having died in that the Christian is no longer an adulteress if she does not live faithfully to the Law but joins herself only to Christ.

The parable's erotic overtones, moreover, are not accidental but absolutely crucial, on my reading, to the whole context, for what has died to the Law is the fleshiness, the being in the flesh, which required the pursuit of an act which bore fruit not for God but for death. The choice of the marital analogy is exact, because being tied to the Law meant the obligation to marry and bear children that the Law enjoins in its command to be fruitful and multiply. No longer married to the Law, since they have died to the flesh—meaning both the fleshly, literal meaning of the commandment and the use of the flesh that it implies and enjoins—, Christians belong to Christ—sexually, as it were, so that as his brides they bear "fruit for God," spiritual children.

Romans 7:5–6 repeat this precise argument in nonparabolic language:

> When we were in the flesh, our sinful passions, aroused by the law, were at work in our members to bear fruit for death. But now we are discharged from the law, dead to that which held us captive, so that we serve not under the old written code but in the new life of the Spirit.

> ὅτε γὰρ ἦμεν ἐν τῇ σαρκί, τὰ παθήματα τῶν ἁμαρτιῶν τὰ διὰ τοῦ νόμου ἐνηργεῖτο ἐν τοῖς μέλεσιν ἡμῶν, εἰς τὸ καρποφορῆσαι τῷ θανάτῳ. νυνὶ δὲ κατηργήθημεν ἀπὸ τοῦ νόμου ἀποθανόντες ἐν ᾧ κατειχόμεθα ὥστε δουλεύειν ἡμᾶς ἐν καινότητι πνεύματος καὶ οὐ παλαιότητι γράμματος

These verses raise several questions: (1) What is the meaning of being "in the flesh"? (2) What is the connection between that fleshly condition and being under the Law? (3) Why does the Law arouse sinful passions? (4) How is being freed of the Law going to prevent the arousal of sinful passions?

There is, in effect, a single answer to all of these questions. Paul speaks of a situation in which "we were still in the flesh," which is the antithesis to having died to the Law. In other words, then, being in the flesh is equivalent to being alive to the Law. This is best understood if "the flesh" is taken to refer to the letter of the Law together with all of its associated fleshinesses: generation and filiation. Being alive to the Law, that is, serving in the old being of the letter—Be fruitful and multiply—, arouses sinful passions in our members to bear fruit for death, that is to have children and thus to participate in the whole disaster of human mortality. In the new life of the spirit, however, even that most fleshly commandment to procreate will be understood in its spiritual sense, namely, as a commandment to spiritual procreation, to that which bears fruit for God and not for death.

Serving under the old written code includes the positive commandment to be fruitful and multiply—the very first commandment in the Torah—, as well as the first negative commandment not to desire (Paul's midrashic gloss, on my hypothesis, on being forbidden to eat of the fruit). Prescribed procreation leads inevitably to forbidden sexuality, and the whole process to the bearing of fruit for death. It is no wonder that Paul, given this set of assumptions, will speak of the law in the second part of Romans 7 as presenting an impossible dilemma, indeed a double bind. Do have sex, in order to bear children, but do not have desire. Dying to the law through the body of Christ relieves one of the obligation to produce children—"fruit for death"—and thus frees one to bear only spiritual fruit, fruit for God.

THE FRUITS OF THIS
INTERPRETATION: ROMANS 6 AND 8

Whether or not the specifics of this interpretation of Romans 7 as Adam midrash bear fruit and multiply, it nevertheless seems to me to be a highly plausible, if not ineluctable, line of interpretation that sees Paul's focus here as on sexuality and the contrast that he is drawing between fleshly life, with its getting of children, and spiritual life, where the propagation is of spiritual fruits for God. One of the ways of testing a new interpretation of a text is, of course, to observe that it renders clear other aspects of its context that were otherwise difficult to understand. Observing the thematic that I have hypothesized for chapter 7 will help us to solve several interpretative conundra in chapters 6 and 8.

The analogies between the nexus of Law and desire in Romans 7:5–6 and the similar one of 6:12–14 are obvious, and we are justified, therefore, in seeing these verses as glossing each other.[16] Here, however, as in the parable that opens chapter 7, there seem to be the same paradoxes about who is dead and who alive:

> We know that our old man was crucified with him so that the sinful body might be destroyed.

> τοῦτο γινώσκοντες ὅτι ὁ παλαιὸς ἡμῶν ἄνθρωπος ουνεσταυ-
> ρώθη, ἵνα καταργηθῇ τὸ σῶμα τῆς ἁμαρτίας.   (6:6)

Paul, having just argued that Christians have been crucified and died, now argues that they have been brought from death to life:

> Do not let sin therefore reign in your mortal bodies, to make you obey their passions. Do not yield your members to sin as instruments of wickedness, but yield yourselves to God as men *who have been brought from death to life,* and your members to God as instruments of righteousness. *For sin will have no dominion over you, since you are not under law but under grace.*

> Μὴ οὖν βασιλευέτω ἡ ἁμαρτία ἐν τῷ θνητῷ ὑμῶν σώματι εἰς τὸ
> ὑπακούειν ταῖς ἐπιθυμίαις αὐτοῦ. μηδὲ παριστάνετε τὰ μέλη
> ὑμῶν ὅπλα ἀδικίας τῇ ἁμαρτίᾳ, ἀλλὰ παραστήσατε ἑαυτοὺς
> τῷ θεῷ ὡσεὶ ἐκ νεκρῶν ζῶντας καὶ τὰ μέλη ὑμῶν ὅπλα δικαιο-
> σύνης τῷ θεῷ. ἁμαρτία γὰρ ὑμῶν οὐ κυριεύσει οὐ γάρ ἐστε ὑπὸ
> νόμον ἀλλὰ ὑπὸ χάριν.   (6:12–14)

There are two cruxes here. The first is the apparently self-contradictory account of the relation of life to death. On the one hand, Christians are enjoined to die with Christ; on the other, they have been brought from death to life. In other words, they have participated in both the death and the resurrection of Christ. But the Christians to whom Paul is speaking are still alive, and in the same bodies they were always in. Paul is speaking, in the past tense, of that which has already happened to Christians, not of future expectation. Second, how is the non-obedience to one's passions equivalent to not being under Law, or even more sharply, how can sin have no dominion over you because you are not under Law? These two interpretative cruxes may both be solved according to the present line of interpretation that precisely the body of sin of which Paul speaks is the sexual body. Thus Christians have through the crucifixion died to a certain mode of living and progressed to another mode of living, *both of which are, however, available in this life.* I interpret this as a reference to a life which is responsible to the needs of the flesh, a fleshy life, the life of procreation, on the one hand, and a life that is dedicated to spiritual pursuits on the other. Christians have already died to the life of the body; they are no longer engaged in the getting of children together with its messy entanglements in passion, heat, jealousy—all that later Christian writers will refer to as concupiscence—which all lead to death. Rather, having been freed from "all of that," they have been brought from a condition of physical death to a condition of spiritual life. This answers, moreover, the second question as well, for it is the Torah, the Jewish Law, which enjoins the procreation of children and thus directly and necessarily stirs the passions. In other words, literally by being not under Law, that is by not being obligated to procreate, the Christian is freed from the dominion of sinful passion, that is free to remove sexuality from her person, and thus able to free herself from being under sin.

Chapter 8 continues the theme of the immortality granted those who abandon the birth and death cycle from which Christ, through his birth and death, has freed them. The hypothesis that I have offered enables us to make sense of at least one passage which has been hardly intelligible until now, verses 9 through 13:

> But you are not in the flesh, you are in the Spirit, if the Spirit of God really dwells in you. Any one who does not have the Spirit of Christ does not belong to him. But if Christ is in you, although your bodies are dead because of sin, your spirits are alive because of righteousness. If the Spirit of him who raised Jesus from the dead, dwells within you, he who raised Christ Jesus from the dead will give life to your mortal bodies also through his Spirit which dwells in you. *So then, brethren, we are debtors, not to the flesh, to live according to the flesh—for if you live according to the flesh you will die, but if by the Spirit you put to death the deeds of the body you will live.* (8:9–13)
>
> Ἄρα οὖν, ἀδελφοί, ὀφειλέται ἐσμὲν οὐ τῇ σαρκὶ τοῦ κατὰ σάρκα ζῆν, εἰ γὰρ κατὰ σάρκα ζῆτε, μέλλετε ἀποθνῄσκειν εἰ δὲ πνεύματι τὰς πράξεις τοῦ σώματος θανατοῦτε, ζήσεσθε. (8:12–13)

These verses have caused interpreters no end of trouble. Now it is particularly the last two (italicized) verses that have caused the trouble. What does Paul mean by saying that Christians are under an obligation, but not one of the flesh? Some commentators assume an otherwise totally un-known and unalluded to gnostic sect in Rome that had practiced obliga-tory libertinism. According to my reading, we need assume no bizarre gnostic obligations to libertinism behind this verse. If we assume that "the flesh" here means the fleshly obligations of the Law, *both* their literal sense *and* the fact that they are concerned with the flesh, then the answer is clear. "Obligated to the flesh" in 8:12 means simply the obligation to procreate. Christians have obligations, but they do not have the obliga-tion of keeping the fleshy commandments of the Torah and particularly, I think, in this context, the commandment to procreate, to which Paul refers as "deeds of the body."

Adam's situation is the situation of the Jews. As Dunn and others have pointed out, then, "when we were in the flesh" must mean simply "in our pre-Christian state," when we considered membership in the literal Israel *according to the flesh* (1 Corinthians 10:18) as decisive for salvation and propagation of the race as a central value and also when we were alive in our fleshly bodies and subject to the Law, before we died to the Law.[17] If you continue in that mode of existence, then you will die, "but if by the Spirit you put to death the deeds of the body [sex and procreation] you will live" (8:13). He furthermore repeats this point at the end of the letter, when he writes, "But put on the Lord Jesus Christ, and make no provision for the flesh that desires be aroused [εἰς ἐπιθυμίας]" (13:14), which ought, on my hypothesis, to be glossed: Be baptized into the body of Christ and the new family of the spirit and make no provision for physi-cal progeny, which provision necessitates the arousal of desires! Dying to the Law in baptism is functionally identical to the baptism of converts into Judaism who are also understood as having died to their old existence and been reborn to a new one, and it is precisely this understanding of baptism that Paul is employing.[18] Paul and the other (formerly Jewish) Christians are no longer "in the flesh" and are thus freed of the conse-quences of being in the flesh.

BRIDES OF CHRIST:
1 CORINTHIANS 6

The topos of spiritual propagation as opposed to and higher than physical procreation is well-known in Paul's world. Found already in Plato's *Sym-posium*,[19] it is also frequently mobilized in Philo, Paul's Jewish contemporary, most notably in his description of the life of the celibate Therapeutae (Harrison, forthcoming). According to my reading, Paul in Romans 6 and 7 also opposes a physical sexuality to a spiritual, that is, allegorical, sexuality. This reading can be strengthened by noting that the same antithesis occurs in 1 Corinthians 6:14–20:

> And God raised the Lord and will also raise us up by his power. Do you not know that your bodies are members of Christ? Shall I therefore take the members of Christ and make them members of a prostitute? Never! Do you not know that he who joins himself to a prostitute becomes one body with her? For, as it is written, "The two shall become one." But he who is united with the Lord becomes one spirit with him. Shun immorality. Every other sin which a man commits is outside the body; but the immoral man sins aginst his own body. Do you not know that your body is a temple of the Holy Spirit within you, which you have from God? You are not your own; you were bought with a price. So glorify God in your body.

The argument in verses 15–16 ("Do you not know . . .") seems strikingly inconsequent, in that it skips from the immorality of sex with a prostitute right over to union with Christ. Moreover, the verse cited, "And the two shall become one," refers in Genesis entirely positively to sexual union between man and wife. I would certainly expect to read here: "Do you know that he who joins himself to a prostitute becomes one body with her? For, as it is written, 'The two shall become one.' But he who is united with his wife becomes one flesh with her. Shun immorality." I think, therefore, that Paul is truly revealing his hand here. For him, sexuality per se is tainted with immorality.[20] Paul looks forward to the becoming-one-flesh of Genesis being entirely replaced by an allegorical becoming-one-spirit with Christ. He proposes displacing this commandment, as well as the commandment to be fruitful and multiply, by their spiritual referents of marriage to Christ and the bearing of fruits of the spirit. Here, however, Paul makes the point not openly but indirectly, through what he does not say, because immediately below he is going to recommend legitimate marital sex for those not gifted as he is with the ability ro remain celibate and who would therefore be in danger of porneia were they not married.[21] Paul says as much openly in 7:1, "It is well for a man not to touch a woman," and 7:7, "I wish that all were as I myself am. But each has his own special gift from God."[22] The value system is crystal clear. It is thus manifest from these verses that the modes of sexuality Paul contrasts are not so much sex with prostitutes as opposed to legitimate sexual intercourse but rather physical union between men and women as opposed to spiritual union between people and Christ.

But what, however, of Paul's dual insistence here on the body as members of Christ and as a temple for the spirit? Neither of these expressions seems in any way a manifestation of an ascetic contempt for the flesh. Paying close attention to this inconsequence in Paul's argument gives us another moment of access to the very special Pauline anthropology that I have explored elsewhere with reference to 1 Corinthians 15 and 2 Corinthians 5. As in those passages, Paul is at great pains to disable those strains of thought—perhaps proto-gnostic—that would claim that the body is of no significance and in radical platonic fashion only to be escaped from and denied. For Paul, not only will there be a body of resurrection, but the body in this life is to be honored and paid its due by keeping it pure and holy. He is alive always to the danger that by devaluing the flesh and its works—positive and negative—he is making room for a libertinism that will achieve the precise opposite of his intention. Thus he must insist both that the body is temple of the spirit and that the Christian in his [sic] body is a member of Christ—but precisely that membership in Christ anticipates the resurrection body which is not a body of flesh. Paul thus distinguishes between the flesh and the body. The flesh, i.e., sexuality, has been dispensed with in the Christian dispensation, precisely in order to spiritualize the body. To be sure, a legitimated marital sexuality is allowed for in Paul's system as the second-best alternative to celibacy, but the ideal is a spiritual union as bride of Christ in which he who "is united with the Lord becomes *one spirit* with him" and not *one flesh* with even his lawful wife. Indeed the connection between chapters 6 and 7 of Corinthians is now much clearer.

WORKS OF THE FLESH
IN GALATIANS 5–6

The same concatenation of themes occurs in Galatians 5–6 as in 1 Corinthians 6, namely, the death and resurrection of Christ which is opposed to the fleshy or sexual nature of humans:

> For you were called to freedom, brethren; only do not use your freedom as an opportunity for the flesh, but through love be servants of one another. For the whole law is fulfilled in one word, "You shall love your

neighbor as yourself." But if you bite and devour one another take heed
that you are not consumed by one another. But I say, walk by the Spirit,
and do not gratify the desires of the flesh. For the desires of the flesh
are against the Spirit, and the desires of the Spirit are against the flesh;
for these are opposed to each other, to prevent you from doing what
you would. But if you are led by the Spirit you are not under the law.
Now the works of the flesh are plain: immorality, impurity, licentiousness, idolatry, sorcery, enmity, strife, jealousy, anger, selfishness, dissension, party spirit, envy, drunkenness, carousing, and the like. . . .
But the fruit of the Spirit is love, joy, peace, patience, kindness, goodness, faithfulness, gentleness, self-control, against such there is no law.
And those who belong to Christ Jesus have crucified the flesh with its
passions and desires.   (5:13–24)

In my view these verses make quite clear the connection of the "paranetic" passage in the last two chapters of Galatians to the first four chapters of the letter.[23] I think they strongly support the point of view that
this part of the letter comes to correct a possible (and very plausible)
misunderstanding of Paul's views as expressed in the rest of the text. Paul
has throughout the letter been presenting a ringing call to Christian freedom in the spirit, as opposed to the Jewish bondage to the norms of a
Law. What could be more expectable than that some people will (mis)-
understand his doctrine as a libertine one—as, I would claim, the Corinthians in fact did?[24] Paul now provides the answer to that possible misreading of his intention in quite a brilliant piece of argument. Paul's very
dualism provides the irrefutable answer to this confusion. Law has been
associated throughout with the flesh, and its opposite, Christian freedom,
with the spirit. Therefore, freedom in the spirit cannot possibly permit
libertinism, which belongs entirely to the realm of the flesh. Paul's denunciation of the Law, on the one hand, and libertinism, on the other, both
issue equally logically from his promotion of the spirit over the flesh! How
ironic it would be were they now to allow that very freedom to be an
opportunity for sins of the flesh to abound, thus giving in to the flesh even
more drastically than they would by observing, say, the law of circumcision. Paul is thus not at all contradicting the message of the first four
chapters of the letter but rather confirming it. If you are truly in the spirit,
then you do not need Law, the Law which belongs wholly to the realm of
the flesh.[25]

This passage, once more, presents certain striking interpretative gaps.
The most obvious is the leap in verse 18 from the discourse on libertinism

or licentiousness in the previous verses to being "under the Law." On my
reading, in this passage Paul is guarding against an obvious danger of misunderstanding aroused by his discourse. As I have shown in detail in the
previous chapter, Galatians 3:12 amounts to a disavowal of Leviticus 18
as the guide to Christian living. Leviticus 18:5 reads "He who *does them*
lives by *them,*" which Paul understands to mean: One who does the commandments lives by *them* and not by faith. But Paul argues: Since we know
from Habbakuk that the righteous live by faith, he who lives by *them* and
not by faith is not righteous—is not justified. Christians, therefore, no
longer live by "them." What is crucial to remember is that Leviticus 18:5
is the introduction to the catalogue of forbidden sexual connections. One
could, therefore, very easily imagine Paul at the end of the letter becoming
aware of the enormous danger for (mis)interpretation that his letter could
produce. If he has repudiated, as it were, Leviticus 18, does it not follow
that its provisions are no longer valid and sexual license is permitted? That
is precisely the conclusion that some Corinthian Christians seem to have
reached, and it is what Paul seeks to counter in chapters 5 and 6 of Galatians. It is, therefore, most attractive to read the passage just quoted as
carrying its obvious sense in which desires and passions of the flesh are just
what would be referred to in a modern use of these terms, namely, sexual
desire and passion. This interpretation affords an elegant bridge over the
apparent gap between verses 17 and 18, in the light of Romans 7. We now
understand precisely the connection between the "desires of the flesh,"
and being "under the Law," for it is the Law which produces the desires
of the flesh and thus the works of the flesh through its insistence on the
bearing of children, leading inexorably to passion and thus to licentiousness, jealousy, and the rest.[26]

An objection has been raised to the sexual interpretation of "the desires
of the flesh," ἐπιθυμίαν σαρκὸς, because the itemized "works of the
flesh," ἔργα τῆς σαρκός, are *not* primarily works of sexual immorality.
The point is well taken, of course, but not, I think, decisive. We must
distinguish between the desires of the flesh and the works of the flesh, that
is, the results of those desires. The desires of the flesh are indeed what
they seem to be, namely, sexual desire, but the works of the flesh are the
social outcome of such desire: "immorality, impurity, licentiousness, idolatry, sorcery, enmity, strife, jealousy, anger, selfishness, dissension, party
spirit, envy, drunkenness, carousing, and the like." Lest this sound far-
fetched, the following parallel from a first-century text is unambiguous:

"But to the spirit of perversity belong a greedy mind and slackness of hands in serving righteousness, evil and lying, pride and a haughty heart, deceit and cruel treachery; hypocrisy in plenty, shortness of temper but full measure of folly and zeal in insolence; deeds abominable in a *spirit of lust* and ways of uncleanness in the service of impurity."[27] This text provides an excellent parallel to Galatians 5, for here we see also how the spirit of lust leads not only to sexual immorality but to deceit, cruelty, treachery, and even shortness of temper, a list quite similar in spirit to the works of the flesh that Paul adduces. Note also that the same concatenation of themes occurs in 1 Corinthians 6, where Paul begins his discourse attacking civil strife and jealousy and seamlessly segues into a discussion of sexual immorality. In other words, those who do not crucify their flesh with its passions and desires are those who produce a society within which not only the obvious immorality, impurity, and licentiousness occur but also idolatry and sorcery—perhaps Paul means the idolatry and sorcery of love charms—as well as enmity, strife, and jealousy.[28] Those, however, who are unmoved by eros are capable of creating a society of agape. Philo also provides an excellent parallel to this idea when he describes first a paradisal condition in which *men* spend their lives in contemplation before the creation of woman but then writes, "Love supervenes, brings together and fits into one the divided halves, as it were, of a single living creature, and sets up in each of them a desire for fellowship with the other with a view to the production of their like. And this desire begat likewise bodily pleasure, that pleasure which is the beginning of wrongs and violation of the law, the pleasure for the sake of which men bring on themselves the life of mortality and wretchedness in lieu of that of immortality and bliss."[29] There is, therefore, no reason to discredit the obvious meaning of "gratifying desires of the flesh" as referring to sexual desire.

The theme is carried further in the continuation in chapter 6, "For he who sows to his own flesh will from the flesh reap corruption; but he who sows to the Spirit will from the Spirit reap eternal life" (6:8), where we find precisely the same metaphorical opposition that Paul uses in Romans 7:4–5. One who sows to the flesh by having children will reap corruption, i.e., the corruption of death, for flesh is mortal. One who sows to the spirit will, however, escape corruption in eternal life. "Sowing," of course, as a metaphor for sexual activity is commonplace.

I think it is a strong conclusion, therefore, that the "desires of the flesh" in Galatians 5–6 are also to be understood as sexual. Christians are freed from sexuality. The final and ultimate fruit of the spirit listed in Galatians 5:23 is ἐγκράτεια, and given the interpretation that I have offered here we can give this word its full technical meaning of self-control and withdrawal from sexuality.[30]

PAUL THE PROTO-ENCRATITE

We thus see that at three points in his discourse Paul repeats the same highly significant sequence of ideas. In their former state of being in the flesh, Jewish Christians had been obligated under the Law. This Law is a law of flesh, because with its emphasis on fleshly obligations and especially procreation, it inevitably leads to passion and desire. However, under the new dispensation afforded to Christians through baptism, which is an enactment of Christ's death and resurrection, they are born again freed of the obligation to the flesh, that obligation which produces sinful desire in the members and fruit for death. The erotic life of Christians is ideally entirely devoted to the new bridegroom, Christ, and the joining with this bridegroom results not in fruit for death but in spiritual fruit for God.

The emphasis on embodiedness involved in being Jewish, in both senses of "flesh," that is, valorizing circumcision and other fleshly practices as well as concentrating on genealogical connections, implies necessarily the obligation to have children. The only solution, then, is to escape from the condition of being in the flesh, to die to the Law and be reborn in the new life of the spirit, which spiritualizes precisely those fleshly, embodied aspects of the Torah, kinship and the performance of Jewish ritual and thus sexuality.[31] Freed from the captivity of the letter, the flesh, the commandment which actually causes us to sin, we can serve God in the freedom of the spirit and escape from that which stirs up our members. It thus constitutes a return to the pre-lapsarian state in which Adam dwelled when he lived apart from the Law, that is, both the law to be fruitful and multiply and the prohibition to eat of the Tree of Knowledge. For the Christian, Christ and dying with Christ constitute return to this state of grace and redemption from the death and the bearing fruit for death which Adam's transgression occasioned, as opposed to the bearing of spiritual fruit for God of Romans 7:4. "In the flesh" here, then, like its equivalent, "in the letter," means simply in literal Jewish existence, in Israel according to the flesh. Just as the Law itself is not sin but causes sin as an inevitable consequence of its commandment to procreate, so being in the flesh, that is, being under the Law, being Jewish and thus committed to physical, Jewish continuity, is not ipso facto evil but leads to sin, once more by preventing the exit from sexuality. Although life in the spirit is obviously superior to life in the flesh, as the allegorical is superior to the literal, "in the flesh" here has no pejorative meaning of its own, that is, it is devalued with respect to the spirit but not figured as something morally or religiously evil in itself. It is primarily, as I am claiming throughout, a hermeneutical term. The state of remaining in the literal, concrete, fleshly situation of the old Israel does, of course, have negative consequences, which Paul emphasizes, largely to disabuse Jews of any sense that the Law makes them superior to the gentiles. Jews bear fruit for death, that is, they have children who will feed the death machine, while Christians bear spiritual fruit, fruit that cannot die.

Paul never once to my knowledge mentions the bearing of children as a positive event, not even as a necessary evil! A rather obvious objection that I am certain will be raised is that Paul is speaking in an extreme eschatological situation, and his views are not to be taken as characteristic of his understanding of sexuality per se. It is unquestionably the case that Paul is indeed working *in extremis*. Indeed, I would go so far as to argue that "For the form of this world is passing away" (1 Corinthians 7:31) is at least in part to be understood as a further argument against procreation (Fredriksen 1991, 533 n. 4). This does not vitiate my point at all, however, for the fact that it is precisely the function of the eschatological moment to free people from sexuality and procreation, that is, to enable them to fulfill spiritual and not physical functions of propagation makes exactly the point about Paul's thought that I wish to make. It is not, after all, in any way a necessity of eschatological expectation that the eschaton lead to an end to sexuality and procreation. As evidence for this, I cite the picture of the eschaton current in rabbinic tradition in which a major feature is "Quickly, O Lord, our God, may there be heard in the hills of Judea the voice of joy and voice of happiness, the voice of the singing of bridegrooms from their bridal chambers and youths from their marriage celebrations."[32] It is no accident, of course, that this same context emphasizes the national restoration in Zion that will take place at the eschaton as well. Further documentation can be provided from two modern Jewish messianic movements, quite different from one another, both characterized by the sort of eschatological tension which marks Paul's thought and both of which engage copiously in procreative activity and place it at the center and zenith of their value systems. I am referring, of course, to the messianic Zionists of Gush Emunim and the messianic Hasidim of Lubavitch (Habad). Both groups are procreating abundantly. Paul's "choice," then, of freedom from sex and procreation as a central marker of redemption is hardly inevitable or without a cultural message. The "law of sin," I conclude, can be very plausibly understood as the commandment to procreate from which the eschatological moment of the crucifixion and resurrection has ideally freed Christians.

I think that if my interpretation of these passages is acceptable, a significant revision of the history of sexuality in Christendom is in order, with the encratic Fathers much closer to Paul than has been previously allowed. The meaning of Romans 7 is that it was the command to be fruitful and multiply that created the inescapable dilemma of Adamic humanity, and the horns of this dilemma were only sharpened by the Jewish insistence on the centrality of the commandment because of its role in the reproduction of the Holy People. The dual effect of the Christ event is that an allegorical interpretation of Jewish existence, one that provides significance and salvation in the promise and not in the flesh, also provides release from the terrible double bind in which first-century Jews seem to have found themselves. Commanded to procreate, for only thus could the holy seed be continued, they were plagued by a constant anxiety and sense of sinfulness about the performance of that very commandment. In one fell swoop, Paul removes the sword of Damocles by telling them that the physical continuation of Jewish peoplehood is no longer necessary. In this end-time after the death and resurrection of Christ, Israel itself is no longer according to the flesh, defined by genealogy, but has been replaced by its spiritual signified, the community of the faithful baptized. The physical command to be fruitful and multiply and thus bear fruit for death has also been replaced by its spiritual signified, to bear spiritual fruit for Christ, fruit that will never die. When Paul is read thus, the encratic forms of Christianity are legitimate (if less compromising) heirs to a vitally important part of Paul's thought.

In Chapter 8 below, further elaboration of Paul's dual relation to the body, highly favoring the spirit but allowing room for the flesh as well, will be mobilized as a means to a renewed understanding of the relation between the Letter to the Galatians and the first Letter to the Corinthians. The notion that Paul valorized the celibate life most highly but did not vilify marriage will be crucial to this reading. For Paul, the celibate or encratite ideal was not the product of a "theological/moral" dualism. It was, rather, the solution, via a cosmological/anthropological duality, of an essentially ethical problem, the search for human autonomy and equality. Only celibates were free of the restrictions of gender, and in particular, only celibate women were free of the ties that bound (and bind) women.

8

"There Is No Male and Female"
Galatians and Gender Trouble

THE UNIVERSAL SPIRIT AND
THE BODY OF DIFFERENCES

Recently, feminist theory has provided us with extraordinarily subtle analyses of the ways that the mind/body split is inextricably bound up with the western discourse of gender. The work of Judith Butler is of particular importance. She argues that the critique of dualism is in fact at the heart of the founding text of modern feminist theory, Simone de Beauvoir's *The Second Sex:*

> Although Beauvoir is often understood to be calling for the right of women, in effect, to become existential subjects and hence, for inclusion within the terms of an abstract universality, her position also implies a fundamental critique of the very disembodiment of the abstract masculine epistemological subject. That subject is abstract to the extent that it disavows its socially marked embodiment and, further, projects that disavowed and disparaged embodiment on to the feminine sphere, effectively renaming the body as female. This association of the body with the female works along magical relations of reciprocity whereby the female sex becomes restricted to its body, and the male body, fully disavowed, becomes, paradoxically, the incorporeal instrument of an ostensibly radical freedom. Beauvoir's analysis implicitly poses the question: Through what act of negation and disavowal does the masculine pose as a disembodied universality and the feminine get constructed as a disavowed corporeality?   (Butler 1990, 12)

I am tracing one of the historical trajectories along which this act of negation, disavowal, and construction takes place. In her book, *The Man of Reason: "Male" and "Female" in Western Philosophy*, Genevieve Lloyd has described the historical process within philosophy wherein the universal mind came to be identified as male, while the gendered body became female (1984, 7, 26). I am trying to do two things: to further specify the cultural mechanisms which rendered this gender ontology dominant in our formation and to show that and how "the Jew" has been constructed analogously to "Woman" within the culture and by a very similar historical vector.[1] As I have argued in the first chapter, the specific historical occasion of the merger in Philo of Plato and Genesis 2 synergistically enhanced this ideological process in the world of Hellenistic Judaism and from hence to much of Christianity. In this chapter, I am going to concentrate on the question of gender through a close and contextualized reading of the crucial Pauline texts.

PAUL'S "BACKSLIDING" FEMINISM

As I have been arguing throughout, Paul was motivated by a Hellenistic desire for the One, which among other things produced an ideal of a universal human essence, beyond difference and hierarchy. This universal humanity, however, was predicated (and still is) on the dualism of the flesh and the spirit, such that while the body is particular, marked through practice as Jew or Greek, and through anatomy as male or female, the spirit is universal. The strongest expression of this Pauline cultural criticism is Galatians and especially 3:28–29. 1 Corinthians, on the other hand, has been read and used within much Christian practice as a powerful defense of a cultural conservatism. Making 1 Corinthians the hermeneutical key to Paul has had fateful cultural consequences, although to be sure such a reading has also been the *product* of the very ideologies that it eventually underpinned. I have been claiming throughout that the major motivating force behind Paul's ministry was a profound vision of a humanity undivided by ethnos, class, and sex. If Paul took "no Jew or Greek" as seriously as all of Galatians attests that he clearly did, how could he possibly—unless he is incoherent or a hypocrite—not have taken "no male and female" with equal seriousness (Fiorenza 1983, 210)? The task of my reading here, among other things, is to articulate a coherent reading of Paul as a social and cultural critic, i.e., reading Galatians very seriously while also making sense of Corinthians (cp. Gager 1983, 226).

I am, of course, not the first critic to attempt this task. In her justly famous feminist reconstruction of Christian origins, *In Memory of Her*, Elizabeth Schüssler Fiorenza reproduces an "apocryphal" female epistle of Phoebe, written by one of Fiorenza's students. This document contains the following lines:

> The second story is one I would like to discuss with Paul who lately seems so concerned with putting women back in "their proper places."

He is so taken up with giving a good impression to the pagans that he is reverting to his rabbinic prejudices I think. As if the proper place of woman was in the home bearing children—"woman is the glory of man" indeed! Surely with his background he would know where Genesis puts woman: "in the image of God he created them; male and female he created them." What a strange man he is. In his letter to us he so firmly emphasized the equality of woman and man in marriage; in the same letter he raged on and on about hairstyles in the assembly. . . . And, even more pointed, are these words from his letter to our Galatian neighbours: "For as many of you as were baptized into Christ have put on Christ. There is neither Jew nor Greek, there is neither slave nor free, there is neither male nor female, for you are all one in Christ Jesus." I do fear that some people hear, not these words of Paul which so clearly reflect the attitude and teaching of Jesus our Wisdom but hear instead his returns to the past before he received the freedom of the Spirit. I shudder to think that some time in the future a leader of one of the churches will say, "Gentiles, slaves and women cannot become part of the ministry of the Word because Jesus did not entrust the apostolic charge to them." When I said that to Paul, he laughed uproariously and exclaimed, "Phoebe you are a person with the strangest notions! If any of my letters do survive, only someone bewitched will fail to see the difference between my preaching of the Good News and my ramblings about cultural problems and situations. People from another age will easily disregard the cultural trappings and get to the heart of the message." If only that distinction were as clear to the rest of us as it is to Paul!   (Fiorenza 1983, 63–64)

Fiorenza, of course, quotes this discourse very approvingly. This student writing, according to her, "can highlight the educational and imaginative value of retelling and rewriting biblical androcentric texts from a feminist critical perspective." What we have here, in fact, is a fairly typical move of certain Christian feminists. One aspect of Pauline discourse, indeed constituted by only one (crucial) verse in Galatians, is rendered the essential moment of his message about gender, while the rest is relegated to an incompletely exorcised demonized Jewish past. I submit here two propositions: The first is that such a reading of Paul will simply not stand up critically and, indeed, trivializes him beyond retrieval. Paul's so-called "ramblings" about cultural problems and situations are, indeed, at the heart of his ministry, as Fiorenza herself indicates (226). The second is that no feminist critical perspective will be progressive if it is dependent on false and prejudicial depictions of Judaism—the Rabbis presumably lacked the background that included reading "in the image of God he created them; male and female he created them"—or, for that matter, prejudicial representations of so-called paganism.[2]

I have not cited Fiorenza here because she is in any way an egregious offender in these respects; if anything, she has made special efforts not to fall into such traps.[3] For that reason, however, this lapse is all the more symptomatic. Her student has failed to produce an acceptable solution, but she certainly has exposed the problem. For there is a major issue here for Pauline studies. On the issue of gender, as on several other matters of equal significance, Paul seems to have produced a discourse which is so contradictory as to be almost incoherent. In Galatians, Paul seems indeed to be wiping out social differences and hierarchies between the genders, in addition to those that obtain between ethnic groups and socioeconomic classes, while in Corinthians he seems to be reifying and reemphasizing precisely those gendered hierarchical differences. Fiorenza's student's answer to this dilemma comprehends, in fact, two types of standard approaches to such problems in Pauline studies. One is that there is conflict within Paul between an unreconstructed Jewish past and his Christian present, and the other is that Paul was given to caving in under external "pagan" pressures, even on fundamental and critical points in his ideology.[4] In a third approach to this and other similar problems, Paul is granted absolution, as it were, from the sin of inconsistency by being absolved of any desire for consistency to start with. According to this version of Paul, he was not a systematic thinker, and all of his pronouncements are oriented toward the local problems with which each of his epistles is dealing (Räisänen 1980; Räisänen 1985). Thus, while writing to the Galatians, Paul emphasized the social equality of the sexes in the new Christian reality, but when writing to the Corinthians, for whom such notions of equality had apparently become spiritually and socially dangerous, he backtracked or backslid and reinstated gender difference and hierarchies.

In my view, none of these ways of understanding Paul is adequate, and I wish to propose here a different way of reading him, one which is generated, no less than the reading produced by Fiorenza's student, by feminist reading practices, politics, and theory. Let me begin by restating the problem. First of all, there is the question of apparent contradiction between Galatians and Corinthians. This contradiction obtains on two levels. First, in the baptismal formula in Galatians 3:28, the phrase "There is no male and female" is included, while in the Corinthians (1 Cor. 12:12–13) version it is dropped. Second, much of the advice on marriage and general discussion of gender in Corinthians seems to imply that there very much is and ought to be male and female in the Christian communities and households, certainly insofar as marriage is to continue. Finally, even within Corinthians itself, there seems to be much tension between "egalitarian" notions of the status of the sexes and rigidly hierarchical ones.[5] I am going to propose a partially new resolution of these contradictions within the context of my overall interpretation of Paul's thought, because these expressions and tensions function within the entire system. I will argue in the end that Paul is caught here on the horns of a dilemma not of his own making, as it were, and one on which we are impaled into post-modernity and (embryonic) post-patriarchy—the myth of the primal androgyne.

The construction I wish to build here is constituted on the following notion: The famous "myth of the primal androgyne," together with the myth of Adam's rib, provides the ideological base of gender in our culture until this day. According to this myth, the first human being was an androgyne who was later split into the two sexes. However—and this is the catch—in the Hellenistic world and late antiquity, the primal androgyne was almost always imagined as disembodied, so that the androgyne was really no-body and dual-sex was no-sex.[6] This myth, I suggest, encodes the dualist ideology whereby a spiritual androgyny is contrasted with the corporeal (and social) division into sexes.[7]

Given this general understanding of the context of Pauline thought and expression, I can begin to set out my interpretation of the differences and apparent contradictions between Galatians and Corinthians on gender. To put it briefly and somewhat crudely: Galatians is, on my reading, a theology of the spirit and Corinthians a theology of the body.[8] In Galatians Paul's major concern is to defend his doctrine of justification by faith as a means of including the gentiles in the Israel of God, and he violently rejects anything that threatens that notion and that inclusion. "For you are all children of God through faith in Christ Jesus. For as many of you as were baptized into Christ have put on Christ: 'There is neither Jew nor Greek; there is neither slave nor freeman; there is no male and female. For you are all one in Christ Jesus.' If, however, you belong to Christ, then you are Abraham's offspring, heirs according to the promise" (Galatians 3:26–29).

But in Corinthians, Paul is fighting against pneumatics who seem both radically anti-body and radically antinomian.[9] He thinks the whole Christian mission is in danger, having fallen into the peril that he anticipated at the end of Galatians of allowing the spirit to provide opportunity for the flesh, because the realities of the flesh and its demands have not been attended to. He produces, therefore, a theology of the body that balances and completes, but does not contradict, the theology of the spirit of Galatians.[10] It is no wonder, then, that this is the text which is richest in "halakhic" prescriptions, and no wonder, as well, that it is this text which inscribes hierarchy between men and women in the marriage relationship. In the life of the spirit, in Paul as in Philo, there may be no male and female, but in the life of the body there certainly is. Next is the fact that in Corinthians there is an explicit and frequent appeal to both Jewish tradition and that of apostolic, Jewish Christianity. Several times in this letter Paul refers to his passing on of tradition ($\pi\alpha\rho\dot{\alpha}\delta\sigma\sigma\iota\varsigma$) that he had received, and all but one of his citations of traditions attributed explicitly to Jesus appear in this letter as well (Tomson 1990, 72–73), while according to Wire's interpretation *all* such citations are in Corinthians (Wire 1990, 272). All this is in direct contrast (not contradiction) to Galatians, in which Paul emphasizes that he is not authorized by tradition, by the teaching of Jesus in the flesh, that he is an apostle not from men but from God, authorized by his visionary experience of the spirit. It is no accident that the Pauline text that most thematizes the body is the one that also most manifests such fleshly concerns as rules and regulations, tradition, literal interpretations, and authority.[11] I suggest that we best read Paul as a middle way between the insistence on literality and corporeality, perhaps even the monism of the Jerusalem Church, on the one hand, and the radical dualism of gnostics (and gnostic-like tendencies in the early Church), on the other.[12] Paul's is a dualism that makes room for the body, however much the spirit is more highly valued. In this light I will reread Paul on gender.

"THERE IS NO MALE AND FEMALE"

In short, what Socrates has shown is that gender is not a pertinent criterion for dividing the human race except in the realm of biology, where childbirth and engendering are distinct functions. In social life, where personal aptitudes are all that matters, sex cannot be the determining characteristic. Was Plato therefore an advocate of equal rights for women, a male who acknowledged the aptitudes and talents of females? Shall we allow ourselves to fall under the spell of his thinking?

If we do, we incur the penalty of Plato's overestimation of the identity of all human beings, his denial of difference.   (Sissa 1992, 59)

Crucial to an understanding of Paul on gender is a proper appreciation of the history of the phrase "There is no male and female" in Galatians 3:28. It has been recognized, at least since the publication of Wayne Meeks's landmark "The Image of the Androgyne," that Paul is here citing Genesis 1:27: "And God created the earth-creature in His image; in the image of God, He created him; male and female He created them" (Meeks 1973). One of the proofs that the verse is being alluded to in the Pauline formula is linguistic: Paul shifts from nouns—Jew, Greek, slave, freeman—to adjectives, using ἄρσεν (male) and θῆλυ (female) instead of the expected ἀνήρ (man) and γυνή (woman). Second, the use of και (and) in place of the οὐδὲ (or) used in the other phrases gives this away. The "ungrammaticality" marks this as a site of intertextuality, sociolinguistic heterogeneity, dialogue in the Bakhtinian sense of the word.[13]

Meeks and more recently Dennis Ronald Macdonald have demonstrated that in this baptismal formula is encapsulated a very early Christian mythic formation and its liturgical expression in the pre-Pauline church (Macdonald 1987 and 1988). What was the meaning of this "original" baptism? According to Meeks, this was a "performative" ritual utterance in which "a factual claim is being made, about an 'objective' change in reality which fundamentally modifies social roles" (Meeks 1973, 182). Whatever the "original meanings," however, I think that the entire context of the passage in Galatians leads rather to the conclusion that what is being referred to is an ecstatic experience, in which are modified not social roles but ontological categories in the pneumatic moment of initiation. Paul's whole claim at this moment is based on an appeal to the Galatians' *memory* of their ecstatic experiences at baptism.[14] This interpretation would tend, of course, to make Pauline baptism more similar to the initiatory rites of the Mysteries, in which, as Meeks himself argues, "the exchange of sexual roles, by ritual transvestism for example, was an important symbol for the disruption of ordinary life's categories in the experience of initiation. This disruption, however, did not ordinarily reach beyond the boundaries of the initiatory experience—except, of course, in the case of devotees who went on to become cult functionaries" (170).[15] Following the researches of Dennis Ronald Macdonald we can further assume that the expression "no male and female" originally referred indeed

to a complete erasure of sexual difference in some forms of earliest Christianity and is cited by Paul here from such contexts (Macdonald 1987).[16]
In such groups, the declaration that there is no male or female may very
well have had radical social implications in a total breakdown of hierarchy
and either celibacy or libertinism.[17] The key to my interpretation of Paul
here is that though he did intend a social meaning and function for baptism, namely, the creation of a new humanity in which indeed all difference would be effaced in the new creation in Christ, he did not—and this
is crucial—he did not think that this new creation could be entirely
achieved on the social level *yet*. Some of the program was already possible;
some would have to wait. This interpretation will be further developed
below. First, I must return for a while to Philo, whose ideas are much
more explicit than Paul's, forming, I claim, an important partial analog
to them.

PHILO'S SPIRITUAL ANDROGYNE

For Philo the first human—the male-and-female of Genesis 1—was in
truth a spiritual androgyne. Thus both myths are comprised in his discourse: a primal androgyne of no-sex and a primal male/secondary female.
Since the two texts, the one in Genesis 1 and the one in Genesis 2, refer
to two entirely different species, he can claim that only the first one is
called "in the image of God," that is, only the singular, unbodied Adam-
creature is referred to as being in God's likeness, and his male-and-
femaleness must be understood spiritually. That is to say that the desig-
nation of *this* creature as male-and-female means really that it is neither
male nor female.[18] We find this explicitly in another passage of Philo:

> After this he says that "God formed man by taking clay from the
> earth, and breathed into his face the breath of life" (Gen. ii. 7). By
> this also he shows very clearly that there is a vast difference between
> the man thus formed and the man that came into existence earlier
> after the image of God: for the man so formed is an object of sense-
> perception, partaking already of such or such quality, consisting of
> body and soul, man or woman, by nature mortal; *while he that was after
> the Image was an idea or type or seal, an object of thought, incorporeal,
> neither male nor female,* by nature incorruptible.   (Philo 1929b, 107)

Philo's interpretation is not an individual idiosyncrasy. As Thomas
Tobin has shown, he is referring to a tradition known to him from before

(Tobin 1983, 32). The fundamental point which seems to be established is that for the Hellenistic Jews, the one-ness of pure spirit is ontologically privileged in the constitution of humanity. This platonic Jewish anthropology is elegantly summed up with respect to Philo by Steven Fraade: "Philo inherits from Plato a radically dualistic conception of the universe. In this view, the material world of sense perception is an imperfect reflection of the intelligible order which emanates from God. The human soul finds its fulfillment through separation from the world of material desires, a world that lacks true reality, and through participation in the life of the spirit and divine intellect; the soul finally reunites *the true self* with its divine source and thereby achieves immortality" (Fraade 1986, 263–64; emphasis added). Since, as we have seen, that primal state is one of spiritual androgyny, in which male-and-female means neither male nor female, this fulfillment would naturally be a return to that state of noncorporeal androgyny. This notion had, moreover, social consequences as well in the image of perfected human life which Philo presents.

In his *On the Contemplative Life,* Philo describes a Jewish sect, the Therapeutae, living in his time on the shores of Lake Mareotis near Alexandria (Kraemer 1989). It is clear from the tone of his entire depiction of this sect and its practice that he considers it an ideal religious community. The fellowship consists of celibate men and women who live in individual cells and spend their lives in prayer and contemplative study of allegorical interpretations of Scripture (such as the ones that Philo produced). Once a year (or once in seven weeks), the community comes together for a remarkable ritual celebration. Following a simple meal and a discourse, all of the members begin to sing hymns together. Initially, however, the men and the women remain separate from each other in two choruses. The extraordinary element is that as the celebration becomes more ecstatic, the men and the women join to form one chorus, "the treble of the women blending with the bass of the men." I suggest that this model of an ecstatic joining of the male and the female in a mystical ritual recreates in social practice the image of the purely spiritual masculofeminine first human of which Philo speaks in his commentary, indeed, that this ritual of the Therapeutae is a return to the originary Adam (Meeks 1973, 179; Macdonald 1988, 289).[19] Although, obviously, the singing and dancing are performed by the body, the state of ecstasy (as its etymology implies) involves a symbolical and psychological condition of being disembodied and thus similar to the primal androgyne. The crux of my argument is that a distinction between androgyny as a mythic notion and one that has social consequences is a false distinction. The myth of the primal androgyne, with all of its inflections, always has social meaning and social significance, for Paul no less than for Philo, for Rabbis, and for Corinthian Christians.

Two points are crucial here as background for a reading of Paul on gender. First of all, the society and religious culture depicted by Philo *do* permit parity between men and women and religious, cultural creativity for women as for men. Second, this autonomy and creativity in the spiritual sphere are predicated on renunciation of both sexuality and maternity.[20] Spiritual androgyny is attained only by abjuring the body and its difference. I think two factors have joined in the formation of this structure—which will be repeated over and over in the history of western religion, including at least one instance within early modern Judaism. On the materialist level, there is the real-world difference between a woman who is bound to the material conditions of marriage and child-bearing/ rearing and a woman who is free of such restraints. Even more to the point, however, is the symbolic side of the issue. Just as in some contemporary feminist philosophy, the category "woman" is produced in the heterosexual relationship, so in Philo as well a female who escapes or avoids such relationships escapes from being a woman. (See also discussion of Tertullian's *On the Veiling of Virgins*, in D'Angelo forthcoming, where precisely the issue between Tertullian and his opponents is whether virgins are women or not!) This division in Philo is reproduced as well in his interpretations of the status of female figures in the Bible, who fall into two categories: women and virgins (Sly 1990, 71–90).[21] Those biblical figures defined as virgins by Philo are not women and thus do not partake of the base status that he accords to women. Any parity between male and female subsists only in the realm of spiritual and ecstatic experience or in the symbolic spiritual myth of the primal androgyne. What about Paul?

Paul never intended for a moment to promulgate a truly "gnostic" doctrine of escape from the body and rejection of it, with all of the social consequences thereby entailed. This is proven by Galatians 5:13–17— "For you were called to freedom, brothers, only do not use your freedom as an opportunity for the flesh"—i.e., Do not misuse your Christian freedom to allow yourself hedonistic pleasure. Nor did he ever imagine a social eradication of the hierarchical deployment of male and female bodies for married people.[22] While it was possible for him to conceive of a total

erasure of the difference between Jew and Greek on the level of the
body—all he had to do was to eliminate circumcision, and Jews were just
like Greeks; female Jews and Greeks having always been bodily alike—,
he, no more than anyone else of his time, could not imagine that male
and female bodies would be in any condition other than dominant and
dominated when they were in sexual relationship with each other, that is,
when they were living "according to the flesh" (Fiorenza 1983, 236). It is
(hetero)sexuality, therefore, that produces gender, for Paul as for Philo
and, we shall see, within crucially paradigmatic texts of the Christian
cultural tradition.[23]

There is thus no contradiction between Galatians and Corinthians on
the question of gender. As I have suggested, Paul's preaching always intended a moderate pneumaticism—but not more, a spirit-flesh hierarchy
in which spirit was, of course, higher than flesh but the flesh, that is,
sexual *morality*, propriety, and ethics, was not thereby canceled (as the
end of Galatians makes entirely clear). Assuming that Paul's original
teaching of the Corinthians was similar to the doctrine of the first four
chapters of Galatians, it is easy to see where they could have gotten their
ideas: no male and female indeed! Galatians 5:25–6:10 shows how
clearly Paul anticipated this danger, which seems to have been realized in
Corinth.[24] If Paul was not troubled in Galatians by the implications (mis-
readings, from his point of view) of the quoted ancient formula, it was
because the "error" in the understanding of Christianity that concerned
him there was in the direction of too much physicality, so the pneumatic, gnostic implications of "There is no male-and-female" were not a
stumbling block. In Corinthians, however, where his problem is with
Christians who have gone too far (from Paul's ideological standpoint) in
the pneumatic direction and he must emphasize, therefore, the theology
and ethics of the body, "no-male-and-female" would be exactly antithetical to the message he wishes to promote. And so it is dropped, because
Paul perceived that it was open to serious misunderstanding as being applicable to life "according to the flesh" as well as "according to the spirit"
(cf. Wire 1990, 137–38). There is thus no contradiction in Paul's thought
at all. He held out the possibility of a momentary ecstatic androgyny but
only that; on the corporeal level of human society, sex/gender difference
was maintained. Paul on gender, it seems to me, represents then neither
the more misogynistic trend of such thoroughly Hellenized Jews as Philo
nor a breakthrough in the politics of gender as some Christian feminists

would have it. His picture of the relations of married people seems most like that of Palestinian Judaism in general, a moderate, "benevolent" domination of women by men, or rather wives by husbands, one which neither permits cruelty to women nor entirely suppresses the subjectivity of women.[25]

PAUL'S ETHIC OF THE BODY

What then is Paul's ethic of the body, his picture of the relations between married men and women, and how does it compare to the detailed rules for married life promulgated by the rabbinic Judaism of the second and following centuries? Careful study of 1 Corinthians 7 supports the conclusion drawn by Peter J. Tomson that Paul's ethic ("halakha") of sexuality and marriage and "Paul's conception of women was not much different from his [Jewish] contemporaries." Thus the famous pronouncement of verses 3–5: "Let the husband give the wife what is due to her, and let the wife likewise also give her husband his due" is identical to the provision of the Mishna which provides the same penalties to the husband who refuses sex to his wife and to the wife who refuses sex to her husband (Tomson 1990, 107).[26] Rabbinic literature preserves, moreover, strong polemics against men who out of desire for holiness cease sleeping with their wives (D. Boyarin 1991 provides extensive documentation and critique on this issue). There is, however, one element in Paul's thought on sexuality which divides him sharply from the later rabbinic tradition and connects him rather with certain other trends in contemporary Judaism, and that is the question of celibacy, which, I argue, is crucial to solving the problem that I am about in this chapter.

Tomson has provided us with a suggestive analysis of the cultural context of Paul's discourse on celibacy in 1 Cor. 7 (Tomson 1990, 105–08). The apostle prefers celibacy both personally, practically, and religiously, but is quite unwilling to consider the married state forbidden, condemned, or even disparaged by God. Moreover, since as stated, in his ethic of the obligations of married people to each other, he is close if not identical to Jewish traditions of his day, those who are presently married must fulfill those obligations. The essential similarity between much of Paul's ethic here and other strains within first-century Judaism can be evoked (if not demonstrated) by the following quotation from the *Testaments of the Twelve Patriarchs:*

> The commandments of the Lord are double,
> and they are to be fulfilled with regularity.
> There is a time for having intercourse with one's wife,
> and a time to abstain for the purpose of prayer.
>
> (Kee 1983, 814)

This practically demands comparison with Paul's pronouncement in 1 Corinthians 7:5: "Do not refuse one another except perhaps by agreement for a season, that you may devote yourselves to prayer." There are some obvious differences of emphasis between these two dicta but clearly the idea of abstention from sex for prayer grows out of the same religious and cultural milieu.

Finally, insofar as Paul himself and Jesus, whom he follows here, seem to reflect a particular attested ancient Jewish tradition against divorce, those who are married ought not to divorce and neither can they separate from their partners to whom they are obligated.[27] We can thus explain all of the details of 1 Corinthians 7 on the basis of the assumption that Paul maintains a two-tiered system of thought regarding sexuality: celibacy as the higher state but marriage as a fully honorable condition for the believing Christian.[28] This is by and large identical to actually attested forms of Palestinian Judaism and not very far from Philo either, except that Philo's tone toward sexuality seems much more negative in affect, reflecting, I think, the greater Greek philosophical influences on him.[29] However, it must be admitted that even Paul, whose dualism was so much less extreme, manifests quite a cold and ambivalent feeling about married sex, regarding it primarily as a defense against lust and fornication. As Peter Brown has written:

> What was notably lacking, in Paul's letter, was the warm faith shown by contemporary pagans and Jews that the sexual urge, although disorderly, was capable of socialization and of ordered, even warm, expression within marriage. The dangers of *porneia*, of potential immorality brought about by sexual frustration, were allowed to hold the center of the stage. By this essentially negative, even alarmist, strategy, Paul left a fatal legacy to future ages. An argument against abandoning sexual intercourse within marriage and in favor of allowing the younger generation to continue to have children slid imperceptibly into an attitude that viewed marriage itself as not more than a defense against desire. In the future, a sense of the presence of "Satan," in the form of a constant and ill-defined risk of lust, lay like a heavy shadow in the corner of every Christian church.   (Brown 1988, 55)

Where I disagree with Brown is when he says, "At the time, however, fornication and its avoidance did not preoccupy Paul greatly. He was concerned to emphasize, rather, the continuing validity of all social bonds. The structure of the household as a whole was at stake. This included the institution of domestic slavery. On this, Paul was adamant: slaves, like wives, must remain in their place" (Brown 1988, 55). On my reading, the situation is exactly opposite. Paul called for freedom and the breaking down of all social bonds. Realizing, however, the unrealizability of that goal— for slaves because of the social unrest and suppression of Christianity that would result, for wives because of porneia—Paul settled for something else, something less than his vision called for, and thus the continuation of the domestic slavery of marriage for those not called to the celibate life (cf. Segal 1990, 172–74). Rabbinic Judaism ultimately went in another direction entirely, increasingly rejecting not only the preferability of celibacy but ultimately even its permissibility. With that rejection, the one avenue of escape into autonomy for women was closed but a much richer and warmer appreciation of sexuality developed (Boyarin 1993).

This interpretation of Paul is coherent with the interpretation of his anthropology in general offered in this book. If celibacy corresponds to "the spirit" and marriage to "the flesh," then the axiological relationship between these two states fits perfectly, for as I have argued throughout, the flesh, while lower than the spirit in Paul's thought, is by no means rejected or despised by him. The analogy with celibacy versus marriage is exact. Marriage is a lower state than celibacy—He who marries a virgin does well and he who does not marry does better (verse 38)—but not by any means forbidden or despised.[30] However, and this is the crux, any possibility of an eradication of male and female and the corresponding social hierarchy is possible only on the level of the spirit, either in ecstasy at baptism or perhaps permanently for the celibate. In other words, I surmise that although Paul does not *cite* the myth of the primal androgyne, his gender discourse seems just as likely to be an outgrowth of that ideological structure as is that of Philo—no male and female—in the spirit, but in the flesh, yes indeed.

"The man is the head of the woman"

The crucial text for strengthening this interpretation, or at least for rendering it plausible, is arguably 1 Corinthians 11:1–16—"in the same letter he raged on and on about hairstyles in the assembly."[31] In this passage, on my reading, Paul makes practically explicit the ratio between the politics of the spirit and the politics of the body. The crucial verses are 3, 7–9, and 11–12:

> I would have you know, however, that every man's head is Christ, but a woman's head is the man, and Christ's head is God.   (11:3)

> For a man must not veil his head, since he is the image and reflection of God but a woman is the reflection of man.[32] For man did not originate from woman, but woman from man. Neither was man created for woman's sake, but woman for man's.   (11:7–9)

> Of course, in the Lord there is neither woman without man nor man without woman. For just as woman originated from man, so, too, man exists through woman. But everything comes from God.   (11:11–12)

These verses have been much discussed from many points of view. It is far beyond the scope of the present chapter to analyze either the theological or hermeneutic issues involved in the text, but however we interpret them, it is clear that Paul explicitly thematizes two (partially opposed) forms of conceptualizing gender, one in which there is an explicit hierarchy and one in which there is none.[33] Paul himself marks this difference (the gap between the hierarchy of verses 7–9 and the "there is neither woman without man nor man without woman" of verse 11) as the situation of "in the Lord" (ἐν κυρίῳ). I do not think it is going too far—nor is it unprecedented in Pauline interpretation—to connect this "in the Lord" with the "in Christ" of Galatians 3:28 and read both passages as a representation of an androgyny that exists on the level of the spirit, however much hierarchy subsists and needs to subsist in the flesh, in the life of society even in Christian communities. These two levels might well correspond, indeed, to the two myths of the origins of the sexes as found in Genesis 1 and 2. The no-male-or-female, which is "in the Lord," or "in Christ," would represent the androgyne of chapter 1, understood, as in Philo, as neither male nor female, while the "since he is the image and reflection of God, but a woman is the reflection of man. For man did not originate from woman, but woman from man," which Paul cites here, would be a reference to the story as found in chapter 2![34] "In the Lord" might even be seen then as an allusion to "in the image of God," and the latter human of chapter 2 would be "in the flesh" in contrast. This perhaps speculative interpretation is dramatically strengthened if Josef

Kürzinger's suggestion is accepted that verse 11 means, "In the Lord woman is not different from man nor man from woman" (Kürzinger 1978). Ultimately, as Karen King suggests, the two myths of gender "are quite compatible in that both imagine the ideal to be a unitary self, whether male or androgynous, whose nature is grounded in an ontology of transcendence and an epistemology of origins."[35]

These verses demonstrate that Paul had not changed his mind or backslid from Galatians; they also explain, given the context of the Corinthian correspondence, why he chose to omit "There is no male and female" in the Corinthian version of the baptism.[36] I suggest, therefore, that for Paul just as much as for the Corinthians, a state of androgyny, a cancellation of gender and sexuality, would have been the ideal. The difference between them lies in the application of the principle.[37] The Corinthians believe that they have already achieved a state of perfection that permits the acting out of the cancellation of gender difference, whereas Paul is skeptical of their achievements (cf. 4:8). This does not, however, imply that for Paul the ideal of androgyny has no social consequences.

There are in fact three (not mutually exclusive) options for a social enactment of the myth of the primal androgyne. Some gnostics (and perhaps the Corinthians) seem to have held that once having attained the spirit, humans transcended gender entirely and forever whether in celibacy or libertinage.[38] Philo, on the other hand, restricts such transcending redemption from gender to celibates, and then only to special ritualized moments of ecstasy. Paul's strictures against women with short hair and the speaking out of women prophets (14:37–38)—if the latter is genuinely Pauline—seem to suggest a third option: For all (not only celibates) there is no male and female, but only momentarily in the ritualized ecstasy of baptism. It is only then, in this life, that people attain the status of life in the spirit, in Christ or in the Lord, in which there is no male and female. Another way of saying this is that Paul holds that ontologically—according to the spirit—there is a permanent change in the status of gender at baptism, but insofar as people are still living in their unredeemed bodies, gender transcendence is *not yet* fully realized on the social level—according to the flesh. Perhaps, we might say, that final realization awaits the Parousia. I am thus inclined to agree with Tertullian's view that the notion of Paul giving celibate women the power to teach, preach, and baptize that is functional, social equivalence to men seems hard to credit.[39] On the other hand, it may not be gainsaid that he had women associates in his ministry, nor that he implied that virgins could achieve spiritual states unavailable to the married (7:32–35). All three of these possibilities are equally dependent, however, on a notion that gender difference exists only at one ontological level, the outer or physical, the corporeal, but that at the level of true existence, the spiritual, there is no gender, that is, they depend on dualism. Much of the immediate post-Pauline tradition seems to have adopted a version of the first option—namely, that celibate women *could* attain a permanent state of the erasure of gender, a development that has had profound effects on the later discourse of gender in European culture.

THEKLA AND PERPETUA; OR, HOW WOMEN CAN BECOME MEN

The myth of the primal androgyne—that is, an anthropology whereby souls are engendered and only the fallen body is divided into sexes—is thus a dominant structuring metaphor of gender for the early church and for the Christian West as a whole. There are many different versions of the application of this myth. In some versions of early Christianity, all Christians *must* remain celibate, and in that spiritual existence a total eradication of gender difference becomes imaginable.[40] In some communities such celibate men and women lived together in the same dwellings, arousing the suspicion and calumny of their pagan neighbors and the ire of more establishment Christian leaders. In other communities, more in tune with the Pauline and deutero-Pauline message, there was a two-tiered society: the celibate, in which some form of gender parity obtained, and the married, for which the hierarchical *Haustafeln* (tables of household practice found in the "deutero-Pauline" Colossians and Ephesians) were the definitive ethic. This could be accompanied by more or less approbation of the married state, more or less privilege for virginity/celibacy over marriage. In every case, however, virginity was privileged to greater or lesser extent over the sexual life, and, more to the point of the present argument, it was only in virginity, that is, only in a social acting out of a disembodied spiritual existence, that gender parity ever existed (Clark 1986). Female humans could escape being "women" by opting out of sexual intercourse. Just as in Philo, virgins were not women but androgynes, a representation, in the appearance of flesh, of the purely spiritual non-gendered, presocial essence of human being.[41] For all of these forms of

Christianity, as for Hellenistic Judaism, this dualism is the base of the anthropology: equality in the spirit, hierarchy in the flesh. As a second-century follower of Paul, Clement of Alexandria, expressed it, "As then there is sameness [with men and women] with respect to the soul, she will attain to the same virtue; but as there is difference with respect to the peculiar construction of the body, she is destined for child-bearing and house-keeping" (Clement 1989, 20). As this quotation suggests and Christian practice enacts, this version of primal androgyny provided two elements in the gender politics of the early Church. On the one hand it provided an image or vision of a spiritual equality for all women—which did not, however, have social consequences for the married;[42] on the other hand, it provided for real autonomy and social parity for celibate women, for those who rejected "the peculiar construction of the body," together with its pleasures and satisfactions.[43] As Clement avers in another place, "For souls themselves by themselves are equal. Souls are neither male nor female when they no longer marry nor are given in marriage" (Stromateis 6.12.100, qu. in Macdonald 1988, 284).

Much of the paradigmatic literature of early Christianity involves this representation of gender and its possibilities. Elizabeth Castelli has described the situation with regard to one of the earliest and most explicit texts of this type, *The Gospel of Thomas:*

> The double insistence attributed to Jesus in the *Gospel of Thomas* saying—that Mary should remain among the disciples at the same time as she must be made male—points to the paradoxical ideological conditions that helped to shape the lives of early Christian women. At once they are to have access to holiness, while they also can do so only through the manipulation of conventional gender categories.   (Castelli 1991b, 33)[44]

As I have suggested, however, these were not the paradoxical ideological conditions only of Christianity but similar indeed to paradoxes of contemporary Judaism as well. The Therapeutrides, too, have the same access to spirituality as their male counterparts—for all of them, however, at the expense of conventional gender categories.[45] One of the most striking representations of such manipulation of gender is the story of the martyr Perpetua, brilliantly analyzed recently by Castelli (1991b).[46] This story enacts both sorts of gender erasure. On the social level, the marks of Perpetua's gendered status are indicated by her leaving of her family, renunciation of her husband (who is not even mentioned), and eventual giving up of her baby, together with a miraculous drying up of the milk in her breasts, that is, a sort of symbolic restoration of virginity. The crux of the story, however, and of Castelli's argument is that in Perpetua's dream in which she becomes a man and defeats her opponent in the gladiatorial ring, her victory is, in fact, paradoxically a representation of her death as a martyr, while defeat for her would have meant giving in to her father, renouncing her Christianity, and continuing to live (42).[47] Life in the spirit represents death in the body and the converse, and the erasure of conventional gender is thus also an event in the spirit. This is, then, a drastic version of Paul's eradication of gender in Christ.

The best representation, however, of an androgynous status for Christian celibate women in late antiquity is the story of Thekla, also treated by Castelli. This apocryphal female companion to Paul refuses to marry, cuts her hair short like that of a man, dresses in men's clothing, and accompanies Paul on his apostolic missions. Castelli notes with regard to this and similar stories:

> It is striking that in all of these narratives, the women who perform these outward gestures of stretching dominant cultural expectations related to gender are also embracing a form of piety (sexual renunciation and virginity) which resists dominant cultural expectations vis-à-vis social roles. (44)

If my reading of Philo and Paul and of the general cultural situation is compelling, however, this connection is not so much striking as absolutely necessary. Insofar as the myth of the primal, spiritual androgyne is the vital force for all of these representations, androgynous status is always dependent on a notion of a universal spiritual self which is above the differences of the body, and its attainment entails *necessarily* one or another (or more than one as in the case of Perpetua) of the practices of renouncing the body: ecstasy or virginity or physical death.[48] We thus see that from Philo and Paul through late antiquity gender parity is founded on a dualist metaphysics and anthropology, in which freedom and equality are for pre-gendered, pre-social, disembodied souls, and is predicated on a devaluing and disavowing of the body, usually, but not necessarily, combined with a representation of the body itself as female.[49] On my reading, then, Christian imaginings of gender bending/blending do not really comprehend a "destabilization of gender identity." Rather, insofar as they are completely immured in the dualism of the flesh and the spirit, they represent no change whatever in the status of gender (cf. Macdonald 1988, 285). All of these texts are mythic or ritual enactments of the "myth of the primal androgyne" and, as such, simply reinstate the metaphysics of substance, the split between Universal Mind and Disavowed Body. It is striking how closely they match Beauvoir's critique of "the very disembodiment of the abstract masculine epistemological subject," as described by Butler:

> That subject is abstract to the extent that it disavows its socially marked embodiment and, further, projects that disavowed and disparaged embodiment on to the feminine sphere, effectively renaming the body as female. This association of the body with the female works along magical relations of reciprocity whereby the female sex becomes restricted to its body, and the male body, fully disavowed, becomes, paradoxically, the incorporeal instrument of an ostensibly radical freedom.

This trap is, I claim, based in the material conditions of heterosexual marriage, if not—even more depressingly—in the material conditions of heterosexuality itself, and precisely to the extent that Paul was unwilling to disallow or disparage marriage, as some of his more radical followers were to do, something like the pronouncements of Corinthians 11 and the *Haustafeln* became almost a necessary superstructure. Rather than "resting on the assumed natural differences between the sexes institutionalized in patriarchal marriage," as Fiorenza puts it, I would imprudently suggest that patriarchal marriage—that is, at least until now—*produces* such naturalized gender differences (Fiorenza 1983, 207). To be sure Christian women had possibilities for living lives of much greater autonomy and creativity than their rabbinic Jewish sisters, but always on the stringent condition and heavy price of bodily renunciation.[50] Let me make myself absolutely clear: I am not allying myself with Christian conservatives who argue that Paul's pronouncements in Galatians 3:28 did not have social meaning. Paul's entire gospel is a stirring call to human freedom and universal autonomy (cf. Fuller 1985). I think that, within the limitations of *Realpolitik*, he would have wanted all slaves freed, and he certainly passionately desired the erasure of the boundary between Greek and Jew (Fiorenza 1983, 210).[51] In arguing that "no male-and-female" did not and could not mean a fundamental change in the status of wives, I am not arguing that he was inconsistent (nor being inconsistent myself) in the name of the preservation of male privilege, but rather I am suggesting that

Paul held that *wives are/were slaves* and that their liberation would have meant an end to marriage.[52] Jews and Greeks need ultimately to cease being Jews and Greeks; slaves need to cease ultimately to be slaves, and the equivalent is that husbands and wives need ultimately to cease being husbands and wives, but Paul feels that the last is unrealistic for most people, even Christians: Because of immorality, let each man have his own wife and let each woman have her own husband (7:2).[53] When Paul says, "the form of this world is passing away" (7:31), it seems to me that he is doing two things. On the one hand, he is emphasizing why it is not necessary to engage in radical, immediate social change, in order to achieve the genuine radical reformation of society that he calls for, and on the other hand, he is explaining why having children and families is no longer important. Procreation has no significance for Paul at all. From Paul on through late antiquity, the call to celibacy is a call to freedom (7:32–34). Virgins are not "women." Rabbinic Judaism, which rejected such dualism and thus celibacy entirely, strongly valorized the body and sexuality but cut off nearly all options for women's lives other than maternity, trapping all women in the temperate and patronizing slavery of wifehood. This should not be read, however, as in any sense a condemnation of Christianity, nor, for that matter, of rabbinic Judaism, for I suspect that all it means is that people in late antiquity had not thought their way out of a dilemma which catches us on its horns even now—in *very* late antiquity.

9

Paul, the "jewish Problem," and the "Woman Question"

In these final chapters of my book, I will be considering the historical effects and reflexes of both the Pauline discourse of the "universal" as well as the rabbinic discourse of the "particular." Once more, I will emphasize, this is a book in which there are no winners and losers. Both poles of this dialectic, the universalist thesis and the particularist antithesis, or, the particularist thesis and the universalist antithesis, present what seem to me to be both enormous ethical and political problems as well as enormous promise, each for reasons quite naturally directly opposite from the other.

ROMANS 11:
PARTICULARIST UNIVERSALISM

If the dough offered as first fruits is holy, so is the whole lump, and if the root is holy so are the branches. But if some of the branches were broken off, and you, a wild olive shoot, were grafted in their place to share the richness of the olive tree, do not boast over the branches. If you do boast, remember it is not you that support the root, but the root that supports you. . . . For if you have been cut from what is by nature a wild olive tree, and grafted, contrary to nature, into a culti-vated olive tree, how much more will these branches be grafted back into their own olive tree.   (Romans 11:16-24)

This is a passage truly astonishing in its richness which I think has been underused in readings of Paul on "the Jews."[1] It seems to me to contain— "contain," in several senses—all of the ambiguity of Paul's understanding of the ratio between the historical, genealogical Israel and the new believ-ers in Christ from the gentiles. Ultimately, what we must remember as we read these verses, clearly intended as a stirring call to gentile Christians not to despise Jews, is that the Jewish root which supports them has been continued solely in the Jewish Christians. The branches which have been lopped off—for all Paul's hope and confidence that they may be rejoined some day—are those Jews who remain faithful to the ancestral faith and practice and who do not accept Jesus as the Messiah.[2] We thus see the peculiar logic of supersession at work here. *Because* Israel has not been superseded, therefore most Jews have been superseded.[3] Let me unpack the paradox some more. The issue is not whether ethnic Jews have been displaced from significance within the Christian community but whether a community of faith (= grace) has replaced a community of flesh (= genealogy and circumcision) as Israel. Precisely *because* the signifier Israel is and remains central for Paul, it has been transformed in its signification into another meaning, an allegory for which the referent is the new community of the faithful Christians, including both those faithful Jews (as a privileged part) and the faithful gentiles but excluding the Jews who do not accept Christ. Of course, Paul does not argue that the term Israel refers only to gentile Christians! How could he have done so, since in so doing he would have left himself, Barnabas, Peter, and even Jesus out? As he himself says, "I ask then: Did God reject his people? By no means! I am an Israelite myself, a descendant of Abraham, from the tribe of Benjamin" (Romans 11:1). This, however, is not proof that Paul's theology is not supersessionist, for the historical understanding of Israel has been entirely superseded in the new, allegorical interpretation (*pace* Campbell 1992, 143). Indeed, I am convinced that the main point of Paul's argument is precisely to persuade gentile Christians of the invalidity of a certain notion of supersession, one found for instance in the gospel of John, to the effect that God has rejected the Jews *tout court* and that the new Israel is entirely gentile Christians (Campbell 1992, 170–75). As I have already argued, supersession can be understood in two ways. Although Paul argues against one version of supersession, I will suggest yet again on the basis of Romans 11 that from a Jewish perspective his theology is nevertheless supersessionist. At the very site of Paul's main argument for tolerance of Jews, I find the focal point of his ultimate and unintended devaluation of Jewish difference.

In the beginning of the passage, Paul writes: "If the dough offered as first fruits is holy, so is the whole lump." The ceremony of the dough offering involves the separation of a small portion of the dough before baking and offering it to a priest as holy food. Paul suggests that if the portion separated is holy, then since it is of the same substance as all of the dough, all the lump must be holy as well. "First fruits" is a commonly used prophetic metaphor for Israel. The metaphor, however, has been transvalued in Paul. The relation of first fruits is no longer of Israel to humanity but of Christian Jews to Jews as a whole.[4] Now the crux of Paul's argument is for the continuing significance of the Jewish People. If the Christian part is holy, so is the rest. Paul, however, subtly shifts the ground upon which he is standing. On the one hand, he argues that the Christian Jews are merely a saving remnant, such as the one that the same prophetic texts would speak of from Elijah to Jeremiah. Here, however, is where the shift comes in, for the saving remnant is no longer, as it was in the prophets, those Jews who are faithful to the commandments, the works of the Torah, but is now defined by grace alone. For the prophets as well, it was clear that a remnant would persist through history that would guarantee the salvation of all Israel at the end-time, so in a sense Paul has changed nothing, but for those very prophets the remnant was defined by faithfulness to works—all works, circumcision *and* charity—while for Paul the ground has explicitly shifted from works to a new, arbitrary election of some of Israel who have been chosen to have faith in Christ now. A new, if temporary, election has been added to the original one. Although ultimately God has not abandoned the original election by grace of Israel, a new act of grace has taken place which replaces those who are faithful to the original covenant with those who have faith in Christ as the remnant of Israel. Surely, those left behind will in the end be gathered into this community of faith, so God's honesty has not been impugned, but for the moment at least, Jews who have not accepted Christ are simply left by the wayside. Precisely, however, as that moment stretched into millennia, this doctrine became inevitably one of supersession even without—indeed, as it may have stood against—the sectarian formulation and violence of a community such as the one that later would produce John's gospel.[5]

Paul's second metaphor in the chapter makes this even clearer. The metaphor is based on the practice of the grafting of fruit trees. Branches of different sub-species and indeed even of different species can be attached to root-stock such that they form effectively one plant. To perform this operation, however, existing branches often have to be pruned in order to make room for the new ones and also to give them a fair chance at the vitality and nutrients of the root. This is Paul's metaphor, then, for his new formation. The root remains Israel, and just as in the case of a graft, the root-stock defines what the plant, in some sense, is and gives it nutriment, so also the new plant of Christians remain defined as Israel.

Branches, however, have been lopped off to make room for the new grafted ones.[6] The branches that have been removed are, of course, those Jews who "refuse" to believe in Christ; that is, those Jews who constituted what used to be called Israel. It follows that the grafted Israel—including both Jewish and gentile believers in Christ—is now the true, living Israel, and the rejected branches are at best vestiges, at worst simply dead. The Old Israel has been superseded and replaced with a New Israel, precisely, as claimed, because Israel itself has not been superseded. The claim of some scholars, therefore, that the notion of the Church as a New Israel that superseded the old first appears in Justin Martyr seems to me falsified by this passage (Gager 1983, 228, citing P. Richardson 1969, 9–14; see also Campbell 1992, 49 and 74–75).[7] Paul holds out to the Jews the possibility of reinclusion in the community of faith by renouncing their "difference" and becoming the same and one with the grafted Israel of gentile and Jewish believers in Christ, but if they do not, they can only be figured as the dead and discarded branches of the original olive tree. There is, on the one hand, what I take to be a genuine, sincere passion for human (re)-unification and certainly a valid critique of "Jewish particularism," but on the other hand, since the unification of humankind is predicated on same-ness through faith in Christ, those humans who choose difference end up effectively non-human (Shell 1991).

Let me put this another way. I think that it is here that the moment of a "cultural reading" of the text comes in, that is, a reading informed by a different culturally defined subject position from the one that normally and normatively has read this text, and I am reading from the point of view of a member of that Jewish group that refuses to believe in Jesus and abandon our ancestral practices and commitments. On the one hand, Paul is clearly arguing against a certain kind of anti-Judaic boasting: "If some of the branches have been broken off, and you, though a wild olive shoot, have been grafted in among the others and now share in the nourishing sap from the olive root, do not boast over those branches. If you do, consider this: You do not support the root, but the root supports you" (17–18). But on the other hand, imagine reading this from the perspective of a broken-off branch, and you will see why it is cold comfort indeed. I think that the very utilization of the sign "Israel" for Paul's discourse both enables and constrains it to be forever caught in a paradox of identity and difference. "Israel" is, almost by definition, a sign of difference (cp. Campbell 1992, 27, who makes substantially the same claim but draws almost the exact opposite conclusion). The story of Israel in the Hebrew

Bible is essentially a myth of tribal identity, not entirely unlike other tribal myths of origin and identity. The appropriation of the story of a particular tribe, with all that marks it as such, as the story of all humanity would inevitably lead to paradox and even contradiction. If one olive tree among all the others has come to be the all-in-all, then any others become necessarily only so much dead wood. It is in this ambivalent symbol, then, that there begins a certain logic of exclusion by inclusion, or "particular universalism" that would characterize Christian discourse historically.[8] In the final chapter below I will suggest that rabbinic Judaism, particularly its strategy of self-deterritorialization, constitutes an attempt to retain the discourse of the tribal myth as such, i.e., without universalizing it, even in drastically changed historical situations, and constitutes therefore the exact antithesis to Paul. To be sure, it is only the story of one olive tree, and to be sure as well, it is convinced of itself that it is the only "cultivated" one and all the others are mere wild olives, but it does leave room for those wild olives to continue living alongside it in the grove. They do not have to be grafted in.

I wish, however, to reemphasize a point that I already made in the last chapter. There is an enormous difference between the nascent Pauline doctrine of supersession, and those of some other later Christian theologies. Paul's doctrine is *not anti-Judaic!* It does not ascribe any inherent fault to Israel, Jews, or Judaism that led them to be replaced, superseded by Christianity, except for the very refusal to be transformed. As in 2 Corinthians 3, it is the denial on the part of most Jews that a veil has been removed and the true meaning of Torah revealed that leads them to become pruned-off branches. I treat Paul's discourse as indigenously Jewish, thereby preempting (or at least recasting) the question of the relationship between Paul and anti-Semitism. This is an inner-Jewish discourse and an inner-Jewish controversy. The only flaw in the rejected branches is their rejection. Indeed, they still retain their character as Israel, and if they will only return they are assured of a successful regrafting. The point will only be clear if we forget for a moment the subsequent history and imagine ourselves into the context of the first century. One way to do that will be through an analogous situation in our own time, where, once again, the meaning of Torah is extremely contested. Reform Jews consider Orthodoxy seriously flawed in its "refusal" to see that the Torah "intended" itself to change with the times, and Orthodox Jews see Reformers as heretics, but no one doubts the Jewishness of either group, nor considers the other "anti-Semitic"! I would argue for the analogous analysis of the situation of first-century Judaism with the Qumran covenanters, Pharisees, Sadducees, Paul, and others all on the same footing as competing and mutually exclusive claims for having the truth of Torah. They all attack each other intemperately but none can be considered *anti*-Judaic.

In that sense, Sanders is absolutely correct in his statement that the only flaw that Paul finds in Jews is that they are not Christians. However—and this is a *very* big qualification—"not being Christian" is, on my understanding, not an arbitrary, christological, or purely formalist disqualification, because I, in contrast to Sanders, understand Paul as moving from plight to solution, namely, from the theological plight of a tension between the universalistic claims of Jewish theology (particularly as reinterpreted subconsciously through the lens of Hellenistic "universalism," as they had been for centuries by now) and the particularistic nature of its prescribed practices (Hengel 1974). This interpretation is verified by Paul's insistence that the remnant is chosen by grace (= faith) and not by works (verses 5–6). Paul had simply taken the first to be the signified of the second, and argued that in the revelation of Christ (in the world and to him individually) the true meaning of the particular practices as signifiers of the universal theology had been revealed. The consequence of refusal, however, of the lesson of that revelation was to be pruned from the branch of Israel, lopped off and left for dead by the roadside, and that was, indeed, the fate of the Jews in Christian history.[9] *Precisely* because we understand "grace" and "works" as sociological markers, then we must understand Romans 11:5–6 as reflecting a replacement of the historical, physical Jewish tribe, with its cultural practices, by another kind of community, defined by grace. Indeed it has always been the case that only part of Israel are the elect, but election until now has been defined through commitment to Israel's historical practice and memory. No longer: The remnant is now defined through its graceful acceptance of Christ. No longer Israel according to the flesh, but Israel according to the spirit— that Israel signified by the physical and historical one.

ISRAEL IN THE FLESH:
THE EMBODIED SUBJECT OF THE JEW

The dialectic between a Christian universalism and a Jewish particularism is perhaps first explicitly enunciated in a remarkable text of the mid second century, *Dialogue of Justin, Philosopher and Martyr, with Trypho, a Jew,* a text for which Galatians provides a vitally significant intertext, even though Paul is never mentioned in it. Trypho quite eloquently represents the puzzlement of a rabbinic Jew confronted with such a different pattern of religion:

> But this is what we are most at a loss about: that you, professing to be pious, and supposing yourselves better than others, are not in any particular separated from them, and do not alter your mode of living from the nations, in that you observe no festivals or sabbaths, and do not have the rite of circumcision.   (Justin 1989, 199)

Circumcision is thus a site of difference in the same way that a female body is a site of difference, and thus a threat to univocity. And so Justin answers Trypho:

> For we too would observe the fleshly circumcision, and the Sabbaths, and in short all the feasts, if we did not know for what reason they were enjoined you,—namely, on account of your transgressions[10] and the hardness of your hearts. For if we patiently endure all things contrived against us by wicked men and demons, so that even amid cruelties unutterable, death and torments, we pray for mercy to those who inflict such things upon us, and do not wish to give the least retort to any one, even as the new Lawgiver commanded us; how is it, Trypho, that we would not observe those rites which do not harm us,—I speak of fleshly circumcision, and Sabbaths, and feasts.   (Justin 1989, 203)

The crucial issue dividing Judaism from Christianity is the relation to the body, in general as a signifier of corporeal existence in all of its manifestations and here, in particular, as a signifier of belonging to a particular kin-group.[11]

The dualism of body and spirit in anthropological terms transferred to the realm of language and interpretation provides the perfect vehicle for this carnal signification to be transcended. Justin repeats accordingly the gesture of Philo in understanding the corporeal rites, the holidays, the Sabbath, circumcision, as being "symbols" of spiritual transformations (Justin, 201), again exceeding Philo, of course, in that for the former the corporeal existence of the signifier was still crucially relevant, while for Justin it has been completely superseded:

> For the law promulgated on Horeb is now old, and belongs to yourselves alone; but *this* is for all universally. . . . For the true spiritual Israel, and the descendants of Judah, Jacob, and Isaac, and Abraham

(who in uncircumcision was approved of and blessed by God on account of his faith, and called the father of many nations), are we who have been led to God through this crucified Christ.   (Justin 1989, 200)

If, however, on the one hand, the allegorization of the commandments on the part of a Christian like Justin creates the attractive possibility of a universalizing discourse, it also contains within itself, perhaps inevitably, the seeds of a discourse of contempt for the Jews.[12] Thus Justin's universalism becomes, to use Jonathan Boyarin's felicitous phrase, "a particularist claim to universality" (J. Boyarin 1992; cf. Connolly 1991, 41): "For the circumcision according to the flesh, which is from Abraham, was given for a sign; that you may be separated from other nations, and from us; and that you alone may suffer that which you now justly suffer; and that your land may be desolate, and your cities burned with fire; and that strangers may eat your fruit in your presence, and not one of you go up to Jerusalem" (Justin 1989, 202). As Castelli has precisely phrased it,

> The call to sameness (with Paul) in [1 Corinthians] 11:1 is paradoxically bound up with the call to exclusivity (difference) from the rest of the world. The action of imitation again has no specified content, but refers rather to a gesture which would set Christians apart as Christians. Unity and exclusivity are two sides of the same coin in the economy of Christian social formation. Each quality is a function of the mimetic relationship, insofar as each is played out in the polarity of sameness and difference.   (Castelli 1991a, 114)

Ultimately, then, E. P. Sanders is right that Paul's main problem with Jews is that they are not Christians. This is, however, not nearly so weak as it might appear, because the not-being-Christian (or Greek or Roman or any universal human) is, in a sense, the very essence of the signifier Jew, and the insistence on difference was also (and remained) a positive content of Jewish self-definition as well. If the "content" of Pauline Christianity is a drive toward sameness, the Jew is the very site of difference which both constitutes and threatens that sameness, and the circumcision of the male Jew's penis is precisely a diacritic. The Pauline critique of one kind of particularism leads to a particularism of another sort, which threatens ideologically and in practice to allegorize the Jews out of existence entirely. On the one hand, Justin argues that Abel, Noah, Lot, and Melchizedek, all uncircumcised, were pleasing to God, a message of universalism, but on the other, "to you alone this circumcision was necessary, in order that the people may be no people, and the nation no nation" (Justin, 204). It is here, building on Paul, that "Christian" becomes, then, reinscribed as universal, and "Jew" becomes the realm of the particular, in almost the very same hermeneutical move that inscribes male as spirit and female as the realm of the senses. "The Jew" in the text is taken as the concrete signifier of a spiritual signified, so "The Jew" in the world becomes demoted precisely to the extent that signifiers are disavowed vis-à-vis signifieds.[13]

THE CONTINUING ALLEGORIZATION OF THE "JEW"

The "Secret Jew" and the "True Jew"

Paul's allegorization of the Jew is, in fact, twofold. On the one hand, Israel is, as I have been arguing throughout, the signifier of the new Israel, ultimately to be the Christian church. For Paul, this seems to be the primary referent of the sign Israel and thus the Jews. On the other hand, there are two textual moments in the Pauline corpus that lend themselves to another, somewhat more sinister, reading of the signifier Jew. I mean Romans 2 and 7, where we can (and a certain tradition does) read the Jew as a symbol for everything that Christ and Paul have come to negate.[14] These two symbolizations of the Jew have their historical continuation in the continued allegorizations of "Jew" in European culture until now. I have called them the trope of the "secret Jew in all of us" and the trope of the "true Jew." The first-mentioned trope continues a traditional reading of Romans whereby the Jew represents *homo religiosus* or some other despised human characteristic, while the second continues the Pauline theme whereby the Jews are the material signifier transcended by their allegorical, spiritual signified.

The "Jew" as Symbol of Inferior Religion: Rudolf Bultmann, Ernst Käsemann, and Robert G. Hamerton-Kelly

The "Secret Jew"   The key text for the neo-Lutheran theological appropriations of Paul by Rudolf Bultmann and his student Ernst Käsemann is Romans 2. In this chapter, Paul addresses a singular, anonymous Jewish interlocutor as "O Jew." This formal usage has lent itself very conveniently to those who wish to see here EveryJew, and indeed to allegorize EveryJew as a contemnable part of Everyman. Bultmann and Käsemann have revived in all its glory the Lutheran tradition whereby Paul stood against everything Jewish as the very essence of that which God hated and which he had sent Christ (and Paul) to strike down.

Having seen one possible reading of the first part of Romans 2 (above in Chapter 4), let us see what happens to it in the hands of Ernst Käsemann, who, it will be remembered, is one of Bultmann's leading neo-Lutheran heirs. As shown there, this chapter is eminently readable as a critique of Jews who believe that merely being Jewish will afford one a place in the economy of salvation; indeed it is an attack on a notion that by grace alone, one may be saved. Paul argues strenuously, indeed, that it is only by good works that anyone is justified. He redefines, however, at the end of the chapter, of what it is that good works consists. These are not, as the Jew would think, those practices that mark them off from the Nations, such as circumcision, but rather those spiritually understood universal allegorical meanings of the practices, such as faith and love. Käsemann, in accordance with his religious ideology inherited from his teacher and ultimately from the whole Lutheran tradition, reads the Jew who is being addressed in this chapter as "religious man." Accordingly, verse 4 becomes for him not a charge against "real" Jews that they forget that God's special regard for the Jews is a demand that they repent—"Or do you think lightly of the wealth of his goodness and of his forbearance and patience, disregarding the fact that the kindness of God is to lead you to repentance?"—but something else entirely:

> The danger of the pious person is that of isolating God's gifts from the claim which is given with them, and of forgetting to relate forbearance and patience to the Judge of the last day. Humans always crave security. They seek to obtain it through moralism, worshipping the gods, or trusting the divine goodness.   (Käsemann 1980, 55)

Paul's "Jew" is no longer as in my interpretation—based on Dunn's—a real Jew at all but a symbol or allegory for the "pious person"—a pejorative in Existential Theology. Käsemann goes on to say that, "The person represented typically by the Jew is determined by σκληρότης [hardness] and, in explication, by the καρδία ἀμετανόητος [impenitent heart]" (56). On the one hand, Käsemann, superficially similarly to Dunn, recognizes as well that these terms are drawn from biblical preaching of repentance itself, but on the other hand, for him the repentance that Paul calls for is not repentance from failure to keep the Law but from success in keeping the Law. This move is brought out clearly in such a statement as the following: "θησαυρίζειν is not used ironically (*contra* Michel). It derives from the good Jewish view that a person accumulates capital in heaven with his works when he is alive. . . . Paul, however, changes the Jewish expectation into its opposite" (57). Hidden in this statement is a truly sinister interpretation of Paul—although one which the entire Lutheran tradition prepares—that Paul is not claiming that Jews who do *not* keep the Law, claiming instead privilege by its mere possession, are storing up wrath for the day of wrath, but that Jews who *do* keep the Law and believe that thus they are storing up merits are, in fact, only accumulating wrath. As Käsemann puts it explicitly in another place, "works of the law . . . [by which Käsemann means all good works and ethical striving] are for Paul a higher form of godlessness than transgression of the law and are thus incompatible with faith" (103)—to which I as a Jew would instinctively reply that such "godlessness" is surely preferable to God than a faith that does not issue in ethics. Now Käsemann clearly recognizes that the next verses (6–8) are extraordinarily difficult for traditional Protestant interpretations of Paul, his among them:

> "who will render to each according to his works." To those who seek
> for glory and honor and immortality by perseverance in doing good—
> eternal life. But to those who out of selfish ambition also disobey the
> truth, being persuaded to unrighteousness—wrath and anger.

These verses are extremely difficult ones for Protestant Paulinism, whereby works not only are insufficient for salvation but actually constitute sinfulness. Indeed well might have "Roman Catholics seized on it, not without malicious joy for their dogmatics," for these verses clearly say that at the last judgment one will be judged by one's works (57).[15] In fact, the problems which this chapter presents are much deeper and more fatal for a Lutheran Paul than Käsemann is willing to admit.[16] The Jew who is addressed by Paul here is *not* a Jew who has confidence in her achievement in keeping the Law and thereby denies God's grace, but exactly the opposite. The Jew whom Paul is addressing and attacking here is a Jew who does not successfully keep the Law, *and relies on God's grace to the Jews to save her at the last judgment.* Paul's adversary is covenantal grace, not good works. Romans 2, I submit, renders the Lutheran reading of Paul, and

with it Käsemann's, simply nonsensical. In the brilliant and biting formulation of Francis Watson: "The Jews teach a doctrine of *sola gratia*, and
this leads them to live by the maxim *pecca fortiter*" (Watson 1986, 112).[17]
The biblical theologoumenon, established in the Torah and repeated in
the Prophets—which Paul knows and even asserts in Romans 9–11—that
in the end salvation is guaranteed to the Jews, could easily lead to the
(mis)understanding that Jews do not even need to keep the commandments in order to be saved, and Paul's argument here is thus one that any
Pharisee would agree with. The doctrine of God's grace is indeed a dangerous one. What is new in Paul is his deduction from the truism that Jews
must keep the Law to be saved that therefore they are in no advantageous
position at all vis-à-vis gentiles when it comes to justification.[18] This chapter, then, strongly supports the tradition of interpretation going back to
F. C. Baur, within which Dunn and I stand, for on our view Paul is not
critiquing *homo religiosus* but *homo non religiosus*, the Jew who does not
keep the Law but thinks it is enough merely to be Jewish and possess or
hear the Law to be saved.[19] Käsemann's attempt to get out of the implication of these verses is simply incomprehensible to me, and I will not even
attempt to paraphrase it.[20]

Käsemann's fullest exposition is found, however, not in his commentary on Romans but in his essay "Paul and Israel," in which he reveals
both a hopelessly confused and confusing understanding of Judaism and
thus of Paul (Käsemann 1969). He achieves this confusion by mixing two
entirely separate categories: On the one hand, an assumption by Jews of
some kind of privilege with God borne of possession of the Torah or
the past of the patriarchs; on the other, "religious achievement" (185),
blithely assuming that all will assent that reliance on ethnic status without
works is equivalent to reliance on commitment to the fulfillment of God's
will. Only the latter is considered "religious achievement" by Jews; the
former is the source of the obligations that Jews have and feel to perform
works. These are both considered by Käsemann equally as examples of a
"distinction that he may have previously conferred upon us," that is, both
ethnic Jewishness and attempting to do his will in the present. This is
simply sleight of hand to cover up the fact that Paul's open expression
here is in direct and obvious contradiction to Lutheran theology.[21]

However, let all that be as it may, and let indeed even the improb-
ability and incoherence of Käsemann's interpretation of Paul rest for a
moment—it has been adequately disposed of by contemporary critics

(Watson 1986, 109–22)—the issue that concerns me here is the moral responsibility which a postwar German must take for allowing himself to utter the following statement, "In and with Israel he strikes *at the hidden Jew in all of us,* at the man who validates rights and demands over against God on the basis of God's past dealings with him and to this extent is serving not God but an illusion" (1969, 186 [emphasis added]).[22] First of all, there is the sheer arrogance of the claim to understand Israel's religion on the part of a man who only knows that religion from secondary sources—Strack-Billerbeck and the *TDNT!*—and indeed those produced by the same hostility to Jews that he shares. On what basis dare he, a German writing after World War II, characterize Judaism as the religion of men [sic] who "validate rights and demands over against God"?—particularly as by then it had been amply demonstrated by Jewish and Christian scholars that such a description of Judaism is a libel. And even more condemnable is the mode of expression, making "Jew" the name and allegory for something shameful about human nature. The notion that there is Jewishness (a Jewish spirit) that is hidden in everyone and must be driven out or overcome was, as Peter Heller has written, "paradigmatic of the most virulent variety of anti-Semitism in the twentieth century," because "the true, fanatical anti-Semite of the Hitlerian type furiously fights what he conceives to be a threatening possibility within himself" (Heller 1981, 102). It is impossible to imagine that Käsemann was innocent of the implications of his use of "the Jew Within" as a trope for human evil, since it was a veritable topos of German anti-Semitism (Aschheim, 1985). If this tradition was abominable before the Nazi genocide, it has only become more so now that its effects have become historically real in such deadly fashion.[23]

Undoubtedly Käsemann himself—known as an opponent of Nazism—imagined that he was striking a blow against anti-Semitism by indicating that "Jewishness" is not the special province of Jews, but in fact he did the reverse. When I say, as I often do, that there is a Nazi hidden in each of us, I am implying the proposition that to be a Nazi is something essentially evil. There is no such thing as good Nazis and bad Nazis. For Käsemann to write such a sentence of a "Jew," and thereby imply such a proposition of Jews, shows that he has learned nothing at all from the events of the Nazi genocide. Postmodern hermeneutics has often been claimed as an escape from moral responsibility. I would claim the exact opposite. Interpretation can no longer serve as a cover for moral and political irresponsibility, since we know that hermeneutical choices are always being made by interpreters. There may be interpretations that the text excludes; it almost never demands only one reading. Thus if Käsemann reads Paul anti-Semitically, then he, Käsemann, must be held responsible for his anti-Semitism. Dunn's example—among others—amply reveals the alternatives. I thus find the following statement almost shocking in its lack of care for Jewish sensibility:

> The approach to Paul taken by the representatives of dialectical theology (one thinks of scholars such as Bornkamm, Fuchs, Conzelmann, Klein and Hübner, as well as Bultmann and Käsemann) should not be lightly dismissed by those who cannot accept it. It represents much the most impressive modern attempt to reach to the heart of Paul's theology, and its theological seriousness compels respect, the more so as it has been engendered in part by the bitter experiences of modern German history. (Watson 1986, 9)

Although I am not familiar with the other theologians that Watson cites, from where I sit and write, the works of Bultmann and Käsemann seem more engendered by the ideology that caused the "bitter experiences of German [!] history" than by those experiences. And I learn from reading Campbell (1992, 193 n. 65) that Markus Barth sought, unsuccessfully, a retraction from Käsemann. To the very great extent that the work of Bultmann and Käsemann is generated by anti-Judaism—which is, by now, in the late twentieth century no longer distinguishable from anti-Semitism— it should not be dismissed lightly but rejected vigorously by all who desire and need to be Christian, for their unconscionable notions could not possibly, I submit, represent the will of God.

Robert G. Hamerton-Kelly: Judaism as the "Paradigm of Sacred Violence"
Neo-Lutherans are not the only source for anti-Semitic appropriations of Paul. Robert G. Hamerton-Kelly's *Sacred Violence: Paul's Hermeneutic of the Cross*, a "Girardian" reading of Paul, endorses the interpretation of Paul as traducer of Judaism with a vengeance (Hamerton-Kelly 1992). Although this by itself does not constitute an argument against its validity, it should nevertheless be emphasized that if accepted it would set back any possibility for a common language between Jews and Christians by centuries. It does, moreover, endorse this interpretation critically but in full collaboration with such a project. A sequel in pseudo (post)modern

terms of the most violent aspects of Christian discourse about Judaism, Hamerton-Kelly's book reads like a medieval *Tractatus adversus judaeos,* not only in content but in form as well.[24] His explicit intent is to delegitimize Jewish culture—or any culture but Christian—as independent cultural alterities in favor of a Christian exceptionalism by which Paul represents the end to religion and the end to "cultural embeddedness." The term is his and used by him as a pejorative—see below.[25]

Hamerton-Kelly ostensibly interprets Paul in such a way that his discourse does not constitute a delegitimation of Jews or Judaism:

> For Paul the church is not another sect, but the community of the new creation. It is ontologically beyond the world of opposites, and so is not a rival religion to Judaism, but a new and inclusive community. It is possible to construe this claim as just another ploy in the game of sectarian rivalry. Unfortunately, Christians down through the ages have certainly read it as such and used it to justify themselves and delegitimize the Jews. Paul left himself open to such an interpretation, but he did not intend it. He would have been appalled to see the community of the end of time becoming another sect in time, subject to the delusions of sacred violence. (146)

Paul's discourse is on this account a discourse of inclusion, an attempt to break down the hierarchical barriers that exist between people. In the passage discussed above in Chapter 3 in which Paul says "our fathers were all under the cloud," precisely the import is all of our fathers, that is, the fathers of us both gentile and Jewish. To the extent, however, that the new and inclusive community demands conformity to certain practices that contradict the practices of the historical Jews, even if those practices be only the confession of certain beliefs, then it is inevitably a rival religion and a delegitimization of the Jews, and indeed all non-Christians. Hamerton-Kelly is, however, wholly oblivious to the fundamental contradictions built into the notion of such a community, namely, its presumption that anyone who does not wish to join the new community of faith is under a cloud of quite a different sort. The very claim to be "ontologically beyond" itself constitutes rivalry!

Paul did not only leave himself open to misinterpretation here; the "misinterpretation" is almost a necessary consequence of such an idea. The obvious fact is that this coercive "new and inclusive community" still excludes (and often violently) those who do not have faith in Christ. Hamerton-Kelly, moreover, reads Paul according to the best possible con-

strual of the "intentions" of his discourse and not even its virtually ineluctable effects (How precisely Hamerton-Kelly claims to know the intention
of Paul better than, say, Justin Martyr did is itself fascinating!), while
Judaism is read by him according to its alleged "actual" practice of killing
dissenters. Thus, Judaism is simply "the impulse to fulfill the Mosaic Law
[that] made him [Paul] a persecutor and had killed Christ" (141).[26]

Hamerton-Kelly is willing to grant that Paul's putative experience does
"not take the whole range of the religion into account" but not willing,
apparently, to consider that the doctrines of Jews that other Jews referred
to as "Zealots" or "Knifers" were marginal and vigorously opposed subcul-
tures of Greco-Roman Judaism.[27] For Hamerton-Kelly, despite occasional
pro-forma disclaimers, these groups represent the true essence of Judaism.
For as he says, "I have endorsed Paul's attack on *Judaism*" (183 [empha-
sis added]). To this should be contrasted Hays's sober and balanced
judgments:

> Only a narrowly ethnocentric form of Judaism, Paul insists, would
> claim that God is the God of the Jews only or that Abraham is the
> progenitor of God's people "according to the flesh," that is by virtue
> of natural physical descent. For the purposes of his argument, Paul
> associates these (evidently false) notions with the (disputed) claim
> that Gentile Christians must come under the Law. Paul, speaking
> from *within* the Jewish tradition, contends that the Torah itself pro-
> vides the warrant for a more inclusive theology that affirms that
> the one God is God of Gentiles as well as Jews and that Abraham is
> the forefather of more than those who happen to be his physical
> descendants.   (1989, 55)

Paul is on this view indeed a Jewish cultural critic, calling Jews to ally
themselves with the progressive understandings contained within their
own tradition and to reject the practices of certain ethnocentric zealots.
In fact, the notion that gentiles are saved without conversion to Judaism
is a doctrine held by many *within* ancient Judaism; indeed, what is new
in Paul is rather the idea that all—Jews and gentiles—must be justified in
the *same* way, through faith in Jesus Christ. Paul dreamed of a day in
which all human distinctions that led to hierarchy would be erased and
not merely one in which there was a place in God's saving plan for all.
These are the grounds of his critique of—not "attack on"—Judaism.

Hamerton-Kelly's account of Judaism, as well as his account of Paul,
like all interpretation, teaches us a great deal about him and his ideology.

For the certainty of faith, we find here substituted a certainty borne of "the preunderstanding we [Hamerton-Kelly] bring to the text," which is "well founded on the evidence not only of the texts it interprets but also on other evidence from the human sciences" (61). For Hamerton-Kelly it is simply a fact that the Jews killed Christ, that their religion was a religion of Sacred Violence, and that God/Paul rejected the Jews because of the essential evil of their "way of life": "The Law had created a way of life founded on sacred violence and the crucifixion of Christ is the logical outcome of such a way of life" (66 and 71)! Hamerton-Kelly does not even present this characterization as Paul's and criticize it but rather produces a discourse supported by "the evidence from the human sciences" [i.e., Girard!] which asserts its authority as a description of Judaism. He interprets Philippians 3:8, in which Paul refers to his former achievement as σκύβαλα (dung), as Paul's characterization of "the Jewish way of life." Hamerton-Kelly somewhat softens the translation to "refuse" and then asserts that this is "what the Law really is" (68). He thus relies ultimately on both the authority of Paul and that of Girard (science) in support of his own political/theological agenda. When we read the Pauline passage in question, however, we find that Hamerton-Kelly's interpretation of it is far from ineluctable. The passage reads:

> Yea doubtless, and I count all things but loss for the excellency of the knowledge of Christ Jesus my Lord: for whom I have suffered the loss of all things, and do count them but dung, that I may win Christ.
>
> ἀλλὰ μενοῦνγε καὶ ἡγοῦμαι πάντα ζημίαν εἶναι διὰ τὸ ὑπερέχον τῆς γνώσεως Χριστοῦ Ἰησοῦ τοῦ κυρίου μου δι᾽ ὃν τὰ πάντα ἐζημιώθην, καὶ ἡγοῦμαι σκύβαλα, ἵνα Χριστὸν κερδήσω.

I think that a reading of this verse much more likely than Hamerton-Kelly's is that Paul is precisely not referring to what his former life "really is," but rather emphasizing that even though it was of value, he counts it now as dung in comparison to the excellency of the knowledge of Christ and in order that he may win such knowledge (Sanders 1983, 44–45; Barclay 1991, 243). In fact, the figure works precisely only if that of which he is speaking is not "really dung." It is not Paul here who is anti-Judaic, unless any disagreement or cultural critique is to be defined as anti-Judaic.

In fact I give Hamerton-Kelly much more credit than he does himself. He claims to have endorsed Paul's attack on Judaism; I think he has created it. For example, Hamerton-Kelly writes:

> The agent of my action in this situation is the sin "that dwells in me";
> namely "in my flesh" (τοῦτ᾽ ἔστιν ἐν τῇ σαρκί μου) (Rom. 7:18).
> In the light of my argument this might be paraphrased, "no good
> thing dwells in me, that is, in my culturally embedded (Jewish)
> self." (147)

Even granting the undecidability of texts, the multivariate nature of hermeneutics, and my own personal investments that lead me to read one way and not another, I find it hard to imagine that anyone who is not already inclined toward Hamerton-Kelly's hatred of Judaism will find his paraphrase in Paul's language, and I think it unnecessary even to produce an alternative reading in this case.[28] Hamerton-Kelly's affirmation of this proposition, whether or not it is Paul's, reveals that he still somehow manages to imagine that there is a self that is not culturally embedded. Paul says nothing so nefarious but certainly does hold out the positive hope of a humanity that will not be differentiated by cultural specificities. Paul can be forgiven his naïveté. Hamerton-Kelly is, however, intellectually and morally unforgivable for his ignorance of the critique of universalism mounted in recent criticism. (His appropriation of "theory" seems limited to Girard, and Girard alone.) In the wake of the horrors that have been perpetrated in the name of such visions of a humanity "not culturally embedded," Hamerton-Kelly's remark is simply inexcusable. I want to underscore this point: If for Hamerton-Kelly, "cultural embeddedness" is the sin that dwells in our flesh, then his politics will be a politics of the eradication of cultural embeddedness, which we know, by now, means the assimilation of all, willy-nilly, to the culture that is defined as not specific—that of white Christian European males.

The obvious charge that suggests itself is that Hamerton-Kelly is engaging in sacred violence and scapegoating of his own. He is certainly aware, although contemptuously dismissive, of this accusation. Indeed, he devotes an entire section of his book to "refuting" it:

> If the solution to sacred violence is the renunciation of rivalry, and if
> faith can take different forms, each of them valid as long as they can
> be classified under the heading of agape, why have I endorsed Paul's
> attack on Judaism? Have I not been engaged in precisely the rival-
> rous behavior that I have been criticizing, rivalrously condemning
> rivalry? (183)

Hamerton-Kelly's answer is that, "Clearly, a religious system that kills innocent people 'righteously' has less rational and moral justification than one that cherishes all in love" (183).[29] It follows, therefore, as the night follows the day, that "the sophistic taunt that Paul scapegoats Judaism is, therefore, unworthy of serious consideration" (184). Indeed, such a "taunt" *would* be inappropriately directed at Paul, because Paul does not mount his critique of Judaism on such false grounds; it can well be directed, however, at Hamerton-Kelly, and it is more than a "sophistic taunt," a formal contradiction. It is a damning charge which discredits entirely any pretense he has to a hermeneutic which claims to "escape mimetic violence into a new community of agapaic cooperation" (184).[30]

The burden of Hamerton-Kelly's book is that the Jews *really are* Christ-killers.[31] Now we do not know if "historically" there were *any* Jews involved in the killing of Christ, nor is there any reason to suppose that even if there were, they represented the whole People or its religion. What we do know, however, is that millions of Jews have been killed in Europe (and in the "Europe" imposed on the rest of the world by Europeans), owing at least partly to this scapegoating slander.

The "True Jew": Romans 2:28–29
and Post-Structuralist "jews"

Bultmann's, Käsemann's, and Hamerton-Kelly's allegories of the Jews represent the continuation of a kind of Christian discourse that can be held partly responsible for Nazi genocide. However, paradoxically, there is a European practice of allegorization of the signifier "Jew" that is a reaction *against* the Nazis but nevertheless, I argue, also deprives "real" Jews of existence. I mean, of course, the "true Jew." There is accordingly an enormous difference between the two tropes. The "secret Jew" owes its very existence as a trope to the Reformation and its reading of Paul; the "true Jew" is explicitly inscribed in the Pauline text. In the early parts of Romans 2, "O Jew" is indeed a trope, but it is not metaphor or allegory. The Jew whom Paul addresses is a synecdoche, a representative member of and corporate part of the "real" historical people Israel, who call themselves "Jews." The Lutheran interpretative tradition turned the synecdoche into a metaphor. On the other hand, Paul, by addressing the Jew as "You who call yourself a Jew," is already preparing the way for a different usage of "Jew" as metaphor; for a split between the material literal signifier of a body which belongs to historical Israel and its spiritual, allegorical referent, "the true Jew" in the end of the chapter.

This other allegorical appropriation of "Jew" owes its origins to the final verses of Romans 2, where Paul explicitly coins and uses the term. In Chapter 4 above, I have read these verses closely, and there is no need to do so again. What is important to reemphasize is that in this passage Paul claims that being a "true Jew" is not at all a matter of genealogy, history, and practice but a matter of an inner disposition. "For he is not a Jew who is one outwardly, nor is circumcision something external and physical. He is a Jew who is one inwardly, and circumcision is a matter of the heart, spiritual and not literal." Anyone at all can be Jewish, and those who "call themselves Jews" are not necessarily Jewish at all. This utterance of Paul's has had fateful consequences for the Jews in the Christian West. Once Paul succeeded, "real Jews" ended up being only a trope and have remained such for European discourse even until today and even in the writings of leftists whose work is positioned as being opposed to anti-Semitism—and even in the writings of Jews. Similarly, it seems, for some poststructuralist writers being a woman is not a matter of having a certain body and the experiences that go with it but of an inner disposition, and therefore anyone at all can be a woman by merely choosing to do so (Culler 1983). It is not surprising, given all that I have been saying about Paul and "the Jews," that this allegorization of Jew is much less offensive than the Lutheran's "secret Jew," or Jew as religious man, since the "true Jew" is at least a positively marked trope. Although well intentioned, any such allegorization of "Jew" and indeed of "woman" is problematic in the extreme for the way that it deprives those who have historically grounded identities in those material signifiers of the power to speak for themselves and remain different. In this sense the "progressive" idealization of "Jew" and "woman," or more usually, "jew" and "Woman," ultimately deprives difference of the right to be different.

"jews": Lyotard's diacritique of Jewishness   The critical text which has gone furthest in employing "the jew" as an allegorical trope for otherness is Lyotard's recent *Heidegger and "the jews"* (Lyotard 1990). I am going to propose in this section that Lyotard's essay on "the jews" continues in highly significant fashion the Pauline dualist allegory of the Jews.[32] The title tells the story: Heidegger gets a capital "H," but "the jews" are in lower case. This is done, as the back cover copy explains, "to represent the outsiders, the nonconformists: the artists, anarchists, blacks, homeless, Arabs, etc.—and the Jews." The Jews are doubtless chosen as exemplary both because the voices of some Jews are so prominent in Euro-

pean modernism and because of the enormous challenge of Nazi genocide to Enlightenment thought. But the name as used here is *essentially* a generic term standing for the other. And indeed Lyotard's book is all about the danger of forgetting that one ("one" in a position of relative power, that is) has always already forgotten the Other.

But why does Lyotard feel free to appropriate the name "the jews"? What does it mean for David Carroll, the author of the introduction to the American edition of Lyotard's book, to write, in reference to Lyotard's citation of "Freud, Benjamin, Adorno, Arendt, Celan," that "these are ultimately 'the jews' we all have to read and even in some sense to become, 'the jews' we always already are but have forgotten we are, 'the jews' that Heidegger forgets at great cost for his thinking and writing" (xxiv)?

What Lyotard refuses to forget, remembering the negative example of Heidegger, is not so much upper *or* lower-case Jews as Christian European crimes against humanity. In other words, Lyotard takes history seriously as an implication of philosophy, doubtless a vital exercise. This sketch of a critique, therefore, is not intended as an exposé of Lyotard but as a further implication of the universalizing, allegorizing traditions of Hellenistic philosophy as absorbed into Christian culture.

Lyotard basically repeats Sartre's thesis about the production of the Jew by the anti-Semite: "What is most real about real Jews is that Europe, in any case, does not know what to do with them: Christians demand their conversion; monarchs expel them; republics assimilate them; Nazis exterminate them. 'The jews' are the object of a dismissal with which Jews, in particular, are afflicted in reality" (3). Let us stop a second on the first words here, and try a paraphrase: how would it work if a man or a woman said, "What is most real about real women is that men continually try to dominate them." The condescension of Lyotard's statement immediately becomes evident.

It would have been quite different if Lyotard had written rather, "What matters most to me here about those usually called 'Jews' is that Europe does not know what to do with them." For there is no gainsaying the power of his insight: Europe indeed does not know what to do with "real Jews." But what of European philosophy? Is Lyotard not Europe here? Might we not fairly say, "Europe does not know what to do with them; philosophers allegorize them," et cetera? To which one might comment that in doing so, they continue another particularly Christian practice with regard to upper-case Jews, one which begins with Paul.

And here we can see more analytically what is wrong with Carroll's rhetoric about us all becoming once again "the jews we always already are but have forgotten we are." We must resist the seduction of these sentiments, for they deny, they *spiritualize* history. For some contemporary critics—indeed, those most profoundly concerned with the lessons of the encounter between Jewish identity and European self-adequation—it seems that the real Jew is the non-Jewish jew. What does this say about the "reality" of those Jews—most of those who call themselves Jews, of course, are the untheorized, unphilosophical, unspiritualized Jews—who would think the phrase "non-Jewish Jew" to be nonsense? Is it politically correct to "forget" them and to fashion an imaginary dialogue with the Other who is, in fact, the already-sanctioned, official model of the "non-Jewish Jew," the Kafkas and Benjamins? For as we know, the vast majority of the Nazis' Jewish victims were unredeemed "real" Jews.[33]

Against this incipient critique stands precisely the force implicit in Lyotard's act of allegorizing the name "jew." Radiating out from the sun of philosophy, remembering the other by writing the "jew," Lyotard challenges all those who would fetishize their particular difference, insisting that we learn how to imagine ourselves as blacks, as Arabs, as homeless, as Indians. This is a political challenge, but Lyotard does not suggest how those who are themselves "real Jews" could respond to it. Indeed, he explains that one reason for his avoidance of the proper noun, of the uppercase "Jews," is to make clear that he is not discussing a particularly Jewish political subject, which he identifies as Zionism (3). I want to insist in response to Lyotard that there is a loss and a danger either in allegorizing away real, upper-case Jews or in regarding them primarily as a problem for Europe. My claim entails in turn a responsibility to help articulate a Jewish political subject "other" than Zionism, which in fundamental ways merely reproduces the exclusivist syndromes of European nationalism. Zionism itself is predicated on a myth of autochthony. I will be suggesting in the next chapter that a Jewish subject position founded on memories of genealogy, not genealogy *tout court* but that which has since antiquity been called "race," provides for a critical Jewish identity.

Jean-Luc Nancy and the Jews   Sometimes the reference to the allegorized Jew is implicit or made in passing; in other recent works it is an explicit and central trope. An example of the former is contained in Jean-Luc Nancy's recent *The Inoperative Community*. As Jonathan Boyarin has recently shown, Lyotard's allegorizing move on the signifier "Jew" is repeated at other moments as well in post-Nazi, post-structuralist appropriations of the signifier Jew (Boyarin and Boyarin 1993). Nancy's central problem in that work is to formulate a notion of community which will not violate the standard of non-coercion. That standard holds that community is "the com-pearance [*comparution*] of singular beings." For Nancy, such singularity and the simultaneity which is a condition of it appear to imply an evacuation of history and memory. So many brutalities, so many violations of any notion of humanly responsible community have been carried out in the name of solidary collectives supposed to have obtained in the past, that Nancy seems to have renounced any possible recourse to memory in his attempt to think through the possibility of there ever being community without coercion. Of there ever *being:* the only community which does not betray the hope invested in that word, Nancy argues, is one that resists any kind of stable existence (Nancy 1991, 58).

The problem is that Nancy has in fact attempted a generalized model of community as *non-being.* Hence any already existing "community" is out of consideration by its very existence, relegated through philosophical necessity to a world we have lost or which never existed. Following Nancy's rhetoric, the only possible residues of that lost world are false community appearing as either a serial, undifferentiated collective in the same analytic category as the Fascist mass or, alternatively, an assemblage of unrelated individuals. The individual in turn "is merely the residue of the experience of the dissolution of community" (3), and furthermore, "the true consciousness of the loss of community is Christian" (10).

Although Nancy is silent on the relations among history, memory, and community, he considers at some length the apparently tortured relation between "myth" and community. For Nancy myth—that necessary fiction which grounds the insistent specialness of the existent communal group—is an irreducible component of community and at the same time necessarily pernicious in its effects. Therefore Nancy asserts a search, not for the eradication of myth but rather for its "interruption": "interruption of myth is therefore also, necessarily, the interruption of community" (57). In a footnote Nancy elaborates on an earlier comment by Maurice Blanchot:

> Blanchot . . . writes: "The Jews incarnate . . . the refusal of myths, the abandonment of idols, the recognition of an ethical order that manifests itself in respect for the law. What Hitler wants to annihilate in the Jew, in the 'myth of the Jew,' is precisely man freed from myth." This is another way of showing where and when myth was definitively interrupted. I would add this: "man freed from myth" belongs hence-

forth to a community that it is incumbent upon us to let come, to let write itself.   (Nancy, 162 n. 40, citing Blanchot, "Les Intellectuels en Question," *Le Débat,* May 1984)

I want to press, in a sense by literalizing, the opening offered here. The quote from Blanchot seems ambiguous if not contradictory: Do the Jews literally "incarnate . . . the refusal of myths," or is that one of Hitler's myths? Let me first pursue the first reading, which is both the more flattering and the more dangerous. This reading would tell us that community without myth was once the special possession of the Jews. Nancy's "addition" would then explore the consequences of the release of that secret to "us," as a result of the genocide. What else, after all, can "henceforth" mean? Now I deeply respect that this and other work of Nancy's is explicitly motivated by the desire to understand and unwork the complicity between philosophy and twentieth-century violence (Lacoue-Labarthe and Nancy 1990). Nancy would doubtless be horrified at the suggestion that his rhetoric is complicit in perpetuating the annihilation of the Jew, yet it seems clear that this is one potential accomplishment of his further allegorization of Blanchot. *That which the Jew represented before "he" was annihilated is that which "we" must let come, must let write itself.* The word "henceforth" indeed implies that the secret of freedom from myth has passed from the Jews to a community which does not exist, which is only imaginable in and by theory. The secret becomes potentially available to all who await a second coming of this sacrificed Jew. I insist: This plausible yet "uncharitable" reading cannot be stretched to an accusation of anti-Judaism. On the contrary, it is clear that Nancy and thinkers like him are committed to a sympathetic philosophical comprehension of the existence and annihilation of the Jews. My claim is rather that within the thought of philosophers such as Nancy lies a blindness to the particularity of Jewish difference which is itself part of a relentless penchant for allegorizing all "difference" into a monovocal discourse.

THE DE(CON)STRUCTION OF WOMEN

One at least has to recognize that positing woman as a figure of displacement risks, in its effects, continually displacing real material women.   (Fuss 1989, 14)

What I wish to suggest here, very briefly, is that post-structuralist deconstruction of the sign "woman" once more reproduces and continues the "western" (Pauline) tradition of attack on real identities, on difference. In other words, once more here I would suggest that women and Jews are analogous terms vis-à-vis the dominant discourse. The political claim about post-structuralism is not new; what is new is only the suggestion that post-structuralism here continues—as opposed to opposing—the discourse that it seeks to disrupt. For some post-structuralists, it seems, "Woman" has become a sign in almost strict analogy to the way that "jew" has become a sign for Lyotard and Nancy. Thus Diana Fuss remarks of Lacan, "Of real material women . . . Lacan has nothing to say, readily admits his knowing ignorance. But of 'woman' as sign Lacan has everything to say (especially since women, as we shall see, cannot say 'it' themselves)" (Fuss 1989, 11).[34] "Woman" is, for Lacan, the being who (whether male or female in body) has ecstatically transcended—gone beyond—the phallus and attained the status of "Woman." It seems that Lacan ultimately reinscribes here the myth of the primal androgyne, however—and this is not to be ignored—inscribing the androgyne as a female and not a male one. We still end up with no male and female in Christ— quite precisely in Christ; Saint Theresa is, after all, Lacan's ideal type of one who has gone beyond the phallus.

Fuss has thus shown how central is the distinction between penis and phallus for Lacan's system (11).[35] I speculatively suggest that the precise source of the scandal of circumcision in western culture lies in its threat to the idealization of the phallus, to its conversion from biological organ to logos. Because of circumcision, the flesh cannot become Word. The insistence on a physical cutting interrupts the dematerialization of the penis and thus of its semiotic transformation into phallos and logos. And paradoxically we find this brought out even at the very site of the theoretical attack on this structure, Derridean post-structuralism. As Barbara Johnson has written:

> The letter, says Lacan, cannot be divided: "But if it is first of all on the materiality of the signifier that we have insisted, that materiality is *odd* [singulière] in many ways, the first of which is not to admit partition." This indivisibility, says Derrida, is odd indeed, but becomes comprehensible if it is seen as an *idealization* of the phallus, whose integrity is necessary for the edification of the entire psychoanalytical system. With the phallus safely idealized and located in the voice, the so-called signifier acquires the "unique, living, *non-mutilable integrity* [emphasis added, DB]" of the self-present spoken word, unequivocally pinned down to and by the *signified.* "Had the phallus been per(mal)-

> chance divisible or reduced to the status of a partial object, the whole
> edification would have crumbled down, and this is what has to be
> avoided at all cost." (Johnson 1987, 225)

But the penis, of course, *is* divisible. In circumcision it is divided. It is
striking to me that the penis has been so spiritualized in European tradition that even when its Lacanian idealization is being opposed by a hypothetical, Derridean mutilable, divisible phallus, the very mutilation of
the penis which is at the center of the tradition of the Jewish Other is not
mentioned. For Derrida, standing in antithesis to Lacan, even castration
remains allegorized. "The phallus, thanks to castration, always remains in
its place, in the transcendental topology . . . In castration, the phallus is
indivisible, and therefore indestructible" (Derrida 1987, 185, 194–95).
This rather invites speculation on the legend [?] of Origen's castration and
on the reason why in some cultural contexts circumcision is identified *with*
castration and in others as its very opposite. Once the signifier no longer
possesses a "non-mutilable integrity," then the "idealization of the phallus" is no longer possible. I would argue that this idealization is necessary
not only for the edification of the psychoanalytic system but for any logocentric (allegoretical) system.[36] But since it is precisely this transformation
that allows for the putative de-essentialization of "Woman" in Lacan's
(and ultimately even in Derrida's) thinking, we see once more the sources
of this strange and persistent association of Jews and women in western
culture. Women in their bodies and Jewish (males) in their altered ones
keep reminding "us" that *the* phallus is after all (only) *a* penis, and *the*
logos is after all (only) some body's utterance. According to midrash, even
the Torah is given in the speech of human beings.[37]

THE SECRET OF THE JEWS

Now let me pursue an alternate reading of Blanchot, and of Nancy's gloss.
Its implications are both more modest and more conducive to my project
of constructing a progressive and strong Jewish subjecthood. According to
this second reading of Blanchot, the Jews' freedom from myth was primarily, if not exclusively, significant as a myth that murderously irritated
Hitler. Nancy would then be saying not that "we" have inherited the
secret of the Jews but rather that it is incumbent upon us—the pronoun
this time not excluding in any way Jews living after the Nazi genocide—
to assume the challenge of the myth of freedom from myth, to let come a

community that is free from myth. I will suggest in the final chapter below that, especially in the experience of Diaspora, which has constrained Jews to create forms of community that do not rely upon one of the most potent and dangerous myths—the myth of autochthony—living Jews may have a particular contribution to make to that general effort. As I have already suggested, the tendency of postmodern thought continues willy-nilly the trajectories that Paul set in motion in Christian/European thought. Reactions against this disembodying move, however, prove equally as dangerous, if not more so. Let Heidegger be an exemplum. This conclusion raises, however, frightening specters with regard to Jewish existence in the world.

10

Answering the Mail

Toward a Radical Jewishness

> There is no Jew nor Greek.
> Paul

> פּאָולוס איז געווען דער ערשטער באָלשעוויק
> Paul was the first Bolshevik.
> Hillel Kempinsky, late archi-
> vist of the Bund in New York

Throughout this book I have been arguing that Paul's writing poses a significant challenge to Jewish notions of identity. I have suggested that Paul
was impelled by a vision of human unity that was born of two parents:
Hebrew monotheism and Greek longing for universals. As I have argued,
however, and will pursue further, Paul's universalism seems to conduce to
coercive politico-cultural systems that engage in more or less violent projects of the absorption of cultural specificities into the dominant one. Yet
Jews cannot ignore the force of Paul's critique just because of its negative
effects, for uncritical devotion to ethnic particularity has equally negative
effects. Thus, while Jewish discourse both limits its claims to hegemony to
what is, after all, a tiny piece of land (in contrast to the whole world
staked out by "Christendom") and, moreover, does not consider conversion of others a desideratum or a requirement for their "salvation" (Shell
1991), modern Jewish statist nationalism has nevertheless been very violent and exclusionary in its practices vis-à-vis its others, and traditional
Judaism was often offensively contemptuous toward them.

On the political or ethical level, then, Paul presented (and presents)
Jews with a set of powerful questions that cannot be ignored. Echoing
Alan F. Segal, I claim that Paul's letters are letters addressed to us—to
me, as a (post)modern Jew. I conclude this book, then, with a highly
personal and engaged, perhaps not always completely satisfactory, attempt
to answer Paul's letters to me. How can I ethically construct a particular

identity which is extremely precious to me without falling into ethnocentrism or racism of one kind or another? This is particularly poignant since, as we shall see, the latter are protean and can disguise themselves in many forms. In this chapter, this book will significantly change its tone and its focus. The effort of this final chapter is to articulate one individual notion of Jewishness—and by analogy, other forms of particular identity—that will attempt to answer the challenge of Paul's letters to enroll in and commit to a universal human solidarity as well.

CARNALITY AND DIFFERENCE

> Plotinus, the philosopher of our times, seemed ashamed of being in the body. As a result of this state of mind he could never bear to talk about his race or his parents or his native country.
>
> Porphyry, *Life of Plotinus*

Traditionally, group identity has been constructed in two ways: as the product of either a common genealogical origin or a common geographical origin. The first type of figuring has a strongly pejoratized value in current writing, having become tainted with the name "race" and thus racism,[1] while the second is referred to by the positive, even progressive-sounding, "self-determination"—in spite of the evident fact that either or both of these discourses can equally be used to justify acts of enormous violence.[2] The negative evaluation of genealogy as a ground for identity can be traced to Paul, the fountainhead, as I am claiming, of western universalism. In his authentic passion to find a place for the gentiles in the Torah's scheme of things and the brilliance of the radically dualist and allegorical hermeneutic he developed to accomplish this purpose, Paul had (almost against his will) sown the seeds for a Christian discourse that would completely deprive Jewish ethnic, cultural specificity of any positive value and indeed turn it into a "curse" in the eyes of gentile Christians. As Augustine was to write:

> Behold Israel *according to the flesh* (i Cor. 10:18). This we know to be the carnal Israel; but the Jews do not grasp this meaning and as a result they prove themselves indisputably carnal.[3]

This characteristic Augustinian text further enables us to understand the conjunction of Jews with women as the terms of a difference which is opposed to allegorical univocity. Just as the female body with its disturbing two-ness (both by being different from the male body and by being "a sex which is not one") is the site of difference and fallen corporeality, so also the Jews, by refusing to be allegorized into a spiritual disembodiment, remain the site of difference and fallen corporeality.[4]

Elizabeth Castelli has focused most sharply on the extent to which the drive for sameness was constitutive of Pauline discourse by analyzing the function of imitation and its political effects in his letters:

> The language of imitation, with its concomitant tension between the drive toward sameness and the inherent hierarchy of the mimetic relationship, masks the will to power which one finds in Pauline discourse. Paul's appropriation of the discourse of mimesis is a powerful rhetorical move, because this language identifies the fundamental values of wholeness and unity with Paul's own privileged position vis-à-vis the gospel, the early Christian communities he founded and supervises, and Christ himself. *Here is precisely where he makes his coercive move. To stand for anything other than what the apostle stands for is to articulate for oneself a place of difference, which has already implicitly been associated with discord and disorder.* To stand in a position of difference is to stand in opposition, therefore, to the gospel, the community and Christ. (Castelli 1991a, 87)

Castelli describes the personal will to power implicit in the Pauline rhetorical drive toward sameness. The same analysis can be applied, however, to the politics of group relations even after the apostle's death. What I am suggesting here is that as Paul became ultimately not an embattled apostle for one kind of Christianity contending with others but gradually the source of Christianity *tout court*, and as so-called pagans faded from the scene, the function of those who "stand in a position of difference" came to be filled almost exclusively in the discourse by the Jews, and the "coercive move" toward sameness became directed *at* the Jews.[5] The place of difference increasingly becomes the Jewish place, and thus the Jew becomes the very sign of discord and disorder in the Christian polity. That this is so can be shown from the fact that as other "differences" appear on the medieval European scene—the Lollards, for example—they are figured in literature as "Jews."[6] The association of Jews and women as parallel terms of difference throughout western discourse is a further example of the reduction of Jewishness to a diacritic, a signifier of difference per se.

Paul's allegorical reading of the rite of circumcision is an almost perfect emblem of his hermeneutics of otherness. In one stroke, by interpreting circumcision as referring to a spiritual and not corporeal reality, Paul made it possible for Judaism to become a world religion. It is not that the rite was difficult for adult gentiles to perform—that would hardly have stopped devotees in the ancient world—it was rather that it symbolized the genetic, the genealogical moment, of Judaism as the religion of a particular tribe of people. This is so both in the very physicality of the rite, grounded in the practice of the tribe and marking the male members of that tribe, but it is even more so as a marker on the organ of generation, representing the genealogical claim for concrete historical memory as constitutive of Israel. By substituting a spiritual interpretation for a physical ritual, Paul was saying, the genealogical Israel, "according to the flesh," is not the ultimate Israel; there is an "Israel in the spirit." The practices of the particular Jewish People are not what the Bible speaks of, but faith, the allegorical meaning of those practices. It was Paul's genius to transcend "Israel in the flesh."

Porphyry exposes with rare incandescence the intimate connection between the corporeality of the individual and his or her connection with "race," filiation, and place and the neoplatonic revulsion from both. As Porphyry writes of his hero Plotinus, it was Plotinus's disdain for the body that led him to disdain as well race, parentage, and native country. The Pauline move, while considerably less extreme in every way than that of Paul's younger (by a century) near contemporary, was very similar in structure. I am proposing that Paul's there-is-no-Greek-nor-Jew grew out of substantially the same platonistic cultural themes that drove a Plotinus. This interpretation furnishes us a key to understanding the resistance of the Rabbis to platonism as well.[7] If commitment to "the One" implied a disdain for the body, and disdain for the body entailed an erasure of "difference," then commitment to such differences as race, parentage, and native country entailed a commitment to the body and to "difference" in general. The ancients certainly well understood the connection between notions of the body and ideologies of ethnic identity. As I will try to show, this issue is inextricably bound up in the feminist controversy on essentialism; now, just as in antiquity, the issues of ethnicity and gender are inextricable, and analogies between Jews and women can be pursued for productive purposes. There are ways in which gender is to sex as ethnicity is to race, an analogy that will, moreover, call into question both sets of oppositions.[8]

As Etienne Balibar has argued, the very way that the modern individual is valorized in an opposition between universal and individual, on the one hand, and the particular and gregarious, on the other, reestablishes a hierarchy that performs exactly the same function as the old racism:

This latent presence of the hierarchic theme today finds its chief expression in the priority accorded to the individualistic model (just as,
in the previous period, openly inegalitarian racism, in order to postulate an essential fixity of racial types, had to presuppose a differentialist
anthropology, whether based on genetics or on *Völkerpsychologie*): the
cultures supposed implicitly superior are those which appreciate and
promote "individual" enterprise, social and political individualism, as
against those which inhibit these things. These are said to be the cultures whose "spirit of community" is constituted by individualism. In
this way, we see how the *return of the biological theme* is permitted and
with it the elaboration of new variants of the biological "myth" within
the framework of a cultural racism.   (Balibar 1991a, 25 [emphasis
original])

In other words, by placing a certain model (a Protestant, Paul-derived
model) in a superior position as Culture vis-à-vis those cultures within
which significant aspects of identity and practice are derived from the
group, the ideology of individualism reinscribes the precise hierarchy of
peoples (West and East, or North and South) that racism had. My point
is not, of course, to argue that Paul and his modern posterity are somehow
complicit with racism but rather to show that either ideology, in itself,
can serve racist ends, understood as the organization of hierarchical structures of domination between groups. The insistence on the value of bodily
connection and embodied practice emblematic of Judaism since Paul thus
has significant critical force over against the isolating and disembodying
direction of western idealist philosophies. This very critical force is, however, not devoid of its own dark and frightening aspect.

POWER, IDENTITY, VIOLENCE

The Jewish religion was admirably fitted for defense, but was never designed for conquest.
                    Gibbon, *The Decline and Fall of the Roman Empire*

My thesis is that rabbinic Judaism and Pauline Christianity as two different
hermeneutic systems for reading the Bible generate two diametrically opposed, but mirror-like, forms of racism—and also two dialectical possibilities of anti-racism.[9] In the discussion that follows I shall try to pay attention equally to all four terms of this dialectic.

The genius of Christianity is its concern for all of the peoples of the
world; the genius of rabbinic Judaism is its ability to leave other people

alone.[10] This is grounded theologically in rabbinic Judaism in the notion that in order to achieve salvation, Jews are required to perform (or better, to attempt to perform) the entire 613 commandments, while non-Jews are required only to perform seven commandments given to Noah that form a sort of natural, moral Law. Jewish theology understands the Jewish People to be priests performing a set of ritual acts on behalf of the entire world. Clearly, the temptation to arrogance is built into such a system, but not the temptation to "Sacred Violence" that leads to forced conversion, whether by the sword, ridicule, or the Pound, or deculturation in the name of the new human community. Christianity is the system that proposes that there is something which is necessary for all: faith in Jesus Christ.

And the evils of the two systems are the precise obverse of these genii. If in Christian churches today, one may be uplifted by the expression of concern—and often activist intervention—on behalf of the oppressed peoples of the world, one is equally troubled, often enough, by the missionizing activities and discourses of those same churches. On the other hand, in most traditional synagogues one would be hard put to discover that gentiles exist, except as enemies of the Jews or potential enemies, friends of the Jews or potential friends, but at least no one is proposing to convert or change those gentiles into Jews. Indeed, the explicit theological notion is that they may earn a place in the Next World without even hearing of Jews, let alone converting to Judaism.

Pauline universalism even at its most liberal and benevolent has been a powerful force for coercive discourses of sameness, denying, as we have seen, the rights of Jews, women, and others to retain their difference (Connolly 1991, 42 ff.). As Balibar has realized, this "universalism" is indeed a racism:

> This leads us to direct our attention towards a historical fact that is
> even more difficult to admit and yet crucial, taking into consideration
> the French national form of racist traditions. There is, no doubt, a
> specifically French brand of the doctrines of Aryanism, anthropometry
> and biological geneticism, but the true "French ideology" is not to be
> found in these: it lies rather in the idea that the culture of the "land of
> the Rights of Man" has been entrusted with a universal mission to edu-
> cate the human race. There corresponds to this mission a practice of
> assimilating dominated populations and a consequent need to differen-
> tiate and rank individuals or groups in terms of their greater or lesser
> aptitude for—or resistance to—assimilation. It was this simultaneously

> subtle and crushing form of exclusion/inclusion which was deployed in
> the process of colonization and the strictly French (or "democratic")
> variant of the "White man's burden."   (Balibar 1991a, 24)

This discourse was characteristic of liberal Germany, as Marc Shell points
out,[11] and still persists in the United States of today in such "liberal"
expressions as "too Jewish."[12] Shell documents such notions in the discourse of the contemporary Russian ideologue Igor Sharevich, who argues
that Jews must abandon their difference if they wish to be full citizens of
Russia (Shell 1991, 332). The paradox in such discourse is that nearly
always, as Shell emphasizes, the justification for coercing Jews to become
Christian, Russian, citizens of the world is paradoxically the alleged *intolerance* of—the Jews. The parallels between this modern liberal discourse
and that of Paul—and perhaps even more so of Justin Martyr as discussed
above—seem obvious to me.

The Rabbis' insistence on the centrality of Peoplehood can thus be read
as a radical critique of Paul as well, for if the Pauline move had within it
the possibility of breaking out of the tribal allegiances and commitments
to one's own family, as it were, it also contained the seeds of an imperialist
and colonizing missionary practice. The very emphasis on a universalism
expressed as concern for all of the families of the world turns very rapidly
(if not necessarily) into a doctrine that they must all become part of our
family of the spirit, with all of the horrifying practices against Jews and
other Others which Christian Europe produced. The doctrine of the
Apostle of the Free Spirit can be diverted, even perverted, to a doctrine
of enslaving and torturing bodies. As Henri Baudet has remarked of late-
fifteenth-century Portugal:

> Although the bodies of Negroes might be held captive, this very fact
> made it possible for their souls to achieve true freedom through con-
> version to Christianity. And so the enslavement of Negroes took on a
> kind of missionary aspect. It was in keeping that christened Negro
> slaves should enjoy certain small privileges above their fellows.
> (Baudet 1965, 30)[13]

Paul had indeed written, with notorious ambiguity, "For though absent in
body I am present in spirit, and if present I have already pronounced
judgment in the name of the Lord Jesus on the man who has done such a
thing [lived with his father's wife]. When you are assembled and my spirit
is present, with the power of our Lord Jesus, you are to deliver this man

to Satan for the destruction of the flesh, that his spirit may be saved in the day of the Lord Jesus" (1 Corinthians 5:3–5). It is surely Paul's own sense of self as divided into body and spirit, so that his spirit can be where his body is not—and he means this literally, not as metaphor—, that permits some of his followers to practice torturing and killing bodies to save the souls. (I am not, of course, suggesting that this was Paul's "intent.") Disdain for the bodies of others, when combined with concern for their souls, can be even more devastating than neglect of both.

As sharply, however, as this coercion to conform must be exposed as a racism, we must also be prepared to recognize that Jewish difference with its concomitant nearly exclusive emphasis on caring for other Jews—even when Jews are powerless and dominated—can become an ugly lack of caring for the fate of others and thus another form of racism, logically opposed to the first but equally as dangerous. The insistence on *difference* can produce an *indifference* (or worse) toward Others. The ways in which "benign neglect" can and have become malignant in Jewish texts can readily be documented. From the retrospective position of a world which has, at the end of the second Christian millennium, become thoroughly interdependent, each one of these options is intolerable. A dialectic that would utilize each of these as antithesis to the other, correcting in the "Christian" system its tendencies toward a coercive universalism and in the "Jewish" system its tendencies toward contemptuous neglect for human solidarity might lead beyond both toward a better social system. At present, rather than the best of the two cultures being allowed to critique each other, the most pernicious aspects of both of these hermeneutic systems are in an unholy alliance with each other, so that ethnic/racial superiority has been conjoined with spatial, political domination and the constraint towards conformity in the discourse of nationalism and self-determination. For five hundred years we have seen the effects of such a conjunction in the practices of Christian Europe, and now we see its effects *mutatis mutandis* in many of the practices of the Jewish state. Jewish difference can indeed be dangerous, as the Palestinians know only too well, but Christian universalism has been historically even more dangerous, as Jews, Muslims, Native Americans, Africans, and others have been forced to demonstrate with their bodies. Insistence on genealogical identity and its significance has been one of the major forms of resistance against such violence. In other words, the rabbinic Jewish insistence that there is a difference between Jew and Greek and that that difference has

value can be a liberatory force in the world, a force that works for a contemporary politics of the value of difference—feminist, gay, multicultural,
postcolonial—against coercive sameness. In the next section I am going
to make the perhaps surprising claim that genealogy as a grounding of
identity, while suspiciously close to being racist and always in danger of
becoming such, need not function politically as racism. Indeed, I suggest
that grounding in genealogy is necessary for any secular notion of Jewish
identity at all and further that it plays the political role for Jewishness that
essentialism plays for feminism and gay identity politics (cf. Sedgwick
1990, 75–85).

JEWS AND OTHER DIFFERENCES; OR,
ESSENTIALISM AS RESISTANCE

> It could be said that the tension produced by the essentialist/construc-
> tionist debate is responsible for some of feminist theory's greatest in-
> sights, that is, the very tension is constitutive of the field of feminist
> theory. But it can also be maintained that this same dispute has cre-
> ated the current impasse in feminism, an impasse predicated on the
> difficulty of theorizing the social in relation to the natural, or the theo-
> retical in relation to the political.   (Fuss 1989, 1)

Although it is inflected differently for race, sex, and sexuality, there are
ways that the essentialist/social constructionist dichotomy operates similarly for all of these categories.

We must start with a recognition that essentialism has no essence (Fuss
1989, 4, 21). There are as many essentialisms as there are differences to
be essentialist about (Boswell 1992, 135). Although they have been often
analogized, essentialism with regard to gender seems to me quite different
from essentialism with regard to sexuality—and both, it seems, are entirely different from essentialism with regard to race and to whatever Jewishness is as well. To begin to understand the dimensions of this difference, a typical definition of the question with regard to sexualities will be
sufficient. Contrasting definitions of essentialism with regard to feminism
and gayness will bring out this point clearly. A recent writer on gay identity has defined the controversy in the following manner:

> "Essentialists" treat sexuality as a biological force and consider sexual
> identities to be cognitive realizations of genuine, underlying differ-
> ences; "constructionists," on the other hand, stress that sexuality, and
> sexual identities, are social constructions, and belong to the world

of culture and meaning, not biology. In the first case, there is considered to be some "essence" within homosexuals that makes them
homosexual—some gay "core" of their being, or their psyche, or their
genetic make-up. In the second case, "homosexual," "gay," and "lesbian" are just labels, created by cultures and applied to the self.
(Epstein 1992, 241–42)

This quotation should by itself point up how the meaning of essentialism
will be different when applied to the category "woman" than when used
for the category/ies gay and lesbian, for virtually no one will doubt the
reality of the division into sexes or its historical and cultural universality.[14]
Essentialism, then, with regard to the category "woman" has to do rather
with whether attributes beyond the obvious and physical ones—women
menstruate, conceive and bear children, and lactate; men lack all of
these capabilities—are to be associated with these physical differences or
whether all such associated characteristics are culturally constructed and
thus detrimental to the autonomy of individual women to define their own
essence. (My illogical usage of "essence" at the end of the sentence is
conscious and proleptic of the position I will take.) On the other hand,
the debate about sexuality is whether or not in other cultures or in the
past of our culture, which is the same thing, there were homosexuals and
heterosexuals as categories of people, or only homosexual and heterosexual acts. With regard to sexualities, I claim, the question of essentialism is first a historical and ethnographic question, almost an empirical
one; with regard to sexes, it is a philosophical one.

The following description of what essentialism means in a feminist context should further clarify the point:

If most feminists, however one may classify trends and positions—
cultural, liberal, socialist, poststructuralist, and so forth—agree that
women are made, not born, that gender is not an innate feature (as
sex may be) but a sociocultural construction (and precisely for that
reason it is oppressive to women), that patriarchy is historical (especially so when it is believed to have superseded a previous matriarchal
realm), then the "essence" of woman that is described in the writings
of many so-called essentialists is not the *real essence,* in Locke's terms,
but more likely a *nominal* one.   (De Lauretis 1989, 5; see Fuss 1989,
4–5)

The crucial words in this paragraph for my limited purposes here are "as
sex may be"; in other words, the division into sexes is (or at least may be)
an innate feature, even for those who are anti-essentialist feminists.[15]

There are men and women "really"; the question is what does this mean, or what are they like, or are there any essential differences beyond the obvious ones, while the question with regard to gay people is: Have "they" always existed, or have "we" "made them up"? Have they perhaps made themselves up—at a certain point in cultural history (Hacking 1992)?[16]

In a paper published in a recent collection, Steven Epstein poses the issue in a sharply focused and politicized manner. "I take as given that power inheres in the ability to name," he writes, "and that what we call ourselves has implications for political practice. . . . Legitimation strategies play a mediating function between self-understanding and political programs, and between groups and their individual members" (Epstein 1991, 241). The great virtue of Epstein's paper is its constant attention to the *political* function of claims to essence. In the following statement, while I think he seriously misconstrues social constructionism, he nevertheless clearly articulates this political function:

> A "folk constructionism" comes to be disseminated: the view that sexual identities are willful self-creations. And in reaction against this folk constructionism, which denies the experience of a non-voluntary component to identity, lesbians and gays operating within the liberal discourse slide to the opposite extreme: they assert that there is something "real" about their identity, and then try to locate that felt reality in their genes, or their earliest experiences, or their mystical nature. (261)[17]

This alleged "folk constructionism" bears no relation, typological or genetic, to social constructionism—it certainly predates these theories—, so Epstein is setting up a paper tiger here, but nonetheless, the positive part of the argument seems undoubtedly correct to me. Claims for essence are legitimation strategies for identity politics and, as such, are attacked at great peril to causes of difference and liberation of differences. As Ed Cohen has put it, "How individuals come together to act for change, how these actors are changed by their activities, and how these acts and actors crystallize as movements cannot be adequately imagined if the powerful effects *felt* by acting subjects are 'theoretically' disappeared" (Cohen 1991, 82). This formulation appears in a generally appreciative discussion of Judith Butler's work, in which Cohen has also written:

> In its attempt to rethink "agency" so that it is "constituted" in terms of "construction," it obviates any concern with what brings individuals together to effect changes in the social imagination/organization of

their shared life-world, implicitly portraying collective action as "simply" voluntaristic.   (83)

And thus, I would add, it paradoxically reinscribes the "Protestant" ideology of the individual. Picking up on Cohen's overall argument, I would suggest that only a grouping which has some somatic referent can allow itself the possibility of reinventing its essence: "For if we can begin to gather together on the basis of constructions that 'we' are constantly and self-consciously in the process of inventing, multiplying, and modifying, then perhaps 'we' can obviate the need for continuing to reiterate the fragmenting oscillations between identity and difference that have been the legacy of post 1960s progressive politics" (88). As Cohen quite brilliantly suggests here, there has to be some referent for a we that is not in quotation marks in order for the cited, constructed "we" to function as such. With regard to women and gay people, there is some "objective reality," some somatic referent, it seems, about which to even ask the question of essence. At least ostensibly, the category of women is defined by something they are in their bodies, and gay and lesbian people by something they do with their bodies. There is, in both cases, as I have said, something about which to ask the question regarding essence, although I have argued that it is a different question in each of these two cases. But what about Jews? In what sense does this category exist—even as a nominalist category? I suggest that only genealogy can fill that function for Jews.

The most common language for the description of Jewishness historically is the language of race, γένος. Race, however, certainly did not mean in the premodern period anything like what it means today. The term has taken on an entirely different set of connotations in a recent epistemic shift, analogous to the epistemic shift that Foucault and especially Arnold Davidson have identified in the discourse of sexuality (Davidson 1992). If Foucault could write, "Our epoch has initiated sexual heterogeneities" (Foucault 1980), we can also claim that our epoch has initiated racial heterogeneities in almost the same fashion (Cohen 1991, 78–79). "Race," which was once the signifier of a set of relations with other human beings determined in the first instance by a common kinship and historical connection, has become the signifier of distinct, heterogeneous human essences, at just about the same time that sexual practices were transformed into the signifiers of different categorical essences of human beings. As Lloyd Thompson has put it:

In these old and ever-popular usages, "race" bears two sometimes over-
lapping connotations: on the one hand, an ethnic group, a people, or
a nation; and, on the other hand, a somatic type defined in terms of
perceived skin colour, hair type, and morphology—a concept of "race"
that dates from the latter part of the seventeenth century.   (Thompson 1989, 13)

This shift in meaning has, of course, enormous implications; the fact that
it took place in tandem must also be meaningful.

Let us begin, then, by exploring the sense that "race" might have had
for premodern and particularly late-antique people. Symptomatic perhaps
of this shift is the following statement from Dio Cassius, "I do not know
the origin of this name [Jews], but it is applied to all men, even foreigners,
who follow their customs. This race is found among Romans" (Gager
1983, 91). Now it is quite clear from this quotation that for Dio the word
"race" does not imply some sort of biological essence, since it can be
applied to Romans who have chosen to follow the customs of Jews. In
short, one can *convert* to a race. "Race" is thus the signifier of a concept
for which we have no word at all in our language, something like family
writ very large. Just as family for us is primarily the signifier of a genealogical, that is, biological connection, but one that does not in any way
presuppose some biological essence, so also "race" in premodern usage.
Furthermore, just as family includes people who are not in the primarily
physically defined grouping but have joined it secondarily, either through
marriage or adoption, so also people can join a race in Dio's usage.

Jewishness was, therefore, in antiquity, something—I do not say an
essence—that could be referred to via the language of race. We no longer
do so, although oddly enough, it seems that the modern sense of race has
been constructed originally precisely against the Jews. This occurred at
two points in the development of the modern concept. The first is in the
Spanish "purity of blood," *limpieza de sangre,* to which I will have further
reference below. This term signified one whose blood had not been tainted
with the blood of *conversos,* converted Jews, and was, therefore, purely
Spanish and purely Christian.[18] The second is at the development of modern "scientific" racism, which is, originally, the founding ideology of anti-
Semitism.

There are significant differences between Jewishness and the modern
sociopolitical senses of race. The primary dissimilarities involve the fact
that people can convert to Judaism, which would seem to suggest that it

is merely a confession, and that there are no "racial" characteristics that mark Jews off from other human groups, as there are, for instance, for Japanese people or Europeans.[19] More revealingly, however, the convert's name is changed to "ben Avraham" or "bas Avraham," son or daughter of Abraham. The convert is adopted into the family and assigned a new "genealogical" identity, but also, since Abraham is the first convert in Jewish tradition, converts are his descendants in that sense as well. There is thus a sense in which the convert becomes the ideal type of the Jew (see, however, Davies 1974, 168n. 3).

On the other hand, Jews do not sense of themselves that their association is confessional, that it is based on common religion, for many people whom both religious and secular Jews call Jewish neither believe nor practice the religion at all. This kind of "racialism" is built into the formal cultural system itself. While you can convert *in* to Judaism, you cannot convert *out*, and anyone born of Jewish parents is Jewish, even if she doesn't know it. Jewishness is thus certainly not contiguous with modern notions of race, which have been, furthermore discredited empirically. Nor are Jews marked off biologically, as people are marked for sex; nor finally, can Jews be reliably identified by a set of practices, as for example gay people can. On the other hand, Jewishness is not an affective association of individuals either. Jews in general feel not that Jewishness is something they have freely chosen but rather that it is an essence—an essence often nearly empty of any content other than itself—which has been inscribed—sometimes even imposed—on them by birth.

How can this sense of genealogically given essence be distinguished from racism? What it comes down to, finally, is this. Any claimed or ascribed essence has two directly opposed meanings depending simply on the politics of the given social situation (Foucault 1980, 101–02). For people who are somehow part of a dominant group, any assertions of essence are ipso facto products and reproducers of the system of domination. For subaltern groups, however, essentialism is resistance, the insistence on the "right" of the group to actually exist.[20] Essence, as such, always makes an appeal to the body, to the "real," the referential. For women, the appeal is to the difference in the reproductive, sexual body; for gay people the appeal is to the difference in their sexual practices; for Jews, the appeal is to filiation. What we see in each of these cases is that the very things appealed to in order to legitimate the subaltern identity are appealed to as well by dominating groups in order to exploit the dominated. The valence of the claim shifts from negative to positive with the political status of the group making the claim. Therefore, I suggest, that which would be racism in the hands of a dominating group is resistance in the hands of a subaltern collective. In order, then, to preserve the positive ethical, political value of Jewish genealogy as a mode of identity, Jews must preserve their subaltern status. I wish to set out, at least *in nuce,* a notion of identity, which I will call Diaspora identity, which will be of value beyond the articulation of Jewishness alone.

DIASPORIZING IDENTITY

The most violent practice that rabbinic Judaism ever developed vis-à-vis its Others was playing cards on Christmas Eve or walking around the block to avoid passing a pagan or Christian place of worship. Something else was needed for the potential racist implications of genealogical particularism to become actualized. That necessity is power over others. This idea was already predicted by the medieval Jewish philosopher, Yehuda Halevi, who in his *Kuzari* has God say to the Jews: Your modesty is a function of your powerlessness; when you have power you will be as cruel as any other people.

Etienne Balibar has been willing, at least initially, to grant the progressive value of "anthropological culturalism," the insistence on the value of maintaining cultural differences (1991a, 21). He remarks: "Its value had been confirmed by the contribution it made to the struggle against the hegemony of certain standardizing imperialisms and against the elimination of minority or dominated civilizations—'ethnocide'" (21–22). He argues, however, citing the example of Claude Lévi-Strauss's "Race and Culture," that the latter ends up embroiling himself in rightist arguments against the mixing of cultures and the danger to humanity from ignoring the "spontaneous" [read "natural"] human tendency to preserve their traditions. And Balibar remarks: "What we see here is that biological or genetic naturalism is not the only means of naturalizing human behaviour and social affinities. . . . *Culture can also function like a nature,* and it can in particular function as a way of locking individuals and groups a priori into a genealogy, into a determination that is immutable" (Balibar and Wallerstein 1991, 2). Moreover, it also can serve as a rational justification for arguments that, purporting to be preventives against racism, propose that to avoid racism, you have to avoid that "abstract" anti-racism which fails to grasp the psychological and sociological laws of human population movements; you have to respect the "tolerance thresholds," maintain "cultural distances" or, in other words, in accordance with the postulate that individuals are the exclusive heirs and bearers of a single culture, segregate collectivities (the best barrier in this regard still being national frontiers).   (Balibar 1991a, 23)

Balibar has thus exposed critical flaws in discourses of "differential racism" as an antidote to racism. The question is whether, then, all discourses of strong cultural identity will necessarily produce such negative effects.[21]

Diaspora culture and identity can, I think, move us beyond this dilemma, for it allows (and has historically allowed in the best circumstances, such as Muslim Spain), for a complex continuation of Jewish cultural creativity and identity at the same time that the same people participate fully in the common cultural life of their surroundings. The same figure, a Nagid, Ibn Gabirol, or Maimonides can be at one and the same time a vehicle of the preservation of traditions and of the mixing of cultures. Nor was this only the case in Muslim Spain, nor even only outside of the Land. The Rabbis in Diaspora in their own Land also produced a phenomenon of renewal of Jewish traditional culture at the same time that they were very well acquainted indeed and an integral part of the circumambient late-antique culture. Diasporic cultural identity teaches us that cultures are not preserved by being protected from "mixing" but probably can only continue to exist as a product of such mixing. All cultures, and identities, are constantly being remade. Diasporic Jewish culture, however, lays this process bare, because of the impossibility of a natural association between this people and a particular land, thus the impossibility of seeing Jewish culture as a self-enclosed, bounded phenomenon. The critical force of this dissociation between people, language, culture, and land has, I think, been an enormous threat to cultural nativisms and integrisms, a threat that is one of the sources of anti-Semitism, and perhaps one of the reasons that Europe has been much more prey to this evil than the Middle East. In other words, diasporic identity is a disaggregated identity.[22]

I am a Jew, I would claim, and it is both right and good (for me and for humanity) that I continue to maintain my cultural practice and cultural identity—the very fact of difference is positive—, but at the same time that does not form an "immutable determination." The truth of my being

244 Answering the Mail

Jewish is not compromised by the fact that I am also American, very profoundly so, that in the morning I may go to the synagogue and in the evening to hear Emmylou Harris, and both practices are of very great importance to me. Lest this point get lost, let me emphasize that the first practice is not only, nor often even primarily, a religious practice but rather a cultural practice. When, for instance, I have the prayer for the sick said in synagogue, this is not because my skeptical self believes— much as I would like to—in the efficacy of petitionary prayer, but because this is the way that Jews express solidarity with sick people. Furthermore, as the example chosen—Emmylou Harris—should make clear, this is not an opposition between a particular and a universal identity—i.e., not a version of "be a Jew at home and a human being abroad"—but a concatenation of two equally particular identities in the same polysystem. I am *not* contrasting the Jewish to the American as the particular to the universal, nor certainly as the private to the public, as expected of Jews in Napoleonic France—which would completely undermine my point—but as two particularities.

Jewishness disrupts the very categories of identity, because it is not national, not genealogical, not religious, but all of these, in dialectical tension with one another. When liberal Arabs and some Jews claim that the Jews of the Middle East are Arab Jews, I concur with them and think that Zionist ideology occludes something very significant when it seeks to obscure this point. Maxime Rodinson has articulated this somewhat differently when he wrote, "Jewish nationalism has special peculiarities. For one thing, it applies to a very disparate human group, whose members have possibilities of self-understanding and action other than those afforded by the ideology of the nation. The best proof of this is the persistent, recurrent, and obstinate effort of Jewish nationalists to rally the mass of their potential adherents behind them, often by dubious means" (Rodinson 1983, 11). The promulgation of a nationalist ideology of a pure Jewish cultural essence that has been debased by Diaspora seems precisely such a dubious means to me. I am proud to hear that in the Cairo University, Rabbi Saʿadya Gaon is being studied as an important Arab and Egyptian philosopher. On the other hand, the very fact that this makes me, an American Ashkenazi Jew, feel proud shows that identifying the rabbi as an Egyptian Arab of the Jewish faith is not the answer either. To continue the personal tone, I feel deeply injured when I hear certain leftist anti-Zionist compatriots deny the very existence or significance of my connection with the eighth-century Egyptian rabbi or with a modern Egyptian Jew, or hers with Rashi or with me. Statist nationalisms seem to require that we choose one or the other. Diasporized, that is, disaggregated identity, allows for Rabbi Saʿadya to be an Egyptian Arab who happens to be Jewish and also a Jew who happens to be an Egyptian Arab. Both of these contradictory propositions must be held together. Similarly, for gender, I think that a diasporization of identity is possible and positive. Being a woman is some kind of special being, and there are aspects of life and practice that insist on and celebrate that speciality. But this does not imply a fixing or freezing of all practice and performance of gender identity into one set of parameters. Human beings are divided into men and women—sometimes—but that does not tell the whole story *of their bodily identity.* Rather than the dualism of gendered bodies and universal souls, or Jewish/Greek bodies and universal souls—the dualism that, as I have argued throughout this book, is offered by Paul—we can substitute *partially* Jewish, *partially* Greek bodies, bodies that are *sometimes* gendered and *sometimes* not. It is this idea that I am calling diasporized identity.

Paradoxically, however, I would also insist that genealogy as a shared historical memory, most fully (but not exhaustively) represented in the actual, physical identity of child of one's parents is crucial to the maintenance of cultural identity. It is the analog for Jews of possession of the womb for women. It is that which produces some sense of reference, of real anchoring, for difference. To be sure, I remark once more, this genealogy has been denaturalized in Judaism for thousands of years through the mechanism of conversion, but as I have indicated such de-naturalization serves at the same time to reinforce the general symbol of genealogical connection through the ascription of it to the convert. Diasporic Jewish identity has been founded on common memory of shared space and on the hope for such a shared space in an infinitely deferred future. Space itself is thus transformed into time. Memory of territory has made deterritorialization possible, and paradoxically, the possession of territory may have made Diaspora Jewishness impossible.

The tragedy of Zionism has been its desperate—and I believe misdirected—attempt to reduce real threats to Jews and Jewishness by concretizing in the present what has been a utopian symbol for the future. Diasporized identities seem threatened ones, and one of the responses to such threats is separatism, an attempt at a social structure that re-aggregates the disaggregated, re-integrizes the non-integral, by closing off the borders, by indeed attempting to prevent mixing, whether biological or cultural. Zionism, like separatist feminism, is such an attempt. Zionism is a particular reading of Jewish culture and especially of the Bible. I do not, and could not, given my hermeneutic theories, argue that it is a wrong reading or that there is a right reading that can be countered to it. I do argue, however, that it is not the only reading.

RACISM AND THE BIBLE

In his brilliantly suggestive recent paper, Marc Shell has discussed the history of the ideologeme of "pure Spanish blood" (Shell 1991). Thus, Shell argues, the Spain of the *Reconquista* "plays a central role in the European history of the idea of caste or race," and when that is combined with the Christian doctrine of "All men are brothers," we end up with a dehominization of all who are not Christian Spaniards. Since they are not brothers, they must not be human (Shell 1991, 308–09)! The result was expulsion of Jews and Muslims and even religious mass murder, such as the slaughter of the innocents in California, practices which, as Shell points out, were *nearly* unknown under Muslim rule. The doctrine of "purity of blood" (*limpieza de sangre*) that developed in this period, whereby a Christian was defined as someone whose ancestors had "always" been Christian, seems a signal departure from everything that Paul stood for.[23] It cannot be solely located in a biblical milieu, either, for in every variety of biblical or post-biblical Judaism that I know of, notwithstanding the enormous emphasis on ethnicity, converts were of *exactly* the same status as Jews "by blood." As Shell remarks, the biblical polity had, moreover, a built-in "law of tolerance" for non-Israelites in their midst, which served as a model for European liberals (328–29). It took the combination of two elements, Shell argues, Pauline "universalism" and racism, to produce unspeakable horror—including an important contribution to the "pure blood" doctrines of both Italian and German fascism (312).[24]

Where, however, did the element of racism come from? Shell locates it exclusively in the absence in Paul of any category between "brothers" and animals, of any category of "others" whose sameness of kind is asserted even while their difference as non-kin is maintained. On the one hand, I am in complete sympathy with Shell's denial that racism is "the Jewish aspect of Christianity" (329). On the other, I think that Shell seriously overplays his hand when he totally denies *any* role at all to the Bible and

"Jewish particularism" in the origins of Spanish racism, and this denial takes on a peculiarly apologetic flavor at times in his work. While there is no gainsaying the enormous cultural significance of biblical "toleration" of the stranger, there is also no gainsaying the dark currents of violence toward certain strangers in the Land—"the seven nations," which are to be exterminated—nor the presence in Ezra-Nehemiah, for example, of a strong tendency toward some kind of family (if not racialized) *limpieza*. A story like that of Abraham refusing to bury his dead among the dead of the Land and insisting on separate ground, understandable perhaps within a certain tribal cultural economy, may certainly have played even an unconscious part in the production of such a cultural theme as *limpieza de sangre*.

On the other hand, critics of Zionism, both Arab and other, as well as anti-Semites, both Jewish and non-Jewish, have often sought to portray Jewish culture as racist to its very foundations, as essentially racist. This foundational racism is traced to the Hebrew Bible and described as the transparent meaning of that document. Critics who are otherwise fully committed to constructionist and historicist accounts of meaning and practice abandon this commitment when it comes to the Hebrew Bible— assuming that the Bible *is*, in fact and in essence, that which it has been read to be and that it authorizes univocally that which it has been taken to authorize.[25] In what is otherwise an astonishingly sophisticated discussion, we find written, "For certain societies, in certain eras of their development, the scriptures have acted culturally and socially in the same way the human genetic code operates physiologically. That is, this great code has, in some degree, directly determined what people would believe and what they would think and what they would do" (Akenson 1992, 9). No interpretation is necessary; Scripture speaks with perfect transparence.[26] Another recent writer holds: "But the distinctions raised in the covenant between religion and idolatry are like some visitation of the khamsin to wilderness peoples as yet unsuspected, dark clouds over Africa, the Americas, the Far East, until finally even the remotest islands and jungle enclaves are struck by fire and sword and by the subtler weapon of conversion-by-ridicule (Deuteronomy 2:34; 7:2; 20:16–18; Joshua 6: 17–21)" (Turner 1988, 45; cf. Jonathan Boyarin 1992b, 134). Local historically and materially defined practices of a culture far away and long ago are made here "naturally" responsible (like the khamsin, the Middle Eastern Santa Ana) for the colonial practices of cultures entirely other to it, simply because those later cultures used those practices as their authorization.

Even the primitive command to wipe out the Peoples of Canaan was limited *by the Bible itself* to those particular people in that particular place, and thus declared no longer applicable by the Rabbis of the Talmud. The very literalism of rabbinic/midrashic hermeneutics prevented a typological "application" of this command to other groups.[27] Does this mean that rabbinic Judaism qua ideology is innocent of either ethnocentric or supremacist tenets? Certainly not! What it argues is rather that Jewish racism, like the racism of other peoples, is a facultative and dispensable aspect of the cultural system, not one that is necessary for its preservation or essential to its nature. Perhaps the primary function for a critical construction of cultural (or racial or gender or sexual) identity is to construct such identity in ways that purge it of its elements of domination and oppression. Some, however, would argue that this is an impossible project, not because of the nature of Jewishness but because *any* group identity is oppressive, unless it is oppressed.

In a recent marxian analysis of both race and racism, Balibar has argued that "racism" has two dissymmetrical aspects. On the one hand, it constitutes a dominating community with practices, discursive and otherwise, that are "articulated around stigmata of otherness (name, skin colour, religious practices)." It also constitutes, however, "the way in which, as a mirror image, individuals and collectives that are prey to racism (its 'objects') find themselves constrained to see themselves as a community." Balibar further argues that destruction of racism implies the "internal decomposition of the community created by racism," by which he means the dominating community, as is clear from his analogy to the overcoming of sexism which will involve "the break-up of the community of 'males'" (Balibar 1991a, 18). This is, however, for me the crucial point, for the question is obviously: If overcoming sexism involves the breaking up of the community of males, does it necessarily imply the breaking up of the community of females? And does this, then, not entail a breaking up of community, *tout court?* Putting it another way, are we not simply reinscribing the One once more in such a formulation, once more imposing a coercive universal? On the other hand, if indeed the very existence of the dominant group is dependent on domination, if identity is always formed in a master-slave relationship, is perhaps the price not too high? What I wish to struggle for theoretically is a notion of identity in which there are only slaves but no masters, that is, an alternative to the model of self-determination, which is, after all, in itself a western, imperialist imposition on the rest of the world. I propose Diaspora—to be sure, an idealized Diaspora generalized from those situations in Jewish history when Jews were both relatively free from persecution and yet constituted by strong identity, those situations, moreover, within which promethean Jewish creativity was not antithetical to, indeed was synergistic with, a general cultural activity—as a theoretical and historical model to replace national self-determination.[28] Another way of making the same point would be to insist that there are material and social conditions in which cultural identity and difference will not produce even what Balibar has called "differential racism," that is, a "racism whose dominant theme is not biological heredity but the insurmountability of cultural differences, a racism which, at first sight, does not postulate the superiority of certain groups or peoples in relation to others but 'only' the harmfulness of abolishing frontiers, the incompatibility of life-styles and traditions" (1991a, 21). To my understanding, it would be an appropriate goal to articulate a theory and practice of identity which would on the one hand respect the irreducibility and the positive value of cultural differences, the harmfulness not of abolishing frontiers but of dissolving of uniqueness, and the mutual fructification of different life-styles and traditions.[29] I do not think, moreover, that such possibilities are merely utopian. I would certainly claim that there have been historical situations in which they obtained, to be sure, without perfect success in this radically imperfect world. The solution of political Zionism, Jewish state hegemony, except insofar as it represented an emergency and temporary rescue operation, seems to me the subversion of Jewish culture and not its culmination, in that it represents the substitution of a European, western cultural-political formation for a traditional Jewish one that has been based on a sharing—at best—of political power with others and which takes on entirely other meanings when combined with political hegemony.[30]

For example, Jewish resistance to assimilation and annihilation within conditions of Diaspora—to which I will return below—generated such practices as communal charity in the areas of education, feeding, providing for the sick, and the caring for Jewish prisoners, to the virtual exclusion of such charity directed at others. This exclusive attention to "one's own," however, when in a subaltern situation simply does not have the same political meanings as it would have when Jews (or others) are domi-

nant politically. In Israel, where power is virtually exclusively concentrated in Jewish hands, this practice has become a monstrosity, whereby
an egregiously disproportionate portion of the resources of the State of
Israel is devoted to the welfare of only one segment of the population. A
further, somewhat more subtle and symbolic example, is the following:
That very practice I mentioned above of symbolic expression of contempt
for places of worship of others becomes darkly ominous when it is combined with temporal power and domination, i.e., when Jews have power
over places of worship belonging to others. To cite one example among
many: It is this factor, I would claim, that has allowed the Israelis to turn
the central Mosque of Beersheba into a museum of the Negev and to allow the Muslim cemetery of that city to fall into ruins.[31] Insistence on
ethnic speciality, when it is extended over a particular piece of Land, will
inevitably produce a discourse not unlike the Inquisition in many of its
effects. We already see a certain nearly inexorable logic at work here. Thus
the declaration of a Jewish State has led, because of its (inevitable and
only partially willed) violence toward the Palestinians, to a Palestinian
counter-discourse of desire for a Palestinian State.[32] We thus have now an
acting out of precisely the theory that Balibar exposed of postulating the
necessity of ethnic/cultural separation behind closed borders in order to
prevent the cultural mixing that leads to violence. In their rightist forms,
these arguments call for expelling the Other. In their liberal forms, these
arguments call for the formation of two states that are sealed off from each
other.[33] Both are racist programs.[34]

My argument is that capturing Judaism in a State transforms entirely
the meanings of its social practices. Practices which in Diaspora have one
meaning—e.g., caring for the feeding and housing of Jews and not "others"—have entirely different meanings in a situation of political hegemony. E. P. Sanders has gotten this just right:

> More important is the evidence that points to Jewish pride in separat-
> ism. Christian scholars habitually discuss the question under the im-
> plied heading "What was wrong with Judaism that Christianity cor-
> rected?" Exclusivism is considered to be bad, and the finding that Jews
> were to some degree separatist fills many with righteous pride. We shall
> all agree that exclusivism is bad when practiced by the dominant group.
> Things look different if one thinks of minority groups that are trying to
> maintain their own identity. I have never felt that the strict Amish are
> iniquitous, and I do not think that, in assessing Jewish separatism in
> the Diaspora, we are dealing with a moral issue. (The moral issue

would be the treatment of Gentiles in Palestine during periods of Jewish ascendancy. How well were the biblical laws to love the resident
alien [Lev 19:33–34] observed?)   (Sanders 1990, 181; cf. Davies
1992, 133–38)

The inequities—and worse—in Israeli political, economic, and social
practice are not aberrations but inevitable consequences of the inappropriate importation of a form of discourse from one historical situation to
another, a discourse of intimacy and resistance to the claims of others,
from a situation in which Jews were a dominated minority to one in which
they are a dominating majority and in which power, concern, freedom,
and resources have all to be aggregate. In the final section of this chapter,
I wish then to begin to articulate a notion of Jewish identity that recuper-
ates its genealogical moment—family, history, memory, and practice—
while at the same time problematizing claims to autochthony and indigeneity as the material base of Jewish identity.

DETERRITORIALIZING JEWISHNESS

The Tanak and other sources of Judaism reveal certain ideas concerning The Land that reflect, or are parallel to, primitive Semitic, other
Near Eastern, and, indeed, widespread conceptions about the significance of their land to a particular people. Israel is represented as the
centre of the Earth. . . . The religious man desires to live as near to
this sacred space as possible and comes to regard it, the place of his
abode, his own land, as the centre of the world.   (Davies 1992, 1, 87)

There are two diametrically opposed moments in the Jewish discourse of
the Land. On the one hand, it is crucial to recognize that the Jewish
conception of the Land of Israel is absolutely and essentially similar and
contiguous to the discourse of the Land of many (if not nearly all) "indigenous" peoples of the world. Somehow, the Jews have managed to retain a sense of being rooted somewhere in the world through twenty centuries of exile from that someplace, and organicist metaphors are not out
of place in this discourse, for they are used within the tradition itself.

There is accordingly something profoundly disturbing about Jewish attachment to the Land being decried as regressive in the same discursive
situations in which the attachment of Native Americans or Australians to
their particular rocks, trees, and deserts is celebrated as an organic connection to the Earth which "we" have lost. Recently at a conference an

aboriginal speaker from Australia began her lecture with greetings from her people to the indigenous people of the United States, of whom there were two representatives at the conference, whom she addressed by name. Much of her lecture consisted of a critique of the rootlessness of Europeans. I had a sense of being trapped in a double bind, for if the Jews are the indigenous people of the Land of Israel, as Zionism claims, then the Palestinians are indigenous nowhere, but if the Palestinians are the indigenous people of Palestine, then Jews are indigenous nowhere (J. Boyarin 1992b, 119; Rabi 1979). I have painfully renounced the possibility of realizing my very strong feeling of connection to the Land (or rather, deferred it to some Messianic redemption, when all will be clarified) in favor of what I take to be the only possible end to violence and movement toward justice. Am I now to be condemned as a person who has lost his roots? I think that the uncritical valorization of indigenousness (and particularly the confusion between political indigeneity and mystified autochthony) must come under critique, without wishing, however, to deny the rights of Native Americans, Australians, and Palestinians to their lands precisely on the basis of real and not mystified political claims.[35] Thus I find the arguments of some Palestinians that they are the direct descendants of the Jebusites and therefore exclusively entitled to the Land frightening in their implications, for the same reason that I find such claims frightening in the mouths of Jews. If Jews are to give up hegemony over the Land, this does not mean that the profundity of our attachment to that Land and the crucial cultural significance of a large grouping of Jews in one place, speaking, writing, and creating in Hebrew, can be denied; these also must have a political expression in the present. The cultural rights of a Jewish collective or collectives must be protected in any future Palestine as well.

The biblical story is not one of autochthony but one of always already coming from somewhere else. As Davies has so very well understood, the concept of a Divine Promise to give this land, which is the land of Others, to His People Israel is a marker and sign of a bad conscience at having deprived the others of their Land (Davies 1992, 11–12).[36] Thus, at the same time that one vitally important strain of expression within biblical religion promotes a sense of organicistic "natural" connectedness between this People and this Land, a settlement in the Land, in another sense or in a counter-strain, Israelite and Jewish religion is perpetually an *unsettlement* of the very notion of autochthony.

Traditional Jewish attachment to the Land, whether biblical or post-biblical, thus provides a self-critique as well as a critique of identities based on notions of autochthony. One Jewish narrative of the Land has the power of insisting on the powerful connection without myths of autochthony, while other narratives, including the Zionist one, have repressed memories of coming from somewhere else. These very repressions are complicitous with a set of mystifications within which nationalist ideologies subsist. We have two alternative modes *in the Bible itself* for the construction of Jewish identity, one based on genealogy and one on autochthony. Paul leveled his primary attack on the former, while I am suggesting that it is the latter that is primarily responsible for racist effects in Jewish cultures. As Harry Berger argues, "The alienation of social constructions of divinity and cosmos by conquest groups resembles the alienation of socially constructed kinship and status terms from domestic kin groups to corporate descent groups—in anthropological jargon, from the ego-centered kinship system of families to the more patently fictional ancestor-centered system of lineages" (Berger 1989, 121). Distinguishing between forms of "weak transcendence" and "strong transcendence," Berger argues that "family membership illustrates weak kinship; tribal membership, strong kinship" (121). Strong transcendence is that which is more aggressive, because it is more embattled and doing more ideological work in the service of, according to Berger, land control: "Status that depends on land is generally more precarious and alienable than status inscribed on the body; mobile subsistence economies tend to conceptualize status in terms of the signifying indices of the body—indices of gender, age, and kinship—rather than of more conspicuously artificial constructions, and are closer to the weak end of the weak-to-strong scale." Thus Berger, following Brueggemann, contrasts two covenants, one the Mosaic, which rejects "the imperial gods of a totalitarian and hierarchic social order," and one the Davidic, which enthrones precisely those gods as the one God. I could similarly contrast the two trajectories, the one toward autochthony and the one against it in the same way: the former promotes status that depends on land while the latter provides for status "in terms of the signifying indices of the body." The first would serve to support the rule of Israelite kings over territory, while the second would serve to oppose it:[37] "The dialectical struggle between antiroyalism and royalism persists throughout the course and formative career of the Old Testament as its structuring force. It sets the tent against the house, nomadism against agriculture, the wilderness against Canaan, wandering and exile against settlement, diaspora against the political integrity of a settled state" (123). My argument, then, is that a vision of Jewish history and identity that valorizes the second half of each of these binaries and sees the first as only a disease constitutes not a continuation of Jewish culture but its subversion.

What, however, of the fact that Berger has also implicated "ancestor-centered systems of lineages" as ideological mystifications in the service of state-power of conquest groups—seeming to agree with Paul that claims of status according to the flesh are retrograde—, while I have held such an organization up as the *alternative and counter* to statism? Empirically, tribal organization with its concomitant myths of the eponymous ancestor, e.g., Abraham, is nearly emblematic of nomadic peoples, not of states. Berger's own discourse, moreover, is inconsistent here, for only a page later, he refers to the pre-monarchic period of Israel ("roughly 1250 to 1000 B.C.") as a social experiment in "the rejection of strong transcendence in favor of a less coercive and somewhat weaker alternative, the tribal system that cuts across both local allegiances and stratificational discontinuities" (123). Thus Berger puts tribalism first on the side of "strong transcendence" and then on the side of "weak." Against Berger's first claim on this point and in favor of his second, I would argue that talk of the eponymous ancestors, of the Patriarchs, is conspicuously less prominent in the "Davidic" texts of the settlement than in the "Mosaic" texts of the wandering. As Berger himself writes, "[David] tried to displace the loyalties and solidarity of kinship ties from clans and tribes to the national dynasty" (124). I would suggest that descent from a common ancestor is rather an extension of family kinship and not its antithesis and thus on the side of wilderness and not on the side of Canaan. Even the myth of descent from common ancestry belongs rather to the semantic field of status through the body and not to the semantic field of status through land. Diaspora, in historical Judaism, can be interpreted then as the analog in a later set of material conditions of nomadism in the earlier, and thus as a continuation of the "sociological experiment" which the Davidic monarchy symbolically overturns.[38] With the "invention" of Diaspora, the "radical experiment of Moses" was advanced. The forms of identification typical of nomads, those marks of status in the body, remained, then, crucial to this formation. Race is here on the side of the radicals; space, on the other hand, belongs to the despots. Paul has, on my view, like many of his followers even of good will, misread the promises and possibilities of the Jewish discourse of deterritorialized, genealogical identity. But then, in my view, so has Zionism.

One modernist story of Israel—the Israeli Declaration of Independence—begins with an imaginary autochthony: "In the Land of Israel this people came into existence," and ends with the triumphant return of the People to their natural Land, making them re-autochthonized, "like all of the nations." Israeli state-power, deprived of the option of self-legitimation through appeal to divine king, discovered autochthony as a powerful replacement.[39] An alternative story of Israel begins with a people forever unconnected with a particular land, a people that calls into question the idea that a people must have a land in order to be a people:

> The Land of Israel was not the birthplace of the Jewish people, which
> did not emerge there (as most peoples have on their own soil). On
> the contrary it had to enter its own Land from without; there is a sense
> in which Israel was born in exile. Abraham had to leave his own land
> to go to the Promised Land: the father of Jewry was deterritorialized.
> (Davies 1992, 63)[40]

For this reading, the stories of Israel's conquest of the Land, whether under Abraham, Joshua or even more prominently, David, are always stories that are more compromised with a sense of failure of mission than they are imbued with the accomplishment of mission, and the internal critique within the Tanakh (Hebrew Bible) itself, the dissident voice which is nearly always present, does not let us forget this either. Davies also brings into absolutely clear focus a prophetic discourse of preference for "Exile" over rootedness in the Land (together with a persistent hope of *eschatological* restoration), a prophetic discourse which has been, of course, totally occluded in modern Zionist ideological representations of the Bible and of Jewish history but was pivotal in the rabbinic ideology (15–19). Ultimately, I would argue, then, that Israel is indeed a product of European colonialism and cultural imperialism but in a sense that the other nation-states of the postcolonial world are as well. The ultimate product of western imperialism is the extension of the very system of nation-states over the entire world, and it is this that must be resisted. As Balibar has put it:

> There is indeed an institution which the world bourgeoisie shares and
> which tends to confer concrete existence upon it, above and beyond
> its internal conflicts (even when these take the violent form of mili-
> tary conflicts) and particularly above and beyond the quite different
> conditions of its hegemony over the dominated populations! That in-
> stitution is the *system of states* itself, the vitality of which has become

particularly evident since, in the wake of revolutions and counter-
revolutions, colonizations and decolonizations, the form of the nation-
state has been formally extended to the whole of humanity.   (Balibar
and Wallerstein 1991, 5; cf. Basil Davidson 1992)

The Rabbis produced their cultural formation within conditions of Diaspora—that is, in a situation within which Jews did not hold power over
others—, and I would argue that their particular discourse of ethnocentricity is ethically appropriate only when the cultural identity is that of a
minority, embattled or, at any rate, non-hegemonic. The point is not that
the Land was devalued by the Rabbis but that they renounced it until the
final Redemption, because in an unredeemed world, temporal dominion
and ethnic particularity are, as I have argued in the last section, impossibly
compromised. I think that Davies phrases the position just right when he
says, "It was its ability to detach its loyalty from 'place,' while nonetheless
retaining 'place' in its memory, that enabled Pharisaism to transcend the
loss of its Land" (1992, 69).[41] My only addition would be to argue that
this displacement of loyalty from place to memory of place was a necessary
one, not only to *transcend* the loss of the Land but to *enable* the loss of the
Land. It was political possession of the Land which most threatened the
possibility of continued Jewish cultural practice and difference. Given
the choice between an ethnocentricity which would not seek domination
over others or a seeking of political domination that would necessarily
have led either to a dilution of distinctiveness, tribal warfare, or fascism, the Rabbis de facto chose the former. Secular Zionism has unsuccessfully sought the first choice, dilution of distinctiveness; religious Zionism has unfortunately (but almost inevitably) led to the second and third
choices.[42] Either way, Zionism leads to the ruination of rabbinic Judaism,
founded on intense, concrete "tribal" intimacy, and it is no wonder that
until World War II Zionism was a secular movement claiming very few
adherents among religious Jews, who saw it as a human arrogation of a
work that only God should or could perform. This is, moreover, the basis
for the anti-Zionist ideology of such groups as *Natorei Karta* until this
day.[43] It was the renunciation of sovereignty over the Land that allowed
Jewish memory to persist.

The dialectic between Paul and the Rabbis can be recuperated for cultural critique. When Christianity is the hegemonic power in Europe and
the United States, then the resistance of Jews to being universalized can
be a critical force and model for the resistance of all peoples to being

Europeanized out of particular bodily existence. When, however, an eth-nocentric Judaism becomes a temporal, hegemonic political force, it be-comes absolutely, vitally necessary to accept Paul's critical challenge—although not his universalizing, disembodying solution—and develop an equally passionate concern for all human beings. We, including religious Jews—perhaps especially religious Jews—must take the theological di-mension of Paul's challenge seriously. How *could* the God of all the world have such a disproportionate care and concern for only a small part of His world?! And yet, obviously, I cannot even conceive of accepting Paul's solution of dissolving into a universal human essence, even one that would not be Christian but truly humanist and universal, even if such an entity could really exist.[44] If, on the one hand, rabbinic Judaism seems to imply that Israel is the true humanity, a potentially vicious doctrine of separa-tion and hierarchy, Paul argues that humanity is the true Israel, an equally vicious doctrine of coerced sameness and exclusion.

Somewhere in this dialectic a synthesis must be found, one that will allow for stubborn hanging on to ethnic, cultural specificity but in a con-text of deeply felt and enacted human solidarity. For that synthesis, Dias-pora provides the model, and only in conditions of Diaspora can such a re-solution even be attempted. Within the conditions of Diaspora, many Jews discovered that their well-being was absolutely dependent on principles of respect for difference, indeed "that no one is free until all are free." Complete devotion to the maintenance of Jewish culture and the his-torical memory were not inconsistent with devotion to radical causes of human liberation; there were Yiddish-speaking and Judeo-Arabic-speaking groups of marxists and anarchists, and a fair number of such Jews even retained a commitment to historical Jewish religious practice. The "cho-senness" of the Jews becomes, when seen in this light, not a warrant for racism but precisely an antidote to racism. This is a Judaism which mobi-lizes the critical forces within the Bible and the Jewish tradition rather than mobilizing the repressive and racist forces that also subsist there.

The alternative story I would tell of Jewish history has three stages. In the first stage, we find a people—call it a tribe—not very different in certain respects from peoples in similar material conditions all over the world, a people like most others that regards itself as special among hu-manity, indeed as The People, and its land as preeminently wonderful among lands, indeed as The Land. This is, of course, an oversimplifica-tion, because this "tribe" never quite dwelled alone and never regarded itself as autochthonous in its Land. In the second stage, this form of life increasingly becomes untenable, morally and politically, because the "tribe" no longer dwells alone, as it were. This is, roughly speaking, the Hellenistic period, culminating in the crises of the first century, of which I have read Paul as an integral part. Various solutions to this problem were eventually adopted. Pauline Christianity is one; so, perhaps, is the retreat to Qumran, while the Pharisaic Rabbis "invented" Diaspora, *even in the Land,* as the solution to this cultural dilemma.

The rabbinic answer to Paul's challenge was, therefore, to renounce any possibility of dominion over Others by being perpetually out of power:

> Just as with seeing the return in terms of the restoration of political rights, seeing it in terms of redemption has certain consequences. If the return were an act of divine intervention, it could not be engineered or forced by political or any other human means: to do so would be impious. That coming was best served by waiting in obedience for it: *men of violence would not avail to bring it in.* The rabbinic aloofness to messianic claimants sprang not only from the history of disillusionment with such, but from this underlying, deeply ingrained attitude. It can be claimed that under the main rabbinic tradition Judaism condemned itself to powerlessness. But recognition of powerlessness (rather than a frustrating, futile, and tragic resistance) was effective in preserving Judaism in a very hostile Christendom, and therefore had its own brand of "power."   (Davies 1992, 82)

As before, my impulse is only to slightly change the nuance of Davies's marvelously precise reading. The renunciation of temporal power (not merely "recognition of powerlessness") was to my mind precisely the most powerful mode of preservation of difference and, therefore, the most effective kind of resistance. The story of Rabbi Yohanan ben Zakkai being spirited out of besieged Jerusalem to set up the Academy at Yavneh rather than staying and fighting for Jewish sovereignty is emblematic of this stance. The *Natorei Karta,* to this day, refuse to visit the Western Wall, the holiest place in Judaism, without PLO "visas," because it was taken by violence. And, I would argue: This response has much to teach us.[45] I want to propose a privileging of Diaspora, a dissociation of ethnicities and political hegemonies, as the only social structure which even begins to make possible a maintenance of cultural identity in a world grown thoroughly and inextricably interdependent. Indeed, I would suggest that Diaspora, and not monotheism, may be the important contribution that Judaism has to make to the world, although I would not deny the positive role that monotheism has played in making Diaspora possible. The very current example of eastern Europe should provide much food for thought, where the lesson of Diaspora, namely, that peoples and lands are *not* naturally and organically connected, were it taken to heart, could prevent much bloodshed. Diaspora can teach us that it is possible for a people to maintain its distinctive culture, its difference, without controlling land, a fortiori without controlling other people or developing a need to dispossess them of their lands. Thus the response of rabbinic Judaism to the challenge of universalism, which Paul, among others, raised against what was becoming in the end of the millennium and the beginning of the next, an increasingly inappropriate doctrine of specialness in an already interdependent world, may provide some, by no means all, of the pieces to the solution to the puzzle of how humanity can survive now as another millennium draws to its close with no Messiah yet on the horizon. I would argue, therefore, that only a precise reversal of the synthesis of domination and racism could provide any answer to the question of how humanity might continue to survive. Renunciation of sovereignty, autochthony, indigeneity (as embodied politically in the notion of self-determination), on the one hand, combined with a fierce tenacity in holding onto cultural identity, on the other, might yet have something to offer. For we live in a world in which the combination of these two kills thousands daily, yet where the renunciation of difference seems both an impoverishment of human life and an inevitable harbinger of oppression.

TOWARD A DIASPORIZED
(MULTICULTURAL) ISRAEL

For those of us who are equally committed to social justice and collective Jewish existence some other formation must be constituted. I suggest that an Israel which reimports diasporic consciousness, a consciousness of a Jewish collective as one sharing space with others, devoid of exclusivist and dominating power, is the only Israel which could answer Paul's and Lyotard's and Nancy's call for a species-wide care, without eradicating cultural difference. I would propose an Israel in which individual and collective cultural rights would become an essential part of its structure, no longer coded as a Jewish State but as a bi-national, secular, and multicultural one. For historical models, one might look to the millet system of the Ottoman Empire, on the one hand, and to that multiculturalism now struggling to be born in the United States on the other. The point would be precisely to avoid both the coercive universalism of a France, the Pauline option, on the one hand, and the violence of a joining of ethnic particularism and state-power, contemporary Israel, on the other.

Reversing A. B. Yehoshua's famous pronouncement that only in a condition of political hegemony is moral responsibility mobilized, I would argue that the only moral path would be the renunciation of near-exclusive Jewish hegemony.[46] This would involve, first of all, complete separation of religion from state, but even more than that the revocation of the Law of Return and such cultural, discursive practices that code the state as a Jewish State and not a multinational and multicultural one.[47] The dream of a place that is ours founders on the rock of realization that there are Others there, just as there are Others in Poland, Morocco, and Ethiopia. Any notion, then, of Redemption through Land must either be infinitely deferred (as *Natorei Karta* understand so well) or become a moral monster. Either Israel must entirely divest itself of the language of race and become truly a state which is equally for all of its citizens and collectives, or the Jews must divest themselves of their claim to space.[48] Race and space, or genealogy and territorialism, have been the problematic and necessary (if not essential) terms around which Jewish identity has revolved. In Jewish history, however, these terms are more obviously in dissonance with each other than in synergy. This allows a formulation of Jewish identity not as a proud resting place, indeed not as a "boast," but as a perpetual, creative, diasporic tension.

Notes

ACKNOWLEDGMENTS

1. William Wrede, *Paul* (1908; reprint, Lexington: American Library Association, 1962), 85, quoted in Stephen Westerholm, *Israel's Law and the Church's Faith: Paul and His Recent Interpreters* (Grand Rapids, Mich.: William B. Eerdmans, 1988), 16.

INTRODUCTION

1. See the very similar points made in Segal (1990, xi ff. and 48). I think that Segal's remark there that "Paul's letters may be more important to the history of Judaism than the rabbinic texts are to the interpretation of Christian Scriptures" is right on the mark. Readers of both books will perceive both my debt to my distinguished predecessor (and colleague in graduate school) as well as my disagreements with him. Some of these will be pointed out in the notes. For the question of Josephus's alleged Pharisaism, see the excellent discussion in Segal (1990, 81–83).

2. It is one of the distinct achievements of Jacob Neusner to have clearly seen this point.

3. The idea of this analysis originally came to me when participating in a seminar of his at the School of Criticism and Theory at Dartmouth in the summer of 1987, where he referred briefly to Paul and Spinoza on circumcision.

4. Cosgrove 1988 is an excellent example of a reading of Paul that is explicit and self-aware in its choice of starting point and the hermeneutic effects of that choice. See p. 2 of that book. I do not believe that the reading of Galatians offered in this book is incompatible with the one offered there; indeed, I hope that they complement each other with their significantly different emphases. Incidentally, this example shows how the choice of a center even within a single letter makes a big difference; where Cosgrove reads Galatians through 3:1–5, I read it through 3:28–29. There is absolutely no Archimedean point from which to adjudicate such choices—on this issue I quite disagree with Cosgrove who does seem to hold that there are criteria which enable such choices (6)—but they should not result, it seems to me, in mutually exclusive interpretations.

5. Gager's remarks on "loose ends" as well as his comment that "I do not take it as a given that the interpretation proposed here is the new, correct view of Paul on these matters. I do assume, or rather will undertake to demonstrate that it is a good interpretation, a valid one" (1983, 208–09) could serve as hermeneutical models. I offer my somewhat different interpretation in precisely the same spirit.

6. Obviously, I hold that the Gaston-Gager interpretation fits into the first category. Despite its appeal ethically and religiously, it ultimately leaves us with a very weak reading of Paul. Furthermore, as I will argue below in Chapter 2, it falls down on exegetical grounds as well. I believe that my own reading of Paul answers many of the same theological and ethical needs that Gaston's does, but in a way that preserves the enormous force of Paul's critique of ethnicity. By reading Paul as a Jewish cultural critic, criticizing aspects of Judaism from within, I can preserve the power of his critique without turning him into an "anti-Semite." (I reserve the term "self-hating Jew" for pathological instances, such as Otto Weininger and those Zionists who detested European Jews and saw them in the same light as anti-Semites did.)

7. The desire for the One seems, in fact, to go back to much earlier Indo-European roots, as witness the *Rgveda* (Kuschel 1992, 181–82). Note the contrast with biblical myth in which God begins his creative work with pre-existent matter. Completely incidentally, a rather bizarre moment in this book is the identification of Emil Schürer as "a great Jewish historian" (198), an artifact, I assume, of the translation. The error, however, ends up particularly grotesque given Kuschel's constant interpretation of scholars according to their religious affiliations.

8. Some feminists may claim of my book—with justice—that it is interested more in the question of ethnicity than of gender, indeed, that it gives gender relatively short *Schrift*. While that is so, I think nevertheless that my argument has implications for feminist theory, since if I am right in certain ways the fates of ethnic and gendered "difference" are common in western culture without, of course, either one being epiphenomenal to the other.

9. William S. Campbell's work begins with a very similar problematic and intuition, to wit, that Paul's situation and his texts have much to teach us about our own cultural situations and dilemmas (Campbell 1992, vii). In some ways, however, his reading of Paul is quite different from mine. My dialogue with Campbell will be specifically marked at several points in the book in footnotes.

10. Some of this reception history will be sketched out below in Chapter 2.

11. Thus, interpretations of Paul (such as Campbell's) that claim that he did not mind whether Jews continued to circumcise their children and keep kosher, i.e., that he allowed for Jewish Christianity, do not disturb my claims. Only interpretations such as that of Lloyd Gaston and John Gager, discussed in Chapter 2, that would have Paul arguing that Jews need not believe in Christ in order to be saved would disrupt my argument.

12. Hays (1989). See now also Wright (1992a, 140). In future work, however, I intend to argue that Paul's exegesis of Torah is closer to rabbinic exegesis than Wright allows; nor is rabbinic exegesis to be identified with "fanciful" or arbitrary prooftexting, *pace* Wright 168 n. 45 and passim.

13. Baur (1875) and see selection in Meeks (1972, 277–88). I had essentially arrived at my interpretation before coming upon the work of Baur and was quite astounded to discover how often I hit on his ideas and formulations. I hope that my reformulation, however, in modern critical terms—taking into consideration other more recent interpretations of Paul as well—will lead to a reconsideration and reevaluation of Baur's contribution.

14. Compare the excellent formulation of John Gager: "We do not find a self-

confident paganism aggressively and unanimously set against Judaism as a 'barbaric superstition,' but a prolonged debate *within* an increasingly anxious culture over the status of Judaism as a religion of universal humanity" (Gager 1983, 31). Gager is referring, of course, to the prolonged debate over the status of Judaism within "pagan" culture, but this is the "flip side" of seeing the internal Jewish debate within that "increasingly anxious culture," *over precisely the same issue.*

CHAPTER 1

1. In Chapter 7 below, there will be a detailed analysis of this passage.

2. It is very important to note that Philo himself is just the most visible representative of an entire school who understood the Bible and indeed the philosophy of language as he did. On this see Winston 1988.

3. See Chadwick. The notion that Paul has a background in Hellenistic Judaism has been advanced fairly often. It has generally had a pejorative tinge to it, as if only Palestinian Judaism was "authentic," and terms like "lax" or, surprisingly enough, "coldly legal," are used to describe Paul's alleged Hellenistic environment. Recently, this idea has been rightly discarded on the grounds that there is no sharp dividing line between Hellenistic and Palestinian Judaism. If we abandon the ex post facto judgments of history, moreover, there is no reason to accept the previous notions of margin and center in the description of late-antique Jewish groups, no reason why Philo should be considered less authentic than Rabban Gamaliel. The question of cultural differences between Greek- and Hebrew-speaking Jews can be reapproached on different non-judgmental territory. In that light, I find the similarities between Paul and Philo, who could have had no contact with each other whatsoever, very exciting evidence for first-century Greek-speaking Jews.

4. I have limited the scope of this claim to allow for other types of allegory, including such phenomena as Joseph's interpretations of Pharaoh's dreams, as well as an untheorized allegorical tradition in reading Homer. When I use the term allegory, therefore, this is to be understood as shorthand for allegoresis of the type we know from Philo and on.

5. See Chapter 3 for further discussion of this point with regard to 1 Corinthians 15.

6. Note how this approach solves exegetical problems resulting from apparent contradictions between Romans 11 and, e.g., Romans 9. See Watson (1986, 168). Cf. also Davies (1965, 143–44).

7. Frederic Jameson has articulated this point well:

> A criticism which asks the question "What does it mean?" constitutes something like an allegorical operation in which a text is systematically *rewritten* in terms of some fundamental master code or "ultimately determining instance." On this view, then, all "interpretation" in the narrower sense demands the forcible or imperceptible transformation of a given text into an allegory of its particular master code or "transcendental signified": *the discredit into which interpretation has fallen is thus at one with the disrepute visited on allegory itself.*
>
> (Jameson 1981, 58).

It is going to be very tricky to distinguish the allegorical mode of relating to a master code from the midrashic, but that is just what I am going to have to do my best to accomplish below.

8. David Dawson has recently brilliantly articulated the relation between the "literal" and the allegorical in the following terms:

> Allegorical interpretation thus seems almost inevitably to challenge prior, nonallegorical readings. Naturally, those for whom that prior reading is meaningful and authoritative in its own right will resist the allegorical challenge, especially when challenge turns into outright replacement. But should a community of such "literalists" subsequently come to embrace the allegorical meaning as the obvious, expected meaning, that allegorical meaning would have become, in effect, the new "literal sense."
>
> (Dawson 1992, 8)

Such a diachronic relationship cannot by definition exist between a midrashic and a literal/allegorical reading because of the way that midrash resists, inherently, the status of "obvious, expected meaning." The politics of this kind of resistance, resistance to allegory and not through allegory, is one of the major themes of this book and will be most fully developed in the final chapter.

9. Indeed, much of her book from page 93 on is devoted to arguing this thesis. However, even she agrees that "over the last two and a half millennia . . . Plato has stood securely, heir to Parmenides' *kouros*, as the founder of 'idealist' philosophy, asserting the existence of a world beyond the senses, one comprehensible only to the intellect, *one that unifies by abstracting from particulars of the world that we experience with our senses*" (92, emphasis added). It is, of course, the Plato of this tradition that interests me here and not the "true" Plato.

10. My next book will be devoted entirely to this theme, in which, however, I will read it as a positive, utopian moment in Jewish masculine subjectivity and not as an anti-Semitic canard. Garber has, in fact, shown the way toward such a reappropriation (227).

11. The longing for univocity runs even deeper than this in Hesiod, on which see Saxonhouse (1992, 23–24). On the other hand, I do not want to show here a fear of diversity in characterizing Greek culture, for Saxonhouse is very careful not to homogenize the Greeks on this issue. See, for instance, her description of the difference between Heraclitus, who celebrates sexual difference as productive, and Parmenides, for whom childbirth and intercourse are "hateful mingling" (Saxonhouse, 38):

> Among the differences that morals introduce with their naming of discrete objects are those that appear to separate the sexes and that lead to the "hateful mingling" of opposites mentioned above. In the world of "what is," there can be no mingling because there are no opposites, and nor is there the "hateful birth" that results from the hateful mingling of the sexes. There is no generation at all. By transforming sexual intercourse (here we cannot forget Aphrodite) and childbirth into what is hateful Parmenides underscores the radical nature of his poem. Rather than attack war, death, and disease, he attacks the traditional pleasures (and the re-

sults) of sexuality. No Helen waits for her Paris to be lifted from the bloodshed of war and brought back to her chambers. The pleasures of sex entail
hated opposites rather than the unified whole of "what is." Such pleasures
seduce men's senses, make them delight in opposites, when in fact they
should dismiss opposites as false divisions of a beautiful whole.

(Saxonhouse, 44)

In this book I am arguing that such themes and affects deeply inform the
culture of Hellenistic Judaism with Philo and Paul, each in his own distinct way,
representative figures. I think that in Paul already—as very explicitly in only
slightly later figures that follow him—this Greek revulsion from sexuality, childbirth, and gender (which is a product of them) comes to one possible resolution. See Chapter 7 below for further discussion particularly with regards to
Romans 7.

12. This is, of course, only a partial list. Below briefly, and in my next book
extensively, I will discuss the transformation of meaning which the signifier/sig-
nified opposition undergoes in Lacan.

13. Recently, Pierre Vidal-Naquet has remarked on the "series of events that
were completely unforseeable. . . . In the second and third centuries A.D., the
Mediterranean world began to turn Christian. Particularly for the intellectuals
who sought to come to terms with the change, this meant replacing their mythology and history, from the War of the Giants down to the Trojan War, with
the mythology and history of the Hebrews and the Jews, from Adam to the birth
of Christ" (Vidal-Naquet 1992, 304). What Vidal-Naquet does not take into
sufficient consideration, in my opinion, is how much the way was prepared for
this "replacement" by the allegorizing platonization of Judaism by Paul and Philo
and their successors. We have not so much a replacement but a syncretization,
whereby the Jewish stories are made to carry Hellenic cultural values.

14. I am thus in near total disagreement with the interpretation of Philo on
gender produced by Giulia Sissa, who writes, "A biologist, who, out of curiosity,
looked into *De opificio mundi* would probably see the text as a mythological commentary on mythology [sic; should this be "biology"?]. He [sic] might notice that
masculine and feminine are symmetrical and appear simultaneously. The notion
that Adam came first and that Eve was later created from one of his ribs is not
Philo's; for him male and female are both essential aspects of the concept of human
being" (Sissa 1992, 54). Sissa ignores entirely the fact that Philo claims that there
were two creations of two "races," *genoi*, of humanity.

15. Philo contradicts himself on this point in several places. I am not interested here in sorting out Philo's different interpretations and their sources, which
has already been very well done in Tobin (1983). My interest here is rather in how
the reading given here enters into a certain politics of the gendered body. For
further discussion of this passage in Philo and his followers, see Tobin (108–19)
and J. Cohen (1989, 74–76 and 228).

16. Note the platonic disdain for poetry. Philo's attitude toward "myth" is
virtually identical to that of his near contemporary, the Hellenistic interpreter of
Homer, Heraclitus, for which see Dawson (1992, 39).

17. For a precise delineation of the modality of this synergistic process by

which allegorical interpretation transforms culture through a transformational combination of two discourses, see Dawson, who writes:

> That is, precisely through an allegorical reading, other, formerly nonscriptural meanings may become "textualized" by being associated with the preallegorical, literal reading. For example, the preallegorical, literal reading of Exodus might concern the escape of Hebrews from Egypt. If I draw on Platonic theories of the soul's origin and destiny in order to read this biblical story allegorically as an account of the soul's ascent from bodily distraction to mental purity, I may do so because I want to reinterpret Plato's account by placing it within a scriptural framework. But in so doing, I may in fact subtly alter the meaning that Plato's account has on its own terms by making the once-eternal soul now directly created by God. When functioning in this way, allegorical readings can subvert previously nonscriptural meanings (i.e., meaning that prior to the allegorical reading would not have been associated with scripture); the allegorical reading can enable the preallegorical or "literal" reading to critique or revise those nonscriptural meanings.
>
> (1992, 11)

18. In Chapter 8 below, I will be coming back to this comparison between Paul and Philo on gender.

19. See Chapter 9.

20. Upon presenting this material orally to the community of Pauline scholars at venues such as the Society of Biblical Literature, I was several times confronted by claims that it is ridiculous to make this text central to an interpretation of Paul, since it is so "transparently" marginal to his writing. I cannot imagine on what grounds one can determine centrality or marginality in this fashion. The fact that it is a citation of liturgy surely does not militate against its authority for Paul! Even Hamerton-Kelly's move (discussed below in Chapter 9) of reading all of Paul through the lens of 1 Thessalonians 2:14 cannot be disproven but only deplored. Certainly the fact that Paul cites the "no Jew or Greek" formula at a crucial point in an explicit defense of his gospel argues for its validity in his thought, however we will interpret it, as do his repeated citations of versions of it in other places. Most of Chapter 8 below will be devoted to sorting out the differences between the citation in Galatians 3:28 and 1 Corinthians 12:13. For a recent discussion of this passage, see Campbell (1992, 106–10).

21. Cp. Betz, especially, "If Paul means his words in this sense, ἐν ὑμῖν would have to be rendered as 'within you': Christ 'takes shape' in the Christians like a fetus and is born in the hearts of the believers; simultaneously they are reborn as 'children.' But ἐν ὑμῖν can also refer to the creation of the Christian community as a living organism, the 'body of Christ'" (1979, 234–35).

22. Indeed, this is his major focus, for when he repeats this formula in Corinthians, he notoriously drops the clause about "male and female." In Chapter 8, I treat this issue in Pauline interpretation more fully.

23. See now the brilliant interpretation of Galatians 3:15–20 in Wright (1992a, 164–67).

24. Note how early and how deeply rooted in Greek culture are the associ-

ations of spirit/mind with the universal and of physical/sensual with difference. As Saxonhouse writes, "The attack on senses [in Heraclitus!], though, is not simply because they are unreliable, but because they separate men from one another as the mind does not. . . . Knowledge is thus unified in the *logos* and the *logos* in its turn unifies humans. This unity, though, can come only from the soul and not from the senses" (Saxonhouse 1992, 31–32). Saxonhouse argues, in fact, that in Plato these notions are somewhat problematized.

25. According to H. A. Wolfson (1968, 369) Philo allowed for the possibility of uncircumcised "spiritual" proselytes. On the other hand, there is a very striking report of Suetonius that Augustus remarked: "Not even a Jew, my dear Tiberius, observes the Sabbath fast as faithfully as I did today" (cited in Gager 1983, 75).

26. "The real member of the Old Israel is he who has appropriated to himself the history of his people: he has himself been in bondage in Egypt, has himself been delivered therefore. We may also add that he has himself received the Torah" (Davies 1965, 104).

27. The circumcision of the Egyptians appears in a very early (late-first-century) polemic against "The Jews," *The Epistle of Barnabas* (9:6), where the author writes, "But you will say, 'But surely the people were circumcised as a seal.' But every Syrian and Arab and all the idol-worshipping priests are circumcised; does this mean that they, too, belong to their covenant? Why, even the Egyptians practice circumcision!" (Lightfoot and Harmer 1989, 174). What was a defense in Philo's apology for Judaism vis-à-vis "pagans" becomes an attack in this apology for Christianity vis-à-vis Judaism.

28. There are, of course, other ways of interpreting this Pauline complex of ideas. Cp. Meeks (1983, 183–85), who interprets this differently, but see there 187–88. This interpretation, however, makes a great deal of sense to me. In baptism, the Christian is translated in this life from a physical existence to a spiritual one. In the ecstasy of the baptismal experience, this is both an experiential fact and an ontological one. Thus Paul explains in Galatians, "For through the Law I died to the Law, in order that I might live for God. I have been crucified with Christ; and it is no longer I who live, but Christ lives in me; and what I now live in the flesh I live in faith in the Son of God who loved me and gave himself up for me" (2:19–20). This is an account not of a moral transformation but of a thorough ontological and spiritual one. It thus follows that there are more possibilities than future resurrection versus righteous life in the present for interpreting such passages as Romans 8:10–11 (*pace* Gundry 1976, 44). The third alternative is a life in the here and now, which is only apparently in the flesh but in reality "Christ living in the person." This form of life is a type or even an anticipation of the resurrection, as is strongly implied by the Galatians passage. (See also Gundry 1976, 46, 57ff.)

29. The term *platonistic*—as opposed to *platonic*—will be used to identify ideas belonging to the middle- or neo-platonist traditions but which are not necessarily platonic in origin.

30. It is not clear to me precisely what is the source of the profound resistance to any imputation of platonism in Paul in contemporary Pauline scholarship. One very important source of insight into this question is surely Smith (1990, esp. 1–36), where the history of seeing "platonism" and "philonism" as a contamina-

tion of the pure waters of early Christianity is documented extensively. Given such a set of prejudices, and particularly the notion that Catholicism is the misbegotten child of this illicit union, one can begin to understand the allergy that Protestant scholarship has for attributing dualism to Paul. Further, those schools of interpretation which have treated Paul as Hellenist in the past have been implicated in anti-Semitic attempts to de-Judaize him (or anti-Paulinic attempts to implicate him in anti-Semitism), further explaining why scholars who wish to rehabilitate Paul historically have emphasized the "purity" of his Jewish cultural connections. But of course, and this is just the point, precisely that pure Jewish cultural world that Paul grew up in was thoroughly Hellenized and platonized—and this is not to be seen as contamination.

31. Cp. Smith (1990, 83). I do not, of course, suggest that the "absolutely new" is therefore necessarily superior to that from which it was constituted. I do, however, suggest that Smith is somewhat unfair to Aune here who, while revealing an apologetic tendency in his unfortunate choice of "transcending" to refer to the relation of Christianity to Jewish and Hellenistic traditions, does not claim Christianity as *sui generis* in some theological sense but as a unique development of given historical traditions. This strikes me as quite different from the polemic purposes of the earlier scholarly apologetics for Christianity which Smith is attacking.

32. Note how similar and yet how different this is from Bultmann's famous claim that for Paul theology is anthropology (Bultmann 1951, 191).

33. Note that in later Christian iconography, according to Leo Steinberg, representations of Christ's genitalia and of his circumcision represent the human aspect of his Incarnation (Steinberg 1983). See also Davidson (1992, 102–10).

34. See the elegant exposition in Martyn (1967, 270–71).

35. I am struck by how infrequently Romans 9:5 is cited in connection with 2 Corinthians 5:16. Even in Fraser's compendium of the possible options for interpreting this verse, it seems not to have been mentioned even once (Fraser 1970–71, 301–03).

36. I discuss this passage in detail in the next chapter.

37. Note how this interpretation clarifies a point at issue between Pauline scholars, namely, the question of the "historical Jesus" in Paul's thought. Some hold that the human, living Jesus held no importance whatsoever for Paul, while "W. L. Knox however rightly regarded Paul as valuing the historical Jesus, for this marked the difference of Christianity from the mystery religions. Yet he regarded II Cor. v. 16 as somehow setting aside the historical Jesus. Therefore he could describe the verse as 'an incautious outburst,' in spite of which 'Jesus as the risen Lord of the Church, remained the concrete figure of the Gospels'" (Fraser 1970–71, 297).

38. Contrast the reductive views of Francis Watson, for whom any such antitheses, whether in Paul or Qumran (or presumably the Pythagoreans), serve only to "express the ineradicable distinction between the sect (in which salvation is to be found) and the parent religious community (where there is only condemnation)." Watson entirely begs the question of why salvation is to be found only in the sect (Watson 1986, 46). Is it not possible that these very antinomies and antitheses are what led to the creation of the "sect"?

39. These are not, strictly speaking, binary oppositions for Paul, but rather bipolar oppositions on a continuum. There is not an absolute opposition of spirit and flesh in Paul, but entities can be more and less spiritual or carnal. Thus the resurrection body can be a spiritualized body. The analogical structure holds up, but with great subtlety and polyvalence, a polyvalence which enabled ultimately the multifarious directions that successors to Paul could take, from gnostic rejection of the material to the wallowing in it of medieval resurrection theory.

40. See next chapter for detail.

41. "This rigorously ecclesiocentric allegory is not an anomaly but a heightened expression of themes that repeatedly surface when Paul turns to interpreting Scripture" (Hays 1989, 111).

42. Allegory here is not in the slightest "related to the *exemplum* and the metaphor" and is therefore *not* "among the *figurae per immutationem*" (*pace* Betz 1979, 239–40). That refers to the construction of an allegorical device in rhetoric, while here Paul is interpreting the Bible in allegorical fashion in order to finally hammer down and home his point that following the coming of Christ the promise to Abraham has been fulfilled. Far from being a weak and merely persuasive device, this allegory is the climax of his whole argument and thus of the letter.

43. Cp. the following account of Plato on kinship:

> They [i.e., the Homeric representation of the friendship of Achilles and Patroclus] invoke kinship and conjugality, in other words, only to displace them, to reduce them to mere *images* of friendship. This dialectic will ultimately prove to have had pregnant implications for the later history of the representation of the relations between family and community, between *oikos* and *polis*, in Greek culture: in Plato's *Republic*, for example, the utopian effort to unite all the citizens of the just city in the bonds of fraternal love effectively does away with the social significance of real brothers and sisters, of both kinship and conjugality, altogether.
>
> (Halperin 1990, 85–86)

It seems hardly stretching the point to see Paul's thinking as within this ethos.

44. It should be noted that in the biblical text, it is not stated that Abraham "knew Sarah his wife" after the "annunciation." There may have even been, then, a tradition that the conception of Isaac was entirely by means of the promise. The birth of Isaac would be, then, an even more exact type of Jesus' birth. This would also explain Paul's application of Isaiah 54:1, in which Hagar is called "she who has a husband," to whom Sarah is contrasted. The point would be that Hagar had sex with a man in order to conceive, but Sarah did not! Indeed, given that the verse in Isaiah explicitly refers to Jerusalem as the barren one, and contrasts her with another city who is figured as "her who has a husband," it is neither surprising nor startling that these two cities are read as the two Jerusalems, nor that they are mapped onto Sarah and Hagar respectively (Hays 1989, 118–19). See also Philo, *On the Cherubim*, 40–52 for the virgin births of the patriarchs' wives, whereby God begets their children! Such notions were abandoned very quickly, it seems, in the post-Christian environment.

45. See also Martyn (1985, 418–20). I am quite unconvinced by Martyn's interpretation that Paul's discourse is intended to discredit such oppositions.

46. Parenthetically, I would like to remark that I think Hays underestimates Paul when he avers that the statement that Ishmael persecuted Isaac was "shaped significantly by the empirical situation of the church in his own time. The fact is that Torah advocates are persecuting those who carry out the Law-free mission to the Gentiles; consequently, given the way Paul has set up the allegory, the text must be read in a way that portrays Ishmael as the persecutor" (1989, 118). I think, rather, given the evidence of to be sure later rabbinic readings to which Hays refers, Paul must have already known of a tradition which reads מצחק as some form of persecution or harassment of Isaac by Ishmael.

47. See Dawson (1992, 15–17 and esp. 256–57n. 56), and cp. Hays (1989, 115–17) and Sang (1991, 7).

48. Cp., for instance, Sallust, for whom, "despite the apparent vicissitudes of the mother of the gods and Attis this myth in fact tells of *eternal and unchanging realities*" (cited in Wedderburn 1987, 127–28).

49. Months after I wrote the above sentence, Timothy Hampton's important paper appeared, which includes the following sentence: "To speak of the other is to make metaphors" (1993, 66). It is altogether quite astonishing how many themes of the present work are approached in that paper from quite a different direction.

50. By a hermeneutic error I mean two things, which are only partly related to each other but converge nevertheless in my claim. On the one hand, I am making a fairly conventional interpretative claim to the effect that a theme that is never mentioned in a major text of a given corpus cannot be identified as the motivating moment of the entire corpus taken as a whole. In other words, unless we are prepared to separate Paul out into separate parts—as some critics are perfectly prepared to do, on, e.g., chronological or situational terms—the expectation of the Parousia, as important as it is, cannot be seen as the central, motivating force of Paul's work. On the other hand, I am claiming that this is a hermeneutic error in the other sense of hermeneutics, as that which makes a text useable to us. For those of us not living in the end-time, in the sense of in the immediate expectation of that end, a Paul who is fully or largely explained as thinking only in that context will become simply irrelevant. Of course I also see Paul as apocalyptic in the sense that the Christ-event has resulted for him in a fundamental change in the structure of history. It is the content of that change that reveals—Apocalypsis—Paul to us. I come back to this point in Chapter 7 in my discussion of Paul on sexuality.

51. See also the very helpful remarks of Gerard Caspary (1979, 17–18 and 51–60) on the relationship between the Old Testament and the New in Paul and Origen and also Robbins 1991.

52. On the last, see Caspary (1979, 60–62). It seems to me even more the case that food rules and the observance of Sabbaths and festivals would not in themselves have prevented gentiles from converting were it not for their symbolic, theological significance to the effect that one had to be Jewish in order to be Christian. Thus arguing that Paul abandoned circumcision in order to make it easier for gentiles to convert begs more questions than it answers, *pace* Watson (1986, 28). I find Watson's account reductive; for example, he contrasts a theological motivation for Paul's abandonment of circumcision, kashruth, and Sabbaths

with a purely utilitarian one, "to make it easier for Gentiles to become Christians" (34–38): "Paul's theological discussions about the law are therefore attempts to justify this essentially non-theological decision" (36). It is not even clear to me what this claim could mean. If Paul held that keeping the Law was important for being saved, then what was he accomplishing by winning souls for Christ who would not be saved anyway? On the other hand, if he did not consider the Law important for being saved, what could be more theological than that? 1 Corinthians 9:19–21 does not prove what Watson claims it proves, since it could easily be interpreted that keeping the Law is adiaphora for Paul—i.e., totally indifferent *theologically*—and then he makes the sociological decision to adapt himself to whatever community he preaches to. On the other hand, I find salutary Watson's clear understanding that not keeping the commandments was not a liberalization of Jewish practice but a break with it, a break with precisely that which made being Jewish Jewish.

CHAPTER 2

1. Of course, Paul is ever designated such only in the highly unreliable account of Acts. I use the name here, therefore, for rhetorical purposes, rhetorical purposes similar to those of Acts.

2. I first learned of this term through participating in the Cassassa Conference on Cultural Reading of the Bible at Loyola Marymount University in March 1992.

3. Campbell has pointed out predecessors to Ruether but remarks, "However, it was only in the seventies that biblical scholars took up this theme with full earnestness, and Ruether's study was at least partly instrumental in causing them to do so" (1992, 12–13).

4. Campbell is more precise. He refers to the "German Lutheran understanding of his [Paul's] theology" (Campbell 1992, iv). Two important pieces of this puzzle are that the Scandinavian Lutheran tradition has been quite different (Campbell 1992, 36n.6—Stendahl and Westerholm are prime examples) and that the Barthian tradition of Christian exceptionalism ("Christianity is not a religion") is not altogether different from the Bultmannian; Hamerton-Kelly is an excellent example here. (For *my* kinsmen according to the flesh, I add that Barth was a prominent Reformed [Calvinist] thinker.) The identification of the "old Paul" as a Lutheran one seems to go back to F. C. Baur himself (1876, 313).

5. The mutual exclusiveness of these two propositions seems to have escaped most of these interpreters!

6. I have tried as much as possible to confine technical discussions of other scholars' work to the notes.

7. It is, in a sense, unfortunate that Gager's book, *The Origins of Anti-Semitism* (Gager 1983), has become so heavily identified with this thesis, which represents only a small part of what is otherwise a signally important and absolutely convincing piece of work. The many positive citations of this book throughout my work attest to its value in my eyes.

8. To a great extent Davies is a real predecessor of this view: "There was no reason why Paul should not reject the view that Gentiles should be converted to Judaism before entering the Messianic Kingdom and at the same time insist that

for him as a Jew the Torah was still valid. In so doing he was being true both to the universalist tradition of Judaism and at the same time showing his identification with Israel according to the flesh: he was being true to the 'new' and the 'old' Israel" (1965, 73). No reason why not indeed, but as lovely as this vision would be, I just do not see it in Paul's texts for reasons that I adduce all through the book. I do not share Davies's willingness to accord credence to reports in Acts which seem to me to contradict the doctrine and practice of the letters. This solution, I would add, is precisely that of rabbinic Judaism.

9. By *exegetically*, I mean that it is founded and founders on the assumption that "works of the Law" means works that the Law does, as it were. Gaston could not know when he wrote that the Hebrew equivalent (perhaps original) for "works of the Law," namely מעשי התורה, was to appear in Qumran as the title of a work detailing the requirements of the Law, just as the traditional interpretation of Paul would have it. See also Westerholm, who compares such phrases as τὰ ἔργα τοῦ θεοῦ in John 6:28, "deeds demanded by God," and especially "works of the Lord" in Jer. 31:10 (Sept.) and Baruch 2:9, where "his works τὰ ἔργα αὐτοῦ are explicitly said to be 'works which he has commanded us'" (1988, 116).

There seems to me, moreover, to be a fundamental implausibility at the heart of the Gaston-Gager hypothesis, namely, its assumption that gentiles could become part of Israel without observing the Law, *and that this would not result in a fundamental redefinition of what being part of Israel meant!* Thus Gager writes:

> Peter Richardson, whose *Israel in the Apostolic Church* is a valuable contribution just because he carefully delineates the circumstances surrounding the Pauline letters, tends to lose sight of these circumstances in his concluding paragraphs. Thus after demonstrating that Paul's argument in Galatians is that Gentile Christians need not be circumcised in order to become part of Israel, his summary reads like a universal claim: "No more do Law and circumcision enter the picture." But surely, as his own analysis has demonstrated, his sentence should read, "No more do law and circumcision enter the picture *for Gentiles.*"
>
> (Gager 1983, 207)

This is, to my mind, a very problematic claim on several grounds: (1) As I have said, the notion that one could be part of Israel and not be subject to the Law issues in a fundamental redefinition of the notion of Israel; (2) The possibility that Paul intended that there would be mixed Christian communities in which some would observe the Law and others not, resulting, e.g., in inability to eat together, is structurally implausible and directly contradicted by the report of the Antioch confrontation as I interpret it below in Chapter 5; (3) This interpretation of Paul is contraverted by such characteristic Pauline expressions as "For in Christ Jesus neither circumcision nor uncircumcision is of any avail, but faith working through love" (Galatians 5:6). In short, I think that Richardson is correct. Where Gaston and Gager (and their predecessors and followers) are clearly correct, in my opinion, is in their stipulation that Paul was not critiquing some essential fault in the Law or in the Jews' observance of it but passionately trying to extend it to all folks. This extension, however, could not but result in a fundamental, cataclysmic redefinition of the Law and of the People Israel. So, once more, Paul was *not* in my opinion anti-Judaic, but he did undermine *any* traditionally understood notions of what being Jewish meant, just as Sanders has claimed.

10. Watson has strongly argued this case (1986, 94–96). The Alexandrian Jewish philosopher and predecessor of Philo, Aristobolus, refers to those who are committed to the literal interpretation of the Law as "having neither strength nor insight," τοῖς δὲ μὴ μετέχουσι δυνάμεως καὶ συνέσεως ἀλλα τῷ γραπτῷ μόνον προσκειμένοις (cited in Hengel [1974, 164], who has no occasion there, of course, to refer to the possible Pauline parallel). Willingness to leave the literal, the written (note the similarity with Paul's terminology), was thus referred to as a sign of intellectual and spiritual strength. See also Jewett 1971, 42–46. The three categories of Jews for Paul, then, are those who have been lopped off, because they have no faith in Jesus; those who are Christian but keep the Law because they are weak; and those—like he himself—whose faith is so strong that they no longer need to keep the Law. Jewish Christians who keep the Law thus take a place in Paul's value hierarchies similar to the married who marry, because of porneia! This is no anti-Judaism in the later sense, of course, but it is certainly not a valuing of Judaism either. Lest I be misunderstood, once more, the point is not to judge Paul but to see in what way his cultural theory can be useful for us.

11. Although Sanders later substantially revises this impression, at this point in the book one could easily conclude that the issue of inclusion of the gentiles has still not been recognized by him as central to Pauline religion.

12. This point has already been made by Charles H. Cosgrove (1988, 12). However, in spite of the impressive vigor and clarity of Cosgrove's argumentation (23–38), I am equally unconvinced that his decision to hang the entire letter on the beginning of chapter 3 is necessary. Paul's argumentation from the ecstatic gifts the Galatians have shared with him is a very significant point in the letter, and I have tried to treat it as such, but I also think it is secondary to the motivating force of Paul's gospel. Moreover, I do not think that it is so neatly isolatable from the question of Jews and gentiles in the People of God. In short, I stand by my claim that the choice of starting point is essentially arbitrary, although some will generate stronger readings than others.

13. Sanders quotes Georg Eicholz very approvingly: "The encounter with Christ has for Paul the consequence that Christ *becomes the middle of his theology,* just as previously Torah must have been the middle of his theology" (cited 1983, 151). But at the risk of belaboring the point, what then caused the encounter with Christ if we are not prepared to accept supernatural explanations or ones drawn from the realm of psychopathology?

14. Indeed, I would suggest that the only place in which we find solution to plight explicitly encoded in Paul's writing is a passage in which he is granting an assumption to his opponent (Peter) in order to persuade him of the absurdity of his position. Sanders himself senses the anomaly of Paul's utterance here in the context of Pauline expression: "Although Paul has shown in Gal. 2:15 that he knew the standard distinction between being a Gentile 'sinner' and a righteous Jew, his general tendency, in evidence in Rom. 6:1–7:4 as well as in Gal. 3: 19–4:10 was to universalize the human plight. All were under sin and in need of redemption; all were under the law" (1983, 72). To my mind, these positions

are so fundamentally incompatible that it is impossible to accept 2:15 as Paul's statement of his own position, though it reads perfectly as granting Peter a point in order to catch him in a sort of reductio argument.

15. Toward the very end of his book, Sanders allows this as a possible alternative to the thesis he has been defending throughout:

> We can never exclude with certainty the possibility that Paul was secretly dissatisfied with the law before his conversion/call. If one is to look for secret dissatisfaction, however, it might be better to look to his stance toward the Gentiles than to his possible frustration with his own situation under the law, or to his analysis of Jews under the law. It is by no means inconceivable that he had native sympathy for the Gentiles and chafed at the Jewish exclusivism which either ignored them or which relegated them to second place in God's plan.
>
> (153)

Despite Sanders's disclaimer that "This, like other attempts to penetrate Paul's precall thought, is entirely speculative," I obviously find it a much more satisfactory account than one that assumes that "out of the blue" Paul had a mystical vision for which nothing in his past had prepared him. I believe there is ample evidence in Paul's preoccupation with this theme in both Galatians and Romans to support the construction of this prior-to-Christ dissatisfaction with Jewish ethnocentricity, particularly as I have already suggested, when we consider the evidence for widespread concern with this issue among Greek-speaking Jews in the first century.

16. See especially the summary on pp. 143–44, where Sanders argues that Paul had definite ideas about soteriology and christology but never solved the problem of the Law in a way that he deemed adequate. His "contradictions" on this question are the record of a life-long struggle never resolved. This position is, in itself, a possible but by no means necessary one as I hope to be showing throughout this book. In the latter book, Sanders claims that his former work was misunderstood to imply that "Paul had no substantial critique of his native faith" (154) and refers the reader to Sanders 1977 (550–52). This very reference, however, only demonstrates further what a marginal role this critique plays in Sanders's account of Paul!

17. Cf., however, Westerholm (1988, 114–15).

18. Note that commentators otherwise as opposed to each other as James Dunn and Charles Cosgrove both observe this principle implicitly and explicitly (Cosgrove 1991, 90ff.; Dunn 1983 and 1990).

19. With regard to Judaism we are not in the situation that we are in with regard to the Superapostles of 2 Corinthians or the women prophets of 1 Corinthians, where we have only Paul with which to reconstruct his opposition. Wire 1990 is a simply brilliant example of just how much can be accomplished convincingly using such methods in the absence of actual data. But where there *are* data, it is impossible to rely on reconstructions through Paul's rhetoric. Wire's reconstruction, moreover, of these Corinthian women is more sympathetic and more critical of Paul's view of them than the reconstructions of Judaism that most Pauline scholarship has produced.

20. For extensive discussion of this book, see now Campbell (1992, 122–32). On the whole, I am much more inclined to Campbell's interpretation of Romans than to Watson's, although I dissent from the conclusions of Campbell's studies regarding the valence of Paul's "tolerance."

21. See, however, p. 165, which is then undercut on p. 167. It is, it seems to me, quite impossible to see Paul as a universalist and then identify his primary motivation as causing his "readers to distance themselves from the Jewish community." See also p. 183, n. 16.

22. Sanders, already in 1983, had demonstrated, to my mind quite successfully, the inadequacy of the view that Paul tried first to preach to Jews and only turned to gentiles after failing with the Jews that is one of the pillars of Watson's sociological reconstruction of the origins of Paul's alleged "sectarianism" (Sanders 1983, 187–88 and esp. 190).

23. Davies (1965, 61–68) is a model itself of a cultural criticism which is not anti-Judaic. Neither apologizing for Jewish "particularism" nor condemning it as an essentialized exclusiveness or innate sense of superiority, Davies anticipates as well my thesis that Paul's critique arose in an environment in which many Jews were increasingly feeling an "uneasy conscience." He well understands that Jewish isolation was a fence that preserved Jewish difference, and also that "a fence while it preserves, also excludes. The Torah, which differentiated the Jew from others, also separated him from them." See also Kuschel (1992, 202).

24. For Epictetus, conversion to Judaism was used as an analogy for becoming a true Stoic, suggesting, as Gager argues, that it was so common as to have become virtually proverbial.

25. See also Thielman (1989, 24) and Westerholm (1988, 117–18). Westerholm makes some remarkable claims in support of his thesis, e.g.:

> Nor do the occurrences of the phrase in Romans (3:20, 28) support Dunn's contentions. Dunn claims that, since Paul has just refuted "Jewish presumption in their favoured status as the people of the law, the 'works of the law' must be a shorthand way of referring to that in which the typical Jew placed his confidence, the law-observance which documented his membership of the covenant." But the only commandments of the law mentioned by Paul before his reference to "works of the law" in Rom. 3:20 are taken from the Decalogue (2:21–22), and do not refer to Jewish "identity markers." Circumcision has been touched upon, but it is treated (rather curiously) as though it were not a part of the law to be observed (2:26–27); in this context at least it can hardly serve as a prime referent of the phrase "works of the law" in 3:20.
>
> (118–19)

The verses Romans 2:25–29 hardly just "touch upon" the question of circumcision; they are central to the entire argument of the chapter, namely, that circumcision—i.e., mere membership in the physical People of Israel and bearing its identity markers—does not justify, while adherence to the Law does. The "curious" contrast between the Law and circumcision, far from being a refutation of Dunn, provides in fact very strong support for Dunn's contention that Paul's target is those practices that mark off Israel as separate and saved alone. Romans 3:20 does mount a theoretical attack on "works of the Law" in a general sense (as do other verses as well); the purpose of this critique, however, is once more immediately revealed in 3:27–30, where again circumcision is emphasized and devalued. Verse 4:16 is even more explicit: "That is why it depends on faith, *in order that the promise may rest on grace and be guaranteed to all his descendants—not only to the adherents of the law, but also to those who share the faith of Abraham, for he is the father of us all.*" In Romans, no less than in Galatians, Paul's primary motive is the universalization of soteriology.

And again: "That Paul supports his rejection of the 'works of the law' in Rom. 3:20, 28 by showing that Abraham was justified by faith, not works (4:1–5), is positively fatal to Dunn's proposal. . . . For the 'works' by which Abraham could conceivably have been justified, and of which he might have boasted (4:2), were certainly not observances of the peculiarly Jewish parts of the Mosaic code" (119). I just do not know what Westerholm is talking about here, since circumcision and attendant Jewish privilege is *the* central issue in Romans 4. When Westerholm interprets Romans 4 (170–71) he simply elides the crucial verse 16. Salvation must rest on grace and not on works so that it will be granted to all and not only to ethnic Jews, those for whom Abraham is "ancestor according to the flesh"; this simply continues Paul's cry from the heart in 3:27: "Is God the God of Jews only? Is he not the God of Gentiles also?" Paul does *not* mention universal sinfulness here as the explanation at all. These passages are as sturdy a support for Dunn as he could want. On the other hand, Westerholm's argument here and throughout that Paul condemns failure to keep the Law and not wrong attitudes, boastfulness, or self-righteousness attendant on keeping the Law seems to me absolutely convincing. Of course, Dunn overstates his case when he claims, as he sometimes seems to, that "works of the law" lexically means only the identity markers. His insight, however, that this is what Paul has in mind as the letter which kills, opposed to the spirit which gives life, seems to me absolutely sound. For discussion of this last issue, letter ~ spirit, see the next chapter.

26. Schreiner sums up his interpretation of Paul thus:

> When Paul says that no one can receive the Spirit or obtain righteousness by "works of law," his argument is directed against those who thought such righteousness could be merited by performing the law. Paul rules out righteousness by "works of law" because no one can obey the law perfectly. He does not oppose obeying the law in principle. What he opposes is the delusion of those who think they can earn merit before God by their obedience to the law, even though they fail to obey it.
>
> (244)

The ultimate problem with this thesis is that there do not seem to have been any Jews who thought that works were sufficient for salvation or that perfect performance was possible for anyone. Accordingly, if that were the force of Paul's critique it would be bursting through an open door, and Jews could answer easily: We agree. No one (least of all us) can keep the Law entirely. God's grace is necessary, but trying to keep the Law is a necessary condition for God's grace to come. His critique would be then no critique, and ineffective. The great advantage of the interpretation that the focus and force of Paul's critique is on the ethnocentrism of Jewish doctrine and practice is that it is a critique of a real Judaism and not one that has to be made up ex nihilo to explain Paul. The issue is, as Schreiner correctly observes, not whether the critique is anti-Semitic but whether it made sense!

27. It seems that here again I have reproduced Baur's intuitions as summed up in Bultmann (1967, 14). See also Barclay (1991, 94).

28. Alan Segal has phrased this particularly well:

> Paul does not distinguish between ceremonial laws and moral laws exactly. He distinguishes between flesh and spirit. But the effect of his distinction, as I will show, is to valorize moral life while denigrating ceremonial life. In other words, it is Paul's opinion that the gentiles must be transformed by their faith in the risen, spiritual Christ so that they are to be treated as righteous gentiles and not to be made to observe any part of the ceremonial law.
>
> (Alan Segal, "Universalism in Judaism and Christianity," unpublished paper, 1992)

CHAPTER 3

1. Howard Eilberg-Schwartz explains this, in part, as owing to a misunderstanding on the part of these Greek philosophers of the nature of biblical religion. They thought that the Mosaic prohibition on the making of images of God was indicative of a spiritualized conception of divinity that resisted imagining the deity in human form, while in fact the opposite might be claimed, namely, that such spiritualized theological conceptions (and I am *not* claiming them as better) only developed in the wake of the contact with Greek philosophical thought (Eilberg-Schwartz forthcoming; Boyarin 1990a).

2. Note how this completely revises older paradigms, in which Judaism and Hellenism are considered as *alternative* options for explaining Paul. See, e.g., the account of H. A. A. Kennedy's and A. D. Nock's work in Smith (1990, 65–71). To this day, however, in much Pauline scholarship we find statements not unlike those of Kennedy's to the effect that Paul is fully explicable as a development of biblical religion pure and simple in an apocalyptic framework. Even more to the point, however, are the recurrent figurations of Hellenism or "platonism" as taints or contaminants which must be exorcised from the Pauline corpus. Nock described the New Testament as "the product of an enclosed world living its own life, a ghetto culturally and linguistically!" (qu. in Smith 1990, 71).

3. Compare the "standard" account of the historical origins of universalism out of monotheism offered (critically) by Wallerstein (1991, 30).

4. Compare the similar views of Gundry (1976, 31 and esp. 84). Although I tend to agree with his view in general, I think he overstates the case when he writes, "Nor does the difference and separability of the corporeal and the incorporeal in man imply any inferiority on the part of the corporeal." Gundry also distinguishes between "radical dualism" and "duality," while I prefer to use the term "dualism" and suggest that the relative axiological weight placed on body and soul is a separate function from the dualism itself.

5. This is an attempt not at super-PCness but simply at emphasis of the

fact that the universal, spiritual human almost always ends up being universally male—and Christian. See Chapter 9 below.

6. Philo, however, can refer to the body as "a sacred dwelling place or shrine fashioned for the reasonable soul" (*Op* 137), a much less misomatist but just as dualist image. See also D. Boyarin (1992b, n. 6).

7. For the notion of the disembodied self as "naked" and its Greek roots, see Lucian's account of Charon's charge to a "client": "Off with your beauty then. Off with your lips, kisses and all. Off with that lovely long hair, and those rosy cheeks—in fact off with your whole body" (Lucian 1961, 66). See also 1 Corinthians 15:35–49, a notoriously difficult passage, and discussion in Conzelmann (1976, 280–88).

8. I think that Gundry has rather missed the point when he writes, "In view of the evidence, it is difficult to comprehend failure to see duality in rabbinic anthropology" (1976, 93). Of course, the Rabbis also believed in a soul that animates the body. The point is, rather, that they identified the human being not as a soul dwelling in a body but as a body animated by a soul, and that makes all the difference in the world. Gundry similarly misses the same distinction with respect to the Hebrew Bible. There is no evidence among the data that he cites (117–34) that the soul has an individual personality or that it is the essence of the self, a fortiori no notion that an individual could be rewarded with a disembodied bliss after death. To the extent that such ideas appear widely in Hellenistic Judaism and to some extent in rabbinic Judaism (not at all "standard for Judaism" [!] as Gundry (148) would have it), they are indeed, it seems, a product of the Hellenistic culture of which Judaism was a part at that time (*pace* Gundry, 148n.2). See also Barclay (1991, 184n.11), who has leveled a somewhat similar critique at Gundry's work. See also the very important discussion in Kuschel (1992, 183–84 and passim).

9. I accordingly respectfully dissent once more from Davies's interpretation here to the effect that "Paul calls the earthly body a σκῆρος and although there are abundant parallels to this, as we saw, in Hellenistic literature, the term would also be quite natural to a Rabbi" (1965, 313). In the parallel that Davies cites there from Genesis Rabbah, it is *not* the body which is referred to as a clay vessel but the entire person, and this makes all the difference. On the other hand, Josephus provides a perfect parallel to Paul (*Wars* 7, 8, vii), adopting, however, the much more negative metaphors of prison and corpse for the body in which the soul is captured until released by death. Another elegant argument for this interpretation of Paul's anthropology is provided by Philippians 1:19–26, for which see Gundry: "'To depart' is to die bodily death. 'To be with Christ' is to be absent from the body (cf. II Cor 5:7–9)" (Gundry 1976, 37). Contrast this with Bultmann (1951, 1, 194). However, even Bultmann is constrained to admit, "From the very fact that Paul conceives the resurrection-life as somatic, it is apparent that his understanding of the self was not shaped by this dualism. But, on the other hand, he sees so deep a cleft within man, so great a tension between self and self, and so keenly feels the plight of the man who loses his grip upon himself and falls victim to outside powers, that he comes close to Gnostic dualism. That is indicated by the fact that he occasionally uses *soma* synonymously with *sarx* ('flesh')" (Bultmann 1951, 199).

10. For a full catalogue of Hellenistic parallels to 2 Corinthians 5, see Knox (1939, 128 ff.) and discussion in Davies (1965, 311–13). For the seen and the unseen, cf. also Romans 1:20. Arlene Saxonhouse traces this theme back to the pre-Socratics: "It is, then, in the fragmentary writings of the pre-Socratics, of Thales, Anaximander, Heraclitus, and Parmenides, that we discover the early fear of diversity and how that fear leads them to dismiss what is seen in favor of what is unseen. . . . They search for a unity in the natural world that can overcome the experience the senses have of a vast multiplicity" (1992, x–xi).

11. Bultmann thus contradicts his own view as quoted above in n. 9. I think here we see Bultmann the exegete contradicting Bultmann the systematic theologian, a point that I develop below. It has long been recognized that Romans 1 shows clear signs of Alexandrian influence. See Charles (1913, 28). For a critical discussion of this view (a critique that I do not find entirely convincing), see Davies (1965, 28–31). Strikingly, even Davies writes, "Unconsciously of course, he follows Plato, who in order to understand justice in the soul drew a large-scale picture of justice in the state" (30).

12. But I cannot, of course, understand what allows Bultmann then to say, "It would be an error in method to proceed from such passages as these to interpret the *soma*-concept that is characteristic of Paul and determines his fundamental discussions" (202). To be sure, "soma" has other meanings in Paul and his dualism does not involve the denigration of the body that we associate with certain gnostics or with a Plotinus, for example, but given these differences it seems to me methodologically sound to proceed from such passages to an understanding of Paul's anthropology, like his ontology, christology, and hermeneutics, as fundamentally dualistic.

13. It is important to note that Paul does not use σάρξ here for the physical but rather ψυχή, but I would not make too much of this, as it is possible that he uses the latter term for the sake of the midrash. In any case, ψυχή and σάρξ seem quite close in Pauline anthropology.

14. See also Bultmann (1951, 204) on this passage. Once more he produces essentially the same reading that I do ("Paul is influenced by Gnostic usage"), and then undermines its import, because it does not suit his theology. Even stranger is his assertion (233) that "flesh and blood here means humanity as such, human nature." There is no doubt at all in my mind that "flesh and blood" here means physical bodies and nothing else!

15. See the following surprising convergence on this point:

> As in Freud's account of moral masochism, Reik's typical subject seems ardently given over to self-mortification of one kind or another . . . but the psychic dynamics are otherwise quite different. To begin with, an external audience is a structural necessity, although it may be either earthly or heavenly. Second, the body is centrally on display, whether it is being consumed by ants or roasting over a fire. Finally, behind all these "scenes" or "exhibits" is the master tableau or group fantasy—Christ nailed to the cross, head wreathed in thorns and blood dripping from his impaled sides. What is being beaten here is not so much the body as the "flesh," and beyond that sin itself, and the whole fallen world.
>
> (Silverman 1992, 197)

16. Another way of approaching this question would be through N. T. Wright's typology of dualisms. Thus Paul's would fit Wright's "cosmological duality: the classic position of Plato . . . a mainline belief of the Greco-Roman (and modern Western world)" and his anthropological duality, which is the human-centered counterpart of the cosmological, but would avoid "theological/moral duality," which sharply divides the world into good and bad principles with the body/material on the side of the bad (not necessarily the product, however, of an evil god). I have added to Wright's typologies a hermeneutical dualism which is the counterpart for language of the cosmological and anthropological dualisms. Once this distinction between these (and other) types of what has been called dualism is clearly made, I think that objections to referring to Paul's dualism should be greatly lessened. (Wright 1992b, 253–54). See also Vincent Wimbush, who writes:

> Thus, what was now required was "salvation"—from the self, or from the "house" (σῶμα, κόσμος) in which the self abides. Almost universally (Panhellenistically) "salvation" entailed some form of ascetic behavior, namely, some form of renunciation of the world, or part thereof.
>
> (1987, 2–3)

17. All of the following summary is drawn directly from Jewett's very useful *Forschungsgeschichte*. I am only citing certain of the major views that I find interesting in particular as background for my proposals here, so for the full history, Jewett must be consulted directly. Jewett several times remarks of scholars that they have remained "aloof from previous or contemporary discussion" and therefore have produced interpretations that "could about as well have been written in the last century" (1971, 76). This suggests to me—although not to Jewett, apparently—that perhaps the last century was on to something. I feel strongly that this is the case with regard to the profound denial of any platonistic-dualist moments in Paul's religious culture. Jewett's own ideas are bound up in a neo-Reformation theology within which "strict obedience to the law" is sarkic because it is a "human revolt against God" (94). One of the advantages, I believe, of the view of σάρξ which I am promulgating here is that it allows us to understand why Paul refers to the Law as the flesh without making the assumption that he believed that those who kept the Law were *thereby* in revolt against God and ipso facto sinners.

18. Jewett's main argument for this suggestion is that Paul does not use the term σάρξ in the allegedly parallel Thessalonian situation (108–14), but this argument is dependent on a very specific interpretation of the Galatian situation as being one of libertinism and a "serious outbreak of sensuality," for which I see not the slightest shred of evidence in Galatians. My interpretation of Galatians 5 takes it as evidence only for Paul's concern for possible misunderstanding of his gospel of freedom, an interpretation which 5:13 strongly supports. See Chapter 7 below for extensive discussion of this point. If the strong analogy with the Galatian situation falls, all Jewett is left with is a particularly weak form of argument from silence, i.e.: If Paul had had the spirit ~ flesh opposition why did he not use it in Thessalonians? This claim is based on so many presuppositions that it would be better not to use it at all.

19. Even Galatians 5:13ff. is not sufficient to establish an independent agency

for the flesh as Jewett and others claim (102–08). Paul could certainly be speaking in very vivid metaphor here when he says that the desires of the spirit are against the flesh, and the desires of the flesh are against the spirit. The intrapsychic dualism is, nevertheless, striking here. The only cosmic agent in Paul which is opposed to God is "Sin."

20. See the partial anticipations of this interpretation already in Robinson:

> In this connection, σάρξ, again like the basar in the Old Testament, stands especially for the solidarities of sex ("the twain shall become one flesh," 1 Cor. 6.16; Eph. 5.31) and of race ("my kinsmen according to the flesh," Rom. 9.3, contracted to "my flesh" in Rom. 11.14). So, in Rom. 4.1, Paul speaks of "Abraham, our forefather according to the flesh," and says of Christ that He was "born of the seed of David according to the flesh" (Rom. 1.3) and was an Israelite τὸ κατὰ σάκα, in what concerned race (Rom. 9.5).
>
> This usage constantly tends to fall over into a contrast (already implicit in the τό of Rom. 9.5) between mere external, racial connection and what is of real, spiritual, divine import. "Israel after the flesh" (1 Cor. 10.18) is distinguished from the Christian Church, the true Israel of God. In Gal. 4.23 and 29, the son born "after the flesh" is contrasted with the one born "through the promise" and "after the Spirit." in Rom. 8.9, the antithesis becomes quite stark: "It is not the children of the flesh that are the children of God."
>
> (Robinson 1952, 21–22)

Robinson's extraordinary exegetical good sense comes aground, however, for him as well, on the shoals of existential neo-Lutheran theology:

> Consequently, as Bultmann rightly stresses, "the mind of the flesh" stands primarily for a denial of man's dependence on God and for a trust in what is of human effort or origin. Thus, when Paul asks the Galatians, "having begun in the Spirit, are ye now perfected in the flesh?" (Gal. 3.3), he refers, not to a lapse into sensuality, but to a return to reliance upon the law. The flesh is concerned with serving "the letter" (Rom. 7.6; 2.28 f), which is "of men" (Rom. 2.29) and represents human self-sufficiency (2 Cor. 3.5 f).
>
> (Robinson 1952, 25)

2 Corinthians 3:5 is, of course, totally irrelevant, as it speaks of Paul's competence as an apostle and his credentials and has nothing to do with the Law at all. There is accordingly nothing whatever in the cited verses that supports the notion that what troubles Paul is human self-sufficiency! Nor does Romans 2:29 say that the Law is of men!

21. I think, however, that even Martin's discussion of the text itself contradicts this interpretation. If the Christ κατὰ σάρκα, whom they have known until now is "Christ in his worldly accessibility, before his death and resurrection," or even according to the views that the adverbial modifies the knowing and not the object of the knowing, so we have *known* Christ according to the flesh, it still is impossible, in my view, to gloss this as "without reference to God"! Even Christ

according to the flesh, or known according to the flesh, was by no means without reference to God. Martin's tacit attempts to overcome this difficulty only point it up all the more, in my opinion: "It would be a human achievement (σάρξ, 'flesh'; cf. Phil. 3:3), and Paul cannot accept such knowledge because it is narrowly circumscribed, i.e., he denies that this way of knowing Christ has any scope in a person's relationship to God."

22. To be sure, the sociological twist on this interpretation is new to Segal (and Watson), but the denial of hermeneutical significance to the flesh and spirit has become near-orthodoxy.

23. See the discussion of 2 Cor. 5:16 below. See also 1 Cor. 3:3–4, but note that Paul there uses different adverbial forms: σαρκικός and σάρκινος and not κατὰ σάρκα, which I am claiming has an hermeneutic Sitz im Leben. He does, on the other hand, use κατὰ ἄνθρωπον περιπατεῖν in the same context where it clearly is to be taken axiologically.

24. A point made by Barclay (1991, 212). I think, however, that my notion of semantic multi-valence is far superior to Barclay's styling of Paul's usage of σάρξ as ambiguous. It is not ambiguity that Paul is exploiting but the rich generative possibilities of a polysemic word and its cultural associations. The association of both keeping the Law and libertinism with σάρξ is not some kind of a rhetorical trick on Paul's part but the very essence of his thought.

25. Thus, to take only one example among several, Jewett alleges that Paul's usage of κατὰ σάρκα is inconsistent vis-à-vis ἐν σαρκί, claiming that in 2 Corinthians 10:2–3 the two terms are distinct, while in Romans 7:5 and 8:8–9, they are alleged to be synonyms. Examining the texts, however, in the light of the exegesis proposed in this book shows this not to be the case. Rather there are complicated nuances (as well as a paradox that Paul himself sees). "In the flesh" has indeed two senses. On the one hand, in Romans 7:5 and 8:8–9 it refers to the condition of those who live in the fleshy condition of commitment to the literal law of the flesh. In the Corinthians passage it refers to the condition of being alive in a human body. The paradox is exactly the same paradox that we find *explicitly* recognized by Paul in Galatians 2: "I have been crucified with Christ; and it is no longer I who live, but Christ lives in me; and what I now live in the flesh I live in faith in the Son of God who loved me and gave himself up for me" (2:19–20). The fleshy existence of the Christian is only apparent—precisely what Paul is arguing in the 2 Corinthians passage as well—but the fleshy existence of those who live according to the flesh is real. They are really in the flesh! There is thus no contradiction in Paul's semantics here.

26. Jewett's arguments to the contrary (1971, 162–63) are invalid. Paul, however, throughout addresses his "brothers," who are kinsmen not literally but only in faith, in the spirit, allegorically. Here, therefore, he draws a contrast by referring to his literal kinsmen. Far from being tautological, the adverb is necessary to avoid misunderstanding. Finally, the notion that "Israel according to the flesh" describes the *nature* of the Jews and not the hermeneutical status of their nomination as Israel is incredible. Jewett writes, "If the phrase κατὰ σάρκα was inserted by the Hellenistic congregation in the confession cited in Rom. 1:3 with the intention of deprecating the fleshly existence in contrast with pneumatic existence, should we not expect that it has a similar negative significance in

Rom. 9:5"—where it refers to Christ! Why not argue the exact opposite? If in Romans 9:5 Christ according to the flesh means simply the earthly, physical Christ as opposed to the risen Christ, according to the spirit, then perhaps that is what it means in 1:3 as well, and we need not assume multiple, contradictory glosses in that poor maligned verse. Jewett writes, "And if σάρξ is blandly neutral in v. 5, why does Paul emphasize the phrase with τό and thereby stress that Christ came from Israel *only* insofar as his flesh was concerned?" The question answers itself (see also Robinson's insightful understanding, cited above in n. 20). The whole point of Romans 9–11 is to emphasize the positive but limited role of physical Israel.

27. On my reading, even if the church is (and I think it is) the spiritual Israel κατὰ πνεῦμα, this does not mean for a moment that Paul implies that it could not fall into error (*pace* Hays 1989, 96). Quite the opposite. The Israelites κατὰ σάρκα could very well have been highly spiritual, and the church which is Israel κατὰ πνεῦμα could very well prove itself carnal indeed, which is certainly the danger that Paul's letter to the Corinthians comes to guard against. We must not conflate κατὰ σάρκα with the description of the Corinthians as σαρκικοί (carnal) in 1 Cor. 3:3–4, as Hays does.

28. Cf. also Schweizer in TDNT, VII, 127: "This expression carries with it an evaluation; this is the Israel which understands itself only in terms of descent. In the context, however, this is not the point at issue, and it is no accident that we do not find the antithesis ὁ Ἰσραὴλ κατὰ πνεῦμα."

29. Hays's reading of this entire passage (91–102) is, as usual, astute. For my explicit points of disagreement with it, see below. On the interpretation of "Israel of God" (Galatians 6:16), I am entirely persuaded by the arguments of Dahl (1950) that this means the new community of the faithful, both those of Jewish as well as those of gentile origins. See also Sanders (1983, 173ff.). Sanders wonders how Paul would have referred to his new creation, since other than here, he does not seem to actually use the term "true Israel" or "Israel of God," and he certainly does not use a term like "Christians." I think that at least one further clue is to be found in Philippians 3:3: "for we are the [true] circumcision." Since "the circumcision" is clearly a technical term in Paul for Israel, when combined with Galatians 6:16, I think it is hard to escape the conclusion that the notion of *Verus Israel* was at least embryonic in Paul (*pace* Campbell [1992, 48 and 74–75]).

30. Richard Hays has written to me on this matter (personal communication, March 10, 1993):

> No, for Paul, that which Israel signified (signifies?) is instantiated in the
> historical phenomenon of the early Christian communities. I think that
> you (ironically) here do to the concrete historical Christian community
> what you complain I do to the concrete historical Jewish community: spiri-
> tualize it out of historical existence.

I think that there is a certain (understandable) misunderstanding of my position revealed here, and I had better try to clarify myself. There is no question but that Hays is right in his claim that that which Israel signifies is manifested in the Christian community; however, note that I substitute for "instantiated" "manifested." The question is what the nature of that "historical phenomenon" is. If for the historical, fleshy Israel, it was a life "according to the flesh," that is, a life of historical action in the world, getting and spending, procreating and dying, for the new Israel, it is a life "according to the spirit," that is, beyond dying and birthing. The Christians have conquered death, Paul says repeatedly, and as such, have exited from history, because death is the necessary condition for history! Paul himself is troubled by the paradox of being in the body while living according to the spirit and treats that paradox at least once, when he writes that your seeing him in the flesh is only apparent, but the spirit of Christ lives within him. "For through the Law I died to the Law, in order that I might live for God. I have been crucified with Christ; and it is no longer I who live, but Christ lives in me; and what I now live in the flesh I live in faith in the Son of God who loved me and gave himself up for me" (Galatians 2:19–20). (See my discussion of this passage below, Chapter 5.) It is this sense that Paul constantly communicates of Christians being beyond history that creates his (realistic) anxiety that they will misunderstand and think that ethics no longer applies to them as well, an anxiety that he is quick to allay, on my readings, in Galatians 5–6 and 1 Corinthians.

31. The term "Judaisms" may go back to Claude Montefiore's work on Paul, as I learn from Westerholm (1988, 35).

32. See Fredriksen (1988, 172) for similar notions of the relationship between Paul's "high" christology and his universalism.

33. I say this primarily to exclude the notion that Paul's doctrine of justification by faith and its entire hermeneutic are a secondary part of his thought, "forced upon him, not by vision of the risen Christ, but by developments in his mission to the Gentiles. Practice determined theory rather than the other way around" (Wrede, as paraphrased by Westerholm 1988, 20).

34. See also Davies's precise formulation with regard to 1 Corinthians 15:

> Paul, in his doctrine of the Second Adam, asserts the same truth that the Fourth Gospel proclaims in its insistence that the Word became flesh, in another, Rabbinic way, that the particular is not a scandal. He was impelled to assert this not from philosophical motives but from the mere fact of Christ in history. (52)

The determination, however, of Christ in history as this or that kind of fact is, of course, a product of "philosophical motives."

35. Thus the Rabbis can refer to "circumcision in the flesh" and also "the Covenant of the flesh" to mean circumcision, with, obviously, quite a different valence from its usage in Paul.

36. I therefore disagree with Martyn (1985, 416) that the Law has become an ally of the flesh in the eschatalogical moment. The Law has always been of the flesh; that is its essence. The issue has rather to do with the evaluation of fleshiness within Pharisaism (later Rabbinism) and Hellenistic Judaism, with Paul an extreme representative of the latter. (See Segal: "Philo criticizes the extreme allegorizers for their attempt to ignore daily life, imagining themselves to be disembodied souls. . . . Philo, had he known Paul, would have considered him one of the radical allegorizers. Though Paul certainly did not ignore the body, he preached its radical transformation through death and rebirth in baptism and through a mystical identification with Christ, which opened him to a criticism

similar to Philo's when he claimed to have left behind the body of flesh and entered the one spiritual body of the Lord" [1990, 246].) Moreover, it is impossible for me to follow Martyn in his assumption that the new age obviates the antinomies of the past, when the fundamental antinomy around which all others are organized—the flesh and the spirit—still exists. On the other hand, I see no reason to doubt that for Paul the place of the flesh and all of its concomitants—ethnicity, sexuality, the Law, etc.—has been entirely changed in the realized eschatology of the crucifixion. The pedagogue belongs to a certain historical moment, now transcended. See also Cosgrove (1988, 181–83).

37. This is the transfer that lies at the bottom of the allegory of Galatians 4:21–31 as well, discussed above in the first chapter.

38. In the Septuagint both translate בשר (flesh). There is, of course, in biblical Hebrew no word that distinguishes "body" as opposed to "flesh."

39. There is even a variant reading here which reads τῆς σαρκὸς "deeds of the flesh," thus further suggesting their synonymity. "Deeds of the body" is, apparently, the better reading.

40. I am not convinced by Jewett's explanations for the particular instances. Even with his over-elaborate theories, dependent on very particular and specific analyses of the breakdown of the Corinthian letters, Jewett is still forced to admit that "at times such usage appeared to be motivated and at other times it did not."

41. I am not distinguishing here between soul, spirit, and mind, which all have different referents in philonic anthropology. For the purpose of the present typology, the broad distinction between flesh and spirit or body and soul is sufficient.

42. I am just adding a further (but to my mind crucial) wrinkle to the point already made well in Hays: "Of course, the expression κατὰ σάρκα is a theologically loaded one for Paul. At the superficial level, it refers simply to the process of natural physical descent, but there are at least two other levels of meaning in Paul's usage of the term: it alludes to circumcision and, at the same time, to the mode of human existence apart from God. The meaning of the expression in Rom 4:1 is to be determined not by choosing among these possibilities but by discerning their complex interweaving in the present context" (1985, 86). This seems to me to be just right, except that I add the hermeneutical sense of "literal" to the interwoven senses identified by Hays, and that I would question whether κατὰ σάρκα truly refers to an existence apart from God. This seems to me a relic of another mode of interpreting Pauline discourse.

43. Although nearly every translation I have seen silently supplies here "true," as they do also in Romans 2:28–29 in a similar context, Paul writes just ἡμεῖς γάρ ἐσμεν ἡ περιτομή "For we are the circumcision," i.e., the Jews, Israel.

44. Cf., for instance, 2 Corinthians 5:12: "We are not recommending ourselves to you once more, but rather providing you a suitable basis to boast in us, that you may have something to say to those who are boasting of what is outward and not of what is within," i.e., to have confidence in us that you may have something to say to those who rely on the outer (lit., what is on the face) and not the inner (what is in the heart). The issue is surely not one of false pride or arrogance but of a mistaken placement of trust by the opponents. This point is even clearer if we adopt the reading of several very important manuscripts that have here ὑπὲρ ὑμῶν "have confidence in yourselves" rather than ὑπὲρ ἡμῶν "in us."

This *lectio dificilior* may be difficult from the point of view of Greek syntax and usage. Note that nearly the exact same phraseology also appears in Galatians 6:4: "But let each one test his own work, and this his reason to boast will be in himself alone and not in his neighbor. For each man will have to bear his own burden." Here, once more, "have confidence in" or "rely on" gives better sense than "boast." This interpretation of καυχᾶσθαι has the singular virtue of obviating the need for comments to the effect that Paul uses the verb sometimes positively and sometimes negatively; if we are not speaking of a moral quality, then the verb itself is neutral and the positive or negative valence is a product of the object of the verb. See also Bultmann (1951, 1, 243), who makes substantially the same point: "Very closely related to 'boasting after the flesh'—in fact, even synonymous with it—is *'putting one's confidence in the flesh.'* In Phil. 3:3 it constitutes the antithesis to 'boasting in Christ Jesus'" (emphasis original).

45. For a similar unthematized tension in Bultmann between exactly these two elements, see Watson:

> In Gal. 5:2 ff, Christ and circumcision are contrasted with each other. Bultmann rightly notes that the demand for circumcision means that "the condition for sharing in salvation is belonging to the Jewish people" (*Theology*, I, 55), but he can still claim that Paul's discussion of circumcision brings us to the heart of "the Pauline problem of good works as the condition for participation in salvation" (111). This mental leap from circumcision to a wrong understanding of good works is quite illegitimate. Paul opposes circumcision because it is the rite of entry into the Jewish people, *and for that reason alone.*
>
> (1986, 69)

46. I trust, therefore, that my interpretation will not be subject to the strictures that have met similar proposals to the effect that they "repristinize Paul" as a Hellenistic philosopher (Jewett 1971, 77).

47. It is at least partially this which is meant when all Western philosophy is regarded as footnotes to Plato.

CHAPTER 4

1. Of these three, of course, my general interpretation of Paul is closest to that of Dunn. See also Carras 1992, and Campbell (1992, 156n. 53).

2. See Goodman (1992, 72), who is skeptical about the scope of such exclusivist notions. See also Sanders 1976.

3. My version of this argument is slightly different from that of Dunn himself.

4. Cf. also the text cited by Dunn from the *Wisdom of Solomon* 15:1 ff. (Dunn 1988, 83).

5. For "boast" (καυχάομαι) in the sense of "have confidence" see discussion above in Chapter 3. This further strengthens Sanders's complete rejection of the view that what Paul found wrong with Judaism was the self-righteousness that keeping the law allegedly promoted.

6. See 2 *Apoc. Bar.* 48:22–24, cited in Dunn (1988, 110).

7. I have specifically used the feminine pronouns here to emphasize another

attractive aspect of Paul's spiritualization, namely, his at least partial transcendence of exclusive religious androcentrism.

8. This chapter is a scandal for interpretation only if one has adopted the Lutheran theology, whereby attempting to perform God's will with the body is itself a form of sin! Cf. also Snodgrass 1986. See also next paragraph.

9. This case has been best argued by Alan Segal, in an unpublished paper.

10. I am puzzled by Dunn's remark that "within the Pharisaic Judaism with which Paul was most familiar, such Gentiles were probably only tolerated and were counted acceptable to God only when they actually became members of the covenant people as proselytes" (1988, 99).

11. Note that, in a sense, this interpretation of Paul in Romans 2 is the precise obverse of the "Lutheran" one, for Paul here is denying salvation by "grace" to the Jew owing to the free election of God and insisting that only through works will the Jew be saved, as in 2 : 13, "For it is not the hearers of the law who are righteous before God, but the doers of the law who will be justified." On this verse, which has been a scandal to much Protestant interpretation, see now the excellent discussion in Snodgrass 1986.

12. I am nonplussed by Sanders's gloss:

> The true Jew is one who keeps the law, who does not make an external show, *who may not be physically circumcised* ("in the flesh"), but who is circumcised internally, in secret; it is a spiritual, not a literal, circumcision of the heart (*en tōi kryptōi . . . kai peritomē kardias en pneumati ou grammati*). . . . Thus far we have seen no evidence that at any point in Romans 2 does Paul step outside the Jewish perspective.
>
> (Sanders 1983, 127 [emphasis added]).

But Sanders surely knows how slippery the term "the Jewish perspective" is, and in this case, aside from Philo's allegorists, I know of no other first-century Jews who would regard one who is only circumcised spiritually as a "true Jew." Indeed, I would suggest that Paul himself is here very close in spirit to Philo's allegorizers, and is therefore no less "Jewish" than they are. The difference between arguing that those who glory in Christ, as opposed to those who contemplate the One, are circumcised—or even that those who love their neighbors are circumcised—seems (from *my* Jewish perspective) trivial compared with the difference between all of those views and a view that insists that only those whose foreskins have been cut off are circumcised. In general, one of the few moments in Sanders's work with which I find myself in near total disagreement is his interpretation of Romans 2 (123–35). I hope that my interpretation obviates the need to state, "Romans 2 remains the instance in which Paul goes beyond inconsistency or variety of argument and explanation to true self-contradiction" (147). Similarly, in an otherwise very interesting and thoughtful work, Campbell makes what is to me one simply astonishing remark, namely, that "the fact that Paul concludes chapter 2 with a description of 'the true Jew' is further proof that he neither views Judaism from a sectarian stance, nor is his image of the Jew consistently negative" (Campbell 1992, 141). I trust that the reasons for my astonishment will be, by now, transparent.

13. Although translations of the text customarily add silently the adjectives

"true" or "real" before "Jew" and "circumcision" in the passage, these qualifiers are not there in the Greek. Paul is arguing that a Jew is defined by circumcision of the heart, and nothing else.

14. "If there is a negative ring to the words διὰ γράμματος καὶ περιτομῆς, it is due to the fact that it is only the possession of the *scrolls* of the law, and only *physical* circumcision, which the Jew in question can claim in his favor. We may compare Paul's words in v. 20: 'having the form (μόρφωσιν) of knowledge and truth in the law.' The choice of the word 'letter,' like that of 'form' in v. 20, does indeed stress that it is only the written scrolls, the external form, which the Jew in question possesses, while he lacks the righteous observance to which possession of the 'letter' obligates; but the fault lies in what he lacks, not in what he possesses" (Westerholm 1984, 234–35).

15. Alan Segal has clarified the issue thoroughly (1990, 192–201).

16. A not atypical early modern Rabbi, Rabbi Menahem Mendel of Kotzk would say: "Too many Jews are concerned about a blood-spot on an egg and not a blood-spot on a ruble." But every egg in the Rabbi's house was punctiliously examined for blood-spots!

17. "According to 2 Cor. 3:7–18, when God's Spirit-inscribed people encounter Scripture, a transformation occurs that is fundamentally hermeneutical in character" (Hays 1989, 131).

18. In my article (Boyarin 1990a) I have argued that the Rabbis of the talmudic period generally did not believe in a wholly non-corporeal Godhead, so God could be present in the world without an Incarnation. For a similar analogy (in a startlingly different context) between "incarnation" of divinity and a semiotics that requires going beyond the material, physical language, see Manganaro (1992, 43–44).

19. Wright translates this simply, "which glory was fading," and argues that it is not part of the argument of v. 7 but a foretaste of the argument to come in v. 11 (Wright 1992a, 178).

20. Hooker (1981, 298 and 308n. 7) notes commentators who have previously adopted this view but simply dismisses it (without argument) with "there are great difficulties with this interpretation." For Hooker's other objection—"He has told us that Israel could not gaze on Moses' glory: how, then, does it come about that Christians can now gaze on the overwhelming glory which belongs to Christ"—see below.

21. I think that Hays loses his way a bit on pp. 142–43, where he needlessly complicates the discussion by arguing that Paul is suggesting a dissimile between himself (and other Christians) and Moses, because "Moses' unveiled encounters with the Lord were intermittent, punctuated by times of withdrawal and veiling." I see nothing in the passage which qualifies or discredits Moses' experience even with respect to Paul; rather, the experience being deprecated is that of the Israelites to whom Moses turned and who would/could not see his glory. Further, there is no difficulty occasioned by the veil being moved from over Moses' face to the hearts of the Israelites (*pace* Hays, 145), because the veil always and only existed to prevent the Israelites from seeing that which they could not stand, and never to prevent *Moses* from seeing anything. I find, therefore, the turn in v. 16 less dramatic than Hays (147) does.

22. In Chapter 3 above, I have argued that the typology/allegory opposition is not a valid one—hence my somewhat slippery language here.

23. I note now the similarity of much of this reading with that of Wright (1992a, 180).

24. This does not preclude Wright's interesting suggestion that Paul is proposing that the Corinthians will see God's glory on each other's faces, just as the Israelites, I would add, would have seen God's glory on Moses' face had they had the strength. Wright's view is enhanced considerably by the good sense it makes of τὴν αὐτὴν εἰκόνα in v. 18.

25. I thus see much more virtue in Hooker's interpretation than does Wright (1992a, 181). She attends much more carefully than he does, in this instance, to the biblical text Paul is interpreting. Note the modification of Hooker's view implied by my account. She writes that Paul does not bother to prove his assumption that the glory faded, because he was not writing to Jews (300). In fact, what I am suggesting is that it is at least as possible that Jewish interpreters read this way also, without the typology, of course, and it was only in reaction to Paul's use of this interpretation that it was rejected in Jewish circles.

26. I dissent, therefore, from Hooker's reading also which contrasts Moses himself to the Christians (303). See above n. 21.

27. Although, as I will detail below, I do not agree with those scholars who hold that there was controversy within Judaism as to the necessity of circumcision for converts, I do think that the Judaizers, quasi-Jews, God-fearers, and even apparently the relatively large numbers of converts to Judaism in the Roman period blurred both the extension and intension of the signifiers "Jew" and "Israel." Symptomatic perhaps of this confusion is the following statement from Dio Cassius: "I do not know the origin of this name [Jews], but it is applied to all men, even foreigners, who follow their customs. This race is found among Romans" (qu. in Gager 1983, 91). What I find remarkable about this passage is its self-contradiction: Anyone who follows the customs of the Jews is termed a Jew, but the Jews are nevertheless designated a race. Unless "race" means something very different from what we take it to mean—and, of course, I am aware that it did not refer to genotype, but presumably it had some genealogical connotation—these two sentences are in tension with each other and thus themselves a sign of contestation. This will be further discussed in the final chapter.

CHAPTER 5

1. For a somewhat different account of the interrelationships of these elements, see Smith (1990, 141).

2. For a very judicious discussion of the question of whether Paul responds to these documents or they are later polemics against Paul, see Davies (1965, 50–51). See also Gager (1983, 125).

3. Luke 1:32 is of significance here, for it simultaneously describes Jesus as the son of God and David as the father of Jesus. The formula is thus the same. Luke simply does not feel the need to supply the hermeneutic gloss, according to the flesh, with regard to Jesus' human genealogy.

4. This last argument was pointed out to me by Ruth Clements.

5. If the Peter/Paul opposition as I describe it seems to prefigure the later controversies between orthodox and gnostic Christians, that is no accident, as I read Paul as a moderate "gnostic," somewhere between the monadic corporeality of the Jerusalem church and the extreme spirituality of the later true Gnostics. Cf. Wedderburn: "[Views of Jesus's resurrection] of Christians seem to range through a whole spectrum from the accounts of the crucified body being restored to life, wounds and all (cf. Lk. 24.37–42); Jn 20.25,27), *through Paul's account in 1 Cor 15 which seems to suggest that the resurrection appearances were of the same kind as his own conversion experience*" (1987, 192–93 [emphasis added]). And again there: "Epiphanius mocks the Valentinians as denying the resurrection of the dead, 'saying something mysterious and ridiculous, that it is not this body which rises, but another rises from it, which they call spiritual,' ('Mysterious and ridiculous' perhaps, but still very Pauline)" (215 and see also 216–18). Moreover, this controversy between Peter/James and Paul had political implications similar to those of the later schism as well. See Pagels (1978, 415–30).

6. See, however, αἷμα καὶ σάρκας contrasted with gods in Polyaen. Strat., III, 11, 1 cited in *TDNT* VII, 99.

7. See next section for further discussion of this point.

8. I absolutely agree with Betz (71) that Paul's ἐν ἐμοί here has to be understood as referring to a vision and will further support it later. The question of "internal" or "external" is irrelevant in my opinion. In either case, Paul is referring to a vision with the "eyes of the mind." See further discussion below.

9. Elizabeth Castelli has asked what is at stake in this claim for me, since I make it so emphatically. The answer is that I wish to disrupt what I believe to be a false antithesis between theological and sociological understandings of Paul. While my reading of Paul is one that interprets his work as responsive to particular situations in the churches to which he is writing, and therefore within the modern sociological tradition of Pauline scholarship, at the same time I find it generated by a consistent theological mainspring as well. In this, again, I think that my method of reading Paul, as well as my particular constructions, are perhaps closest to those of F. C. Baur.

10. It is important, however, to note that from a rabbinic Jewish perspective, this very stance puts Paul into direct conflict with Judaism. It is not "tolerance" of Judaism to say that *for Jews* it is a matter of indifference whether or not they are circumcised. This is a dismissal of Pharisaic/biblical Judaism entirely.

11. The perspective here is substantially the same as that of Sanders (1983, 177).

12. I find it impossible to follow the argument of Watson, who writes that "Paul claims in Gal. 2:14 that in eating with Gentiles, Peter has been living 'like a Gentile' (ἐθνικῶς), and if taken literally this would mean that Peter and the Jewish Christians of Antioch had abandoned the observance of the law and their Jewish identity. But it is hard to imagine the apostle to the circumcised doing this, and it is perhaps more likely that Paul has exaggerated the extent of Peter's departure from the law. . . . The example given—eating with Gentiles—perhaps suggests a relaxed attitude toward the law on the part of the Antiochene Jewish Christians, rather than a complete renunciation of the law" (Watson 1986, 33). Watson goes on to write, however: "It is therefore probable that at Antioch too, Gentile

Christians were exempted from the Jewish food-laws," a claim that certainly contradicts the first one. If Peter had been eating with those gentile Christians, then certainly it means that he was eating the same food as they, and if they were exempted from the Jewish food laws, then he also was eating non-kosher food, which constitutes in itself a renunciation of the Law. See also Sanders (1990, 170–89), who has completely discredited the view that James would have encouraged Peter to stop eating with gentiles because of a putative gentile impurity. As Sanders has shown, even the existence of such a category of impurity was very much contested—and apparently the Shammaites, to whom Paul is often assigned, were against the notion—while in any case, the fact of impurity would not prevent one from eating with a person, certainly not in Diaspora, where all are impure (172–76). Moreover, as Sanders demonstrates beyond a shadow of a doubt, only certain very extreme texts proscribe table fellowship with gentiles if the food is kosher (on this point, see also Segal: "There is no law in rabbinic Judaism that prevents a Jew from eating with a gentile" [1990, 231] and Fredriksen: "The discussions preserved in the Mishnah that detail the correct procedure on such occasions [of Jews and gentiles eating together] attest to the frequency with which they occurred" [1988, 151]). Of the alternatives which Sanders suggests for what Peter was transgressing in James's eyes, I find most attractive the notion that he was eating non-kosher food of some sort (185–86). Sanders's reason for assuming that the most plausible interpretation is that James did not want them to eat with gentiles, "because close association might lead to contact with idolatry or transgression of one of the biblical food laws," seems to me less likely, precisely because the gentiles that Peter was eating with were Christians, and either their food was kosher or it was not. Presumably, it was not. Furthermore, it would hardly behoove James to choose the most extreme and marginal version of Jewish practice (precisely on Sanders's account). This is even more the case on the second of Sanders's choices, namely, that "some people had a *general* reluctance to eat *any* Gentile food." This does not mean that Peter had necessarily eaten pork or shellfish of which Sanders is probably right in assuming that hardly any Jew would eat, but could easily refer to meat not slaughtered properly and the like. Any of these would count as "living like gentiles."

13. As I argue below, this point provides key evidence, also, as to the identity of the "opponents" in Galatia. Sanders has put this in a somewhat more positive light: "It was probably Peter's responsibility to the circumcised, which might be hindered if he himself were not Torah-observant, not disagreement with Paul's mission as such, which led him to withdraw from the Gentiles in Antioch" (Sanders 1983, 19, and see there 177).

14. Compare the reading of Gager (1983, 33–35).

15. In spite of our generally different interpretations of Galatians as a whole, I quite agree with Cosgrove (1988, 133–39) on the interpretation of this passage.

16. The difference between Hays's view and mine is that he understands Paul's interlocutors here to be Jews who have adopted the doctrine of justification by faith but not abandoned the Law, whereas I see Paul as arguing against Jews who, having adopted the doctrine, initially drew the conclusion that the Law was no longer obligatory or important but then went back to Law observance for communal reasons to which Paul objects. I think that this interpretation renders his

argument here and later more coherent and strong. I certainly agree with Hays when he says, "In both of these letters [Galatians and Romans], Paul treats the doctrine of justification by faith as an agreed-upon premise *from* which he can construct his position about the relations between Jews and Gentiles and the role of the Law in the life of the Christian community."

17. For the position that Paul is referring to Peter's actions here, see Cosgrove (1988, 138), who interprets exactly as I do, and Barclay (1991, 80 and n. 13).

18. My view is very close to that of Gaventa 1986.

19. For this interpretation, see below n. 20.

20. Jewett (1970, 204–06) interprets in a similar fashion, adducing, moreover, a highly convincing historical background to this group. There are certain differences, however, between our interpretations, and while I think that there are some considerations which favor Jewett's, others favor my version. Jewett argues that the agitators truly believed in circumcision as a necessity for salvation, and that when Paul says they do not keep the Law, he means the Law as he (Paul) understands it (201). This accounts better than my interpretation for the statement that the agitators are promoting another gospel. On the other hand, it seems to me clear from these verses that Paul is claiming that were it not for their fear of persecution, the agitators would not be pressing the Galatians to convert at all. This tension in his account is exemplified in the following sentence: "The nomistic Christians in Judea would have ample reason to boast if they could induce the Gentile churches to enter the ranks of the circumcised, for such an achievement would release them from a mortal threat levelled against all who dared to associate themselves with the ungodly and the uncircumcised" (206). (Presumably, Jewett would argue that this only means that they would have no interest in converting gentiles at all nor *care what they do,* a proposition I for one find less than convincing.) Once it be admitted that the agitators wish to circumcise the Galatians to avoid persecution and not because they believe in the necessity of the gentiles being circumcised for salvation, then it seems best to consider them the anti-type of Peter as presented in the Antiochene parable—that is, essentially on Paul's side *against James and the even more extreme Palestinian nomistic Christians* but afraid of persecution. Finally, I am not persuaded by Jewett's quite brilliant argumentation that the Galatians were libertines. The entire rhetoric of the letter suggests the opposite, that they were strongly drawn to nomism, and as I have suggested elsewhere, that the last part of the letter has to do with a danger that Paul perceives of misunderstanding of his call to Christian freedom. Jewett reads too much, in my opinion, into the phrase "being completed in the flesh" and into the use of "days" for Sabbaths and holidays. The latter is actually quite attested in rabbinic Hebrew parlance.

21. An attractive alternative explanation for this passage is that offered by Segal:

> If you receive circumcision, you are bound to follow the entire law because
> you have *converted* to Judaism. Paul says that what is necessary is that all
> be transformed by the spirit, which is in modern parlance a different kind of
> conversion. It follows that if you are not circumcised you do not have to
> keep the whole law. But it does not follow that you do not have to keep

parts of it; we have seen that many Jews and Christians assumed that part of the law was encumbent upon non-Jews who wish to live with Jews. He even tells us that the Christians who are making this deal are not as pious as Pharisees. And as an ex-Pharisee he has nothing but contempt for that position. . . . So his argument appears to us to be very subtle, but it may have been exceedingly clear to those living in the social situation he addresses. He says that *if you want to be Jewish* you have to go way beyond what the circumcisers are doing. You need to become a Pharisee, as Paul himself was a Pharisee. Evidently, he sees their ordinary Judaism as a kind of watered-down Judaism. They keep some of the laws but not others. And they do not practice the pieties of the Pharisees. This is a kind of hypocrisy.

> (Alan F. Segal, "Universalism in Judaism and
> Christianity," unpublished paper, 1992)

I have the following difficulties with this elegant reading. First of all, what evidence is there that a sort of partial observance of the Law was characteristic of an alleged "ordinary Judaism"? Second, what evidence is there that when Paul says the "whole law," he is referring to the "pieties of the Pharisees" and not to those observances which were the province of all groups of first-century Jews, at least in Palestine? Third, I find that this interpretation is less responsive to the context of the letter to the Galatians than mine in that it does not account for the analogy between the situation of the circumcisers and that of Peter in the Antioch encounter and thus makes the appearance of the narration of that incident less compellingly relevant. On at least some hermeneutic principles, that alone would lead to preference for the explanation offered in the text.

22. I do not think therefore that "justification" has so much to do with "getting in" or "staying in" (*pace* Sanders) as in being saved at the end. It is conceivable that according to some versions of Christianity (and indeed, some versions of Judaism—not rabbinic), being in is sufficient for being saved, but they are still logically distinct categories. Cf. Wright (1992a, 2 and esp. 148), who conflates the two concepts. As its Hebrew contexts show, "justified" simply means, "declared just," which may or may not be a function of membership in the covenantal community. Although I find much exciting and necessary in Wright's work (which reached me just as I was completing this manuscript), his understanding of justification seems to me to seriously weaken his overall claim that Paul is not dealing with soteriology. Somehow the two elements of covenantal theology and individual salvation will have to be integrated in future work. I, moreover, think that "justified" works perfectly well as a translation of the Greek (and Hebrew). See below in this chapter for an actual Hebrew source for this usage in Paul.

23. But Sanders also quotes approvingly Heikki Räisänen's comment: "The Jews' establishment of their own righteousness . . . is . . . identical with their rejection of Christ," and "the root of the evil lies in a christological failure, not in an anthropological one" (Räisänen 1980, 71). Sanders has seemingly abandoned his correct (in my opinion) insight that "their own righteousness" means the righteousness which devolves on them simply by virtue of being Jewish, and thus contains a trenchant critique of Judaism—not, I agree, on the basis of the false

merit-grace distinction—and has, therefore, nothing to do with their "rejection of Christ." It is precisely an "anthropological" (read ethical) failure, but not one of works-righteousness! See also Sanders: "It is the Gentile question and the exclusivism of Paul's soteriology which dethrone the law" (1977, 496–97). Once we have admitted the first (the gentile question), however, we have no need of the second (Paul's exclusivism), *and I would argue that the latter is, therefore, an epiphenomenon of the first factor.*

I think, moreover, that the interpretation of Paul offered here goes a long way toward answering the objections and contradictions that have led Räisänen to his extreme position on Paul's alleged "incoherence." To take one example: Vis-à-vis Romans 2, Räisänen has argued that it is inconsistent to claim on the one hand that all have sinned and, on the other, that there are gentiles who have kept the Law. This is, however, no contradiction at all once we realize that it is not individuals of whom Paul speaks but groups. All have sinned, Jews and gentiles alike, but individual Jews as well as gentiles have kept the Law. Therefore, all—Jews and gentiles as groups—are equal in the sight of God! Incoherence (as well as coherence) is an artifact of hermeneutics (*pace* Räisänen 1986, 103 ff.).

24. Below I will argue that rabbinic Judaism, which we know, of course, only from post-Pauline writings, elaborated a different response to this ethico-spiritual challenge.

25. See also Segal (1990, 277 and 281). Campbell, citing Davies, seems also to have gotten this just right:

> Although Paul exploits Hellenistic forms and literary genres, he takes seriously the scriptures of his people and seeks to deal with the problem in their terms—employing rabbinical and other methods to do justice both to this new emergence, the Christian community, and its matrix, the Jewish people.
>
> (Campbell 1992, 56)

26. First, I am not persuaded of the necessity for the interpretation that Paul substitutes "all flesh" for "all that lives" as an interpretative gloss and then derives from that the principle that works do not justify, since works are of the flesh. (To be sure, it is not *impossible* that such a midrash lies behind Paul's interpretation here. Dunn has made as good a case for it as can be made, here and also in Dunn [1988, 155].) I find it most plausible that in Paul's Bible the text had πασα σάρξ and not the πας ζῶν of the Septuagint. This position is certainly supported by the fact that Paul's version of the text is cited in 1 Enoch 81.5 as well (Charles 1913, 169). I read Paul's argument, therefore, as both deeper and more straightforward than this.

27. Indeed, it is not to be excluded that "faith of Jesus Christ πίστις 'Ιησοῦ Χριστοῦ" here means Jesus Christ's faithfulness, and then Paul is not even making this exegetical extravagance. This would bring the interpretation in line with the use of the same psalm in Romans 3, for which see Hays 1980. Against this interpretation, however, is the fact that Paul here does seem to be strongly asserting the necessity of human faith *in* Jesus Christ: Even we have had faith in Christ Jesus, in order to be justified by the faith of Christ καὶ ἡμεῖς εἰς Χριστὸν 'Ιησοῦν ἐπιστεύσαμεν, ἵνα δικαιωθῶμεν ἐκ πίστεως Χριστοῦ. I do not dis-

pute, therefore, the notion that there is a faithfulness of Jesus Christ of which Paul speaks; rather I wish to disclaim a view that would hold that it follows from this that the faith of humans in Jesus is not, for him, significant.

One could easily interpret that the human faith in Christ is answered by his faithfulness, a perfectly rabbinic notion of measure for measure מידה כנגד מידה, one of the most frequently attested of all theologoumena in rabbinic thought. Westerholm has adduced several other passages (curiously, not this one) in which it is quite clear that the faith in question is human faith in Christ and not Christ's faithfulness toward humans (1988, 111–12). It may be that in all of these places the same movement of מידה כנגד מידה is present. Indeed, even Romans 3:22 can be taken to show this very movement from the faith of the human to the answer of God's faithfulness: The righteousness of God through the faith of Jesus Christ for all who believe δικαιοσύνη δὲ θεοῦ διὰ πίστεως Ἰησοῦ Χριστοῦ εἰς πάν-τας τοὺς πιστεύοντας. (See the discussion of the analogous Galatians 3:22 by Richard B. Hays [1987].) Although in the earlier work, Hays did not pay attention to this double or dialogical movement of faithfulness, in his later work he does (1989, 40–41). The doctrine of justification by faith remains intact—although, to be sure, not in its Reformation form of *sola gratia*. See also Watson (1986, 199 n. 89) and especially Barclay (1991, 78 n. 8).

28. I accordingly think that Thielman (1989, 64–65), who sees here a Pauline argument that no one can keep the Law, has quite missed the point. Also, this interpretation completely obviates Segal's claim that justification has to do with conversion in first-century Judaism or that "Paul could have learned the language of justification from his Christian compatriots after he entered the Christian community" (1990, 177).

29. See Dunn (1990, 207), where he replies to Räisänen on this precise point but fails to use this (to my mind) decisive argument.

30. Westerholm has also made the point that the inability of humans to be justified by works, because they could not or would never fulfill the Law adequately, was a traditional prophetic claim (1988, 163–64). In a sense, his argument about Paul is similar in structure to mine, although very different in conclusion. Taking this traditional theological motif as primary, he argues that Paul went beyond the Prophets in discovering a radical solution. I hardly think that the fact that inability to keep the Law was not an invention of Paul should be relegated to a "postscript" (*pace* Westerholm 1988, 163); it is crucial to realize that, this "plight" having become a common theme of Jewish writing, Paul alone—or nearly alone—arrived at the conclusion that faith was now a fully adequate surrogate for keeping the commandments.

One point that must be made clear, however, is that my reading of Paul as motivated by the question of the inclusion of the gentiles is most emphatically not a sociological one that locates his writing in the practical problems of the first-century church (*pace* Wrede, as cited by Westerholm 1988, 167), but one that is as theologically based as Westerholm's account of a Paul motivated by the failure of the Law to provide an antidote to the poison of sin. Where Westerholm writes that the "fundamental principle" affirmed by "Paul's thesis of justification by faith, not works of the law, is that of humanity's dependence on divine grace; and that conviction, it may safely be said, underlies everything Paul wrote," I would substitute for the fundamental principle the conviction that all humanity is one in the eyes of God and must be saved in the same way, a conviction that, it may safely be said, underlies everything that Paul wrote. The alternative, then, between Paul the profound theological thinker and Paul the practical church politician is, in my view, a false one. I find Westerholm's interpretation compelling, as I do, of course, find my own as well. The question remains whether they are incompatible. Perhaps the ultimate solution will be an understanding of Paul that sees him as operating on both levels at once.

31. In Romans 3:22, which I have discussed briefly in note 27 above, this motive is explicit also, for immediately after asserting that God's righteousness comes to all who believe through the faithfulness of Jesus Christ, Paul asserts: For there is no distinction οὐ γάρ ἐστιν διαστολή, a declaration that prepares the way for the end of the chapter, in which he insists that there can be no discrimination in the way that God justifies Jews and gentiles, because he is the God of the whole world, and therefore the circumcised and the uncircumcised are all justified on account of their faith.

32. Dunn misses this point again when he writes that the "phrase ἐν σαρκί used in the same passage (Rom. 2.28) denotes not merely the physical as opposed to the spiritual, but also the people of Israel in terms of physical identity and racial kinship" (1990, 222). In my view, these are not two separate meanings at all, but two sides of the same coin. The physical is the people of Israel in terms of physical identity and racial kinship, and the spiritual is the allegorical interpretation of that identity and kinship in the Body of Christ.

33. "Thus, when Paul writes in Rom. 3:21 that 'now, apart from Law the righteousness of God has been manifested, witnessed by the Law and the Prophets,' he is making a claim that anyone who had ever prayed Psalm 143 from the heart would instantly recognize: God's saving righteousness, for which the psalmist had hoped, has at last appeared. The witness of the Law and the Prophets to the righteousness of God is not merely, as Christians have sometimes strangely supposed, a witness concerning a severe retributive justice; rather, it is a witness concerning God's gracious saving power, as Psalm 143 demonstrates" (Hays 1989, 52).

34. Menahem Lorberbaum has made an interesting alternative suggestion, namely, that what Paul is saying here is that his former life under the Law was equivalent to a crucifixion which prepared him for the resurrection with Christ.

35. In this sense Alan Segal's characterization of Paul's experience as "conversion" is certainly justified.

36. Bultmann himself, after setting out the parallels, claims to discredit them. While I do not think that Paul was influenced by so-called Mystery Religions, particularly because they are unattested so early, I do think that there are very strong parallels here. Paul could very well have been the source of the influence, or common religious developments could have produced both. The parallels are nevertheless illuminating, despite Bultmann's disclaimers (1967, 23–30). Thus, Bultmann's claim that "of course Paul experienced ecstasy, but for him it is a special charism and not the specifically Christian mode of life (cf. 1 Cor. 12–14)" (24) ignores in my view the very next verses of Galatians, which I am about to

discuss. What, after all, is the outpouring of the Spirit to which Paul refers, if not ecstasy?

37. Later in Romans 6 Paul will interpret this dying and resurrection of the individual Christian as taking place in baptism, which is certainly (already in older Judaisms, as well as in later) a ritual of death and rebirth.

38. See my discussions below in Chapters 7 and 8.

39. Cp. Gaston and Gager (1983, 234) on this verse. Gager himself seems somewhat skeptical.

40. Cp. again the passage quoted above: Now, my child, you see me with your eyes, but what I am you cannot understand when you look at me with your body's eyes and with the physical sight. It is not with those eyes that anyone can see me now, my child (Bultmann 1967, 19).

41. This is how Murray Krieger describes this figure as used by Phillip Sidney with reference to Psalm 114: "Enargeia, the verbal art of forcing us to see vividly. Through the 'eyes of the mind'—an appropriately Platonic notion—we are shown the coming of God and his 'unspeakable and everlasting beauty.' Here, then, are words invoking a visible presence, though, of course, to 'the eyes of the mind' alone. Though God's may be only a figurative entrance through His personified creatures, the poet makes us, 'as it were,' see this entrance. He is there, in His living creation, and absent no longer" (Krieger 1979, 601).

42. This important point was suggested to me by my student, Cecilia Maho- ney, who thus independently arrived at one of the important insights of Cosgrove's book (1988), namely, that Paul and the Galatians shared a charismatic experi- ence. I accordingly disagree with Betz (133) who writes: "Paul does not reflect upon the difference between himself and the Galatians; his conversion was the result of a vision of Christ and not, as it is for them, of the hearing of the Christian message." I would argue that Paul is explicitly connecting the two experiences via the eyes of the mind. Cosgrove and I, however, reach very different interpretations of Galatians starting from our independently arrived at common assumption that the Galatians have had important pneumatic experiences similar to those of Paul and occasioned by his preaching. For these differences, see below passim.

43. Note that this simply obviates the distinction between πίστις Χριστοῦ as faith in Jesus or Jesus' faith, as both are necessary moments in the same motion. See above, n. 27. I reject as well the opposition between "imitating Abraham's faith" and "participating in Christ, who is Abraham's seed," which Boers sets up, as cited in Dunn (1990, 202).

44. I entirely agree with Cosgrove that there is no reason to assume that the Galatians "must be turning to the law without thought for the Spirit." Paul's ar- gument would lose its entire force were that the case. They believe that Law is compatible with spirit, and Paul is proving to them that it is not, because the Law is of the flesh, while the Spirit (Holy) is of the spirit.

45. I therefore disagree with Cosgrove, who claims that circumcision is not mentioned in Galatians 3–4 (51).

46. There is one part of Cosgrove's argument that, if I have understood it, seems to me singularly weak. His interpretation of 2 Corinthians 3:6 requires that we assume that the Super Apostles in Corinth hold that keeping the Law is a

precondition for the continued experience of the spirit (111–12). In other words, they hold that Law and spirit are not ontologically on the same level. But Paul opposes law and spirit as terms which are ontologically (although not axiologically) equal. His assumptions, then, would be so incompatible with those of his opponents that they could hardly even understand each other. In other words, were Cosgrove's reading correct, it seems to me that Paul should have said something like: "The letter kills but faith gives the Spirit," since on his reconstruction the desirability of the spirit is equal to both groups and the issue is whether Law or faith brings the spirit. On my understanding, the verse makes better sense, because the question is indeed whether the letter or the spirit is the desirable means to life. I do not dismiss, however, the possibility that life itself means life in the Spirit, in which Spirit has already a somewhat different sense from "spirit" opposed to letter.

47. Understanding the participle οἱ περιτεμνόμενοι of 6:13 in the sense of "those who advocate circumcision" (Jewett 1970, 202–03).

48. For much more evidence to this effect, as well as an interpretation and consideration of the gender issues involved, see D. Boyarin 1992b. I think that these data are much more to the point than general claims to the effect that Torah observance is necessary for the Holy Spirit, pace Barclay (1991, 84). Note that Balaam, who was not Jewish and not a Law observer, was vouchsafed the Holy Spirit. According to rabbinic tradition, he was born circumcised!

49. Here, of course, only "his" is possible. Circumcision is accordingly a very problematic moment in the constitution of gens and gender from my feminist point of view. All I can do, however, it seems to me at present, is record that problematic. My next book is intended to be a cultural poetics of rabbinic Jewish manhood, centering around circumcision as a psychic structure.

50. Justin Martyr provides an excellent example of a late-antique platonic version of seeing God with the mind's eye (Justin Martyr 1989, 196).

51. Much of the following section is dependent on the material he has gathered in Wolfson 1987a and b.

52. For an almost identical use of Job, see D. Boyarin (1990b, 86).

53. Howard Eilberg-Schwartz's God's Phallus (1994) is a brilliant phenomenology of Judaism along these lines.

54. As Wolfson so persuasively demonstrates, however, the dominant kabbalistic trend was to understand the mystic as male and the Divine element he encountered as female, The Shekhina, or even the Torah represented as female. Then, the circumcision was necessary for penetration of this female, just as it is required for human sexual intercourse (1987b, 210–11). For the Rabbis (of the premedieval period), such a divine female as a solution to the paradox of mystical gender was excluded, and only feminization of the male mystic was possible.

55. For a much fuller account of the rabbinic interpretations and views, see D. Boyarin 1992b.

56. The distinction between ἐν σαρκί as referring to circumcision or to the works of the Law in general is a false one in my view, pace Barclay (1991, 86). The immediate issue is circumcision, according to my hypothesis, the fleshy observance par excellence, but circumcision itself is a synecdoche for all of the works of the Law.

57. This is a modification of a point made by Barclay (1991, 224, and see there, 228).

58. For this term, see Ortner 1973.

59. Sanders simply refuses to apply to Paul the very logical consideration that he utilizes in regard to Philo's allegorizers: "They did not observe the literal law, but they observed its 'real' intent" (118n. 32). Thus even when he decides that a moment in Paul (Romans 2:29) is similar to Philo's allegorizers (131), *he does so only to deny the genuine Pauline character of the passage.* The question in my mind is what is at stake in denying this hermeneutical dimension in Paul? Why do nearly all modern interpreters wish to exclude it?

60. See Chapter 8 below. Also, in Chapter 6 I will argue that the specific usage that Paul made of a verse of Leviticus in Galatians 3:13 could easily have "misled" those who heard his preaching into thinking that incest was permitted to Christians. I think it is this "misreading" of his intentions that Paul is trying to guard against. I am not "siding" with Paul here, but I do assume that the Corinthian crisis can be explained, without assuming outside agitators in Corinth, simply as an interpretation of Paul's preaching of freedom in the spirit as in most of Galatians, an interpretation which he, already here, is at pains to denote as a misinterpretation. It must be remembered that Marcion (the "heretic" who rejected the "Old Testament" entirely) built his edifice on Galatians, and it is not entirely surprising that he could do so. Once more, it seems that unknowingly I have reproduced a position very similar to that of F. C. Baur (1873–75, 1, 263).

61. I thus decline the very opposition between these two possibilities suggested by Barclay when he writes, "This genitive should not be taken in the sense of a law promulgated by Christ but in the looser sense of the law *redefined through Christ*" (134). My interpretation here is thus virtually the same as—but subtly differentiated from—his (132–34). Or rather, I should say that the hermeneutic perspective I have been defending lends considerable weight, in my opinion, to the interpretation that Barclay proposes. Note how this interpretation subtly shifts (while substantially accepting) the view of Hays (1987, 275) that the Law of Christ "is a formulation coined (or employed) by Paul to refer to this paradigmatic self-giving of Jesus Christ."

62. This interpretation also has the virtue of making sense of the talk of spirit in the continuing verses, which are now understood as carrying both senses, that of the human spirit as opposed to the human flesh which sins, as well as the spirit of the Law (love) as opposed to its flesh (circumcision). See also Barclay (1991, 115), who has provided what seems to me by far the best account of the end of v. 17. See also my discussion in Chapter 6 of Romans 13:8.

CHAPTER 6

1. Aside from Galatians 3:10, which I treat here, other verses that allegedly attest to a position that one who does not successfully keep the whole Law cannot be saved are 5:3 and 6:13 of the same letter. Citing the former simply manifests a confusion between two entirely separate concepts: (1) the requirement to keep the whole Law, and (2) success in fulfilling that requirement as a necessary con-

dition for salvation. All Paul is saying is that if one converts to Judaism by being circumcised, then one is obligated to keep the whole Torah, which is certainly true in any form of rabbinic Judaism. He is not saying that a good-faith failure to meet this obligation is damning. As for 6:13, following the interpretation that I will give to this verse below, it is entirely irrelevant to this question. As far as I know, there was no strain of Judaism, whether Qumranian, Hellenistic, rabbinic, or "Shammaite," which held that failure to completely meet the requirements of the Law was damning. Sanders has made the interesting suggestion that "God's strange work" (the Lutheran term for God having given the Torah in order to increase sin) was indeed a genuine Pauline notion in his struggle to make some sense of the existence of the Law, but one that he later abandoned because of its palpable theological inadequacy (1983, 144–45). In a sense, I would agree with Sanders that Paul proposes various solutions to the problem of the Law. I would, however, cast this point quite differently, arguing that for Paul the replacement of the literal, physical κατὰ σάρκα Law by the spiritual, allegorical κατὰ πνεῦμα interpretation was one of his central and immutable ideas. The question becomes displaced then from the problem of "the Law" *per se* to the problem of the *literal* Law.

2. I am in a tradition here of Jewish interpreters of Paul who read these passages as midrashim and interpret them by referring to standard midrashic methodologies, though the details of my interpretation are different from either of the predecessors of whom I am aware, namely, Klein 1918 and Schoeps 1961. It is in this dual sense that this section is entitled "Reading Paul as a Jew," that is, in a tradition of Jewish scholars who have read Paul as integrally connected with Jewish tradition. Note that Davies wrote, regarding Betz: "The neglect of the Jewish connections of the Galatians perhaps accounts for certain aspects of H. D. B.'s interpretation" (Davies 1984, 178). I would, however, suggest that these Jewish connections do not necessarily prove anything about the Galatians themselves, as they could have been primarily intended to be "overheard" by the opponents, who certainly were Jewish Christians. Sanders also writes of this passage, "We see, rather, Paul's skill in Jewish exegetical argument" (Sanders 1983, 26).

I haven't a clue from where Robert G. Hamerton-Kelly draws his notion that in the text that I discuss in this and the following sections, "Paul interprets the death of Christ against the background of a midrash on Numbers 25:1–13, in which Abraham and Phineas are linked by means of Psalm 106" (Hamerton-Kelly 1992, 74). Only his inexorable determination to make Paul's discourse support his slander of Judaism explains this bizarre and unsupported interpretation.

3. For a distinction between Paul's hermeneutic stance, which is not midrash, and his exegetical techniques which often are, see Chapter 5 above.

4. Romans 5:20 would seem to be a counter-argument and often is cited as support for the notion that Paul's theology of the Law was that it was given in order to increase the amount of sin in the world. Dunn, himself, however has provided the answer to this objection by glossing that verse as "God's purpose for the law was not to distinguish Jewish righteous from gentile sinners, but to make Israel more conscious of its solidarity in sin with the rest of Adam's offspring" (Dunn 1988, 286). "Increasing transgression" means, then, increasing awareness of transgression. Another possibility is that Paul is arguing that the Law increases

transgression as an unwanted side effect of its existence. Romans 7 would tend to support such a reading. In this case also, the point of Romans 5:20, as befits its context in Romans, is to convince Jews that they are not privileged vis-à-vis gentiles in soteriology. Not only will the Law not help them get saved; it may hinder them. The Rabbis held very similar notions, also believing that it was *easier* for gentiles to be saved than for Jews.

5. Sanders's dismissal of Schlier's view (1983, 54 n. 26) seems to me totally ungrounded.

6. "Schlier's own solution is to argue from vv. 11–12 that the curse attaches to ποιεῖν itself as it is determined by the law. But this is simply to ignore the fact that Deut 27:6 applies the curse not to those who *do* the law but to those who *do not*" (Cosgrove 1988, 53). The interpretation of the midrash that I offer here answers this objection to Schlier's interpretation, which is the only one that I believe makes theological sense.

7. Richard Hays refers to this passage and remarks that "one could hardly invent a more whimsical inversion" (1989, 4 and cf. 194 n. 9). If I am right, however, in my comparison with Paul, I think that we do not have whimsy here but time-honored hermeneutical principles of midrash, which have to do with a theological understanding of the nature of God's words (not Word).

8. See also my discussion of H. Schlier's interpretation of Galatians 3:10. Note the difference between this view and that of Dunn, who draws the distinction as between "works of Law" and "doing the Law," while mine puts works and doing on the same side over-against fulfilling (Dunn 1990, 202).

9. My interpretation is thus in fine quite different from that of Barclay (1991, 139–40).

10. That is, I am suggesting that although it is not the same word, still by carrying a semantic component of completeness and by not including a semantic component of "mere" performance, it was available for Paul's purpose of drawing a distinction between "doing" and "fulfilling," once the former term, at the end of the verse, is understood as in contrast with the latter.

11. I thoroughly disagree with Schoeps's rendition of this as a midrash based on the hermeneutic resolution of a contradiction, the "thirteenth canon of Rabbi Ishmael" (Schoeps 1961, 177–78), but *not* on the grounds that it could not have existed before the second century (apud Betz 1979, 138, who himself regards this hermeneutic principle to be as old as the Septuagint in another place, 158 n. 49, unless I have misunderstood him). Schoeps has both misconstrued the rabbinic canon (cf. Dahl 1977, 159–77) and also reads in here that which is not here. Schoeps's basic instinct was, however, sound. This is a near perfect example of rabbinic style building up an argument from several verses and, in fact, constitutes the best pendant I know for the antiquity of such style. The Rabbis well recognized that their own methods of hermeneutic could be used to achieve "false" results. See also below.

12. My reading here is completely different from that of Hays (1983), who reads the subject of this verse, "the righteous," as referring to the Messiah.

13. See above Chapter 5 n. 27 discussion of the controversy over the meaning of "faith of Jesus Christ," i.e., whether it is faith in Jesus or the faithfulness of Jesus which is being invoked.

14. This interpretation is similar to that of Sanders (1983, 22).

15. See the convenient summary of earlier interpretations in Sanders (1983, 54n. 30).

16. For a discussion of how Romans 2:13—justification for the doers—fits in here, see above, Chapter 4.

17. Here I must say that I find Dunn's interpretation of the "curse" as the curse of misunderstanding of the Law too narrowly focused for my taste (Dunn 1990, 229). I do think that Paul's christology involves an ontological change in the status of the Law. It is the Law which is called by him pedagogue—not Christ!

18. Ideas of a virgin birth for Isaac were not unprecedented in pre-Christian Judaism. See, for instance, Philo, On the Cherubim, 40–52.

19. In Aramaic זרעית, from the root meaning "seed," is the regular word for family.

20. He simply asserts, without arguing the point, that this is the correct interpretation and that older commentators got it wrong. Presumably, he is relying on arguments in other commentaries.

21. Barclay's argument against Lull that "whether you viewed the restraining influence of the παιδαγωγός as good or bad depended on whether you were the parent employing him or the child under his care!" (1991, 107n. 2) seems to me an uncharacteristically (for Barclay) weak reed. The issue is not how the child in her immaturity would perceive the role of the pedagogue but how an observer from outside would perceive this role, and in this, I think, Lull is entirely correct in assuming that the role would be seen as positive and necessary. Therefore, τῶν παραβάσεων χάριν must mean "to deal with transgressions"—either to prevent or punish them—and not "to generate transgressions." Sanders has made substantially the same point (1983, 66). On the other hand, Sanders continues generally to accept the standard Reformation claim that Paul argues here that "God gave the law, but he gave it in order that it would condemn all and thus prepare negatively for redemption on the basis of faith (3:22, 24, the purpose clauses conveying God's intention)" (68). For my alternative interpretation of these verses, see immediately below.

22. See also next section. Nevertheless, I am entirely unconvinced by Thielman's notion that the only thing that has changed in the eschatological age is that now people have the ability to keep the Law, whereas before they were cursed with inability to do so. His offhand qualification in a footnote (76n. 102) that "all but those portions that distinguish Jews from Gentiles continue to have validity in the age of the Spirit" (emphasis added), rather vitiates his argument, because it begs the question of by what mechanism these have been invalidated while the rest continue as valid! Moreover, the parallels which Thielman offers in these pages from contemporary Jewish literature do not support his argument either. It is obvious that for most Judaisms (including rabbinic Judaism) sin is defined as breaking the Law, and it is also obvious that having the Law makes one more culpable for sin. This does not in any sense constitute a parallel to the alleged Pauline notion of the Law as having been given because of sin and to confine all under sin, however we understand these difficult and contested phrases. For all of the Judaisms that I know of, the Law is the way that God wants Jews (or all humans) to behave, and it is sinful to disregard his will. One who knows the Law is more culpable than one

who does not, for the obvious reason that his or her defiance is willful and not ignorant. This is not what Paul says, on any account, because Paul is at pains (contra Thielman) to argue that the Law as it was understood by Jews, that is, in its outer aspect of physical, ethnically marked observances, is no longer valid after the coming of the Christ. Thielman's basic assumption—namely, that Galatians 5:14, in which Paul identifies "You shall love thy neighbor as thyself" as the whole of the Law, indicates a commitment to keeping the Law, as Jews understood it—is mistaken. To be sure, as I have already pointed out, Rabbi Akiva did understand this verse as "The great principle of Torah," but certainly not as abrogating Sabbath, kashruth, or circumcision! This can only be achieved via the sort of spiritualizing, allegorical hermeneutic that I am positing for Paul.

Thielman over and over again contradicts himself in order to maintain his basic thesis when his often sound and sensible readings raise difficulties for that thesis. As a final example, he remarks on the pedagogue metaphor:

> Thus Paul explains to the Galatians that, far from being able to make them inheritors of the promise and righteous, the law can only point out and punish their mistakes. To submit to it is to step backward from maturity to childhood, from the ability to live according to God's will to the period of constant mistakes and punishment.
>
> (79)

This seems to me to be exactly right, but then he adds, "Again, it is not the law in its every aspect which is spoken of here, but the law as something which points out and punishes sin." This is, I submit, incoherent. Either the Galatians are supposed to keep the Law or they are not. Clearly, Paul is arguing that they should not keep the Law, and for precisely the reasons given in the first part of the quotation from Thielman. What aspect of the Law, then, remains? If it is only the love of Galatians 5:14, then Paul has thoroughly redefined the Law (as I think he has) and abrogated the literal commandments by fulfilling their spiritual sense. Thielman seems so influenced by Paul's own distinctions between Law and Law that he does not hear how revolutionary they truly are. "Gal. 2:15–16, 3:10–14, and 3:19–5:1, therefore, do not propose the cancellation of the law, the *sine qua non* of Judaism. They are instead statements about the law motivated from the conviction that the time of God's redemption of Israel, and of all humanity, from sin has arrived. These passages serve as reminders to the Galatians of the time in which they should be living as those who believe in Jesus Christ, and thus they serve as arguments to persuade the Galatians not to submit again to the yoke of bondage to sin (5:1) by undertaking circumcision, food laws, and Sabbath keeping as if they had some value for justification before God (5:3)" (86). But from a Jewish point of view, circumcision is not a submission to the yoke of bondage to sin; it is The Law, a crucially significant element of the Law. How, then, is it possible to claim in the same breath that Paul does not propose cancellation of the Law, but that circumcision, food laws, and Sabbath keeping have no value before God? The bottom line is that Thielman's hypothesis, essentially the same as Davies's, is that the Law is abrogated in the Messianic Age, and there is no more evidence now for a view that circumcision, etc., would be canceled then in any Judaism than there ever was. All this does not vitiate the many excellent individual exegetical remarks with which the book is studded, several of which I cite in this chapter.

23. This interpretation is different from those which see Paul here as protecting himself from a Marcionite misinterpretation that the Law is evil, e.g., Longenecker (1990, 143). My interpretation seems to me to make much more sense of the sequel than a reading that sees here a defense of the Law.

24. Nils Dahl has already noted this, but for a somewhat different exegetical purpose (Dahl 1977, 174).

25. Cf. Campbell, who writes: "He is not willing to identify himself with those who see the 'old' covenant as obsolete, the law itself as sinful, and Jewish scriptures and culture as being both anachronistic and wrong for all Christians" (1992, 183). Of these propositions, I think that Paul certainly does see the old covenant as obsolete and anachronistic, for otherwise how can we understand this metaphor of the pedagogue? While it may not be methodologically correct to force Romans to mean what Galatians means, neither does it make sense to interpret Romans in ways that directly contradict Galatians. I agree, of course, that it is not the sinfulness of the Law that has led to its supersession but only its ethnic specificity.

26. The best refutation of this strange theological notion is Romans 7 as demonstrated by Gager (1983, 220–23), following Stendahl's classic *Paul Among Jews and Gentiles* (1976, 86 ff. and 92–94). Paul repeatedly asserts the essential goodness of the Law, which would be impossible were the function of the Law *ab initio* to produce and increase sin (*pace* Westerholm 1988, 178). I am afraid, however, that I find the rest of Gager's argument about this chapter unconvincing. To suppose that the "I" that speaks here of his desire to keep the Law and his inability to do so is a gentile (or only a gentile) is to stretch hermeneutical ingenuity to the breaking point. On "Marcionite" interpretations of Paul, see now Campbell (1992, 126).

27. In fact, the term *originally* meant the letters of the alphabet. The philosophical connotations of "fundamental principle or material out of which all things are composed" is a later development associated with Aristotle, so it is possible that Paul here is digging at philosophy as well. For στοιχεῖα, see Saxonhouse (1992, 25) and esp. Kahn (1960, 120).

28. In a more recent article, I think, Thielman has somewhat revised his previous position. See Thielman (1992, 237–40).

29. Alan Segal has got this point just right:

> For Paul and other religiously committed Jews, Torah was a body of divine wisdom that had to be adopted in its entirety, however that entirety was defined. The only question was how Torah was to be interpreted; by means of allegory, *pesher*, or midrash first-century Jews found grounds for latitude in practice. Though Paul had given up Pharisaism, he simply did not recommend that his community observe the ethical requirements of Torah and ignore the ceremonial parts. . . . There is no ready-made vocabulary on which Paul can depend. Paul takes an unprecedented position when he says: "With the mind, I serve the law of God, but with the flesh, the law of sin" ([Romans] 7:25b) He thus invents a new, personal vocabulary for dealing with the ceremonial laws. His vocabulary partakes of Hellenistic

philosophy and apocalypticism simultaneously. Though Paul's mature position about the special laws is unique, it does have certain affinities with the extreme allegorizers to whom Philo gives credit for having found philosophical wisdom. Philo criticizes the extreme allegorizers for trying to be souls without bodies; such a criticism would make sense against Paul as well, although Paul uses a concept of a spiritual body instead of a soul in the philosophical sense.

(1990, 246)

30. As we learn from the fact that Philo had to oppose such views.

31. The Rabbis interpreted the verse which forbids putting a stumbling block in the way of the blind as an injunction against tempting others into (and providing the conditions for them to) sin, and in the early Middle Ages it was actually debated whether there exists in this verse a prohibition against placing stumbling blocks in the way of the blind!

32. In his recent article Thielman refers to this passage to support the notion that Paul held the continuing validity of the Torah (Thielman 1992, 241). Now, on the one hand, he is clearly correct. Paul does appeal to the verse of the Torah as an authoritative source for practice. On the other hand, the allegorical reading offered that verse, such that the concrete law becomes a signifier for something in the Christian situation, is practically emblematic of Pauline hermeneutics as I understand them.

33. Cp. the somewhat similar formulations of Sanders (1983, 171) and the sensitive remarks of Campbell (1992, 133).

CHAPTER 7

1. From my point of view the only seriously mistaken turn that Wright takes in the whole book is in his interpretation of Romans 7, and particularly of the parable in the beginning. Verse 4, "Likewise my brethren, you have died to the law through the body of Christ, so that you may belong to another, to him who has been raised from the dead," clearly means that the Law was the first husband and not "The former husband is the παλαιὸς ἄνθρωπος, the old 'you' that died in baptism," and then: "It is not, then, the Torah, but the 'old man' that died, leaving the self—who clearly plays the part of both husband and wife in the illustration—to be married to the new man, i.e. Christ" (196). This is an exceedingly clever, even brilliant, way to harmonize the parable and the application, but I am simply unconvinced by it. The fact that the "self"—a term which Paul could not have recognized—plays both husband and wife shows that in any case the interpretation will not be smooth. It is not atypical for parables and applications to show some slippage like this, and I am certain that the old interpretation in this case is better.

2. According to Wright, "'The problem of Romans 7,' and for that matter Romans 8.1–8, is emphatically *not* that of 'man under the law' . . . but of 'the law under man,' or, more specifically, under flesh" (1992a, 209), but this does not take into sufficient consideration the passages in which the Law is identified with flesh as the Law of sin at work in our members, of which Wright himself has correctly

insisted that νόμος in them must mean the same Law, the Torah, as in the rest of the passage, or Paul's text becomes shallow and weak (199)! This can, of course, be retrieved if we understand "the Law under flesh" to mean the Law in its fleshly, that is, literal, interpretation in which physical procreation is commanded, but that, of course, is my reading, not Wright's. On my view, then, the Law of the spirit (ὁ νόμος τοῦ πνεύματος) in Romans 8:2 means the Law spiritually understood, and that is, indeed, the "Law of faith (νόμος πίστεως)" of Romans 3:27, in which the universality of this Law of faith is central (209 n. 23).

3. Thus, for my interpretation, as in Wright's, the "Other Law" is the Torah as well, but the Torah has an Other within itself, which introduces an Other into the person, the Law of Sin (v. 25).

4. Some of the material in this subsection is adapted from Boyarin (1993, 67–70). On the other hand, this should also be seen as a partial corrective to the views expressed in there, p. 3 n. 4. I now see Paul's discourse of sexuality as much closer to that of first-century Palestinian Judaism.

5. Note here as well the notion of pure love, which is similar to Paul's agapic love in Galatians 5:22.

6. For comparison of Romans 7 to the Jewish doctrine of the יצר הרע, see Schoeps (1961, 185).

7. One could say that "law" sometimes functions for Paul semantically as מצוה, commandment, does in rabbinic Hebrew.

8. This obviates the sort of difficulty that Dunn runs into, because he does not understand "law" here to mean the Law given to Adam (1988, 292). Furthermore, if the interpretation of Watson that the speaker of Romans 7 is Adam be accepted (see below), then "I was once alive apart from the law" is also no problem (pace Dunn, 291), because Adam is speaking about the time before he was commanded not to eat of the tree of knowledge! Sin was in the world even then but it had not yet come into the world in the sense of being accounted.

9. I wish to dispel one possible source of confusion here. I am not claiming that when Paul refers to Adam as the type of the one who is to come, that this means the Jew or humanity under the Law. As attractive as this interpretation would be for understanding v. 20, Dunn is clearly correct that it is excluded by v. 15, which seeks to draw a contrast between type and anti-type, such that it is obvious that the anti-type is Jesus and nothing else. Nevertheless, I am arguing, Adam is being used (if not mentioned) as the type of transgressor under the Law and thus of the Jews, a crucial point for interpreting Romans 7. Quite incidentally to my argument here but important to understanding Romans 5 is the realization that an argument of de minore ad maiore (קול וחומר [sic]) from sin to grace or from punishment to mercy is a very common one in rabbinic texts. Accordingly, I completely disagree with Dunn (293), who regards vv. 15–17 as a qualifying afterthought of the comparison of Adam to Christ. I think, given the constant use of this type of argument throughout the chapter, Paul is saying here exactly what he wants to say. If through Adam's sin all are punished (the quality of judgment), how much more so that through the free gift (the quality of mercy) will all be redeemed. Retroverted back into Hebrew and without the christology, this could be a sentence in any midrash!

10. For the latter in rabbinic tradition compare the rabbinic dictum that "Any-

one who is greater than his fellow [in Torah], has a greater desire to sin than his fellow," discussed at length in Boyarin (1993, 64–67).

11. For an assessment of the various views on the identity of "I" here, see Moo (1986, 122–23).

12. See also Moo, who writes, "How could Paul feature Adam's experience in a discussion about a law which he presents as entering the historical arena only with *Moses*?" (124). I think his objection is, however, no objection, because Adam is certainly presented as having had at least one commandment, which he transgressed in chapter 5, and he is the *type* of Israel in this respect. We do not need to appeal to a putative Jewish notion (not attested anywhere that I know of) that Adam received the Torah, only to realize that, as Paul says explicitly, Adam's small set of commandments—Be fruitful, and Do not eat of the fruit—had the same function as the Torah. Moo also concedes "the great attraction of the Adamic interpretation. 'Life' and 'death' can be accorded their full theological meanings, referring, respectively, to Adam's state before and after his disastrous confrontation with the divine commandment, and the springing to life of the previous inactive sin can be regarded as a fitting description of the role of the serpent in the garden," but claims, "However, we have seen that, whatever its virtues, the Adamic view cannot satisfactorily be reconciled with the central concern of the text—the Mosaic *torah*" (125). I claim, however, that this Adamic interpretation is eminently reconcilable with the notion that Paul is talking about the Mosaic Torah, for the reason I have already exposed, namely, that Adam and his commands are treated in chapter 5 as the type of Israel and her Torah. If the objection is taken as answered, then the attractions of the Adamic interpretation remain. I am entirely unimpressed by the arguments of Robert H. Gundry (1980) in favor of the "autobiographical" interpretation. It is, on top of all the other inconsequentialities of its argument, dependent on the totally unsupportable assumption that the concept of Bar Mitzva was present in the first century! I do agree, of course, with his assumption that Paul is talking about sexual desire. Since we agree on the sexual content of the chapter, the question of whether this is Paul's autobiography or a midrash on Adamic man becomes quite crucial indeed.

13. *Pace*, e.g., Moo (1986, 123). Cp. Lyonnet (1962).

14. I am in complete agreement with Wright's insistence that νόμος must mean everywhere the same "Law," both in Romans 7 and in Romans 3:27, if we are not to sap Paul's writing of any strength. I think, however, that my interpretation goes much further in establishing this than his does, because for him, this "Law of Sin" must be reduced to the Torah taken over and used by sin, whereas for my reading, the Torah understood literally *is* a Torah of sin, because it commands sexuality. I agree with Wright that "those who are 'in the Spirit,' do now submit to Torah, in the sense of its righteous decree coming true in them. They are not 'under Torah'; they are not bound by 'works of Torah'; but they 'submit to it,' *in the sense of its deepest intention*" (213, emphasis added), and I agree even more that "This exegesis of νόμος in Rom. 8 would give a good viewpoint, were there time and space, from which to examine Rom. 2.13f., 2.25–29, and particularly 3.27." It is this examination which I am attempting in this very book.

15. This argument would be even stronger, of course, if the Septuagint used the word "fruit" in this verse, but it does not. Since, however, the Hebrew does

use the verb from the root for fruit, פרו, Paul could conceivably be either remembering the Hebrew or perhaps alluding to another, more literal Greek rendition of the verse. Even without the verbal echo, the thematic one of bearing fruit, i.e., procreating, is clear.

16. As Westerholm already acutely observed, 7:5–6—"When we were in the flesh, our sinful passions, aroused by the law, were at work in our members to bear fruit for death. But now we are discharged from the law, dead to that which held us captive, so that we serve not under the old written code but in the new life of the Spirit"—is an interpretative gloss on 6:12–14. In order, therefore, to understand the latter we must interpret the former (and vice versa of course) (Westerholm 1988, 54).

17. The paradox that baptized Christians still have bodies of flesh has already been anticipated and answered by Paul in Galatians 2:19–20.

18. Note that baptized converts into Judaism are not considered the children of their natural parents.

19. For the essentially platonistic mood of this entire theme, see *Symposium* 207 ff. Kenneth Dover has summarized this section concisely:

> Procreation, as explained by Diotima, is an expression of the desire of mortal bodies to achieve a kind of immortality, and is shared by mankind with the animals (207ab); anyone, she remarks, would rather compose immortal poems or make enduring laws than procreate mere human children (209cd), and the generation of rational knowledge is the best of all manifestations of the human desire for immortality. Those men who are "fertile in body" fall in love with women and beget children (208e), but those who are "fertile in soul" transcend that limitation and the "right approach" is open to them alone.
>
> (Dover 1989, 162–63)

20. For a reading of this passage almost directly opposed to mine, see Fiore (1990, 139–40). If Ephesians is Pauline (or even if it was written by someone very close to Pauline thinking), then 5:32, in which the writer explicitly calls this verse a "mystery [μυστήριον]" and interprets it allegorically as referring to Christ and the Church, is very significant. It is in that state of spiritual joining into one body, I am suggesting, that "there is no male and female." See also Wire (1990, 77–78) and especially, "Paul's words would be most congenial to women who have used their freedom to live separately from men, although the next chapter shows that he has no intention of ruling out sexual union for those in union with Christ. But his use of the Genesis quotation, 'the two will become one flesh,' to build the stark antithesis of two kinds of union appeals to those whose union with Christ replaces sexual union."

21. Note that in this "concession" Paul is essentially simply reinstating the ethos of Palestinian (pre-rabbinic) Judaism, as illustrated, once again, by the Testaments of the Twelve Patriarchs: "Be on guard against the spirit of promiscuity, for it is constantly active and through your descendants it is about to defile the sanctuary. Therefore take for yourself a wife while you are still young" (Kee 1983, 792).

22. The second of these citations makes it quite clear that in 7:1 Paul is not merely quoting or reflecting the views of the Corinthians in order to dispute them, as some commentators have argued, but in fact agreeing with and then qualifying them. As in Galatians 5–6 (for which, see below), Paul is always concerned lest an overdisdain for the flesh lead paradoxically toward libertinism!

23. The richest discussion of this passage that I know is Barclay 1991. Barclay discusses several strategies for interpreting the relation of the paranetic ending of Galatians to the rest of the letter. He refers to the common strategy (a version of which I hold here) whereby chapters 5 and 6 are read as corrective to the first part, as readings that perceive Paul as being "apologetic" or "defensive" (12–13). On my view, Paul is simply restoring a balance inherent to his two-tier system of thought and preventing a very plausible confusion that his "freedom" language could lead to. For Barclay himself, the paranesis contains an answer to a question that the Galatians have raised (95). They have been attracted to the Law, because it tells them how to live their lives ethically, and now Paul's task at the end of the letter is to convince them of the possibility of ethical life apart from the Law. The difference between the two interpretations is that while according to mine (following a long line of exegetes) Paul is *warning* the Galatians of a possible and dangerous misreading of his gospel, according to Barclay's he is *reassuring* them that his gospel does not have those negative consequences.

As rich and rigorous as Barclay's discussion is, I am ultimately unpersuaded by this aspect of his interpretation. I find the tone of this passage to be hortatory rather than reassuring. Barclay's reading, in my opinion, does not account for the warning implied in the exhortation not to let the freedom be an opportunity for the flesh, μόνον μὴ τὴν ἐλευθερίαν εἰς ἀφορμὴν τῇ σαρκί (5:13), which seems strongly to suggest Pauline anxiety about possible consequences in the future and not an answer to the Galatians' questions. The tone of this verse (and thus its meaning) is, in my view, comparable to 1 Corinthians 8:9: "Only take care lest this liberty of yours somehow become a stumbling block to the weak"—Paul was always alive to the dangers of his radical preaching. On Barclay's view, Galatians 5:13 should rather have been phrased something like: Have no fear, brothers, freedom in the Spirit will not be an opportunity for the flesh! (Barclay, of course, takes account of this verse; however, his claim that it "functions as *an assurance that the Spirit can provide adequate moral constraints and directions*" [219] just doesn't seem to me to capture its tone at all. I think that this is the greatest weakness in his whole argument which otherwise is an enormous contribution. Barclay goes on to admit the sense of warning as an additional interpretation but does not seem to see how it contradicts [not logically, perhaps, but rhetorically] his main claim.) Second, the warning language of 5:21 seems less apt on Barclay's interpretation than on the one adopted here. Moreover, the assumption that the Galatians were drawn to the Law because it offered them an ethic seems, while possible, less than ineluctable. Barclay himself appropriately indicates its speculative nature, "One of the attractions in the agitators' proposals for law-observance *may have been* the security of a written and authoritative code of law; in comparison, Paul's ethical policy *may have appeared* dangerously ill-defined" (106, emphases added). These are, indeed, possibilities. I cannot find anything in the text that indicates, however, that they were the case, while Paul's warning language does seem to support my construction. Finally, as Barclay himself notes, "if the Galatians were hoping for codifiable rules and regulations, they would not have been well satisfied by what Paul offers" (169).

On the other hand, Barclay's point that current interpretations entirely fail to account for the specificities of Paul's maxims and exhortations here seems well taken. He accordingly suggests—somewhat contradicting his general theory of a Galatian appeal for law and order—that these refer to and answer difficulties that had already arisen in the Galatian community. This, however, seems to me to be implausible (not impossible) in the light of the general tendency of the entire letter. I would like to make a quite speculative counter-suggestion. If, as one theory holds, Paul wrote to the Galatians from Corinth and was preaching to the Corinthians the gospel of freedom detailed in the first part of Galatians, it is clear (from 1 Corinthians) that his hypothesized concerns about being misunderstood were well placed. Indeed, it is remarkable how exactly the exhortations at the end of Galatians seem to speak to the situation of the Corinthian church (as Paul saw it), as can be reconstructed from 1 Corinthians. According to this construction, Paul already sensed at the time of writing Galatians the problems of internal strife and libertinism that were to develop into full bloom by the time he would write 1 Corinthians. A somewhat more conservative version of this suggestion would be that these problems were typical of Pauline churches, once the message of Christian freedom was fully taken in—Corinth being an example—and Paul is concerned lest his passionate call for Lawlessness be once more misunderstood as a call to lawlessness! See also the highly illuminating discussion of this issue in Hays 1987.

24. Note how neatly this solves the outstanding exegetical problem phrased most elegantly by Hays: "After a lengthy exposition of justification by faith, why does Paul move into a series of exhortations which sound more appropriate to the situation at Corinth than to the Galatian problem?" (1987, 289). Hays's own solution is also elegant but almost directly opposite to mine, in that for him "the flesh" refers primarily to civil strife rather than, as I claim, civil strife being a consequence of the flesh understood as eros.

25. See also Colossians 2:20–23, which I would quote were I sure that Paul had written it. On the other hand, let me emphasize once more that Colossians and Ephesians may be the best *commentaries* on Pauline doctrine that we possess. I hope to return to this issue in a future work.

26. Cp. the rather similar views of Fiore (1990, 136–38), and contrast Countryman (1988, 104–09, 296–314).

27. Dead Sea Manual of Discipline, 4:10.

28. Cp. the quite different view of Hays (1987, 286). My interpretation brings Paul *somewhat* closer to the Stoics, *pace* Hays, n. 45.

29. Philo (1929b, i, 121).

30. Jewett's interpretation of this passage in Galatians is untenable, and he can make no sense of the warning about sowing, referring to it as "enigmatic" (Jewett 1971, 104). After his excellent insight that "flesh" for Paul means the literal flesh of circumcision (and I add procreation), he quickly reverts to Bultmannian conceptions: "The 'flesh' is Paul's term for everything aside from God in

which one places his final trust. The Jew sought to gain life through the law which offers the obedient a secure future. This element of seeking the good is an essential part of the flesh idea, and may be seen likewise in the situation of the libertinist. The flesh presents to the libertinist objects of desire which man is to satisfy (Gal. 5:16). These objects lure man on because of the promise inherent in them. They seem to offer man exactly what the law and circumcision offered—life" (Jewett, 103). Jewett's interpretation is dependent on assuming that Paul is arguing that one who follows the Law is in danger of libertinism: "The struggle against the flesh is centered in the cross event and with the appropriation of this event for oneself in baptism, the power of the flesh is broken. It can threaten again only if man foolishly places his faith in the flesh again, thus setting his will in line with the flesh's lures" (106). But this is precisely the opposite of Paul's concern here. He is not telling the Galatians that if they ignore his preaching and get circumcised they will be prey to the lures of the flesh but rather he is afraid that if they take in his preaching, they will misunderstand and think that the flesh is permitted to them. That is, after all, what Paul articulates *explicitly* as his concern in 5:13, "For you were called to freedom, brothers, only do not use your freedom as an opportunity for the flesh." Paul does, indeed, argue in other places that keeping the Law leads to sensuality, though not for the reasons that Jewett adduces but, as I claim throughout this chapter, because the Law requires sexuality and all of its fruits!

I submit, then, that flesh is flesh: human flesh. As such it can be involved in the performance of commandments, or it can be involved in sexuality; indeed, among the commandments, the command to have sex is the most fleshy of all. All the commandments belong to the realm of the flesh, and as such, for Paul share an inferior position. Paul has argued strenuously in the first four chapters of Galatians for liberation from the Law because it is fleshy; he now says, in effect, that it would be most ironic, if not tragic, were this liberation to be misunderstood as an opportunity for the very flesh that it was meant to defeat. The possibility for this misunderstanding is palpable, and everything Paul says in this passage is directed against it. The whole point, Paul says, is to enter the Spirit, and therefore, since the flesh and the spirit are entirely opposed to each other in desire and in works, to understand Christian freedom from the Law of the flesh as permission for the flesh would be grievous and tragic misreading indeed, escaping a pit only to plummet into a pitfall. All the other usages of flesh in Paul are derivations from this primary meaning through the chains of association and analogy that I discuss throughout this book.

31. I think Dunn is, therefore, for once absolutely wrong when he writes, "The ἐν ᾧ obviously refers to the law (as most recognize), not to the 'old man,' or the 'being in the flesh' just described." According to my interpretation, these are precisely the same thing!

32. The quotation is from the traditional marriage blessings current from late antiquity until the present. For discussion see Boyarin (1993, 44–45).

CHAPTER 8

1. In drawing this analogy, I should make it clear that I am not reducing the problem of gender domination to an epiphenomenon of difference; nor would I so

reduce anti-Semitism. The analogies seem, nevertheless, illuminating as partial accounts of both and, moreover, help explain the historically very well attested association of Jewishness with femaleness as a topos of European culture.

2. I wish to spotlight the eloquent remarks of Adele Reinhartz: "While I am concerned about the roles of women within the Jewish community and can offer a critique of their ambiguous portrayal in Judaism's foundational documents, I deplore superficial and apologetically motivated attempts to demonstrate the superiority of Christianity to Judaism on the basis of the respective roles they accord women" (1991, 183).

3. See the brief discussion of her work from this perspective by Reinhartz (1991, 166–67). However, I must admit that I find bizarre Fiorenza's comment on Jewish manumission of slaves: "The slave gained complete freedom except for the requirement to attend the synagogue" (214), as if "Christian freedom" did not carry with it also a series of religious obligations. Is the requirement to participate in the Eucharist somehow more free than the requirement to attend synagogue? I feel an echo of a very ancient polemic (and dispute) here.

4. There seems to be little recognition that these two explanations are at least partially contradictory, or at any rate, render each other otiose. If it was the "pagans" who pressured Paul to insist on male-female hierarchy, then what is the function of "rabbinic prejudices" here other than to provide a gratuitous slap at Judaism? Incidentally, at the time of Paul, the rabbinic movement did not yet exist, so "rabbinic prejudices" is in any case an anachronism. In fact, as we shall see below, it is also an inaccurate (although widespread) description of the relationship between Pauline "halakha" and that of contemporary Judaism(s), but I anticipate myself.

5. I am obviously not of the opinion that 1 Corinthians 11:2–16 can simply be excised by fiat from the Pauline corpus, *because of these tensions*. See on this Walker (1975) for the pro position and Murphy-O'Connor, O.P. (1976) and Meier (1978) for the con.

6. The spherical humans described by Aristophanes in the *Symposium*, while obviously related genetically to the myth of the primal androgyne, encode quite a different set of meanings; first of all, they are physical, and second of all they are not all androgynes by any means. Aristophanes's myth comes to provide an etiology for sexualities rather than to be an "articulation of the notion that human perfection is only accessible apart from sexual difference," as Elizabeth Castelli would have it in an article otherwise wholly admirable (1991b, 31). A very important discussion of the Aristophanes text may be found in Laqueur (1990, 52–53 and 260n.82). As I mention below, Philo, who strongly endorses the myth of the primal androgyne in his writing, is thoroughly contemptuous of Aristophanes's story.

7. In Boyarin 1993, I have claimed that rabbinic Judaism successfully resisted the mind-body dualism of Hellenism with, however, both positive and negative consequences for sexual politics. One of the strategies for that resistance, I claim, was a parodic appropriation of the myth of the primal androgyne which *subverted* its ideology. Elizabeth Castelli has asked whether primal androgyny and a primal androgyne are as easily conflated as I am doing and acutely refers to O'Flaherty, who writes: "In religious parlance, androgyny is a much more comprehensive and

abstract concept than is implied in this visual [virtual] image of the androgyne: to say that God is androgynous is very different from saying that God is an androgyne. . . . [To define] the androgyne in the strict sense in which it is convenient to define it here: a creature simultaneously male and female in physical form" (1980, 283). It seems to me, however, that to the extent that we are talking about human beings and not mythical creatures, it is hard to separate androgynes from androgyny, and that is precisely the nub of the whole problem. Either the androgyne is some sort of a universal, abstract, pre-gendered creature—or an *idea* of humanity, which more or less comes down to the same thing—or it is two people joined in intercourse, with all that may entail in terms of power relations. A true androgyne is just an image; in the imaginary we can imagine anything, but what does it mean on the ground, in terms of real human lives?

8. "Of all Paul's letters, 1 Corinthians is thoroughly and intensely concerned with the physical body" (Neyrey 1990, 114). "Word-statistics show a sudden rise in the frequency of *sôma* in I and II Corinthians and Romans. The denigration of the body at Corinth provides the reason" (Gundry 1976, 50). See below other symptoms of the "corporeality" of Corinthians. This approach, which understands Pauline discourse to be functioning on two levels at the same time, promises a solution as well to the famous question of the so-called indicative alongside the so-called imperative moods of Paul's discourse (Bultmann 1967, 8). Note that my approach answers Bultmann's just methodological demand that approaches to this problem *not* trace these two moments in Paul back to two historical, psychological origins. As Bultmann writes:

> Paul's view of flesh-spirit possesses to a considerable degree the character of the metaphysical dualism that is typical of Hellenistic mystery religions. . . . On this basis then, it is possible to arrive at an understanding of the antinomy—the occurrence of indicatives and imperatives side by side—that can claim to grasp it in terms of the material itself. For the mystic, otherworldly salvation is a present reality, and since this is the case the indicatives can be used in a natural way to speak of that salvation. The imperatives do not really conflict with this, since they express the fact that the empirical, concrete human being is to be canceled out.
>
> (22)

I would only modify this formulation, rather, to read that the imperatives do not conflict with this, since they express the fact that the concrete human being *has not yet been canceled out.* Although Bultmann is only setting his formula up in order to tear it down, I think that my reformulation goes a long way to answering the objection he raises: "Can we say that Paul's empirical fate does not concern him any longer? On the contrary, it served the function 'that the life of Jesus may be manifested in our mortal flesh'" (25). On my modified version of the concept, this is no objection at all, because the place of the flesh is still maintained. This does not preclude, of course, the possibility that, in given historical circumstances, Paul would emphasize one or the other of these aspects of his thought, which is what I am claiming for Galatians and 1 Corinthians.

9. There is nothing particularly new in this formulation per se. What is new in my interpretation is that the differences between Galatians and Corinthians,

while contextualized by different discursive, "political" contexts, nevertheless form a consistent pattern and social theory on Paul's part.

10. The difference between this interpretation and others apparently similar is that I do not think that Paul retreated from Galatians to Corinthians; rather, the former represents the ideal (spirit) while the latter represent accommodation with the real (flesh). Lest this sound implausible, once more I cite: But because of *porneia*, let every man have his wife and every woman have her husband. Much follows from that concession to the demands of the unredeemed flesh. Paul argues that when one does not make provision for the flesh, then one gives an opportunity to the flesh! *Pace* Campbell, then, Galatians 3:26–29 is *not* "over-realized eschatology" (1992, 108).

11. It is further fascinating to note that in Sanders's chart of verses that deal with the various issues of Pauline theology, all of the verses that have to do with the fate of Christians who sin are from the Corinthian correspondence (Sanders 1983, 9), and again, "Here [in Corinthians] we see that, when he had to deal in detail with transgression within the Christian community, reward and punishment, and the possibility of postconversion atonement, he did so in a thoroughly Jewish way" (107), that is (on my view) "according to the flesh." Also, "Paul's discussion of marriage (1 Cor. 7:1–16, 25–40), even though he qualifies part of it as only his opinion (7:25, 40), is close to halakhah" (119n. 46).

12. Dawson reads "the emergence and domestication of radical *gnōsis* in its countless forms" as the "common feature in these struggles that recur throughout the [Western] history of interpretation" (1992, 17). Karen King has emphasized to me (orally) that the term "gnostic" itself is highly problematized in current research and has suggested simply abandoning it in this context. I think, however, that as long as we define our terms and use the term to refer to specific spiritual, ideological tendencies, it still serves a useful purpose.

13. By "ungrammaticality" here, I mean the stylistic infelicity of the formal difference between the different clauses of the Pauline formula, that stylistic infelicity which marks formally the site of a citation and thus points to the intertext. This provides the strongest argument for Meeks's view that Gal. 3:28 has a protognostic background (to use J. Louis Martyn's terminology) and not an apocalyptic one. Martyn claims: "Nothing in the text or context of Gal 3.28 indicates that the thought is that of *re*-unification" (Martyn 1985, 423n. 16), but precisely this argument that Paul is citing Gen. 1:27 and alluding to the "myth of the primal androgyne" does constitute an indication of re-unification.

14. Thus, I completely disagree with Fiorenza, who claims that "the immediate context in Galatians speaks neither about baptism" (208). From the very beginning of the chapter until its end, that is all that is being spoken of.

15. Below I will argue further that Pauline baptism functioned in this way, providing a momentary experience of breaking of categories in the experience of "the spirit." I should clarify here, however, that I am *not* claiming that Paul's religion was heavily influenced by or transformed into a mystery. I am entirely convinced by the arguments of Davies (1965, 90–93) as to the implausibility of this thesis that was once quite popular among certain schools of Pauline scholars. Wedderburn 1987 has, I think, finally confirmed Davies's view of this matter de-

finitively. I am very convinced, moreover, by Davies's comparisons of the baptism and Eucharist with the religious experience of the Passover as imagined in rabbinic Judaism. Rather, I am suggesting that in some ways Pauline baptism was *structurally* similar to the experience of initiation in the Mysteries without arguing that it was therefore connected with them—at the very least, because the Mysteries seems largely a second-century phenomenon. Note that while initiation into Judaism, either through the Exodus or conversion, did, of course, include the entry into a historical community, it did not ever imply any erasure of social roles and hierarchies within the community. To be sure, slaves who became Jews were no longer slaves (or rather, slaves who were freed automatically became Jews), and Greeks who became Jews, by definition, were no longer Greeks but Jews, but even these changes in status only emphasized the fact of difference even more. Women, moreover, certainly remained women. Paul's baptismal declaration of the end of difference cannot, I think, be traced simply to Semitic-speaking "Jewish" sources.

16. I am, of course, aware that Macdonald's reconstructions are not universally accepted.

17. Note how far this theme goes back in Greek culture as well. Thus in Aristophanes's *Ecclesiazusae* breakdown of distinctions between male and female leads to a situation in which "private property is abolished and all is held in common. Exclusive relationships between men and women are forbidden; sexual access is open for all. Dichotomies between male and female, public and private, old and young no longer control the relations of citizens and all (except, of course, slaves) become part of one unified family, eating, drinking, and sleeping together" (Saxonhouse 1992, 2–3). Note the connection between the breaching of the household, i.e., private property, and the breakdown in sexual boundaries between household and household as well. Given such traditions, is it any wonder that Paul would be concerned lest *his* breakdown of social distinctions between men and women also lead into such sexual anarchy? Note also how far Paul goes beyond such thinking in imagining an end to class distinctions of slave and free as well. I think he may well be unique in this in antiquity. Could not the communal life of the early Christian churches have seemed to some similar to the utopian vision of the play (cf. Saxonhouse, 12)? Indeed, is it any wonder that some Corinthian Christians might have drawn such conclusions?

18. This interpretation obviates the necessity to understand that Philo punctuated Genesis 1:27 differently than we usually do, for he *does*, on my reading, construe male-and-female with the first incorporeal human as spiritual androgyny, which *means* (in good structuralist fashion) neither male nor female, and that is my whole point. Contrast Wegner (1991, 45 and 47).

19. This hypothesis also explains the otherwise seemingly unmotivated reference in Philo's text to the *Symposium* of Plato and especially to Aristophanes's story of double-creatures (not necessarily androgynes by any means) at the origins of humanity. Philo is counterposing to this "abhorrent" image of physically double bodies an ideal one of spiritually dual humans. Philo's reversal was double-reversed by the Rabbis, who restored the myth as one of a physical androgyne, as I argue in Boyarin (1993, 42–43). This point is valid whether or not the community of Therapeutae ever really existed. In either case, the description is testimony to the

translation of anthropology into social practice in Philo's writing. If they did exist, moreover, we have further strong evidence that Philo is representative of larger religious traditions and groups.

20. Anne Wire has made the valid point that Philo describes the Therapeutrides as "aged virgins," which, given his usage discussed below, might well mean formerly sexually active women. In a sense, then, these women had "had their cake and eaten it too." The symbolic incompatibility, however, between sexuality and spirituality is nevertheless reinforced, and, as we shall see, in many groups the renunciation had been total and permanent. Furthermore, it is important to note that the women of the culture may not have experienced this "renunciation" as a sacrifice but as a liberation, and I am making an open judgment here which draws on my own contemporary values, which is valid to the extent that I am involved here in a critique and analysis of contemporary culture using the ancient materials as one tool of analysis. In any case, however, it is clear that an autonomy predicated on the forced choice of celibacy (in order to achieve autonomy) is a highly compromised autonomy, however it may have been experienced.

It is not to be ignored, of course, that men, too, in these systems are ideally expected to embrace celibacy. Male autonomy and creativity are *not*, however, predicated on such renunciation, except in one sphere. Thus non-celibate men have many avenues of self-expression and freedom together with sexuality and paternity, while women can only choose between an all-encompassing maternity or none at all. There are, to be sure, in both Judaism and Christianity some hints at ruptures in this rule. See Boyarin (1993, 167–96) and Harrison 1990.

21. See, for example, the characteristically philonic usage, "When a man comes in contact with a woman, he marks [makes her marked; note the semiotic terminology] the virgin as a woman. But when souls become divinely inspired, from being women they become virgins" (QE II, 3). Obviously, Philo's usage is influenced by general Greek diction in which παρθένος is often contrasted to γυνή, as for instance in Xenophon's *Anabasis* 3.2.25: γ. καὶ παρθένοι, cited in Liddel-Scott, 363. This Greek usage alone is significant, because it already encodes the idea that virgins are not women. In Hebrew, the word אשה, which also means both "woman" and "wife," can never be contrasted with בתולה "virgin," and indeed אשה בתולה (= a virgin woman) is a common expression. Finally, even in Greek, one can speak of a γυνή παρθένος (= virgin woman), as in Hesiod's *Theogony* 514 (L-S, 1339). The structural opposition between virgin ~ woman in Philo is thus significant and revealing, even if he is only exploiting and developing a sort of quirk of Greek—a fortiori if, as I hold, he is doing more than that.

The passage from *Joseph and Aseneth*, cited by Macdonald (1988, 289) also supports this reading, for Aseneth is told, "because today you are a pure virgin and your head is like that of a young man." When she is no longer a virgin, only then she becomes a woman.

22. Steven Knapp has made the excellent point that the social entailments of a statement like "There is no male and female" could not but "leak from one social space to another," as it were, and Paul's formulations do not have only the consequences that he intended them to have. "On the other hand, there is some reason to think that marriage in what Boyarin calls 'the Christian West' has evolved into a more egalitarian institution than marriage in at least some other

cultures; if so, how would one go about excluding the possibility that this tendency was encouraged by the Pauline ideal of spiritual androgyny?" (from response at Center for Hermeneutical Studies). The answer is that I am not trying to exclude such a possibility at all. I am speaking here of Paul's intent, not as a hermeneutical or historical control on his text, but as a construct in its own right and a way to understand what seem otherwise to be contradictory moments in his discourse. Of course, this "leaking" goes both ways, for ultimately if a certain vision of gender equality that we share owes its origins to perhaps unintended consequences of Paul's discourse, it is perhaps equally the case that the general male-female hierarchy of even celibate Christian communities owes its origin to his discourse on marriage!

23. Note that in Colossians, a text which if not Pauline is certainly from circles close to him, the *Haustafel* follows hard by "there is no Greek and Jew, circumcised and uncircumcised, barbarian, Scythian, slave, free man, but Christ is all and in all" (3:10f.). Fiorenza acutely remarks that "Paul has taken great care to give a double command covering each case of active sexual interaction between husband and wife. However, it would be reaching too far to conclude from this that women and men shared an equality of role and a mutuality of relationship or equality of responsibility, freedom, and accountability in marriage. Paul stresses this interdependence only for *sexual* conjugal relationships and not for all marriage relationships" (224).

24. One consequence of my interpretation is that we need not assume "outside" influences for explaining Corinthian Christianity. This point gains particular cogency if we accept the hypothesis that Galatians was written *while Paul was in residence at Corinth*, thus increasing enormously the plausibility of the assumption that his "doctrine" in Galatians reflected his early preaching in Corinth. For this view, see Watson (1986, 59).

25. For a fairly thoroughgoing account of this "benevolent" gender hierarchy, see Boyarin 1993. Note that in that form of Judaism, for all its genuine discrimination against women, it is not enshrined as law that wives must be obedient to their husbands' rule. The verse which, in certain Christian circles, is usually cited as requiring wifely obedience, Gen. 3:16, "And your desire shall be toward him, but he will rule over you," is interpreted in talmudic law that husbands must be particularly attentive to pay attention to their wives' unspoken need for sex. Philo the misogynist does read this verse as encoding female submissiveness, but even he explicitly remarks that this servitude is not to be imposed through violence (Wegner 1991, 59). None of this remark should be taken, however, as a covering over or apology for either the misogynist tone of some talmudic/midrashic discourse or the pervasive disenfranchisement of women in that culture and particularly their near-total confinement to the roles of wife and mother. If individual men were somewhat restrained in this culture from cruel physical domination of individual women, the culture as a whole certainly was cruel in its restriction of possibilities for female freedom. Once more, as in the case of celibacy, women may not have experienced this as cruel. From our perspective, nevertheless, it is. I am not prepared, however, to dismiss their experience as "false consciousness." As Karen King has remarked, "The difference between men's imaginings of women and women's lives is such that we can affirm that women have found spiritual

fulfillment and salvation in the practice of Judaism and Christianity despite what the texts would lead us to think" (response).

26. Since this is the passage to which Fiorenza's student refers as where "he so firmly emphasized the equality of woman and man in marriage," then his apparent contradiction can hardly be seen as "reverting to rabbinic prejudices." Moreover, such provision for mutual consideration of husband and wife for each other's needs is hardly incompatible with gender hierarchy. As I have argued with regard to rabbinic Judaism and suggest here with regard to Paul as well, the attitude of husband to wife was expected to be one of benevolent dictatorship, which precluded any cruelty or lack of consideration.

What is remarkable about the Corinthians passage is rather its rhetoric, the fact that Paul addresses men and women equally, whereas the implicit subject of the Mishna is always a man who owes obligations to his wife and to whom she is also obligated. This is an important distinction; however, we should not make too much of it, for we do not know what rhetorical form a Pharisaic/rabbinic address to the populace, whether oral or epistolary, would have taken. Paul's rhetorical stance is usually every bit as androcentric as that of the Rabbis: "It is well for a person not to touch a woman"—not "It is well for persons not to have carnal knowledge of other persons." Conzelmann's argument that he used this form "due to the formulation of their question" (1976, 115) represents wishful thinking. Much more convincing is Wire's interpretation: "The immorality he exposes is male. The solution he calls for is marriage, and here, for the first time in the letter, he refers to women as an explicit group. Paul is not telling the offending men to marry. This cannot happen without the cooperation of others and the others cannot be male" (78). This would certainly explain well the shift from androcentric to "egalitarian" rhetoric in 7:2–3. See also her remark that with regard to the virgin, "Paul does not repeat the same words to the woman but continues to the man, 'But if you marry, you do not sin, and if the virgin marries, she does not sin' (7:28). In this way Paul manages to incorporate the rhetoric of equality, although the woman is only talked about, not addressed" (87).

Karen King has contributed some very wise remarks, which I think worth quoting extensively:

> My own work has shown that quite often a pattern can be discerned in men's writings about women: That is, the way that men view their own bodies and sexuality is structurally analogous to how they view women. In a sense, men often use women (or the category of woman) to think with. Control of one's own sexuality and the use and control of women seem to be two sides of the same problem.
>
> For Philo, a man's relationship to himself is one of control pure and simple: the control of the body by the mind. This control constitutes good order and the best interests of the self. Analogously, women are to be under men's control. They are not rejected, but it is understood that the good of society and man's spiritual progress can only be achieved by the subordination of women, for their own good. Women out of control again and again constitute Philo's primary metaphor for spiritual and social disaster. . . .
>
> For Paul, however, the relation to the self is less one of control and

more one of reciprocity. He does not abandon the body, but expects to see it transformed. Sexuality, body, and spirit are more fully integrated in his conceptuality of self than with Philo. Yet as you note, there still exists a clear hierarchical relation between spirit and body. Celibacy models this relation most clearly. It is also the inscription on the body of his ideal of unity expressed in Galatians 3:28. The model for relations between men and women is similarly one of reciprocity, not equality, as is shown in I Corinthians 7 and 11.

(response)

I would only wish to emphasize, following Wire and the logic of King's own statement, that this reciprocity of male and female is hierarchical precisely in the way that spirit and flesh are for Paul, thus further confirming King's approach. King's principle, which I absolutely endorse, has been of major importance in development of my work.

27. See Tomson (1990, 111) for demonstration that there was such a trend of thought in one form of Palestinian Judaism, and that the prohibition was derived from Gen. 1:27[!], just as Jesus had it. In addition, for Paul at any rate there is the general apocalyptic sense that everything should remain just as it is until the imminent Parousia. For this interpretation, see Wimbush 1987.

28. This interpretation carries with it the consequence that certain Orthodox Fathers of the church best represent the "authentic" Pauline tradition—for instance, Clement of Alexandria, whose positive view of marriage is well known, but also such figures as Gregory Nazianzen, who writes "I will join you in wedlock. I will dress the bride. We do not dishonour marriage, because we give a higher honour to virginity" (quoted in Ford 1989, 25). I am also quite persuaded by Ford's description of the later John Chrysostom's ideology of sexuality that his mature view was not very different from that of the Rabbis (49 and passim), but once again it is important to note that with all that, Chrysostom himself was celibate, and as Ford notes, "he continued all his life to consider a life of virginity in dedication to God as an even higher calling" (73). Others of the Cappadocian Fathers, including Gregory of Nyssa, seem also to reflect such positions. See Harrison 1990.

29. It should be noted, however, that since in the biblical text itself, Eve is positively evaluated as the "Mother of All Living," Philo does not assign her or sexuality only a negative value. Moreover, the term "Helper," for all of its connotations of subservience, is one that he can only read as having a positive valence, because help itself is clearly positively marked. On this, see Dillon, "it seems true to say that in Philo's thought there is present the recognition of a female life-principle assisting the supreme God in his work of creation and administration, but also somehow fulfilling the role of mother to all creation. If this concept reveals contradictions, that is perhaps because Philo himself was not quite sure what to do with it" (Dillon 1977, 164). Similarly, in his allegorical interpretation, for Philo, "woman" is the senses, and the import is that they are something that cannot be done without, something that has a positive role to play, however disturbing, in human life. This understanding on the allegorical level has its parallel on the literal level and even in practice, for in Philo, I think, literal women have about the same status as their signified, the senses, do in the allegorical meaning.

30. See Wire (1990, 88) for an excellent discussion of the interpretative prob-

lems of this verse, but the point being made here is not affected. Any way you cut it, the ratio between celibacy and marriage here is the same.

31. I find that Wire's interpretation of this section, 116ff., esp. 118–20, is the only weak part of her argument. I think, moreover, that the reconstruction offered here strengthens her overall reading considerably.

32. The use of δόξα "glory" as a synonym for εἰκών "image" is beautifully explained by Alan Segal as deriving from "God's Glory" which represents his human image (Segal 1990, 41). See also 2 Corinthians 3:18 and discussion in Segal (1990, 60).

33. Once again, let me make clear that even the explicit hierarchy reified by these verses does not necessarily authorize a tyranny of men over women, certainly not a vicious one. Κεφαλή may or may not mean "ruler," but there can be no doubt that structurally there *is* here a hierarchical series of God > Christ > man > woman, whatever the value placed on that hierarchy. I thus find myself here, as in other respects, in complete agreement with Engberg-Pedersen (1992, 681 n. 9). See also Fitzmyer (1989) for a strong argument that this term *does* mean "one having authority over" in Jewish koine.

34. This interpretation was suggested to me by Karen King. Anne Wire has proposed an entirely different reconstruction of the relation of the baptismal formula to Genesis, suggesting that it does not represent a return at all but a new creation which negates the original one. She accordingly disagrees with the Meeks-Macdonald interpretation. My construction of Paul is not crucially dependent on either of these historical reconstructions being "correct," although admittedly it is much neater following Macdonald. I think, moreover, that there is perhaps less reason than Wire thinks to strictly contrast the two versions. Colossians 3, for instance, "and put on the new man, which is renewed in knowledge after the image of him that created him: where there is neither Greek nor Jew" etc. suggests rather that the two go together, i.e., a creation that is new but also a return to the original.

35. From her response at Center for Hermeneutical Studies.

36. Contrast Betz (1979, 200).

37. Compare Macdonald (1988, 286 and esp. 290), who sees a much more fundamental difference between Paul and the Corinthians than I do. Note that my interpretation of "in the Lord" is diametrically opposed to his (291). As in many cases in chapter 7 as well, as Wire points out (passim), Paul grants a point in principle and disagrees in practice. Note, moreover, that the cases are exactly parallel.

38. For the latter, see Meeks (1973, 191 and 199), and Wire's characteristically shrewd remarks: "On the contrary, they [the Corinthians] may claim in their prayer and prophecy to mediate between God and humanity so that through the spirit the perishable does inherit imperishability and the primal dissociation is breached" (23). This breaching of the dissociation between spirit and flesh, raising of flesh to the status of spirit, would be that which transcends gender as well and explains much of the Corinthians' behavior, including paradoxically both their tendencies toward celibacy and libertinage as well as the Corinthian women's apparent adoption of male styles of headdress (Meeks 1973, 202; Macdonald 1988).

It is important to point out that, although less prominently, celibate men were also apparently sometimes imagined as androgynous. Verna Harrison has been doing very important work on this issue. It is tempting to speculate that Origen's self-castration fits into this paradigm as well; a speculation which can take place, incidentally, whether or not it actually happened. See on this point also the important and stimulating remarks in Brown (1988, 169). This pull to celibacy (and androgyny) for men is also a function of being freed from the constraints of the "world and the flesh," correspondingly weaker insofar as those constraints were much less burdensome for men than for women to start with. Note that the priests of Agditis an androgynous form of the Magna Mater used to emasculate themselves (Meeks 1983, 169). Fiorenza's reference to this cult (213) in apparent support of her claim that Galatians 3:28 "does not express . . . 'gnosticizing' devaluation of procreative capacities" seems somewhat inapposite in this light.

39. *De Baptismo* XVII 4–5.

40. The classic study of this phenomenon is Vööbus 1951, and see the excellent chapter in Peter Brown (1988, 83–103).

41. See the important passage in *The Acts of Andrew*, cited by Aspegren (1990, 126), in which the apocryphal apostle begs Maximilla to remain steadfast in her decision to cease having sexual intercourse with her husband in the following terms: "I beg you, then, O wise man (ὁ φρόνιμος ἀνήρ), that your noble mind continue steadfast; I beg you, O invisible mind, that you may be preserved yourself." Here it is absolutely and explicitly clear that through celibacy the female ceases to be a woman. The passage could practically appear in Philo.

42. See, however, n. 22 above.

43. Interestingly, there is a unique historical case which suggests that this structure remained dormant even in Judaism as a marginal possibility. I refer to the one case of a post-biblical Jewish woman who functioned as an independent religious authority on the same level as men, the famous nineteenth-century "Maid of Ludmir," and precisely the same mechanism operates, autonomy and religious leadership for a woman as an equal to men but only because she is celibate and therefore *not a woman*. Indeed, as soon as she engaged in marriage, at the age of forty, at the urging of male religious authorities—and a celibate marriage at that—her religious power disappeared, *because she had revealed that she really was a woman, and not a man in a woman's body,* nor an asexual androgyne. See Rapoport-Alpert 1988.

44. For the antiquity in Greece of the theme of women becoming male, see Saxonhouse (1992, 57–58), who traces it back at least to Aeschylus. Incidentally, Simon Peter's declaration in this text that women do not deserve life should be contrasted to the explicit statement in the Talmud that women must pray just as men do, "because do not women require life?" (Kiddushin 34b).

45. This also suggests that it is not so obvious that the only direction of such gender blending or bending was from female to male, even for a misogynist like Philo, a fortiori for less misogynist Jews and Christians, even though it is not to be denied, of course, that the usual image was of a female becoming male.

46. This story, as well as that of Thekla, has, of course, been discussed by myriad critics and commentators.

47. For martyrdom as victory, see Revelation 3:21.

48. In this light, the fact that the *Gospel of Thomas* most likely originates in

the most rigidly celibate of all early "Orthodox" churches, the Syrian church, takes on particular significance. See Meeks (1973, 194); Richardson 1973.

49. According to Stevan Davies, these texts were produced by women very similar in social status to the "virgins" of Philo, older women who either were unmarried or had left their husbands (1980). Even Dennis Ronald Macdonald (1984), who disagrees with Davies, still agrees that the oral sources of these texts were produced among celibate women.

50. Once more, I emphasize that neither they nor the Jewish women may have experienced their lives the way we predict owing to our own cultural prejudices.

51. Incidentally, Fiorenza errs when she writes there that in rabbinic Judaism, "even the full proselyte could not achieve the status of the male Israelite." This does not affect, however, her larger claim that the constitution of the Christian community through baptism was intended to be something entirely different from the solidarities of physical kinship that characterized Judaism. This fundamental change in the notion of kinship did not produce, however, only and always welcome sociocultural effects, as Jews and Native Americans (among others) know only too well. (See Chapters 1 above and 9 and 10 below for further discussion.)

52. This should not be taken as a totalizing statement denying wives (either in Christianity or in rabbinic Judaism) all freedom and subjectivity; indeed, it is not inconsistent with the notion that married women could have positions of at least partial leadership in the Pauline churches. Cf. Fiorenza (1983, 232–33).

53. In this sense, then, Paul essentially agrees with the Corinthians as to the way to gender equality (cf. Wire 1990, 65 and especially 90), but Paul sees what he takes to be negative social and moral effects of the wrong people attempting to achieve such status. We need not necessarily accept as "historically" accurate Paul's evaluation of the situation. Anne Wire has argued that Paul's position involved a great deal of oppression of the Corinthian women, "Apparently Paul sets out to persuade women to give up what they have gained through sexual abstinence in order that the community and Christ himself may be saved from immorality" (79). I think that Wire's rereading of 1 Corinthians 6 and 7 is of great significance for our *evaluation* of Paul here, although for reasons I shall immediately lay out, not for our *interpretation*. By a very careful and close reading Wire has arrived at the following conclusions vis-à-vis this section of his text: Paul is primarily concerned with male immorality, and his injunctions to marry fall on women to provide legitimate sexual outlets for men, so that they will not fall into porneia. This includes those Corinthian women who have already achieved a high degree of spiritual fulfillment, who are now commanded to renounce this achievement for the sake of providing sexual service to men not called to the celibate life. Paul's discourse is, on this reading, considerably more compromised ethically than I have allowed above, in that its hierarchical imbalance falls on all women, including those successfully called to the celibate life. The consequence of Wire's brilliant reconstruction is "Paul's agreement with the Corinthians concerning gender equality on principle is strictly a rhetorical ploy if he is, as you say, ruled by the 'negative social and moral effects of the wrong people attempting to achieve such status'" (from Wire's response at Center for Hermeneutical Studies).

It is here, however, that I wish to introduce a nuance, which, if it be apologetic, at least is not compromised by being apology for my own religious tradition, although there may be another factor working here: As a male Jew, all too aware of the gap between my own aspirations toward feminism and the shortcomings of my practice, I may be drawn to forgiving perceived—or constructed—analogous failures on the part of a forefather of sorts. Nevertheless, even given all the details of Wire's construction of the Corinthian women prophets and Paul's repressive reaction to them, I think we do not need to conclude that his agreement with them in principle is "strictly a rhetorical ploy," but rather, I think a genuine and failed vision. Whether the baptismal formula in Galatians 3:28 is, as I suppose, a reflection of the primal androgyne interpretation of Genesis 1:28 or a radical re-writing of Genesis in the new creation of Christ, as Wire proposes, I think that it genuinely holds out the vision of social equality for all human beings. Paul, how-ever, I argue, simply cannot think himself to an adequate social arrangement with equality for the sexes other than chastity, which for one reason or another he considers to be an unworkable solution at the present time. And yes, I agree, it may very well be that it is unworkable because of *male* sexual need in his view, and women may be the servants, for him, of that need; nevertheless, I think that he as well as the Corinthians, as opposed to rabbinic Judaism, envisions an end to gender hierarchy. In any case, if on the one hand, Wire points to the devastating history of male oppression of women in the name of Paul, one can also cite at least a nascent discourse and real history of chastity as female autonomy also carried out in his name, in what is, after all, the Acts of Paul and Thekla for notable example. Similarly, with regard to the parallel issue of slavery. Philemon has been used (maybe misused) as a text in the service of slavery. It is just as true, however, that Galatians 3:28 has been mobilized in anti-slavery discourses. The failure of con-sistency here involves not Paul's aspirations but his achievements. Others who come after may indeed be able to put into practice that which in Paul is fraught with contradiction. I think that the ultimate elimination of slavery in all of the Christian world is an eloquent case in point, although it took nearly two thousand years for Paul's vision to be realized here.

Richard Hays, on the other hand, suggests to me that in this verse, Paul is already into his discourse on the already married, and all he is saying is that those who are married should not become celibate. This interpretation would only strengthen my overall case. I am not entirely convinced, however, that this is the only way to read the verse, since then v. 3 would seem redundant. My take on the verse is rather that Paul is echoing—approvingly, and this is crucial—that which the Corinthians had written, namely, that celibacy is ideal. Paul agrees with them strongly, for he later repeats the theme of the free virgin, but qualifies their "extremism." On this whole section, Wimbush 1987 can also be profitably consulted.

CHAPTER 9

1. For exceptions, see Sanders (1983: 193–94). I agree with Sanders's reading, as far as it goes, against that of the Stendahl tradition. Altogether, let me say, with a certain amount of hutzpah, that I find the second section of Sanders's book on the Jews uniformly successful while, as will be clear from my discussions, I have some problems with the first part on the Law.

2. It is thus very hard for me, a Jew, to see how Romans 9–11, even taken by themselves, "could be interpreted in a pro-Jewish sense" (Marxsen, quoted approvingly in Campbell [1992, 28; see also 40n. 37]).

3. The point is that, for me, "upholding the special place of Jewish Christianity" (Campbell 1992, 51) is precisely the essence of supersession. This does not, however, make it illegitimate or "anti-Semitic." My point is rather to maintain the distinctiveness of Paul's version of Judaism over against most other versions contemporary with it and the rabbinic Judaism that developed in the succeeding centuries which insisted on the special task of Jews precisely in maintaining the works of the Law and had no interest in faith in Jesus. This is—translated into our terms—a genuine commitment to the maintenance of cultural difference, not a pseudo-multicultural Christian hegemony in which it does not matter in what language the Mass is sung. Because, however, at any point in my dialectic its antithesis may be forgotten by readers, I emphasize yet again that it is a dialectic, and I will be arguing extensively in these two chapters that both thesis and antithesis have their perils and promises.

4. There is an interpretative tradition that reads the "first fruits" as Christ himself; however, this interpretation is weakened considerably by the parallelism of the second clause.

5. Note that Luther himself was very "friendly" toward Jews at first. He was not, therefore, an anti-Semite. But once he realized that he was not going to be able to convert the Jews, he turned against them with a vengeance.

6. It is precisely at this point that I think that Campbell misses the mark in his reading. He takes v. 19, "You will say 'branches were broken off so that I might be grated in,'" to be that which Paul is disavowing. In fact, Campbell argues, "It is to repudiate such formulations that Paul writes Romans 9–11 and possibly the entire letter" (71). This is simply not the case, however, as the context clearly shows. Paul himself has proposed that the branches have been lopped off only two verses before, and his response to this utterance is "granted!" He does not oppose the doctrine of the lopped-off branches; indeed, it is he who has proposed it; he just does not want the gentile Christians to draw "anti-Semitic" conclusions from the metaphor, a clear and present danger, realized only slightly after his death.

7. A further argument for this point is the fact that Paul already knows of precisely twelve apostles. As Paula Fredriksen argues, the necessity for this precise (and clearly ahistorical) number is the association it bears with the twelve tribes and thus its implicit claim that the Christian community is the New Israel (Fredriksen 1988, 102).

8. See below on Justin Martyr. The notion of particularist universalism is drawn and cited from the work of my brother, Jonathan Boyarin. Compare the interpretation of this passage in Gager (1983, 60–61).

9. Below I will argue, however, that Paul was not *responsible* for that history, in that his position of power vis-à-vis Jews was entirely different from that of the Church—in fact, almost directly opposite. Discourses of resistance have entirely different political, ethical valences from discourses of domination, even when they share identical contents (Foucault 1980, 101–02)!

10. Cf. Galatians 3:19.

11. This should not be understood as an analogical relationship, i.e., of the body of the individual and the social body, but as an actual implication. If I am my body, then I am ontologically filiated with other bodies. The move from family to "nation" or "race" is, however, accomplished via the myth of origin of the cultural group in a single progenitor. For the close connection between "race," filiation, and even place, see the quotation from Porphyry's *Life of Plotinus* in the next chapter.

12. On the other hand, we must take very seriously the differences between the historical situation of Paul, persecuted by Jews (or Jewish Christians), Justin, a co-victim with Jews of Roman persecution but also in some ways underdog in the pagan world vis-à-vis Jews, and Augustine, at the threshold of Christian hegemony and Jewish marginalization. The very important analyses of John Gager are highly relevant here, especially: "We are now able to affirm that wherever Christianity developed abroad in the cities and towns of the Empire, it encountered a well-established, self-confident, and widely appreciated Judaism. Furthermore, this non-Palestinian encounter between the two religions took place at precisely the time when positive elements in pagan views of Judaism appeared with greatest clarity. Once again Christianity had to deal with Judaism from beneath, that is, from a position of cultural and social inferiority" (1983, 114).

13. In a very important communication, Richard Hays writes:

Right. Your analysis is brilliant and telling [I trust I will be forgiven the narcissism that leads me to leave this phrase in.]. The question—the huge question that runs through the whole book—is to what extent that disavowal has actually taken place in Paul. I say it hasn't, you say it has. I think that Paul's thought is dialectical, complex, full of contradictory impulses. A later Christian-Platonist-allegorizing tradition develops one side of Paul's dialectic to the exclusion of the other and thus produces precisely the result you describe. But I would contend that the one-sidedness of the development produces a position fundamentally unfaithful to Paul's vision.
(personal communication, March 10, 1993)

I would agree that any understanding of Paul, as of any truly great and complex cultural production, is likely to be a reduction, but, I would argue, this interpretation of Paul responds to so much that is there that it can hardly be a position "*fundamentally* unfaithful to Paul's vision." To argue such is to (somewhat triumphantly) suggest that the Fathers could not understand Paul and that *only* we can! Rather, I would suggest that in order to be adequate to Paul's dialectics, our interpretations should be allowed to enter into their own dialectics, as precisely the controversy for the sake of Heaven that perdures. For the notion of interpretation as constant dialectic, see Boyarin 1990b. In other words, I am saying that strong readings that develop one side of Paul intensely are more likely to be of hermeneutic usefulness than others. Either we are revealing unresolvable tensions within Paul, or at another level, the dialectic will resolve itself into a synthesis.

14. Compare, however, the readings of these chapters, which I have offered above in Chapters 1 and 2, respectively, of this book.

15. I would like to see what evidence Käsemann has for the malice in this joy at finding a verse which clearly discredits the Reformation Paul.

16. "I regard most of the quoted material [from Käsemann] to be more or less blatant eisegesis, even if eisegesis which rests on long and venerated (perhaps too venerated) tradition. The finding that Paul criticized his kinsmen for zeal for good works is simply bewildering" (Sanders 1983, 155–56).

17. Käsemann would probably detect some "malicious joy" here as well. See also Wilckens (1982, 1 : 177 and passim).

18. That this is a correct reading of Romans 2 is practically proven by Paul's rhetorical question at the beginning of 3. "Then what advantage has the Jew?"!

19. I do not, therefore, accept Watson's conclusion from his excellent analysis that "Paul does not attack Judaism because of any theoretical incompatibility between his own emphasis on grace and the alleged Jewish emphasis on achievement. He attacks it because Jewish failure to respond to the gospel has led him to proclaim a law-free gospel to the Gentiles, and to form congregations living in sectarian separation from the Jewish community. His attack on Judaism serves to establish and maintain that sectarian separation" (113). The first sentence of these two seems impeccable to me; the second could not be less convincing. And they are a non sequitur, because rejection of the Lutheran premise that Paul attacks Judaism as works-righteousness does not yet lead to a conclusion that therefore his critique was not theological or ideological but sociological (Watson makes it almost sound petulant—You don't play by my rules, I'll take my football). I can see nothing in the Pauline texts or even in Watson's reading of them that necessitates such an extreme conclusion, rather than the assumption that Paul turned to the gentiles out of ideological conviction, abandoned the Law (or effectively those parts of it which mark off Jewish identity) because it did not fit his theology, and critiqued those very aspects of the Law as non-salvific. In other words, I am arguing that the formation of a sect comes as a result of Paul's theology and not as the effective cause of that theology. I also find implausible his suggestion that Paul is, in effect, throwing back a Jewish charge—Let us do evil that good may come—at the Jewish leaders "who stress the divine gift of the covenant as the guarantee of salvation to such an extent that obedience to the law becomes superfluous" (113). As Watson himself admits, were this the content of Paul's attack it would be more like a parody than a convincing representation of most authentic views of the Covenant. Much more likely, I think, is an interpretation which simply argues (as most Jews would have argued) that membership in the covenant community without works is meaningless. Once more, Paul would secure the assent of that very Jew whom at the end he is going to accuse. The real payoff of the diatribe is at its end, where Paul redefines entirely what "works" means. On this last point, see next section below.

20. Cf. Watson (1986, 118) who has exposed Käsemann's incoherence and embarrassment.

21. In other words, what I am suggesting is that Käsemann also understands (consciously or unconsciously) that the Pauline text does not support his theology and weasels out of this (again consciously or unconsciously) by treating as identical two things (one that Paul says and one that Luther says) that are entirely different.

22. This is even more shocking when one remembers that this text was originally a radio broadcast. Nor is Käsemann alone in this form of expression, even

among postwar German critics: "For Paul, the Jew represents man in general. . . . This man is indeed not somewhere outside, among unbelievers; he is hidden within each Christian," to which my only response can be: No, I'm not. The quotation is from Bornkamm in Watson (1986, 198 n. 78). Note that Käsemann's usage of the hidden Jew is precisely opposite to Paul's, for whom the hidden Jew is a positive term. It is the ἐν τῷ κρυπτῷ 'Ιουδαῖος who is the true Jew for Paul!

23. Which is not to say that I ascribe the Nazi genocide of the Jews entirely to the Lutheran theological tradition.

24. See, e.g., my comparison with John Chrysostom below. Hamerton-Kelly's book is the very antithesis in every respect, both morally and scholarly, of the work of his teacher, W. D. Davies!

25. See citation below.

26. It is entirely unclear from where Hamerton-Kelly derives his notion that fulfilling the Mosaic Law would have led to the killing of Christ. Cf. on this point the devastating comments of Paula Fredriksen (1988, 108).

27. That is, the sort of violence that Hamerton-Kelly seems to wish to essentialize as "Jewish" per se did exist in certain extreme groups in the first century, but those very groups were marginalized by the terms of opprobrium assigned to them by other groups, including notably the Pharisees!

28. Even though I *do* interpret "When we were in the flesh" to mean when we inhabited the literal, fleshy world of Jewish existence—fleshy because of its commandments to circumcise, to eat this way and not that, and especially to procreate, this does not begin to approach Hamerton-Kelly's gloss of this verse. It would be quite a different thing to say that Paul is saying that sin exploits the situation of being in the flesh, that is, as Paul says explicitly, that sin exploits the commandment of the Torah. See above, Chapter 7.

29. His rhetorical move reminds me of that of John Chrysostom who in his violent attacks on Judaism pauses to remark, "I know that some will condemn me for daring to say that the synagogue is no better than a theater" (cited in Gager 1983, 119), but "he will not be deterred." Such also is Hamerton-Kelly's "courage," vaunted in the blurbs on the jacket. Compare also the discussion of Tertullian's anti-Judaism in Gager, "For him the Jews are the very anti-type [*sic*] of true virtue: they resisted the prophets and Jesus; they insult and persecute Christians; they rebel against God. Their crimes are manifold. They embody the principle of *vetustas*, or obsolescence. In short, what emerges in Tertullian [Hamerton-Kelly] is a rekindling of traditional Christian anti-Judaism in which the full burden of Marcion's assault of the God of the Jews is deflected onto the Jews themselves. And in his case, the intensity of language clearly crosses the boundary between anti-Judaism and anti-Semitism" (164).

30. Girard and Oughourlian have tried to guard against the sort of misreading that Hamerton-Kelly engages in; on pp. 174–75, they explicitly refer to the transformation "of the universal revelation of the founding murder into a polemical denunciation of the Jewish religion"—precisely that which Hamerton-Kelly engages in and which Girard refers to as "a new form of violence, directed against a new scapegoat—the Jew." Not only a bad reader of Paul, therefore, Hamerton-Kelly is also, owing to his anti-Semitic passion, a highly selective and superficial

reader of Girard as well! Girard himself also falls into supersessionist patterns of thought and expression. The following quotation is exemplary:

> I think it is possible to show that only the texts of the Gospels manage to achieve what the Old Testament leaves incomplete [in the transumption of Sacred Violence into harmonious community]. These texts therefore serve as an extension of the Judaic bible, bringing to completion an enterprise that the Judaic bible did not take far enough, as Christian tradition has always maintained.
>
> (Girard 1978, 158)

This is supersessionist because it refuses to recognize that there was/is another "extension of the Judaic bible," which has also continued historical cultural processes that began within the biblical period. Insofar as Girard will refer to Christianity as "the religion which comes from God," while Judaism (and everything else) is relegated to being "religion which comes from man," he can hardly expect non-Christians to be very interested in his work (166), which is ultimately theologically based Christian apologetic triumphalism. However, nothing in Girard's writings, to the extent that I know them, prepares one for the virulence of Hamerton-Kelly's anti-Judaism, which is all his own. Just comparing Girard's account of the crucifixion as having been given "explicit or implicit assent" by "the crowd in Jerusalem, the Jewish religious authorities, the Roman political authorities, and even the disciples" (Girard 1978, 167) with Hamerton-Kelly's "the impulse to fulfill the Mosaic Law [that] made him [Paul] a persecutor and had killed Christ" (141) makes the disparity apparent.

On the other hand, Girard's text is sufficiently problematic on its own, at least in part because of the dialogical (literally as a dialogue) way that it is presented. Girard speaks of a founding murder which lies behind all culture—that is, it is constitutive of hominization, something which is hidden since the foundation of the world, while his interlocutor (Oughourlian) transmutes this into "cultural *differentiation* develops on the basis of the founding murder" (165, emphasis added), and Girard does not protest. It is thus easy to see how a personality dedicated to the erasure of difference and imposition of Christianity on all could find his (mistaken) point of origin in Girard. Girard's text hovers around the pit of a Christian triumphalism (and implicit anti-Semitism) which it avoids, while Hamerton-Kelly jumps right in.

31. He dismisses the challenge of modern Christian New Testament scholars (such as Mack) to the simple veracity of the gospel accounts. He also simply reads Luke into Paul.

32. The discussion of Lyotard and Nancy here owes much to two essays and in general to the thought of my brother Jonathan: "Der Yiddisher Tsenter; or, What Is a Minyan?" (forthcoming), and Jonathan Boyarin and Greg Sarris, "Jews and Native Americans as Living Voice and Absent Other," presented at MLA, December 1991. In general, it has been startling to watch our work converging in recent years. He begins with the present and looks for its genealogies; I begin in late antiquity and observe its effects even now. Much of the language of this and the next section on Nancy has been adapted from a joint paper of ours (Boyarin

and Boyarin 1993). Here, typically, the account of Lyotard and Nancy is his; its connection with Paul is mine.

33. Lest there be confusion, I of course endorse Isaac Deutscher's actual point that modern Jewish radicals who do not practice the Jewish religion nevertheless represent an appropriate way of performing Jewishness in the contemporary world (Deutscher 1968).

34. I am not here pursuing the issue that Fuss argues so well, namely that all constructivist positions are founded on essentialism, and my account of Lacan and Derrida is largely derivative of hers. My concern is rather to demonstrate how "deconstructive" positions are complicitous with idealizations that go back to Paul for Christian Europe and ultimately deeply back into Greek culture.

35. She argues, of course, that the distinction ultimately collapses back on itself, an important point, which is, however, not relevant for my argument here. My entire next book (tentative title *Antiphallus*) will be devoted to this subject.

36. Of course, this remark of Derrida's presupposes a certain interpretation of psychoanalysis, one dissented from by Johnson herself, as well as others. The argument may prove thus more compelling with regard to patristic allegoresis than to Lacanian psychoanalysis.

37. A disclaimer is necessary here to ward off misunderstanding. I am not suggesting that Jewish culture is eo ipso anti-logocentric simply because it retains the literal sense of circumcision, or for any other reason. In fact, I would argue, and have argued elsewhere, that from the early Middle Ages onward, Jewish culture is virtually indistinguishable from Christianity in its hermeneutic stances; by then, both cultures have significantly evolved, so that Christianity has developed material practices and communal identities and memories similar to those of the Jews, while Judaism has been thoroughly imbued with platonism. The result is often a Judaism in the Middle Ages that is quite similar in structure to that of Philo. For a somewhat more extensive version of this claim, see the first chapter of Boyarin 1993. I say this in part in response to two recent critics of my work, who have read an essentialist characterization of "Jewish" versus "Greco-Christian" cultures here. I would hope that the larger context of the argument in this book will displace such misunderstandings. I am proposing rather that Paul emphasized certain strands in the Greco-Jewish culture that he inherited, thus yielding his "universalist" variety of Christianity, while rabbinic Judaism reacted against those very strands, producing a "particularism" even more pronounced than that of the Bible. Both are thus products of the interaction of ancient Hebrew culture with Hellenism. Finally, I have mightily tried to expel any vestiges of a Jewish triumphalism from this dialectical co-critique. I may not have entirely succeeded, for obviously I make no bones about being a critical but committed Jew.

CHAPTER 10

1. See Sander Gilman, who writes, "The concept of 'race' is so poisoned in Western society that it is difficult to imagine how it can be resurrected" (Gilman 1991, 242).

2. Witness the "ethnic cleansing" of Muslims and Croats from the space of

Serbian "autochthony." This double-edged sword of accounts of origin is precisely captured by Spivak: "The notion of origin is as broad and robust and full of affect as it is imprecise. 'History lurks in it somewhere,' I had written, but now I think that sentence would have to be revised: History slouches in it, ready to comfort *and* kill" (Spivak 1992, 781).

3. Augustine, *Tractatus adversus Judaeos*, vii, 9.

4. For the disturbing nature of women, see Saxonhouse: "The poets introduce the female as a constant reminder of the diversity out of which the world was made and as a constant warning against the attempt to see the world as a uniform whole and, therefore, subject to simple answers and rational control" (1992, 53, and see also 57). See also Bloch 1991, 31–32.

5. At least until new "pagans" were discovered in the early modern period. See next note.

6. Lawton 1993 is, inter alia, a remarkable documentation of this process. One of the most stunning moments in this book (from my point of view) is Lawton's citation of the recent (1985) translation of the gospel for the benefit of the Panare People of the Amazon, a translation that reads:

> The Panare killed Jesus Christ
> because they were wicked
> Let's kill Jesus Christ
> said the Panare.
> The Panare seized Jesus Christ.
> The Panare killed in this way.
> They laid a cross on the ground.
> They fastened his hands and his feet
> against the wooden beams, with nails.
> They raised him straight up, nailed.
> The man died like that, nailed.
> Thus the Panare killed Jesus Christ.

Lawton cites this text from Lewis 1988, and then glosses it:

> The new theology is used to predict the Panares' punishment; and that punishment is of course the destruction of their rainforest habitat and the traditional life-style that goes with it. God wants the Panare to wear American clothes, use soap, and have sweet-smelling orifices. The discourse of guilt for the Crucifixion is treated here as a transferable discourse justifying persecution and exploitation. Seeing it in this form, we can recognise it for what it is, and so identify the traditional role of the Jews in it. The Panare are non-Christians; they are therefore blasphemers, and so must be the subject of conversion whether they wish it or not. As blasphemers, they are able to assume the role of the Jews in the trial of Jesus. From the gospels onward, blasphemy is Greek for Jew.

7. This "Jewish" resistance to dualism and the Ideal can even be claimed for the christology of the Jewish Christians, the Ebionites, who into the third century claimed that Jesus was the crucified and risen Messiah but "solely and normally human." This insistence on a single, physical, literal existence for Christ was

paralleled, of course, by literal observance of Jewish Law including, of course, circumcision. (Fredriksen 1988, 213).

8. The analogy itself has been previously remarked by Anthony Appiah (1985, 35).

9. Cp. Balibar (in a quite different historical context): "In fact racism figures *both* on the side of the universal and the particular" (1991b, 54). Also Connolly (1991, 41).

10. Fredriksen cites abundant evidence to the effect that in antiquity Jews permitted gentiles to attend the synagogue without conversion, even if they continued to worship idols (1988, 149–51)! "As long as a group thinks that its moral code applies only to itself, it will make no effort to impose it on others. Orthodox Jews, believing that the dietary laws of *kashrut* are binding only on Jews, have never tried to prevent gentiles from eating pork and shellfish" (Greenberg 1988, 6–7).

11. Thus, as Marc Shell points out, "Moses Mendelssohn in his *Jerusalem* tried to steer the ideology of a universalist Enlightenment . . . away from what he took to be its probably inevitable course towards barbarism. . . . In the Germany of his day Jews were pressured to renounce their faith in return for civil equality and union with the Christian majority. The pressure was kindly, but it was also a form of intolerance towards non-kin" (Shell 1991, 331).

12. On this point see Gilman (1991, 25–27).

13. In California, certain missionaries had thousands of Indian babies killed, so that their souls would be saved before their bodies could sin.

14. "Virtually" no one, because Judith Butler (1990), for one, denies precisely this reality. See also Butler 1991b, 19. My position seems to me closer to that of Luce Irigaray, for instance, who writes, "The human species is divided into *two genders* [*sic*] which ensure its production and reproduction. To wish to get rid of sexual difference is to call for a genocide more radical than any form of destruction there has even been in History" (Irigaray 1993, 12). I have my problems with the apocalyptic tenor of this comment; even disaggregated bodies can, after all, get pregnant. But I do think that it answers to a fundamental sensibility of how culture has always been built on the material base of reproduction, and how, therefore, the difference between male and female may indeed be somatically "hard-wired" into our psyches/cultures. See also in quite a different vein E. Cohen: "You see, I *feel* there *is* something 'different' about the body: I *believe* feeling is the difference that bodies make, a difference that *moves* people to action" (1991, 84).

15. I am not ignoring the qualification in the "may be." This leaves room for positions such as that of Judith Butler.

16. It is important for me to emphasize that it is a category error to assume that social constructionism is coextensive with the notion that gay and lesbian people can change if they want to (Epstein 1992, 242). Sedgwick (1990, 40) has remarked the confusion of these two categories, which she refers to as the "phylogenetic" and "ontogenetic" questions. She is absolutely correct in the ways that the debate has been willy-nilly implicated in homophobic projects, *but only, I would claim, insofar as the question of "ontogeny"—the determination of the causes of heterosexuality in the individual—is concerned.* I, for my part, think that this question of "ontogeny" has never properly been part of the issue to start with. Below I will

return to this question, for I think that in this distinction lies the key to a proper understanding of Aristophanes's speech in the *Symposium* as well. I could not agree more with Sedgwick when she says "that gay-affirmative work does well when it aims to minimize its reliance on any particular account of the origin of sexual preference and identity in individuals" (41). The historical constructionist position has nothing whatsoever to say about the origin of sexual preference in individuals. It has only to do with the sociocultural characterizations which determine whether people who prefer this or that kind of sexual behavior are anatomized as a taxonomically significant human type. Preferable, perhaps, to thinking of the issue as a question of the origins of homosexuality would be thinking of it as having to do with the origins of homophobia—or maybe with the origins of heterosexuality. It certainly has nothing to do with "gay [!] origins" (*pace* Sedgwick 1990, 43). Insisting on a constructionist position will not, then, deprive gay people of the right to their identity but only of homophobia of its claims to be natural.

17. Similarly, Epstein seems to me right on target when he writes that "a gay or lesbian identity might have a clear resonance for individuals without necessarily binding them to any specific definition of what that identity 'means'" (274). I would suggest that this is true of other types of identity as well.

18. "A racism which does not have the pseudo-biological concept of race as its main driving force has always existed, and it has existed at exactly the level of secondary theoretical elaborations. Its prototype is anti-Semitism. Modern anti-Semitism—the form which begins to crystalize in the Europe of the Enlightenment, if not, indeed, from the period in which the Spain of the *Reconquista* and the Inquisition gave a statist, nationalistic inflexion to theological anti-Judaism—is *already* a 'culturalist' racism" (Balibar 1991a, 23). See also Thompson (1989, 16).

19. This last point is, however, an excellent argument for the social constructedness of races, because only fifty years ago there *were* physical characteristics that marked Jews' bodies off from the bodies of others. Sander Gilman's recent book (1991) is a sustained demonstration of this point. Not only gentiles but Jewish doctors were absolutely convinced, for instance, that the Jewish foot was constructed differently from the gentile one.

20. On this point, see also the very moving and convincing discussion by Sedgwick (1990, 42–43).

21. In his remarkable *Identity\difference: Democratic Negotiations of Political Paradox*, William E. Connolly has asked the same question in quite different terms. Referring to the formation of identity as an attempt to solve what he calls the "first problem of evil," he argues that this very formation often produces "a second problem of evil," namely, the violence toward Others that shores up identity. Then, "the Augustinian definition of Manicheanism as heresy and of Greek polytheism as paganism provides two exemplifications of the politics of identity and difference. That politics contains the second problem of evil moving silently inside the first one. The question now becomes: Is it possible to counter the second problem of evil without eliminating the functions served by identity" (8). Although I read Connolly's book just as I was finishing this manuscript, it seems to me that he anticipated in quite different terms some of the directions of my argument here. It is fascinating to me to see the different results achieved when Augustine and not Paul is the starting point for the inquiry into identity and differ-

ence, since Paul, after all, did not set out to define an abject Other in quite the same way that Augustine did.

22. As Connolly argues, "to engage the second problem of evil [see above n. 21], it is necessary to practice the arts of experimental detachment of the self from the identity installed within it, even though these are slippery, ambiguous arts hardly susceptible to full realization" (9).

23. And as such was hotly contested within Spanish Christendom. See Balibar (1991b, 52). Also Simms (1992, 45–46).

24. Among the telling points that Shell makes is the very fact that Spain was defined as a *Germania,* that is, a union of siblings-german, siblings by seed, consanguinity (311).

25. This move is not by any means limited to gentile critics. Certain "liberal Zionists" blame everything that has "gone wrong" with Israel on the residues of biblical sensibility that have not been eradicated successfully enough.

26. Note how such an utterance completely reproduces precisely the ideology that it would question, for the societies under consideration would have us believe that Scripture underwrites their practice directly. Akenson's position, which I will further criticize below, demonstrates a fundamental lack of understanding of, at least, traditional modes of Jewish biblical interpretation. In general, his reading of the Bible is highly unbalanced. He is certainly right in opposing apologists who would gloss over the corrosive or "sulphurous" aspects of the Bible (10), but he is hardly justified, for instance, in his conclusion (based on one verse in a psalm) that "it is a small and natural step in covenantal thinking to affirm that the possession of might (whether in the form of economic prosperity or military power) is evidence that one is morally right" (16), since myriad biblical texts that directly contravene such a claim could be adduced. In other words, those who would derive the "Protestant ethic" from Hebrew Scripture are not obeying a genetic code but producing a reading of the text, one that, like all readings, is tendentious and ideologically informed. By suggesting that it is a "genetic code," then, Akenson simply endorses the hermeneutical stance not only of the society but of its most reactionary elements.

27. The attempt of some modern ultranationalist groups calling themselves Orthodox to reconfigure the Palestinians as the "five nations" and thereby reactivate the command to drive them out of the Land is thus an act of radical religious revisionism and not a continuation of rabbinic Judaism. The so-called ultra-Orthodox in Israel reject such views—as indeed many Orthodox nationalists do also. As I correct proof (in March 1994) I note that such nationalist revisionism has now borne the bitterest fruit of all—the Hebron mass murder.

28. This proposal, of a diaspora deterritorialized Jewish identity, is hardly new. It has a genealogy ranging from the historian Shimᶜon Dubnov to George Steiner and Philip Roth.

29. "It is easy for us now to read, say, Proust as the most expert operator of our modern technologies for dismantling taxonomies of the person. For the emergence and persistence of the vitalizing worldly taxonomic energies on which Proust also depends, however, we have no theoretical support to offer. And these defalcations in our indispensable antihumanist discourses have apparently ceded the potentially forceful ground of profound, complex variation to humanist liberal 'tolerance' or

repressively trivializing celebration at best, to reactionary suppression at worst" (Sedgwick 1990, 24).

30. It should, however, be emphasized that political Zionism is not the only form that the movement historically took. Prior to the formation of the State of Israel, there were various movements calling themselves Zionist that proposed creating concentrations of Jews in Palestine without seeking political hegemony or statehood, including some, indeed, for whom such aspirations were anathema. The ideas of some of these groups, including the highly progressive ones of Judah Magnes and Martin Buber, could come much closer to my notion of multicultural—Diasporized—states than the eventually dominant political Zionism has.

31. A highly ingenuous, or more likely egregiously disingenuous, claim of Abba Eban's (from a letter to W. D. Davies) is given the lie in every page of Israeli history and particularly the last ones. Beersheba may have been "virtually empty," but that provides little consolation to the Bedouin who were and continue to be constantly dispossessed there and in its environs, and the refugees in camps in Gaza as well as the still visible ruins of their villages would certainly dispute the claim that Arab populations had avoided "the land of the Philistines in the coastal plain . . . because of insalubrious conditions." Abba Eban quoted in Davies (1992, 76).

32. Early in the Intifada, the Palestinians, acknowledging that the Zionists would never accept a secular, democratic, binational state in all of Palestine, reverted to the notion of two separate ethnic states. The Palestinian version of this vision still expresses much more interdependence and contact than most "liberal" Zionist versions.

33. As this is being written (June 1993), the Palestinian people are being held behind military roadblocks, cut off from sources of livelihood and even from their cultural, administrative, medical [!] center, Jerusalem. This so-called "closure" has divided the Palestinian West Bank into three hermetically sealed Bantustans—and this by the so-called liberal Labor government with the full support of its coalition partner, "The Citizens' Rights Party." Advertising campaigns in Israeli elections for parties that support "two states" tend to portray their solution as one of (relative) ethnic purification of the Israeli state. Nor, obviously, is this only true in Palestine/Israel, since it is also taking place in both south-central Europe and central Asia as well. (Nor has much changed, in my opinion, as I review these observations in December of that year, famous handshakes notwithstanding.)

34. Note that this point is not incompatible with the notion of Zionism as a national liberation struggle (a description that I neither fully ascribe to nor entirely reject). Balibar has shown the complicity, indeed implicature, between national liberation struggles and racisms. "Racism is constantly emerging out of nationalism. . . . And nationalism emerges out of racism, in the sense that it would not constitute itself as the ideology of a 'new' nation if the official nationalism against which it were reacting were not profoundly racist: thus Zionism comes out of anti-Semitism and Third World nationalisms come out of colonial racism" (Balibar 1991b, 53, and see also 57). Following this line, it is not only anti-Semitism that is "the socialism of fools."

35. For the ideological functions of myths of autochthony, see Saxonhouse (1992, 51–52, and esp. 111–31).

36. Davies remarks there that this sense of "bad conscience" can be found in texts as late as the first century B.C. I think that he underestimates; this factor can still be found much later. The classical midrash on Genesis, Bereshith Rabba, a product of the fourth and fifth centuries C.E., begins with the question: Why does the Torah open with the creation of the world, and answers, so that when the Nations will call Israel robbers for their theft of the Land, they will be able to point to the Torah and say: God created the earth and can dispose of it at his will!

37. See Schwartz (1992, 142) for an even more nuanced reading of tensions within the Davidic stories themselves. Schwartz's forthcoming book will deal with many of the themes of identity in the Bible that this chapter is treating, albeit with quite different methods and often with quite different results.

38. It is important to emphasize that this analysis is indifferent to the historical question of whether there were nomadic Israelite tribes to begin with or the thesis (made most famous by the work of Norman Gottwald [1979]) which ascribes to these tribes a "retribalization" process taking place among "native" Canaanites. For discussion of this thesis, see Berger, 131–32. For my purposes here, the *representations* of the tribes as nomadic and the ideological investments in that representation are indifferent to the "actual" history.

39. Classical Zionism was, after all, a *secular* movement. This is why claims that Zionism is based on the Promised Land theology fall rather flat.

40. Also: "The desert is, therefore, the place of revelation and of the constitution of 'Israel' as a people; there she was elected" (1992, 39). Davies's book is remarkable for many reasons; one of them is surely the way that while it intends to be a defense and explanation of Zionism as a deeply rooted Jewish movement, it consistently and honestly documents the factors in the tradition which are in tension with such a view.

41. I think that Davies occasionally seems to lose sight of his own great insight, confusing ethnic identity with political possession (90–91 n. 10). The same mixture appears also when he associates, it seems, deterritorialization and deculturation (93). It is made clear when Davies writes, "At the same time the age-long engagement of Judaism with The Land in religious terms indicates that ethnicity and religion . . . are finally inseparable in Judaism" (97). I certainly agree that ethnicity and religion are inseparable in Judaism, but fail to see the necessary connection between ethnicity, religion, and territoriality. Moreover, a people can be on their land without this landedness being expressed in the form of a nation-state, and landedness can be shared in the same place with others who feel equally attached to the same land! This is the solution of the *Natorei Karta*, who live, after all, in Jerusalem but do not seek political hegemony over it.

42. This has led, moreover, to a discourse within Israel whereby liberal Israelis, such as the followers of the Meretz party, blame Judaism itself for the racism of Israeli political and cultural life, not noticing the difference in meaning between expressions of dominated minorities and the same expressions in the hands of a dominating majority.

43. I dissent from the conclusion of W. D. Davies that, "For religious Jews, we must conclude, The Land is ultimately inseparable from the state of Israel, however much the actualities of history have demanded their distinction" (1992, 51). Clearly, many religious Jews have not felt that way at all (Rodinson 1983, 56).

Although I do not deny entirely the theological bona fides of religious Zionism as one option for a modern Jewish religious thought, the fact that Zionists are the historical "winners" in an ideological struggle should not blind us to the fact that their option was, until only recently, only one option for religious Jews—and a very contested one at that. Even the theological "patron saint" of religious Zionists, the holy Rabbi Loewe (Maharal) of Prague, who, as pointed out by Davies, "understood the nature and role of nations to be ordained by God, part of the natural order" and held that nations "were intended to cohere rather than be scattered"; even he held that reestablishment of a Jewish state should be left to God (33). Rabbi Nahman of Bratslav's desire to touch any part of the Land and then immediately return to Poland hardly bespeaks a proto-Zionism either (33). Davies seriously nuances his own statement when he remarks "Zionism cannot be equated with a reaffirmation of the eternal relation of The Land, the people, and the Deity, except with the most cautious reservations, since it is more the expression of nationalism than of Judaism" (64). Davies is surely right, however, in his claim that something vital about historical Jewish tradition is surely missing from Petuchowski's statement that there can be a "full-blooded Judaism which is in no need to hope and to pray for a messianic return to Palestine." The desire, the longing for unity, coherence, and groundedness in the utopian future of the Messianic Age is, as Davies eminently demonstrates, virtually inseparable from historical Judaism (66). There is surely a "territorial theological tradition." At issue is rather its status in pre-Messianic praxis. There are (at least two) historically viable and religiously authentic responses. Religious Zionism is only one. The following document will make this alternative Jewish theology absolutely clear:

Statement of the Palestinian Jewish (Neturei Karta) Members of the Palestinian Delegation to the Middle East Peace Conference in Washington, D.C.

We, the Neturei Karta (Guardians of the City—Jerusalem), presently numbering in the tens of thousands, are comprised of the descendants of the pioneer Jews who settled in the Holy Land over a hundred years before the establishment of the Zionist State. Their sole motive was to serve G-d, and they had not political aspirations nor any desire to exploit the local population in order to attain statehood.

Our mission, in the capacity of Palestinian advisers, to this round of the Middle East Peace Conference, is to concern ourselves with the safeguarding of the interests of the Palestinian Jews and the entire Jewish nation. The Jewish people are charged by Divine oath not to seek independence and cast off the yoke of exile which G-d decreed, as a result of not abiding by the conditions under which G-d granted them the Holy Land. We repeat constantly in our prayers, "*since we sinned, we were therefore exiled from our land.*" G-d promised to gather in the exiled Jews through His Messiah. This is one of the principles of the Jewish faith. The Zionists rebelled against this Divine decree of exile by taking the land away from its indigenous inhabitants and established their state. Thus are the Jewish people being exposed to the Divine retribution set down in the Talmud. "*I will make your flesh prey as the deer and the antelope of the forest* (Song of

Songs 2:7). Our advice to the negotiating contingent of the Palestinian delegation will remain within the framework of Jewish theology.

Zionist schoolings dictate a doctrine of labeling the indigenous Palestinian population *"enemies,"* in order to sanction their expansionist policies. Judaism teaches that Jew and non-Jew are to co-exist in a cordial and good neighbor relationship. We Palestinian Jews have no desire to expand our places of residence and occupy our neighbors' lands, but only to live alongside the non-Jewish Palestinians, just as Jews live throughout the world, in peace and tranquility.

The enmity and animosity towards the non-Jewish population, taught to the Zionist faithful, is already boomeranging. King Solomon in Parables 27:19 describes reality: *"As one's image is reflected in water: so one's heart towards his fellow man."* (so an enemy's heart is reflected in his adversary's heart). The Intifada is exhibit A to this King Solomon gem of wisdom. We hope and pray that this face to face meeting with imagined adversaries, will undo the false image created, and that both Jew and Arab in Palestine can once again live as good neighbors as was the life of yesteryear, under a rule chosen by the indigenous residents of the Holy Land—thus conforming with G-d's plan for the Holy Land.

Inchallah!

The last word is the traditional Muslim prayer: "May it be God's [Allah's] will." The document has been transcribed here from the New York Yiddish weekly די אידישע וואכנשריפט, issue dated September 4, 1992.

44. Cf. Judith Butler, "How is it that we might ground a theory or politics in a speech situation or subject position which is 'universal' when the very category of the universal has only begun to be exposed for its own highly ethnocentric biases" (Butler 1991a, 151).

45. This is not to be taken, of course, as an uncritical affirmation of all aspects of *Natorei Karta* society, specifically their gender practices.

46. Shell argues, following Spinoza, that temporal power is necessary for toleration (1991, 328n. 75). I am suggesting the opposite: that only conditions in which power is shared between religions and ethnicities will allow for difference within common caring.

47. There simply is no gainsaying that Israeli definitions of who is and who is not a citizen are most similar to those of Germany, with two major differences: the spouses of ethnic Germans are automatic citizens, while the non-Jewish spouses of Jews are not, and Palestinians living within the Green Line are citizens of Israel, and others (but not Palestinians currently living "outside") can become naturalized as citizens of Israel. Cp. Balibar: "Racism underlies the claims for annexation ('return') to the national 'body' of 'lost' individuals and populations (for example, the Sudeten or Tyrolean Germans) which is, as is well known, closely linked to what might be called the pan-ic developments of nationalism (Pan-Slavism, Pan-Germanism, Pan-Turanianism, Pan-Arabism, Pan-Americanism. . . .)" (1991b, 59 [ellipses in original]). Zionist liberals have tended to think that the solution is a change in the definitions of "Who is a Jew?"—a topic of Israeli public life since the foundation of the State—whereas the whole force of my argument is that

traditional definitions of Jewishness have to stand, or Jewishness ends up meaning nothing and depriving people of "their" identity, and the answer to the Israeli problem is to completely sever Israeliness from Jewishness! Definitions such as "born of a Jewish mother or converted by a Rabbi (even if Conservative, Reform, and Reconstructionist Rabbis are included—the solution of the 'liberals')" cannot possibly be constitutive in any way of citizenship in a democratic state.

48. The first option was the program of the group called "Canaanites," who argued for a total break between the Israelis and the Jews both past and present and the invention of a new People, the Canaanites, former Jews and former Palestinian Arabs, who would together restore the glory of our common "indigenous" ancestors. This is a coherent—if to me unattractive—project in ways that Zionism is not.

Bibliography

Akenson, David Harman
    1992   *God's Peoples: Covenant and Land in South Africa, Israel, and Ulster.* Ithaca, N.Y.: Cornell University Press.

Anderson, Gary
    1989   "Celibacy or Consummation in the Garden? Reflections on Early Jewish and Christian Interpretations of the Garden of Eden." *Harvard Theological Review* 82(2):121–48.

Appiah, Anthony
    1985   "The Uncompleted Argument: Du Bois and the Illusion of Race." In *"Race," Writing and Difference,* Henry Louis Gates, ed., 21–37. Special issue of *Critical Inquiry.* Chicago: University of Chicago Press.

Aspegren, Kerstin
    1990   *The Male Woman: A Feminine Ideal in the Early Church.* Renée Kieffer. Uppsala Women's Studies: Women in Religion. Stockholm: Almqvist & Wiksell International.

Augustine
    Tractatus adversus Judaeos.

Bal, Mieke
    1987   *Lethal Love.* Indiana Studies in Biblical Literature. Bloomington: Indiana University Press.

Balibar, Etienne
    1991a   "Is There a 'Neo-Racism'?" In *Race, Nation, Class: Ambiguous Identities,* Etienne Balibar and Immanuel Wallerstein, trans. Chris Turner, 17–28. London: Verso.
    1991b   "Racism and Nationalism." In *Race, Nation, Class: Ambiguous Identities,* Etienne Balibar and Immanuel Wallerstein, trans. Chris Turner, 37–67. London: Verso.

Balibar, Etienne, and Immanuel Wallerstein
    1991   *Race, Nation, Class: Ambiguous Identities.* Trans. Chris Turner. London: Verso.

Barclay, John M. G.
    1991   [1988] *Obeying the Truth: Paul's Ethics in Galatians.* Minneapolis: Fortress Press.

Baudet, Henri
    1965   *Paradise on Earth: Some Thoughts on European Images of Non-European Man.* New Haven: Yale University Press.

Baur, Ferdinand Christian

1873–75   *Paul, the Apostle of Jesus Christ.* Ed. and trans. E. Zeller. London: William and Norgate.

1875   *The Church History of the First Three Centuries.* London and Edinburgh.

1876   *Paul: His Life and Works.* Trans. A. Menzies. London: Theological Translation Fund Library.

Beker, Johannes C.

1980   *Paul the Apostle: The Triumph of God in Life and Thought.* Philadelphia: Fortress Press.

Berger, Harry

1989   "The Lie of the Land: The Text Beyond Canaan." *Representations* 25:119–38.

Betz, Hans Dieter

1979   *Galatians: A Commentary on Paul's Letter to the Church in Galatia.* In *Hermeneia—a Critical and Historical Commentary on the Bible.* Philadelphia: Fortress Press.

Biale, David

1992   *Eros and the Jews.* New York: Basic Books.

Bloch, R. Howard

1991   *Medieval Misogyny and the Invention of Western Romantic Love.* Chicago: University of Chicago Press.

Borgen, Peder

1965   *Bread from Heaven.* Leiden: E. J. Brill.

1980   "Observations on the Theme 'Paul and Philo': Paul's Preaching of Circumcision in Galatia (Gal. 5:11) and Debates on Circumcision in Philo." In *The Pauline Literature and Theology,* Sigfred Pedersen, 85–102. Teologiske Studier. Århus: Forlaget Aros.

Boswell, John

1992   "Categories, Experience, and Sexuality." In *Forms of Desire: Sexual Orientation and the Social Constructionist Controversy,* 133–73. New York: Routledge.

Boyarin, Daniel

1989   "Language Inscribed by History on the Bodies of Living Beings: Midrash and Martyrdom." *Representations* (25):139–51.

1990a   "The Eye in the Torah: Ocular Desire in Midrashic Hermeneutic." *Critical Inquiry* 16 (Spring): 532–50.

1990b   *Intertextuality and the Reading of Midrash.* Bloomington: Indiana University Press.

1991   "Internal Opposition in the Talmudic Literature: The Case of the Married Monk." *Representations* (36):87–113.

1992a   "'Behold Israel According to the Flesh': On Anthropology and Sexuality in Late Antique Judaism." *Yale Journal of Criticism* 5 (Spring): 25–55.

1992b   "'This We Know to Be the Carnal Israel': Circumcision and the Erotic Life of God and Israel." *Critical Inquiry* 18 (Spring): 474–506.

1993   *Carnal Israel: Reading Sex in Talmudic Culture.* The New Historicism: Studies in Cultural Poetics. Berkeley and Los Angeles: University of California Press.

Boyarin, Daniel, and Jonathan Boyarin

1993   "Diaspora: Generation and the Ground of Jewish Identity." *Critical Inquiry* 20 (Summer): 693–725.

Boyarin, Jonathan

1992a   "Jewish Ethnography and the Question of the Book." In *Storm from Paradise: The Politics of Jewish Memory,* 52–76. Minneapolis: University of Minnesota Press.

1992b   *Storm from Paradise: The Politics of Jewish Memory.* Minneapolis: University of Minnesota Press.

Brandenburger, Egon

1968   *Fleisch und Geist: Paulus und die dualistische Weisheit.* Wissenschaftliche Monographien zum alten und neuen Testament. Neukirchen-Vluyn: Neukirchener Verlag.

Brown, Peter

1988   *The Body and Society: Men, Women and Sexual Renunciation in Early Christianity.* Lectures on the History of Religions, vol. 13. New York: Columbia University Press.

Bruce, F. F.

1990   [1982] *Commentary on Galatians.* New International Greek Testament Commentary. Exeter: Paternoster Press.

Brunner, Emil

1950   *Dogmatics.* Trans. Olive Wyon. Vol. 1: *The Christian Doctrine of God.* Philadelphia: Westminster Press.

Bruns, J. E.

1973   "Philo Christianus: The Debris of a Legend." *Harvard Theological Review* 66: 141–45.

Bultmann, Rudolf

1951   *Theology of the New Testament.* Trans. Kendrick Grobel. Scribner Studies in Contemporary Theology. New York: Scribner's.

1967   "The Problem of Ethics in the Writings of Paul." In *The Old and the New Man,* trans. Keith R. Crim, 7–33. Richmond, Va.: John Knox Press.

Burkert, Walter

1972   *Lore and Science in Ancient Pythagoreanism.* Trans. Edwin L. Miner. Cambridge: Harvard University Press.

Burton, Ernest De Witt

1988   [1920] *A Critical and Exegetical Commentary on The Epistle to the Galatians.* The International Critical Commentary. Edinburgh: T&T Clark.

Butler, Judith

1990   *Gender Trouble: Feminism and the Subversion of Identity.* Thinking Gender. London: Routledge.

1991a   "Contingent Foundations: Feminism and the Question of 'postmodernism.'" *Praxis International* 11(2): 150–65.

1991b   Imitation and Gender Insubordination. In *Inside/out: Lesbian Theories, Gay Theories*, Diana Fuss, ed., 13–31. New York: Routledge.

Bynum, Caroline Walker

1986   "'. . . And Woman His Humanity': Female Imagery in the Religious Writing of the Later Middle Ages." In *Gender and Religion: On the Complexity of Symbols*, Caroline Walker Bynum, Stevan Harrell, and Paula Richman, eds., 257–89. Boston: Beacon Press.

1991   "Material Continuity, Personal Survival and the Resurrection of the Body: A Scholastic Discussion in Its Medieval and Modern Contexts." In *Fragmentation and Redemption: Essays on Gender and the Human Body in Medieval Religion*, 239–98, 393–417. New York: Zone Books.

Campbell, William S.

1992   *Paul's Gospel in an Intercultural Context.* Studies in the intercultural history of Christianity. Frankfurt am Main: Peter Lang.

Carras, George P.

1992   "Romans, 2, 1–29: A Dialogue on Jewish Ideals." *Biblica* 73(2): 183–207

Caspary, Gerard E.

1979   *Politics and Exegesis: Origen and the Two Swords.* Berkeley and Los Angeles: University of California Press.

Castelli, Elizabeth A.

1991a   *Imitating Paul: A Discourse of Power.* Literary currents in biblical interpretation. Louisville, Ky.: Westminster/John Knox Press.

1991b   "'I Will Make Mary Male': Pieties of the Body and Gender Transformation of Christian Women in Late Antiquity." In *Body Guards: The Cultural Politics of Ambiguity*, Julia Epstein and Kristina Straub, eds., 29–49. New York: Routledge.

Chadwick, H. E.

1966   *Early Christian Thought and the Classical Tradition.* New York: Oxford University Press.

Chadwick, Henry

1966   "St. Paul and Philo of Alexandria." *Bulletin of the John Rylands Library* 48 (Spring): 286–307.

Charles, R. H., ed.

1913   *The Apocrypha and Pseudepigrapha of the Old Testament.* Oxford: Oxford University Press.

Clark, Elizabeth A.

1986   "Ascetic Renunciation and Feminine Advancement: A Paradox of Late Ancient Christianity." In *Ascetic Piety and Women's Faith: Essays in Late Ancient Christianity*, 175–208. New York: Edwin Mellen Press.

Clement, of Alexandria

1989   *Clement of Alexandria.* Alexander Roberts and James Donaldson, eds. In *The Fathers of the Second Century.* The Anti-Nicene Fathers. Grand Rapids, Mich.: Wm. B. Eerdmans Publishing Company.

Cohen, Ed

1991   "Who Are 'We'? Gay 'Identity' as Political (E)motion: (a Theoretical Rumination)." In *Inside/out: Lesbian Theories, Gay Theories,* Diana Fuss, ed., 71–92. New York: Routledge.

Cohen, Jeremy
1989   *"Be Fertile and Increase, Fill the Earth and Master It": The Ancient and Medieval Career of a Biblical Text.* Ithaca: Cornell University Press.

Collins, John J.
1985   "A Symbol of Otherness: Circumcision and Salvation in the First Century." In *"To See Ourselves as Others See Us": Christians, Jews, "Others" in Late Antiquity,* Jacob Neusner and Ernest S. Frerichs, eds., 163–86. Scholars Press Studies in the Humanities. Chico, Calif.: Scholars Press.

Connolly, William E.
1991   *Identity\difference: Democratic Negotiations of Political Paradox.* Ithaca: Cornell University Press.

Conzelmann, Hans
1976   *1 Corinthians: A Commentary on the First Epistle to the Corinthians.* Trans. James W. Leitch. Bibliography and references prepared by James W. Dunkly. George W. S. J. MacRae, ed. In *Hermeneia—a Critical and Historical Commentary on the Bible.* Philadelphia: Fortress Press.

Cosgrove, Charles H.
1988   *The Cross and the Spirit: A Study in the Argument and Theology of Galatians.* Macon, Ga.: Mercer University Press.

Countryman, L. W.
1988   *Dirt, Greed and Sex: Sexual Ethics in the New Testament and Their Implications for Today.* Philadelphia: Fortress Press.

Cox Miller, Patricia
forth-   "Dreaming the Body: An Aesthetics of Asceticism." In *The Ascetic*
coming   *Dimension in Religious Life and Culture,* Richard Valantasis and Vincent Wimbush, eds. New York: Oxford University Press.

Crouzel, Henri
1989   *Origen: The Life and Thought of the First Great Theologian.* Trans. A. S. Worrall. San Francisco: Harper & Row.

Culler, Jonathon
1983   *On Deconstruction: Theory and Criticism After Structuralism.* Ithaca: Cornell University Press.

D'Angelo, Mary Rose
Forth-   "Veils, Virgins, and the Tongues of Men and Angels: Women's
coming   Heads in Early Christianity." In *The Female Head: Pub(l)ic Meanings of Women's Hair, Faces and Mouths,* Howard Eilberg-Schwartz and Wendy Doniger O'Flaherty, eds.

Dahl, Nils A.
1950   "Der Name Israel: Zur Auslesung von Gal. 6. 16." *Judaica* 6:161–70.
1977   *Studies in Paul: Theology for the Early Christian Mission.* In collaboration with Paul Donahue. Minneapolis: Augsburg.

Davidson, Arnold
1992   "Sex and the Emergence of Sexuality." Reprinted from *Critical In-*

quiry 14 (Autumn 1987), pp. 16–48. In *Forms of Desire: Sexual Orientation and the Social Constructionist Controversy*, Edward Stein, ed., 89–132. London: Routledge.

Davidson, Basil

1992   *The Black Man's Burden: Africa and the Curse of the Nation-state.* New York: Random House.

Davies, Stevan

1980   *The Revolt of the Widows: The Social World of the Apocryphal Acts.* Carbondale, Ill.: University of Southern Illinois Press.

Davies, W. D.

1965   [1955] *Paul and Rabbinic Judaism: Some Rabbinic Elements in Pauline Theology.* 2d ed. London: Society for the Promotion of Christian Knowledge.

1974   *The Gospel and the Land: Early Christianity and Jewish Territorial Doctrine.* Berkeley and Los Angeles: University of California Press.

1984   *Jewish and Pauline Studies.* Philadelphia: Fortress Press.

1992   [1982] *The Territorial Dimension of Judaism: With a Symposium and Further Reflections.* Minneapolis: Fortress Press.

Dawson, David

1992   *Allegorical Readers and Cultural Revision in Ancient Alexandria.* Berkeley and Los Angeles: University of California Press.

De Lauretis, Theresa

1989   "The Essence of the Triangle; or, Taking the Risk of Essentialism Seriously: Feminist Theory in Italy, the U.S., and Britain." *Differences* 1 (Summer): 3–37.

Derrida, Jacques

1976   [1974] *Of Grammatology.* Trans. Gayatri Chakravorty Spivak. Baltimore: Johns Hopkins University Press.

1987   "The Purveyor of Truth." In *The Purloined Poe*, John P. Muller and William J. Richards, eds., 173–212. Baltimore: Johns Hopkins University Press.

Deutscher, Isaac

1968   *The Non-Jewish Jew and Other Essays.* London: Oxford University Press.

Dillon, John

1977   *The Middle Platonists: 80 B.C. to A.D. 220.* Ithaca: Cornell University Press.

Dover, K. J.

1989   *Greek Homosexuality.* Revised ed. Cambridge, Mass.: Harvard University Press.

Dunn, James D. G.

1983   "The New Perspective on Paul." *Bulletin of the John Rylands Library* 65:95–122.

1988   *Word Biblical Commentary.* Vol. 38a: *Romans 1–8.* Dallas: Word Books.

1990   *Jesus, Paul and the Law: Studies in Mark and Galatians.* Louisville, Ky.: Westminster/John Knox Press.

1991   "The Theology of Galatians: The Issue of Covenantal Nomism."

In *Pauline Theology*, Jouette M. Bassler, ed., vol. 1, pp. 125–46. Minneapolis: Fortress Press.

Dynes, Wayne R.
1992   "Wrestling with the Social Boa Constructor." Reprinted from *Out in Academia 2* (1988), 18–29. In *Forms of Desire: Sexual Orientation and the Social Constructionist Controversy*, Edward Stein, ed., 209–38. London: Routledge.

Eilberg-Schwartz, Howard
1991   "The Nakedness of a Woman's Voice, the Pleasure in a Man's Mouth: An Oral History of Ancient Judaism." Paper presented at Annenberg Research Institute's Colloquium, "Women in Religion and Society." Philadelphia.
1994   *God's Phallus and Other Problems for Moses, Masculinity and Monotheism*. Boston: Beacon Press.

Engberg-Pedersen, Troels
1992   "1 Corinthians 11:16 and the Character of Pauline Exhortation." *Journal of Biblical Literature* 110(4):679–89.

Epstein, Steven
1992   "Gay Politics, Ethnic Identity: The Limits of Social Constructionism." In *Forms of Desire: Sexual Orientation and the Social Constructionist Controversy*, Edward Stein, ed., 239–94. New York: Routledge.

Fee, Gordon D., ed. and trans.
1987   *The First Epistle to the Corinthians*. The new international commentary on the New Testament. Grand Rapids: William B. Eerdmans Publishing Company.

Fiore, Benjamin
1990   "Passion in Paul and Plutarch: 1 Corinthians 5–6 and the Polemic Against Epicureans." In *Greeks, Romans, and Christians: Essays in Honor of Abraham J. Malherbe*, David L. Balch, Everett Ferguson, and Wayne A. Meeks, eds., 135–43. Minneapolis: Fortress Press.

Fiorenza, Elizabeth Schüssler
1983   *In Memory of Her: A Feminist Theological Reconstruction of Christian Origins*. New York: Crossroad.

Fitzmyer, Joseph, S.J.
1989   "Another Look at ΚΕΦΑΛΗ in 1 Corinthians 11:3." *New Testament Studies* 35:503–11.

Fletcher, Angus
1970   [1964] *Allegory: The Theory of a Symbolic Mode*. Ithaca: Cornell University Press.

Ford, David Carlton
1989   *Misogynist or Advocate? St. John Chrysostom and His Views on Women*. Ph.D. diss., Drew University.

Foucault, Michel
1980   *The History of Sexuality*. Trans. Robert Hurley. Vol. 1: *An Introduction*. New York: Random House, Vintage.

Fraade, Steven D.
1986   "Ascetical Aspects of Ancient Judaism." In *Jewish Spirituality from*

the Bible Through the Middle Ages, Arthur Green, ed. World Spirituality: An Encyclopedic History of the Religious Quest. New
York: Crossroad.

1991   *From Tradition to Commentary: Torah and Its Interpretation in the
Midrash Sifre to Deuteronomy.* Judaica: Hermeneutics, Mysticism,
and Religion. Albany: State University of New York Press.

Fraser, John W.

1970–71   "Paul's Knowledge of Jesus: II Corinthians V. 16 Once More." *New
Testament Studies* 17:293–313.

Fredriksen, Paula

1988   *From Jesus to Christ; the Origins of the New Testament Images of Jesus.*
New Haven: Yale University Press.

1991   "Judaism, the Circumcision of Gentiles, and Apocalyptic Hope:
Another Look at Galatians 1 and 2." *Journal of Theological Studies*
42 (October): 532–64.

Fuller, Daniel P.

1985   "Paul and Galatians 3:28." *Theological Students' Fellowship Bulletin*
9(2):9–13.

Fuss, Diana

1989   *Essentially Speaking: Feminism, Nature & Difference.* New York:
Routledge.

Gager, John

1983   *The Origins of Anti-Semitism: Attitudes Toward Judaism in Pagan and
Christian Antiquity.* New York: Oxford University Press.

Garber, Marjorie

1992   *Vested Interests: Cross-dressing & Cultural Anxiety.* New York:
Routledge.

Gaston, Lloyd

1982   "Israel's Enemies in Pauline Theology." *New Testament Studies* 28
(July): 400–423.

1987   *Paul and the Torah.* Vancouver: University of British Columbia Press.

Gaventa, Beverly

1986   "Galatians 1 and 2: Autobiography as Paradigm." *Novum Testamentum* 28:309–26.

Gilman, Sander

1990   "'I'm Down on Whores': Race and Gender in Victorian London."
In *Anatomy of Racism,* David Theo Goldberg, 146–70. Minneapolis: University of Minnesota Press.

1991   *The Jew's Body.* London: Routledge.

Girard, René

1978   *Things Hidden Since the Foundation of the World.* Collaborators Jean-
Michel Oughourlian and Guy Lefort; trans. Stephen Bann and
Michael Metteer. Stanford, Calif.: Stanford University Press.

Goodman, Martin

1992   "Jewish Proselytizing in the First Century." In *The Jews Among Pagans and Christians in the Roman Empire,* Judith Lieu, John North,
and Tessa Rajak, eds., 53–78. London: Routledge.

Gottwald, Norman K.

    1979   *The Tribes of Yahweh: A Sociology of the Religion of Liberated Israel, 1250–1050 B.C.* Maryknoll, N.Y.: Orbis.

Greenberg, David F.

    1988   *The Construction of Homosexuality.* Chicago: University of Chicago Press.

Gundry, Robert

    1976   *SOMA in Biblical Theology, with Emphasis on Pauline Anthropology.* SNTSMS. Cambridge: Cambridge University Press.

Gundry, Robert H.

    1980   "The Moral Frustration of Paul Before His Conversion: Sexual Lust in Romans 7:7–25." In *Pauline Studies: Essays Presented to F. F. Bruce,* D. A. Hagner and J. Murray, eds., 228–45. Grand Rapids, Mich.: Wm. B. Eerdmans.

Hacking, Ian

    1992   "Making up People." In *Forms of Desire: Sexual Orientation and the Social Constructionist Controversy,* Edward Stein, ed., 69–88. New York: Routledge.

Hadarshan, Shimʿon

    1960   *Numbers Rabbah.* Tel-Aviv: Moriah.

Halperin, David M.

    1990   *One Hundred Years of Homosexuality and Other Essays on Greek Love.* New York: Routledge.

Hamerton-Kelly, Robert G.

    1992   *Sacred Violence: Paul's Hermeneutic of the Cross.* Minneapolis: Fortress Press.

Hampton, Timothy

    1993   "'Turkish Dogs': Rabelais, Erasmus, and the Rhetoric of Alterity." *Representations* 41 (Winter): 58–82.

Handelman, Susan

    1982   *The Slayers of Moses.* Albany: State University of New York Press.

Harrison, Verna E. F.

    forth-   "The Allegorization of Gender: Plato and Philo on Spiritual Child-
    coming   bearing." In *The Ascetic Dimension in Religious Life and Culture,* Richard Valantasis and Vincent Wimbush, eds. New York: Oxford.

    1990   "Male and Female in Cappadocian Theology." *Journal of Theological Studies* 41 (October): 441–71.

    1992   "Allegory and Asceticism in Gregory of Nyssa." *Semeia* 57:113–30. In *Discursive Formations, Ascetic Piety and the Interpretation of Early Christian Literature,* Vincent L. Wimbush, ed.

Hays, Richard B.

    1980   "Psalm 143 and the Logic of Romans 3." *Journal of Biblical Literature* 99(1):107–15.

    1983   *The Faith of Jesus Christ: An Investigation of the Narrative Substructure of Galatians 3:1–4:11.* SBL Dissertation Series. Chico, Calif.: Scholars Press.

    1985   "'Have We Found Abraham to Be Our Forefather According to the

Flesh?': A Reconsideration of Rom 4:1." *Novum Testamentum* 27(1):76–98.

1987   "Christology and Ethics in Galatians: The Law of Christ." *Catholic Biblical Quarterly* 40 (April): 268–90.

1989   *Echoes of Scripture in the Letters of Paul.* New Haven: Yale University Press.

1993   Personal communication.

Hecht, R.

1984   "The Exegetical Contexts of Philo's Interpretation of Circumcision." In *Nourished with Peace: Studies in Hellenistic Judaism in Memory of Samuel Sandmel*, F. Greenspan, E. Hilgert, and Burton Mack, eds., 51–79. Chico, Calif.: Scholars Press.

Hengel, Martin

1974   *Judaism and Hellenism: Studies in Their Encounter in Palestine During the Early Hellenistic Period.* Trans. John Bowden. London: SCM Press.

Henkin, David M.

1991   "Faith and Patricide: Paul, Judaism and the Question of Paternity." Unpublished paper.

Hooker, Morna D.

1981   "Beyond the Things That Are Written? St. Paul's Use of Scripture." *New Testament Studies* 27:295–309.

Howard, George

1990   [1979] *Paul: Crisis in Galatia. A Study in Early Christian Theology.* 2d ed. SNTSMS. Cambridge: Cambridge University Press.

Irigaray, Luce

1993   *Je, Tu, Nous: Toward a Culture of Difference.* Trans. Alison Martin. New York: Routledge.

Jameson, Fredric

1981   *The Political Unconscious: Narrative as a Socially Symbolic Act.* Ithaca: Cornell University Press.

Jewett, Robert

1970   "The Agitators and the Galatian Congregation." *New Testament Studies* 17:198–212.

1971   *Paul's Anthropological Terms: A Study of Their Use in Conflict Settings.* AGAJU. Leiden: E. J. Brill.

Johnson, Barbara

1987   "The Frame of Reference: Poe, Lacan, Derrida." In *The Purloined Poe.* John P. Muller and William J. Richards, eds., 213–51. Baltimore: Johns Hopkins University Press.

Kahn, Charles H.

1960   *Anaximander and the Origins of Greek Cosmology.* New York: Columbia University Press.

Käsemann, Ernst

1933   *Leib und Leib Christi. Eine Untersuchung zur paulinischen Begrifflichkeit.* Tübingen: J. C. B. Mohr (Paul Siebeck).

1969   "Paul and Israel." In *New Testament Questions of Today*, 183–87. London.

1980 *Commentary on Romans.* Trans. and ed. Geoffrey W. Bromiley. Grand Rapids, Mich.: William B. Eerdmans.

Kee, H. C., trans. and introduction

1983 "Testaments of the Twelve Patriarchs, the Son of Jacob the Patriarch." In *The Old Testament Pseudepigrapha,* vol. 1: *Apocalyptic Literature and Testaments,* James H. Charlesworth, ed. Garden City, N.Y.: Doubleday.

Klein, Gottlieb

1918 *Studien über Paulus.* Stockholm: Bonniers.

Knight, Chris

1988 "Menstrual Synchrony and the Australian Rainbow Snake." In *Blood Magic: The Anthropology of Menstruation,* Thomas Buckley and Alma Gottlieb, eds., 232–55. Berkeley and Los Angeles: University of California Press.

Knox, W. L.

1939 *St. Paul and the Church of the Gentiles.* Cambridge: Cambridge University Press.

Kraemer, Ross

1989 "Monastic Jewish Women in Greco-Roman Egypt: Philo on the Therapeutrides." *Signs: A Journal of Women in Culture and Society* 14(1):342–70.

Krieger, Murray

1979 "Poetic Presence and Illusion." *Critical Inquiry* 5:597–620.

Kürzinger, Josef

1978 "Frau und Mann nach 1 Kor 11, 11f." *Biblische Zeitschrift* 22(2): 270–75.

Kuschel, Karl-Josef

1992 *Born Before All Time?: The Dispute Over Christ's Origin.* Trans. John Bowden. New York: Crossroad.

Lacoue-Labarthe, Phillipe, and Jean-Luc Nancy

1990 "The Nazi Myth." *Critical Inquiry* 16 (Winter): 291–312.

Laqueur, Thomas

1990 *Making Sex: Body and Gender from the Greeks to Freud.* Cambridge, Mass.: Harvard University Press.

Lawton, David

1993 *Blasphemy.* Philadelphia: University of Pennsylvania Press.

Levinas, Emmanuel

1990 [1934] "Reflections on the Philosophy of Hitlerism." Reprinted from *Esprit.* Trans. Sèan Hand. *Critical Inquiry* 17 (Autumn): 62–71.

Lewis, Norman

1988 *The Missionaries: God Against the Indians.* London: Arena.

Lightfoot, J. B., and J. R. Harmer, trans.

1989 [London: 1891] *The Apostolic Fathers.* 2d ed. Rev. Michael W. Holmes. Grand Rapids, Mich.: Baker Book House.

Lloyd, Genevieve

1984 *The Man of Reason: "male" and "female" in Western Philosophy.* Minneapolis: University of Minnesota Press.

Longenecker, Richard N.
  1990   *Word Biblical Commentary.* Vol. 41: *Galatians.* Dallas: Word Books.
Lucian
  1961   *Satyrical Sketches.* Trans. Paul Turner. Bloomington: Indiana University Press.
Lull, David J.
  1986   "The Law Was Our Pedagogue: A Study in Galatians 3:19–25." *Journal of Biblical Literature* 105:481–98.
Lyonnet, S.
  1962   "'Tu ne convoiteras pas' (Rom. 7.7)." In *Neotestamentica et Patristica: Eine Freundesgabe, Herrn Professor Dr. Oscar Cullmann zu seinem 60. Geburtstag überreicht,* 158–64. Novum Testamentum Suppl. 6. Leiden: E. J. Brill.
Lyotard, Jean-François
  1990   *Heidegger and "the jews."* Trans. Andreas Michel and Mark Roberts; int. by David Carroll. Minneapolis: University of Minnesota Press.
Macdonald, Dennis Ronald
  1984   "The Role of Women in the Production of the Apocryphal Acts of the Apostles." *Iliff Review of Theology* 40:21–38.
  1987   *There Is No Male and Female: The Fate of a Dominical Saying in Paul and Gnosticism.* Harvard Dissertations in Religion. Philadelphia: Fortress Press.
  1988   "Corinthian Veils and Gnostic Androgynes." In *Images of the Feminine in Gnosticism,* Karen L. King, ed., 276–92. Philadelphia: Fortress Press.
McEleney, Neil J., C.S.P.
  1974   "Conversion, Circumcision and the Law." *New Testament Studies* 20:319–41.
Malherbe, Abraham
  1989   *Paul and the Popular Philosophers.* Minneapolis: Augsburg Fortress.
Manganaro, Marc
  1992   *Myth, Rhetoric, and the Voice of Authority: A Critique of Frazer, Eliot, Frye, and Campbell.* New Haven: Yale University Press.
Martin, Ralph P.
  1986   *Word Biblical Commentary.* Vol. 40, 2 *Corinthians.* Waco, Tex.: Word Books.
Martyn, J. Louis
  1967   "Epistemology at the Turn of the Ages: 2 Corinthians 5:16." In *Christian History and Interpretation: Studies Presented to John Knox,* W. R. Farmer, C. D. F. Moule, and R. R. Niebuhr, eds., 269–87. Cambridge: Cambridge University Press.
  1985   "Apocalyptic Antinomies in Paul's Letter to the Galatians." *New Testament Studies* 31:410–24.
Meeks, Wayne, ed.
  1972   *The Writings of St. Paul.* Norton Critical Editions. New York: W. W. & Norton.

Meeks, Wayne A.
    1973   "The Image of the Androgyne: Some Uses of a Symbol in Earliest Christianity." *Journal of the History of Religions* 13(1):165–208.
    1983   *The First Urban Christians: The Social World of the Apostle Paul.* New Haven: Yale University Press.

Meier, John Paul
    1978   "On the Veiling of Hermeneutics (1 Cor 11:2–16)." *Catholic Biblical Quarterly* 40 (212–26).

Michaels, Walter Benn
    1992   "Race Into Culture: A Critical Genealogy of Cultural Identity." *Critical Inquiry* 18 (Summer): 655–86.

Moo, Douglas J.
    1986   "Israel and Paul in Romans 7.7–12." *New Testament Studies* 32: 122–35.

Mopsik, Charles
    1989   "The Body of Engenderment in the Hebrew Bible, the Rabbinic Tradition, and the Kabbalah." In *Fragments for a History of the Human Body* 1. Michel Feher et al., eds., 48–73. New York: Zone Books.

Murphy-O'Connor, Jerome, O.P.
    1976   "The Non-pauline Character of 1 Corinthians 11:2–16?" *Journal of Biblical Literature* 95 (December): 615–21.

Nancy, Jean-Luc
    1991   *The Inoperative Community.* Minneapolis: University of Minnesota Press.

Neyrey, Jerome H.
    1990   *Paul, in Other Words: A Cultural Reading of His Letters.* Louisville, Ky.: Westminster/John Knox Press.

Nolland, J.
    1981   "Uncircumcised Proselytes?" *Journal for the Study of Judaism in the Persian, Hellenistic and Roman Periods* 12:173–94.

O'Flaherty, Wendy Doniger
    1980   *Women, Androgynes, and Other Mythical Beasts.* Chicago: University of Chicago Press.

Ortner, Sherry B.
    1973   "On Key Symbols." *The American Anthropologist* 75:1338–42.

Pagels, Elaine
    1978   "Visions, Appearances, and Apostolic Authority: Gnostic and Orthodox Traditions." In *Gnosis: Festschrift für Hans Jonas*, B. Aland, ed., 415–30. Göttingen.

Paglia, Camille
    1992   "Junk Bonds and Corporate Raiders: Academe in the Hour of the Wolf." Reprinted from *Arion*, Spring 1991. In *Sex, Art and American Culture*, 170–248. New York: Vintage.

Pardes, Ilana
    1989   "Beyond Genesis 3." *Hebrew University Studies in Literature and the Arts* 17:161–87.

Philo

1929a   Legum Allegoria. In *Loeb Classics Philo*, vol. 1. London: Heinemann.
1929b   On the Creation. In *Loeb Classics Philo*, vol. 1. London: Heinemann.
1932   The Migration of Abraham. In *Loeb Classics Philo*, vol. 4. London: Heinemann.
1937   The Special Laws. In *Loeb Classics Philo*, vol. 7. London: Heinemann.

Rabi, Wladimir

1979   *Un peuple de trop sur la terre?* Paris: Presses D'aujourd'hui.

Räisänen, Heikki

1980   "Legalism and Salvation by the Law: Paul's Portrayal of the Jewish Religion as a Historical and Theological Problem." In *The Pauline Literature and Theology*, Sigfred Pedersen, 63–84. Teologiske Studier. Århus: Forlaget Aros.
1985   "Galatians 2.16 and Paul's Break with Judaism." *New Testament Studies* 31:543–53.
1986   [1983] *Paul and the Law*. Philadelphia: Fortress Press.

Rappaport-Alpert, Ada

1988   "On Women in Hasidism." In *Jewish History: Essays in Honour of Chimen Abramsky*, Rappaport-Alpert and Steven Zipperstein, eds., 495–525. London: P. Halban.

Reinhartz, Adele

1991   "From Narrative to History: The Resurrection of Mary and Martha." In *"Women Like This": New Perspectives on Jewish Women in the Greco-Roman World*, Amy-Jill Levine, ed., 161–85. Society of Biblical Literature: Early Judaism and Its Literature. Atlanta: Scholars Press.
1993   Personal communication.

Richardson, Cyril C.

1973   *The Gospel of Thomas: Gnostic or Encratite?* Orientalia christiana analecta. Rome: Pontificium Institutum Orientalum Studiorum.

Richardson, Peter

1969   *Israel in the Apostolic Church*. Cambridge: Cambridge University Press.

Robbins, Jill

1991   *Prodigal Son/Elder Brother: Interpretation and Alterity in Augustine, Petrarch, Kafka and Levinas*. Chicago: University of Chicago Press.

Robinson, John A. T.

1952   *The Body: A Study in Pauline Theology*. Chicago: Henry Regnery.

Rodinson, Maxime

1983   *Cult, Ghetto, and State: The Persistence of the Jewish Question*. Trans. Jan Rothschild. London: Al Saqi Books.

Ruether, Rosemary

1974   *Faith and Fratricide*. New York: Seabury.

Sanders, E. P.

1973   "Patterns of Religion in Paul and Rabbinic Judaism: A Holistic Method of Comparison." *Harvard Theological Review* 66:455–78.

1976 "The Covenant as a Soteriological Category and the Nature of Salvation in Palestinian and Hellenistic Judaism." In *Jews, Greeks and Christians: Religious Cultures in Late Antiquity*, 11–45. Leiden: E. J. Brill.

1977 *Paul and Palestinian Judaism: A Comparison of Patterns of Religion.* Philadelphia: Fortress Press.

1978 "On the Question of Fulfilling the Law in Paul and Rabbinic Judaism." In *Donum Gentilicum (in Honor of David Daube)*, E. Bammel, C. K. Barrett, and W. D. Davies, eds., 103–26. Oxford: Oxford University Press.

1983 *Paul, the Law, and the Jewish People.* Philadelphia: Fortress Press.

1990 "Jewish Association with Gentiles and Galatians 2:11–14." In *The Conversation Continues: Studies in Paul and John in Honor of J. Louis Martyn*, Robert T. Fortna and Beverly R. Gaventa, eds., 170–89. Nashville: Abingdon Press.

Sang, Barry R.
1991 "Paul's Allegory (?) in Galatians 4:21–31." Paper presented at Society of Biblical Literature. Kansas City.

Saxonhouse, Arlene W.
1992 *Fear of Diversity: The Birth of Political Science in Ancient Greek Thought.* Chicago: University of Chicago Press.

Schlier, Heinrich
1965 *Kritisch-exegetischer Kommentar über das neue Testament begründet von Heinrich August Wilhelm Meyer.* Vol. 7: *Der Brief an die Galater: Übersetzt und erklärt von Heinrich Schlier.* Göttingen: Vandenhoeck & Ruprecht.

Schmithals, Walter
1971 *Paul and the Gnostics.* John E. Steely. Nashville: Abingdon Press.

Schoeps, Hans Joachim
1961 [Tübingen: 1959] *Paul: The Theology of the Apostle in the Light of Jewish Religious History.* Trans. Harold Knight. Philadelphia: Westminster.

Schreiner, Thomas R.
1991 "'Works of Law' in Paul." *Novum Testamentum* 33(3):217–44.

Schwartz, Regina M.
1992 "Nations and Nationalism: Adultery in the House of David." *Critical Inquiry* 19 (Autumn): 131–50.

Schweizer, Eduard
1957 "Der Glaube an Jesus den 'Herrn' in seiner Entwicklung von den ersten Nachfolgern bis zur hellenistische Gemeinde." *Evangelische Theologie* 17:17–21.

Sedgwick, Eve Kosofsky
1990 *Epistemology of the Closet.* Berkeley and Los Angeles: University of California Press. A Centennial Book.

Segal, Alan F.
1990 *Paul the Convert: The Apostolate and Apostasy of Saul the Pharisee.* New Haven: Yale University Press.

1992   "Universalism in Judaism and Christianity." Unpublished paper.
Shell, Marc
1991   "Marranos (pigs); or, from Coexistence to Toleration." *Critical Inquiry* 17 (Winter): 306–36.
Silverman, Kaja
1992   *Male Subjectivity at the Margins.* New York: Routledge.
Simms, Norman
1992   *The Humming Tree: A Study in the History of Mentalities.* Urbana: University of Illinois Press.
Sissa, Giulia
1992   "The Sexual Philosophies of Plato and Aristotle." In *From Ancient Goddesses to Christian Saints.* In *A History of Women in the West,* George Duby and Michelle Perot, eds., 46–83. Cambridge, Mass.: Harvard University Press (Belknap).
Sly, Dorothy
1990   *Philo's Perception of Women.* Brown Judaica Series. Atlanta: Scholars Press.
Smith, Jonathan Z.
1990   *Drudgery Divine: On the Comparison of Early Christianities and the Religions of Late Antiquity.* Chicago Studies in the History of Judaism. Chicago: University of Chicago Press.
Snodgrass, Klyne R.
1986   "Justification by Grace—to the Doers: An Analysis of the Place of Romans 2 in the Theology of Paul." *New Testament Studies* 32: 72–93.
Spidlík, Tomás, S.J.
1986   [Rome: 1978] *The Spirituality of the Christian East: A Systematic Handbook.* Trans. Anthony P. Gythiel. Cistercian Study Series, no. 79. Kalamazoo: Cistercian Publications.
Spivak, Gayatri Chakravorty
1992   "Acting Bits/Identity Talk." *Critical Inquiry* 18 (Summer): 770–803.
Steinberg, Leo
1983   *The Sexuality of Christ in Renaissance Art and Modern Oblivion.* New York: Pantheon.
Stendahl, Krister
1976   *Paul Among Jews and Gentiles.* Philadelphia: Fortress Press.
Stillman, Norman
1979   *The Jews of Arab Lands: A History and Source Book.* Philadelphia: Jewish Publication Society.
Theodor, Jehuda, and Hanoch Albeck, eds.
1965   *Genesis Rabbah.* Jerusalem: Wahrmann.
Thielman, Frank
1989   *From Plight to Solution: A Jewish Framework for Understanding Paul's View of the Law in Galatians and Romans.* Supplements to Novum Testamentum. Leiden: Brill.
1992   "The Coherence of Paul's View of the Law: The Evidence of First Corinthians." *New Testament Studies* 38 (April): 235–53.

Thompson, Lloyd A.
    1989   *Romans and Blacks.* Norman: University of Oklahoma Press.
Tobin, Thomas H., S.J.
    1983   *The Creation of Man: Philo and the History of Interpretation.* The
                Catholic Biblical Quarterly Monograph Series. Washington, D.C.:
                The Catholic Biblical Association of America.
Tomson, Peter T.
    1990   *Compendia Rerum Iudaicarum Ad Novum Testamentum.* Vol. 3, 1:
                *Paul and the Jewish Law: Halakha in the Letters of the Apostle to the
                Gentiles.* Philadelphia: Fortress Press.
Trible, Phyllis
    1978   *God and the Rhetoric of Sexuality.* Overtures to Biblical Theology.
                Philadelphia: Fortress Press.
Turner, Frederick W.
    1980   *Beyond Geography.* New Brunswick, N.J.: Rutgers University Press.
Vernant, Jean-Pierre
    1989   "Dim Body, Dazzling Body." In *Fragments for a History of the Human
                Body: Part One,* Michel Feher, Ramona Naddaff, and Nadia Tazi,
                eds.; trans. and ed. Siri Hustvedt; trans. Anne Cancogne et al.,
                18–47. New York: Zone.
    1991   "Psuche: Simulacrum of the Body or Image of the Divine?" In *Mor-
                tals and Immortals: Collected Essays,* by Jean-Pierre Vernant; ed. and
                trans. Froma I. Zeitlin, 186–92. Princeton: Princeton University
                Press.
Vidal-Naquet, Pierre
    1992   "Atlantis and the Nations." Trans. Janet Lloyd. *Critical Inquiry* 18
                (Winter): 300–326.
Vööbus, Arthur
    1951   *Celibacy. A Requirement for Admission to Baptism in the Early Church.*
                Papers of the Estonian Theological Society in Exile. Stockholm.
Walker, William O., Jr.
    1975   "1 Corinthians and Paul's Views Regarding Women." *Journal of
                Biblical Literature* 94(1):94–110.
Wallerstein, Immanuel
    1991   "The Ideological Tensions of Capitalism: Universalism Versus Rac-
                ism and Sexism." In *Race, Nation, Class: Ambiguous Identities,*
                Etienne Balibar and Immanuel Wallerstein, trans. Chris Turner,
                29–36. London: Verso.
Watson, Francis
    1986   *Paul, Judaism, and the Gentiles: A Sociological Approach.* Society for
                New Testament Studies Monograph Series. Cambridge: Cambridge
                University Press.
Wedderburn, A. J. M.
    1987   *Baptism and Resurrection: Studies in Pauline Theology Against Its
                Graeco-Roman Background.* Tübingen: J. C. B. Mohr.
Wegner, Judith Romney
    1991   "Philo's Portrayal of Women: Hebraic or Hellenic?" In *"Women
                Like This": New Perspectives on Jewish Women in the Greco-Roman*

World, Amy-Jill Levine, ed., 41–66. Society of Biblical Literature: Early Judaism and Its Literature. Atlanta: Scholars Press.

Weinrich, James

1992   "Reality or Social Construction?" Reprinted from James Weinrich, *Sexual Landscapes: Why We Are What We Are, Why We Love Who We Love* (New York: Charles Scribner's Sons, 1987), ch. 5. In *Forms of Desire: Sexual Orientation and the Social Constructionist Controversy,* 175–208. New York: Routledge.

Westerholm, Stephen

1984   "Letter and Spirit: The Foundation of Pauline Ethics." *New Testament Studies* 30:229–48.

1988   *Israel's Law and the Church's Faith: Paul and His Recent Interpreters.* Grand Rapids, Mich.: William B. Eerdmans.

Wilckens, Ulrich

1982   *Der Brief and die Römer.* Evangelisch-katholischer Kommentar. Cologne: Benziger.

Williamson, Ronald

1970   *Philo and the Epistle to the Hebrews.* ALGH, vol. 4. Leiden: Brill.

1989   *Jews in the Hellenistic World: Philo.* Cambridge Commentaries on Writings of the Jewish & Christian World, 200 B.C. to A.D. 200. Cambridge: Cambridge University Press.

Wimbush, Vincent L.

1987   *Paul the Worldly Ascetic: Response to the World and Self-understanding According to 1 Corinthians 7.* Macon, Ga.: Mercer University Press.

Winston, David, ed. and trans.

1981   *Philo of Alexandria: The Contemplative Life, the Giants, and Selections.* The Classics of Western Spirituality. New York: Paulist Press.

1988   "Philo and the Contemplative Life." In *Jewish Spirituality from the Bible Through the Middle Ages,* Arthur Green, ed., 198–231. World Spirituality: An Encyclopedic History of the Religious Quest, vol. 13. New York: Crossroad.

Wire, Antoinette Clark

1990   *The Corinthian Women Prophets: A Reconstruction through Paul's Rhetoric.* Minneapolis: Fortress Press.

Wolfson, Elliot R.

1987a   "Circumcision and the Divine Name: A Study in the Transmission of Esoteric Doctrine." *Jewish Quarterly Review* 78 (July–October): 77–112.

1987b   "Circumcision, Vision of God, and Textual Interpretation: From Midrashic Trope to Mystical Symbol." *History of Religions* 27 (November): 189–215.

Wolfson, Harry Austryn

1968   *Philo: Foundations of Religious Philosophy in Judaism, Christianity and Islam.* Rev. 4th ed. Cambridge, Mass.: Harvard University Press.

Wright, N. T.

1992a   *The Climax of the Covenant: Christ and the Law in Pauline Theology.* Minneapolis: Fortress Press.

1992b   *The New Testament and the People of God.* Christian Origins and the
             Question of God. Minneapolis: Fortress Press.

Zeitlin, Froma
     1990   "The Origin of Woman and Woman as the Origin: The Case of
                 Pandora." Unpublished paper.

Index

Biblical citations are referenced only where they are extensively treated.

Compositor:	G & S Typesetters, Inc.
Text:	10/13.5 Goudy
Display:	Goudy
Printer:	Edwards Brothers, Inc.
Binder:	Edwards Brothers, Inc.